Fighting the Kaiser's War

The Saxons in Flanders 1914/1918

ANDREW LUCAS & JÜRGEN SCHMIESCHEK

Pen & Sword
MILITARY

First published in Great Britain in 2015 by

PEN & SWORD MILITARY

an imprint of
Pen & Sword Books Ltd
47 Church Street
Barnsley
South Yorkshire
S70 2AS

ISBN 9781783463008

Layout: Jürgen Schmieschek

Typeset in AGaramond

Printed and bound in India by Replika Press Pvt. Ltd.

Pen & Sword Books Ltd incorporates the imprints of Pen & Sword Archaeology, Atlas, Aviation, Battleground, Discovery, Family History, History, Maritime, Military, Naval, Politics, Railways, Select, Social History, Transport, True Crime, and Claymore Press, Frontline Books, Leo Cooper, Praetorian Press, Remember When, Seaforth Publishing and Wharncliffe.

For a complete list of Pen & Sword titles please contact
PEN & SWORD BOOKS LIMITED
47 Church Street, Barnsley, South Yorkshire, S70 2AS, England
E-mail: enquiries@pen-and-sword.co.uk
Website: www.pen-and-sword.co.uk

Contents

PREFACE

Our subject would have been instantly recognisable to the generation who fought in the Great War. Saxony was prominent in the old Anglo-German culture before 1914, and once as familiar to the more cosmopolitan Englishman as Bavaria or the Rhineland. British soldiers' memoirs, contemporary newspapers and early unit histories often refer to the Saxons, and few accounts of the Christmas Truce (even from Prussian-held sectors) fail to mention them. Under the Soviet occupation after the Second World War Saxony sadly became *terra incognita* to the English-speaking world. We hope this book will go some way toward rectifying this situation.

This book focuses on primary sources, most of which have never seen print in any language. We aim to give enough background on units and sectors to put the photos and accounts into context, and to provide starting points for further research on the British or German side. Despite limiting our scope to Flanders we unearthed far more relevant material than we could include in a book of this size, and aim to make more available on our website **www.royalsaxonarmy.co.uk**.

We are profoundly indebted to all those who lovingly preserved these historical documents over the past century. We owe a still greater debt to the countless Saxon servicemen (many sadly anonymous) who chose to record their experiences, and to the lax censorship regime which allowed them to do so. We hope we have been fair and respectful to the memory and common humanity of all individuals and units (of all nations) who appear in this book.

For the avoidance of ambiguity, ease of reference with German sources and historical flavour we have used German time throughout and retained much terminology (especially the names of units) in the original German; please refer to the glossary on pp. 255–256. The use of reference works on the German military and the campaigns in Flanders is highly recommended. Except within quotations place names in Belgian Flanders are given in their modern Flemish forms with the exception of those such as Ypres which are far better known in another form. Major variants are noted in the index of places (pp. 252–253), which acts as key to both the text and the maps. We hope our book will be a useful companion to any of the numerous guidebooks to the relevant areas, and that readers will spare a thought for the individuals and units we describe when they visit the places where they lived and died.

Providentiae Memor!

Andrew Lucas and Jürgen Schmieschek

October 2014

ACKNOWLEDGEMENTS

This book would not have existed without the enthusiastic support of Jon Cooksey at *Stand To!* We also owe a deep debt of gratitude to Rupert Harding at Pen and Sword, for unflagging support during its long and difficult gestation. We are very grateful to Frank Peter Große for material on IR 354, and to Jan Vancoillie both for some fine images and for his invaluable knowledge of Flanders. We also wish to thank the staff of The National Archives and Imperial War Museum in London, and of the *Sächsisches Hauptstaatsarchiv* in Dresden for help during our visits.

Andrew would also like to thank the following:

My greatest debt is to my great-grandfather Arno Bierast. Though I never met this brave and principled man, his wartime photos inspired my work. I am deeply grateful to my grandmother Margot Hemmings (née Bierast) for her affectionate support and for taking me to see Berlin and Dresden. I am profoundly indebted to my parents Michael and Ann Lucas for their love and patient assistance. Without experience gained on my father's book *The Journey's End Battalion* or his help with British sources I could not have attempted such a huge project. I wish to thank my long-suffering housemates, most of all Diana Zachau for single-handedly finding us a new home during the writing process. Hearty thanks are due to both her and our good friend Hauptfeldwebel a. D. der Luftwaffe Simon Groeger for help with translations. I am fondly grateful to Cleo (RIP), Bunny, Peggy and the Herr Feldwedel for their soothing presence. I also wish to thank my supportive employers Creative Virtual. Special thanks are due to Jack Sheldon for aid and encouragement early in my research. Without his pioneering work this book would have been immeasurably harder to write. I am also grateful to Jean Polak for early assistance. Finally I must express my heartfelt gratitude to my co-author, who answered all my naïve and clumsy early queries with *sächsische Höflichkeit* and became my staunchest comrade and friend in Great War research.

Jürgen would also like to thank the following:

I am grateful to my family and especially my dear Ute, who patiently accepted that I could spend much less time with them than we would have liked during many phases of the creation of the book. I would also like to warmly thank my co-author Andrew for taking the trouble, on top of all his time-consuming research, to make working through all the language problems as easy and pleasant as possible for me. I am very happy that our long-standing friendship has been greatly deepened by our harmonious work together on this book.

Surviving personal documents from a century ago offer interesting glimpses of the system that produced them and of life under it. This *Verkehrs-schein* (travel permit) for René Deruyter of Lambresart was authorised in 1915 by 24. Feldartillerie-Brigade / 24. Infanterie-Division as *Ortskomman-dantur* of that town, and clearly saw heavy use. Note that contemporary identity documents carried by German soldiers did not include a photo.

- 10 - -   1916.

III.Batl.R.I.R. 22 ab. Ablösung verläuft ohne Störung. Die Nacht
ist ruhig. Schneewetter. Stellung ist sehr gut ausgebaut. (Siehe
Skizze, Anlage 5).

    Tag verläuft ruhig. Fast gar kein feindliches Artilleriefeuer.   8. März
Starker Schneefall, Kälte. Keine Verluste.

    Nacht und Tag verlaufen ruhig. Wenig feindliches Feuer. Keine   9. März
Verluste.

    Ruhig, keine Verluste.   10. März
Verpflegstärke: 28 Offiziere, 1106 Mannschaften, 61 Pferde,   11. März
Gefechtsstärke: 21   "   , 1054   "
Zugang: 12 Mannschaften aus Lazaretten.
Abgang: 14 Mann verwundet.
        Erkrankt: 9 Mann
        Versetzt: 1 Mann.

    Ruhig. Keine Verluste. Am Abend Ablösung durch I. Bataillon.
II. Bataillon bezieht mit Stab und 5. und 8. Komp. Ortsunterkunft
in Comines, 6. und 7. Kompagnie in Gardedieu.

Ruhe. - Nachts einige Gruppen zum Schanzen.   12. März
Ruhe in Comines und Garde-Dieu. Während dieser Zeit ist das Bata-   13. März bis
illon Korpsreserve.   17.März.

    Am Abend in Stellung bei Wytschaete. Ablösung des I. Bataillons
R.I.R. 242.

    Feind unruhig. Artillerie und Infanterie lebhafter. Sehr rege   18. März
feindliche Fliegertätigkeit. Verluste: 1 Mann schwer, 1 Mann leicht
verwundet.

    Während der Nacht und des Vormittags ruhig. Am Nachmittag zeit-   19. März
weilig Artilleriefeuer, das durch unsere Artillerie erwidert wird.
    Verluste:1Mann tot, 4 Mann verwundet.

    Nacht ruhig. Tagsüber einige feindliche Schrapnelle auf vorde-   20. März
re Stellung. Verluste: 3 Mann verwundet. Sehr rege feindliche Fliegertätigkeit.

Verpflegstärke: 28 Offiziere, 1102 Mannschaften, 61 Pferde.   21. März
  Gefechtstärke: 21   "   , 1050   "
Zugang: 3 Mann aus der Heimat,
    18 Mann aus Lazaretten und durch Versetzung.
Abgang: 1 Mann gefallen.
   10 Mann verwundet.
    Erkrankt: 14 Mann.

    Nacht ruhig. Gegen 6 Uhr vormittags starkes feindliches Artille-
riefeuer auf erste und zweite Linie des Abschnitts, wodurch einige
Stellen des Grabens erheblich beschädigt werden und eine Anzahl
Verluste eintreten. Unsere Artillerie erwidert trotz sofortiger
Anforderung das Feuer erst nach ungefähr 20 Minuten; die Verbin-
dung mit der Artillerie war sehr mangelhaft, die Telephonisten der
Artillerie meldeten sich nicht, schienen zu schlafen.

    Verluste: 5. Kompagnie, 4 Mann leicht verwundet,
        7.   "   6   "   "   ,
        8.   "   3   "   gefallen und
                   1   "   leicht verwundet.

    Tagsüber einzelnes Schrapnell- und Granatfeuer. Abends 12.30 Uhr
wird 6. Kompagnie aus Bereitschaftstellung durch 10. und 1/3 11.
Kompagnie R.I.R.215 abgelöst und rückt nach Comines in Ortsunterkunft. (Siehe Befehl, Anlage 6 u.7.)

    Nacht verlief ruhig. Gegen 10.15 Uhr abends großer Feuerschein   22. März
in Richtung vom Kemmel weit hinter der feindlichen Linie beobach-
tet. Patrouillen stellen fest, daß unsere Drahthindernisse an eini-
gen Stellen beschädigt sind. Verschiedene Beobachtungen (Feuertä-
tigkeit, Leuchtpatronen) lassen darauf schließen, daß uns ein ande-
rer Gegner gegenüberliegt.

    Abends wird der Stab, 5. 7. und 8. Kompagnie durch II.Bataillon
R.I.R.215 abgelöst und Ortsunterkunft in Comines bezogen. Verluste:
1 Mann leicht verwundet.

Original typescript page from the war diary of Reserve-Infanterie-Regiment 242 for March 1916, when the regiment was near Wytschaete.

The old and new faces of the Royal Saxon Army: a young infantryman in wartime *feldgrau* walking-out dress and an NCO in the 'colourful' (corn-flower blue and white) pre-war uniform of the Garde-Reiter-Regiment, the most prestigious of Saxon cavalry units; on parade his helmet spike would be re-placed by a gilt lion (see photo on p.10). In wartime this regiment wore *feld-grau*, but the heavy cavalry's traditional 'butcher boots' and metal helmet (albeit with a canvas cover) were retained even for dismounted action.

The Royal Saxon Army (*Königlich Sächsische Armee*) was the national army of the Kingdom of Saxony (*Königreich Sachsen*), one of four states of the German *Reich* to retain its own armed forces. While the various duchies, principalities and free cities provided men, money and traditions to the army of the dominant Kingdom of Prussia (*Preussen*), the three other kingdoms formed and administered entire army corps. Each enjoyed a precisely defined and jealously guarded degree of independence befitting its political weight. Of the twenty-five corps extant on the eve of war, nineteen were Prussian, three Bavarian, two Saxon and one Württemberg. As the largest minor army, that of Bavaria (*Bayern*) only came under the command of the Kaiser in wartime and was excluded from the numbering system used by all other German units. As well as its own corps of officers and general staff, Bavaria even maintained an independent *Kriegsakademie* for staff training. Conversely, the small army of Württemberg had to make its officers partly interchangeable with the Prussians in order to fill all of the posts in the XIII. Armeekorps. The Saxon position lay between these two extremes. Saxon officers trained with the *Kadettenkorps* in Dresden, but if aspiring to a staff career went on to the Prussian *Kriegsakademie* in Berlin. Saxon soldiers swore both loyalty to their king and obedience to the Kaiser, and their units were counted in the 'German' sequence. The Royal Saxon Army was organised, trained and equipped based on regulations formulated in Berlin and ratified in Dresden. These regulations were interpreted and implemented locally, under the watchful eye of *2. Armeeinspektion* in Berlin (which also inspected the Prussian *Gardekorps*). The King of Saxony was commander in chief and appointed all Saxon officers, but the Kaiser could veto appointments of corps commanders.

Although it played a prominent part in the Great War, the Royal Saxon Army has been little studied since 1945. Until 1989 Saxony lay entirely behind the Iron Curtain in the German Democratic Republic, and its archives were believed lost like those of Prussia. Since reunification an extraordinary flood of unpublished primary sources has come to light, and shows no signs of abating. The present work aims to use such sources to describe the Saxon war experience on part of the Western Front of special interest for English-speaking readers, comprising Belgian and French Flanders from the coast to the La Bassée Canal.

Friedrich August III, King of Saxony (25 May 1865–18 February 1932) with his children on the eve of war; from left Ernst Heinrich, Margarete, Maria Alix, Anna, Friedrich Christian and Crown Prince Georg. The portrait on the right is their grandfather King Georg. Their mother Luise of Austria came into scandalous conflict with the strict old King's rigidly Catholic court, and was separated from her husband before his succession. During the war all three princes served as staff officers in Flanders, and Ernst Heinrich in a combat role with Feldartillerie-Regiment 115.

Since 1815 the borders of the Kingdom of Saxony corresponded roughly to the current *Freistaat Sachsen*. With an area of 5,787 square miles it was the fifth largest German state geographically, but third by population. Blessed with fertile soil, abundant mineral wealth and enlightened rulers (and both blessed and cursed with a strategic location at the heart of Europe) its economy was booming in 1914. Partly due to immigration from other German states, it was the most densely populated and urbanised state in the *Reich*. A little over half of the nearly five million inhabitants lived in the towns and cities, principally Dresden (the capital), Leipzig and Chemnitz. The overwhelming majority were German Protestants, with about 12,500 Jews in 1914 and a largely Catholic Slav minority known as Sorbs or Wends in the northeast. In addition to mining and heavy industry, Saxony accounted for a quarter of German textile production and much of the publishing industry. Its most famous export was Meissen porcelain, which still enjoys a world-class reputation. The rulers of Saxony had long been keen patrons of learning, music and the arts. Of the four universities they founded only Leipzig remained within the post-1815 borders, but the kingdom still boasted one of the most literate populations in Europe. While this high level

of education and urbanisation had great economic advantages, it also provoked discontent with the country's moderate constitutional monarchy, making Saxony a major focus of social democratic politics in Germany. Its shrewd and genial ruler King Friedrich August III had therefore followed a path of cautious modernisation and cultivated a casual and down-to-earth personal image. The king gained great popularity by his habitual use of the local dialect (considered ridiculous by many other Germans) and habit of wandering Dresden incognito and unguarded.

In contrast to its economic and cultural achievements, Saxony had been less successful in the political sphere. The decline of Saxon power since the middle ages can be partly traced by the widespread use of variations of the name beyond the kingdom's borders. The original tribal homeland of the Saxons included Lower Saxony (*Niedersachsen*) on the North Sea coast, from which some raided and ultimately settled in England. However the Electorate (*Kurfürstentum*) and later Kingdom of Saxony descended from the Margraviate of Meissen on the Elbe, ruled since the eleventh century by the House of Wettin. The family gained the electorate in 1423 but were late and inconsistent adopt-

Final peacetime dispositions of the Saxon Army. At mobilisation most units left an *ersatz-bataillon*, *-abteilung* or *-eskadron* behind to train replacements. *Ersatz-bataillonen* were also set up for reserve and *landwehr* infantry in August 1914, and the 'active' infantry and *jäger* formed second battalions in 1915. *Ersatz* units were later created for machine-gunners (Königsbrück and Zeithain), *minenwerfer crews* (Königsbrück), *Kraftfahrtruppen* (Zwickau) and aviators (Grossenhain). Each corps HQ left a *stellvertretendes generalkommando* (deputy corps staff) behind to organise the *ersatz* units (see p. 242).

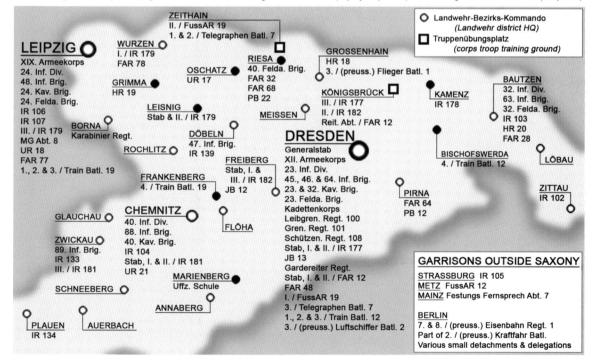

Kaiser Wilhelm und König Friedrich August begeben sich an der Spitze der verschiedenen Fürstlichkeiten zum Denkmal.

Kaiser Wilhelm II and King Friedrich August III at the dedication of the *Völkerschlachtdenkmal* at Leipzig on 18 October 1913. This imposing monument commemorates the decisive 'Battle of the Nations' against Napoleon in 1813, during which most of the Saxon Army switched sides.

ers of primogeniture, resulting in the existence of many small duchies to the west of the future kingdom ruled by branches of the Ernestine Wettin line. Of these, *Sachsen-Weimar-Eisenach*, *Sachsen-Altenburg*, *Sachsen-Meiningen* and *Sachsen-Coburg und Gotha* still existed in 1914. The last of these merged with the British royal house in 1840 when Queen Victoria married Prince Albert, as a result of which the queen's surname technically became Wettin.

The Protestant Reformation began in the sixteenth century at the then Saxon capital of Wittenberg, under the protection of the electors. As a result Saxony was devastated in the religious wars of the sixteenth and seventeenth centuries. In 1697 the ambitious Elector Friedrich August I 'the Strong' (*'August der Starke'*) returned to Catholicism in order to become King of Poland. His wars and extravagances ruined both Saxony and Poland, and his son Friedrich August II was the last Saxon to hold the Polish crown. After a period of renewed prosperity the French brought fresh turmoil. Defeated by Napoleon at Jena alongside Prussia, Elector Friedrich August III chose to join the Confederation of the Rhine. On 20 December 1806 Saxony became a kingdom under Napoleonic patronage. Crowned as King Friedrich August I, the former elector also ruled the puppet Duchy of

Warsaw from 1807. After the deaths of thousands of Saxon soldiers in the invasion of Russia, the war came to Saxony in 1813. Forced to remain on the French side by Napoleon's threats to devastate his country, the king saw much of his army desert at Leipzig in October. The kingdom was occupied by Prussia and over half annexed, mostly joining the Prussian Province of Saxony (*Provinz Sachsen*). Remarkably the king was wildly popular on his return from captivity in 1815, due to intense public hostility to the Prussians.

Renewed peace was disturbed by revolutionary unrest in 1848, and broken by war with Prussia in 1866. In the dispute over German unification, King Johann preferred a looser *'Großdeutschland'* of all the German states to a Prussian-dominated *'Kleindeutschland'* excluding Austria. Under Crown Prince Albert the Saxons proved to be Austria's most resolute and effective allies, but could not save them from defeat at Königgrätz. The kingdom avoided the annexation suffered by Hanover and several smaller states, mainly due to its value in rebuilding Austro-Prussian relations. Nevertheless it was forced to pay an indemnity of 10,000,000 Thalers and join the Prussian-led *Norddeutscher Bund*. The continued existence of its army was seriously in doubt, with King Wilhelm I and Bismarck initially favouring its full

Pre-war visit by heavy artillerymen of Fußartillerie-Regiment 12 (garrisoned in peacetime in the border fortress of Metz) to the *Sachsendenkmal* on the old battlefield of Gravelotte-St. Privat, where the Saxon XII. Armee-Korps played a major role in the German victory of August 1870.

absorption under Prussian officers. However senior Prussian generals managed to convince them that the Saxons would be far more loyal and effective under their own leaders. In 1867 the kingdom integrated its army into the forces of the *Bund* as **XII. (I. Kgl. Sächs.) Armee-Korps**, comprising **23. (1. Kgl. Sächs.)** and **24. (2. Kgl. Sächs.) Infanterie-Division**. Organisation, training and terminology were all adapted to Prussian norms, under the efficient direction of Saxon war minister Genltn. Alfred von Fabrice and the careful scrutiny of the Prussians. The new system of dual German / Saxon unit numbering produced many oddities. Saxon infantry regiments received the 'German' numbers 100–108, but had far longer traditions than many lower-numbered Prussian units. Having absorbed all the old Saxon field batteries, 1. Kgl. Sächs. Feldartillerie-Regiment Nr. 12 inherited the traditions of the entire Saxon artillery arm back to 1620 and became officially the 'oldest' German regiment.

Fearful of Prussian power and masterfully manipulated by Bismarck, France declared war on the *Norddeutscher Bund* in July 1870. To the horror of the French, the remaining south German states sided with the *Bund* and Austria remained neutral. Once again the Saxons fought with great distinction under Crown Prince Albert, notably in the attack on St. Privat at the

decisive Battle of Gravelotte on 18 August. In a clear affirmation of Prussian faith in their once-reluctant allies, the prince was given command of 4. Armee the next day. On 18 January 1871 Kaiser Wilhelm I was proclaimed in the Hall of Mirrors at Versailles, and the new French government signed a peace treaty with the new German *Reich*. A large swathe of predominantly German-speaking territory conquered by France in the seventeenth and eighteenth centuries was brought under direct imperial rule as the *Reichsland Elsass-Lothringen*, and the French forced to pay 5,000,000,000 Francs in reparations.

Crown Prince Albert became king on 29 October 1873. While major constitutional and welfare reform took place during his reign, the Royal Saxon Army remained his primary interest. Protected by his formidable military reputation and confidently administered by General von Fabrice (elevated to the title of Graf von Fabrice in 1884), its semi-independent status was rigorously defended against all political threats. As an intrinsically 'particularist' institution it was distrusted by nationalists, to whom the old loyalties to the historic German states were obstacles to the cause of 'Germany above all'. They were especially suspicious of the numerous former Hanoverian officers who had entered Saxon service after their country's annexation, since the deposed King Georg V remained a bitter enemy of Prussia until his death in 1878 (even raising a small private army in French exile) and his son only reconciled with the Kaiser in 1913. Within Saxony this influx of talent also provoked resentment among native-born officers, due to the effect on their own career prospects. During the 1870s the Saxon *Kadettenkorps* in Dresden and its Hanoverian head Oberstltn. von Bülow were repeatedly attacked in the 'national liberal' press for subversive particularism. It was certainly favoured by the sons of the Hanoverian nobility, though most sought commissions in Prussian regiments. More broadly the Saxon officer corps established a reputation as a more cultured and progressive alternative to Prussian service. In Prussian eyes the army was often seen to embody the stereotype of the Saxons as a people – 'cosy' (*gemütlich*), slightly effete and lacking in aggression. Nevertheless its independence was assured by its rigorous professionalism, the reputation of its leaders and not least the 'particularism' of the Prussians themselves, who did not wish to dissolve their own identity in monolithic 'German' institutions. The death of King Albert in 1902 without issue and succession of his elderly brother Georg made little difference, since the new king had also served with distinction in 1870.

Saxony's share of the French reparations had been used to construct the *Albertstadt* on the northern edge of Dresden, at the time the largest contiguous barracks complex in Germany; unlike the city centre, it was not firebombed in 1945 and many of the original buildings survive. After an expansion of the artillery in 1872–1873, enough infantry units were formed from 1881 onwards to create the **32. (3. Kgl. Sächs.) Infanterie-Division** in 1887. Rapid economic and demographic growth allowed further expansion from 1897, leading to the formation of the **40. (4. Kgl. Sächs.) Infanterie-Division** and **XIX. (II. Kgl. Sächs.) Armee-Korps** in 1899 and raising the prospect of a Saxon field army in wartime. The unpopular King Georg died in 1904 and was succeeded by his son Friedrich August, who had only seen peacetime service. By force of personality, the new king soon won the confidence both of the Kaiser and of his people. His peacetime reign saw the introduction of the subdued *feldgrau* uniform, universal issue of machine-guns to the infantry and the formation of enough new units to equalise the strength of the two corps. His wartime reign would see the downfall of both Saxony and Germany.

All four German kingdoms were required to contribute to the garrison of the imperially-administered *Reichsland Elsass-Lothringen*. In addition to the artillery at Metz, Saxony provided Infanterie-Regiment 105 – seen here during an oath-taking ceremony (*vereidigung*) at Oberhausbergen in Alsace. Infanterie-Regiment 105 served with Prussian 30. ID / XV. Armee-Korps and belonged to the Strassburg garrison in peacetime, but upon mobilisation established its Ersatz-Bataillon in its actual recruiting area at Werdau in West Saxony (with a 2. Ersatz-Bataillon at Meerane in 1915–1917).

Private soldier (*husar*) of Husaren-Regiment 19 in full parade uniform – light blue with white braid. His *sabretache* bears the royal cypher 'AR', awarded to this regiment and to Husaren-Regiment 'König Albert' 18 in 1891. Traditionally both the Garde-Reiter-Regiment and Leib-Grenadier-Regiment 100 bore the cypher of the ruling monarch (since 1904, 'FAR') on their shoulder-straps, as did Feldartillerie-Regiment 12 and 32 (above a flaming bomb and crossed cannon respectively).

Einjährig-freiwilliger (shown by green and white twist piping on his shoulder-straps, which bear a red hunting horn above the number) of Schützen-(Füsilier-)Regiment 'Prinz Georg' 108 in full wartime marching order. The unique Austrian-influenced *tschako* of the Saxon *jäger* and *schützen* was worn with a black horse-hair plume (as seen here, over the camouflage cover) even in the field. Like the Prussian *jäger*, these units wore *graugrün* (greener than *feldgrau*) in wartime.

The Saxon military oath (*Fahneneid*)

Ich ... schwöre zu Gott dem Allmächtigen und Allwissenden, dass ich seiner Majestät dem Könige Friedrich August von Sachsen während meiner Dienstzeit als Soldat treu dienen, seiner Majestät dem Kaiser und den Kriegsgesetzen Gehorsam leisten und mich stets als ein tapferer und ehrliebender Soldat verhalten will.
So wahr mir Gott helfe und sein heiliges Wort, durch Jesum Christum, unsern Erlöser. Amen.

I, (name) swear by almighty and all-knowing God that I will loyally serve His Majesty King Friedrich August of Saxony during my period of military service, be obedient to His Majesty the Kaiser and the laws of war and conduct myself always as a brave and honourable soldier. So help me God and His holy word, through Jesus Christ our saviour. Amen.

For Jewish soldiers the last line was simply "*so wahr mir Gott helfe*". Further variations existed for subjects of other German states (or of the *Reichsland*) serving with the Royal Saxon Army. The oath was sworn in the presence of a clergyman, on a unit colour (*fahne*) or a gun for artillery units. An officer's sword was often used in wartime.

Unidentified Saxon infantry relaxing at a rear-area *'Sachsenheim'* somewhere in Flanders circa 1915. The patriotic sign-painter has made a classic error – the green diagonal *rautenkranz* (the 'rue crown') should run downward from left to right across the black and gold striped field.

Like soldiers of other nations, Saxons often bestowed familiar names from home (as well as those of their leaders) on trenches, streets and landmarks in their sectors. Since military maps were produced by corps-level topographical survey teams (*vermessungs-abteilungen*), the Saxon Vermessungs-Abteilung 19 decided the official German names of many places on the Armentières / Ploegsteert front – here the 'Leipziger Straße' spanning French and Belgian Comines.

CHAPTER 2
ROYAL SAXON ARMY AT WAR 1914–1918

Remarkably casual studio portrait of an 'old sweat' from 1. Kgl. Sächs. Jäger-Bataillon Nr. 12 (Freiberg) immediately before departure for the front, showing the typically Saxon habit of rolling the trouser legs over the boot tops and a likewise typically casual attitude to his uniform and equipment.

The King was on a mountaineering holiday at Taufers in Tyrol when he learned that the Austro-Hungarian heir apparent Archduke Franz Ferdinand von Österreich-Este had been murdered at Sarajevo by Serbian-sponsored terrorists. While horrified, His Majesty was optimistic that the crisis would result in no more than a short, sharp punishment of the rogue state, perhaps due to the friendly relations between Saxony and Russia (which had provoked Prussian outrage when the Tsar was made honorary *chef* of Feldartillerie-Regiment 28 without consulting the Kaiser). As the clouds of war gathered the royal family hurried back to Dresden. Though kept closely informed, the King was powerless to intervene in foreign policy. However it is hard to imagine that even a fully independent Saxony would not once again have sided with its ancient ally. His Majesty's youngest son Prince Ernst Heinrich later wrote: '*In Dresden the population was greatly agitated by these events; a general excitement was abroad, which in part assumed a violent character. Tens of thousands gathered at the Dresdner Schloss and in the Theaterplatz, singing the* Deutschlandlied *and* Wacht am Rhein *and shouting 'hurra' until the King showed himself on the balcony.*'[1]

Russia mobilised on 31 July and Germany on 1 August. In the *Reichstag* a rare political unity prevailed, and the Kaiser declared '*Ich kenne keine Parteien mehr, ich kenne nur noch Deutsche!*' (henceforth I recognise no parties, only Germans) The die had been cast, and the Royal Saxon Army prepared to join the all-out effort to bring the war to a swift and victorious conclusion. Prince Ernst Heinrich recalled: '*Adorned with flowers and accompanied by the population, the regiments of the Dresden garrison marched in field grey to the railway stations where they embarked. I accompanied my father, who saw them off there. The carriages were decorated by the soldiers with every possible inscription. I will never forget one of them:* "Paris muß sächsisch werden" [Paris must be Saxony's]'.[1]

The co-author's great-grandfather Gefreiter Arno Bierast (kneeling with blanket roll) with fellow volunteers at the *Leipziger Bahnhof* in Dresden in autumn 1914, about to join Feldartillerie-Regiment 48 on the Aisne. He served with 23. ID and 241. ID for the duration and was promoted at least to sergeant. As a former trade union leader, he spent Hitler's war in Berlin in active conspiracy against the regime and died peacefully in 1959.

The mobilisation plans called for the immediate formation of a Saxon reserve corps (based around a cadre of regular personnel and otherwise formed of trained reservists). Unlike some reserve formations formed simultaneously elsewhere in Germany, this **XII. Reserve-Korps** (**23.** and **24. Reserve-Division**) was equipped to a standard close to that of the 'active' units; six of its eight infantry regiments had a full machine-gun company from the outset, and each division could boast three quarters of the field artillery strength of its active counterpart (nine batteries rather than twelve) rather than the typical half. This reserve corps and both active corps (themselves raised to wartime strength with reservists) marched out in August 1914 under a Saxon staff as Germany's **3. Armee**, initially accompanied by (Prussian) XI. Armee-Korps. While the titular commander was former Saxon war minister Generaloberst Max Freiherr von Hausen, his chief of staff was the Prussian General-major von Hoeppner (later the first commander of the Imperial German Air Force, the *Luftstreitkräfte*).

In addition to these three corps, virtually all remaining fit and trained manpower was mobilised in an array of smaller units. One Prussian and two Saxon cavalry brigades formed **8. Kavallerie-Division**, fighting in Lorraine in August before being transported to the East for the remainder of the war. Seven Landwehr infantry regiments were formed from older reservists in their thirties, four of which were grouped into the all-arms (*gemischte*) **45.** and **47. Landwehr-Brigade** for the Western Front. As dictated by a 1911 amendment to the mobilisation plans, the bulk of the remaining younger reservists formed the provisional and incompletely equipped **19. Ersatz-Division**, which was sent to the Vosges. This comprehensive mobilisation led to an acute shortage of fit and experienced personnel when the new Saxon / Württemberg **XXVII. Reserve-Korps** (**53.** and **54. Reserve-Division**) began formation from the thousands of untrained *ersatz-reservists* and war volunteers who flocked to the colours in August. It also left only token forces to face the Russians. In addition to three Landwehr infantry regiments, most of the newly formed *ersatz-bataillons* of the reserve and Landwehr infantry were relocated to the Prussian border fortresses of Breslau, Graudenz, Thorn and Posen. More significantly Fussartillerie-Regiment 19 moved its main depot to Posen, together with three reserve and Landwehr battalions armed with 15cm howitzers.

The advance of 3. Armee into Belgium was to be the last battle fought by the Royal Saxon Army as a body. During the Battle of the Marne in September, the **XII.** and **XIX. Armee-Korps** were sent to reinforce 2. and 6. Armee respectively.

In an especially harsh blow to Saxon military pride, the elderly Freiherr von Hausen (who had fought the Prussians in 1866) was relieved of his command on 12 September due to a bout of typhus and replaced by the Prussian General von Einem. Further humiliation followed in October, when Genltn. von Carlowitz (von Hausen's successor as war minister) led XXVII. RK to disaster in Flanders and was replaced by a Prussian. General von Schubert's tenure (until August 1916) was to be the only instance of a non-Saxon commanding a Saxon corps during the war.

By the end of 1914, Saxon dispositions in the West had settled into a pattern which remained largely consistent until 1916. The XXVII. RK and **IR 105** (with 30. ID/XV. AK) were established around Ypres and XIX. AK facing Armentières. XII. AK held the Aisne valley between the Chemin des Dames and Reims, with 47. Landwehr-Brigade on its left. 45. Landwehr-Brigade was dissolved at the end of 1914 and its elements widely dispersed. In the Champagne, XII. RK

Saxon commanders in 1914: 1. Gen. d. Infanterie d'Elsa (XII. AK); **2.** Genltn. Edler von der Planitz (32. ID); **3.** Gen. d. Infanterie von Carlowitz (XXVII. RK); **4.** Gen. d. Kavallerie von Laffert (XIX. AK); **5.** Gen. d. Artillerie von Kirchbach (XII. RK); **6.** Gen. d. Kavallerie Krug von Nidda (24. ID).

Sachsen in großer Zeit, vol. II, p. 48

British field guns captured 'at Ypres' (probably in spring 1915) on display in the *Marktplatz* at Leipzig, in front of the *Siegesdenkmal* commemorating 1871. This fine memorial survived the Second World War, but was destroyed under the Soviet occupation regime in 1946.

(still with 3. Armee) held the front Moronvilliers – Aube-rive – St. Souplet. Finally 19. Ersatz-Division held the line Lagarde – Blâmont – Cirey-sur-Vezouze in the Vosges south-west of Saarburg.

After rebuilding over the winter, the spring of 1915 brought fresh expansion. Mindful of the fate of the young reserve corps at the First Battle of Ypres, the Germans now sought to build new units via 'donations' from existing ones in the field, whilst replenishing donor formations with new recruits. The traditional 'square' division (two infantry brigades each of two regiments) was to be superseded by the 'triangular' division (one infantry brigade of three regiments); meanwhile field artillery batteries were being reduced as standard from six guns to four. The resulting surplus of men and guns allowed formation of the Saxon/Württemberg **58. Infanterie-Division** (from XIX. AK and XIV. RK) at the beginning of March, and the purely Saxon **123. Infanterie-Division** (from XII. AK and XII. RK) on 1 April. Both were designated as 'independent' from the out-set, with no 'permanent' attachment to a corps, and some traditional corps assets (such as heavy artillery) at divisional level. The Saxons did not attempt to 'triangularise' further divisions until 1917, as the XXVII. RK and 19. Ersatz-

Division (which only formed its provisional battalions into regiments in February 1915) first needed to achieve normal levels of equipment and organisation. In the meantime how-ever a more modest expansion scheme began, with XIX. and XII. AK using donations from many existing regiments to build Infanterie-Regiment 183 (in May) and 192 (in July) respectively. Each soon became part of an independent brigade with the same number, together with non-Saxon regiments formed in a similar manner. **192. Infanterie-Brigade** possessed a Saxon staff and other Saxon units, and was destined to become a full Saxon division – as was the slowly expanding 47. Landwehr-Brigade, formally design-ated *Division Müller* by Autumn 1915.

The sectors of XII. and XIX. AK remained largely quiet throughout 1915, allowing them to provide significant re-inforcements to other parts of the Western Front threatened by Entente offensives. The new independent divisions and brigades played a still larger role as strategic reserves. 58. ID fought the French at Vimy Ridge (May–June), then transferred to the Eastern Front (July–October) and the Vosges (October–December). 123. ID briefly held various quiet sectors before being entrusted with the defence of the crucial Souchez salient in late August; after resisting both the French and British autumn offensives it returned to Flanders. XII. RK fought in the First Battle of Champagne (December 1914–March 1915) and suffered massive losses in the Second (September–October 1915), during which **183.** and 192. Infanterie-Brigade also fought with 3. Armee.

Meanwhile in the East, most of the motley assortment of Saxon garrison regiments and battalions had been sent into the field with Prussian formations (the battalions as part of new 'mixed' regiments); the Saxon **46. Landwehr-Brigade** (*Brigade Graf Pfeil*) left the fortress of Graudenz for the front in July. More ambitiously, Saxony formed **Etappen-Inspektion *Süd*** (comprising countless medical, logistic and transport units) in January for the new *Südarmee*, supporting the Austrians in the Carpathians.

1916 brought expansion and consolidation. In June the provisional *Division Müller* became 47. Landwehr-Division. Meanwhile the (all-arms) **408. Infanterie-Brigade** became the first combat unit of its size formed in Saxony since 1914, and met up with Württemberg 407. Infanterie-Brigade on 31 July in Flanders to form **204. Infanterie-Division**. It was to be the final 'joint venture' between the two kingdoms. After an exchange of units in October,

54. RD became purely Württemberg (and left XXVII. RK), 192. ID purely Saxon and 183. ID purely Prussian; the latter two had been upgraded from brigades in June. This was followed in late December by the 'Württembergisation' of 204. ID and 'Saxonisation' of 58. ID. However ongoing Saxon attempts to wrest IR 105 from Prussian command remained unsuccessful. In this context the creation of **212. Infanterie-Division** in September (with a Saxon staff and field artillery, but otherwise Prussian) seems odd, but its composition would change radically in 1917. Summer 1916 also brought major changes for the six battalions of Saxon *jägers*, all now separated from their divisions. From August JB 13, RJB 25 and RJB 26 formed Jäger-Regiment 7 with Prussian 197. ID in Galicia (Austrian Ukraine). JB 12, RJB 12 and RJB 13 transferred to the Balkans, and spent the rest of the war supporting the Bulgarians in the mountains of Macedonia.

The early months of 1916 were dominated by the Verdun Offensive. By April most of the Saxon heavy artillery on the Western Front was involved, principally the 21cm *mörser* battalions of Fussartillerie-Regiment 12. IR 105 arrived with 30. ID in late February, and left in early October for the Somme. 58. ID fought at Bois de la Caillette in March and April, suffering grievous losses. 192. IB arrived in March and

A *lausejagd* (louse hunt) in the primitive dug-outs of Leib-Grenadier-Regiment 100 near Berry-au-Bac at Whitsun (*Pfingsten*) 1915.

Frontschweine of IR 134 crouch in the squalid trenches of *Fourreaux-wald* (High Wood) during the Battle of the Somme in August 1916.

A Saxon infantry company somewhere in Galicia, taking a welcome break from the march during the scorching summer of 1917. A brief note on the back is dated 12 July, in the days between the collapse of the Russian Kerensky Offensive on the front of the *Südarmee* and the start of the decisive counter-offensive.

remained on this front as a division until 1918. Further south in the Vosges, 19. Ersatz-Division conducted diversionary attacks for the offensive, and transferred to Verdun in October. The Battle of the Somme was a far more severe trial for the Saxon Army. IR 183 (183. ID) was first to arrive on 6 July near Pozières, followed by 123. ID at Guillemont/Maurepas from the 8th. Both were relieved later in July, though IR 183 endured a second tour (September–October) before changing divisions. By the end of the year XII. RK (July–August and October–December), XIX. AK (August and October), XXVII. RK (September), 58. ID (September and November) and IR 105 (October–November) had all fought north of the river. XII. AK at first remained on the Aisne and sent a provisional '*Division Francke*' (from parts of both divisions) to oppose the French south of the river in late July, with the entire 23. ID committed from the end of August for the remainder of the year. 32. ID was re-formed in September and left for the Argonne, reappearing north of the Somme in November; the divisions and corps staff of XII. AK were now permanently separated. By the end of the year, XII. RK was south of Arras, XIX. AK in Flanders, and both IR 105 and 58. ID back at Verdun. 123. ID had been in the East since August. From November XXVII. RK (minus 54. RD) was in Galicia, where personnel from 53. RD played a major part in forming the

Sturmbataillon der Südarmee (later Sturmbatl. 8) in December with German, Austro-Hungarian and Ottoman elements.

The spring of 1917 saw the Royal Saxon Army reach its peak strength of nineteen divisions. In January **219. Infanterie-Division** was formed in the Vosges (from elements of XII. RK and 19. ED) and **241. Infanterie-Division** in Saxony; the latter included numerous teenage recruits from the class of 1919 and spent the year in the East. Also in January 212. ID was 'Saxonised' in Rumania by absorbing 408. IB and IR 182. In March, assorted Saxon Landwehr regiments and battalions in the East were concentrated as **45. Landwehr-Division** and 46. LB became a division. Finally in April **96. Infanterie-Division** was formed in the East with contributions from 19. ED and 53. RD. 1917 also saw the separation of all German corps staffs from their divisions, and their redesignation as geographical *gruppen* – first XII. RK (April), then XIX. AK (end of June) and finally XXVII. RK (end of November).

In February and March 23. ID, 32. ID and XII. RK took part in *Alberich*, the German scorched-earth withdrawal to the *Siegfriedstellung*, and 47. LD in the evacuation of civilians from St. Quentin and reinforcement of the new defensive lines. In April the French launched their ruinous offensive on the Aisne, and 23. ID, 32. ID, 58. ID and IR 105 all contributed to the German victory; 23. ID remained on this front until February 1918. On 7 June the Messines detonations interrupted the relief of XIX. AK as *Gruppe Wytschaete*; between July and November 23. RD, 32. ID, 58. ID and a massive concentration of Saxon artillery all became involved in the hellish battle that followed. In December 24. RD and IR 105 fought in the German counter-offensive at Cambrai.

With the arrival of 58. ID (April), 24. RD (May) and 47. LD (June) the Saxons on the Eastern Front reached a peak of ten divisions that summer. 24. RD, 53. RD (still under XXVII. RK) and 241. ID fought alongside Prussian, Austrian, Hungarian and Ottoman divisions with the *Südarmee* in the decisive defeat of the final Russian offensive and the subsequent pursuit. 24. RD, 58. ID, 123. ID and 53. RD all returned to the West by the end of the year, followed by 241. ID in January 1918, Jäger-Regiment 7 (with 197. ID) in February, then 23. RD and 40. ID (both of which had only arrived in the East in October) and finally 96. ID in early April. Ultimately only the three Landwehr divisions, 212. ID and 219. ID would remain in the East, donating their younger and fitter men to the divisions going westward.

8. KD was dissolved in April 1918 and its elements dispersed on police duties.

In the West, 192. ID, 19. ED and 40. ID at Verdun and 96. ID in the Vosges remained on the defensive in spring 1918. The remainder were all designated attack divisions for Ludendorff's offensives. When the *Kaiserschlacht* opened on 21 March, 24. RD and 53. RD attacked side by side at Cambrai on the southern flank of 17. Armee, with 24. ID in army reserve further north. 23. ID was with 18. Armee in the thrust west of St. Quentin, also initially in reserve. On 28 March 23. RD took part in the *Mars-Angriff* on the right flank of 17. Armee north of Arras. 53. RD joined the attack of 18. Armee at the beginning of April, with IR 105 arriving a few days later for the subsequent defensive fighting. Meanwhile 32. ID and 58. ID fought in the *Georgette* Offensive in Flanders. 241. ID drove forward southwest of Laon in April (*Archangel*) and again in late May to June (*Blücher-Yorck*); Jäger-Regiment 7 also fought in the latter offensive. On 15 July, 23. ID and 123. ID attacked southwest of Reims in the abortive *Friedensturm* with IR 105 in reserve. 18 July, the opening of the French-led counter-offensive, could well be called the 'Black Day of the Saxon Army'. By its conclusion on 6 August, 23. ID, 40. ID, 24. RD,

The King visiting Crown Prince Georg in the field at Thiaucourt on 7 May 1918, two weeks before the end of the prince's tenure in command of Infanterie Regiment 'Kronprinz' 104. Marked with an 'x' at the front is Hptm. Max Koch, company commander of 2./104 in August 1914 and architect of the '*Kratzbürste*' raid in May 1916 (see p.114). Koch was killed in action leading I./104 at Ervillers on 23 August 1918.

53. RD, 19. ED, 241. ID and IR 105 had all endured heavy fighting, and all the ground gained here since March had been lost. Conversely the Battle of Amiens launched on 8 August could be judged a local defensive success for the Saxons, with 24. ID and 192. ID holding their sectors south of Plessier against the full weight of the French attack until withdrawn. 23. ID, 40. ID and 58. ID resisted the British August offensive in the Bapaume area, with 58. ID and IR 105 engaged in heavy rearguard fighting between Cambrai and the Sambre from September to November. On 17 August the French attacked at Noyon and thrust toward La Fère, with 24. ID, 24. RD, 53. RD, 241. ID, 19. ED and Jäger-Regiment 7 all involved in desperate defensive fighting which continued into September. 24. RD resisted the subsequent advance to the Serre for the remainder of the war.

On 12 September the Americans began the reduction of the St. Mihiel salient on the Meuse; 123. ID and 192. ID both saw heavy fighting, the latter narrowly escaping encirclement when the Austrian division on its flank disintegrated. The Saxon Army was now plainly bleeding to death; on 26 September the battered 53. RD and its infantry regiments were ordered dissolved, and the survivors

sent to reinforce the other depleted Saxon divisions. On 28 September the Entente began their final advance in Flanders, with 23. ID, 40. ID and 23. RD all heavily engaged until the Armistice. On the 29th the British and Americans crossed the St. Quentin Canal with numerous tanks; in the resulting battle 241. ID was practically destroyed, 24. ID so mauled that it never fought again and 197. ID dissolved due to losses together with its Prussian regiments. Jäger-Regiment 7 was transferred to 241. ID, which joined 32. ID, 123. ID and 192. ID (all engaged there since October) in resisting the Franco-American Meuse-Argonne Offensive in the final days of the war.

On 13 November Friedrich August III voluntarily abdicated, releasing the surviving officers and men of the Royal Saxon Army from their military oath. Legend states that the saddened and exhausted monarch addressed his quarrelsome republican successors with the words 'Nu, da machd doch oiern Drägg alleene' ('well then, do your filthy business by yourselves'). From a pre-war population of almost five million, the Kingdom had mobilised around 750,000 men. According to semi-official estimates in 'Sachsen in großer Zeit' (1920), 212,783 Saxon servicemen had been killed, 334,000 wounded and 42,023 taken prisoner.

Clowning for the camera in civilian and enemy clothing, *landsers* of Reserve-Infanterie-Regiment 106 (123. Infanterie Division) put a brave face on their imminent departure from the Bezonvaux sector (Verdun) in June 1918 to take part in the ill-fated *Friedensturm* Offensive.

CHAPTER 3
THE YEAR 1914

Two friends from 2. Kgl. Sächs. Pionier-Bataillon Nr. 22 about to depart
for the front (as shown by the traditional flowers) in full marching order,
probably at the battalion's garrison
town of Riesa. Differences from infantry equipment include smaller ammunition pouches and long-handled
digging tools (a pickaxe and a shovel),
both later adopted by 'storm troops'.
Saxon *pioniere* differed from those of
the other armies of the *Kaiserreich* in
having 'German' tunic cuffs (like the
Saxon infantry) instead of the 'Swedish'
style (as worn by the *telegraphist* on
p. 171); they were also distinguished
by the traditional pick and shovel em-
blem above the unit number on their
shoulder-straps.

1914 in Flanders

The Saxons arrived in Flanders in October 1914 during the great strategic gamble later known as the *Erster Flandernschlacht* (First Battle of Ypres). From 11 October **XIX. Armeekorps** fought on the right of 6. Armee, taking Lille and establishing a strong defensive front east of Armentières. Further north, **XXVII. Reserve-Korps** was one of four hastily raised corps forming the bulk of 4. Armee, which launched its offensive on 20 October. **Infanterie-Regiment 105** arrived on their left on 30 October, during the first of two major efforts to regain the initiative on the Menin Road.

The desperate and ruinously costly efforts of 4. Armee to break through toward the channel ports became the stuff of legend. Like the first day of the Somme in Britain, the scale of the slaughter left a deep mark on the national consciousness, as survivors and bereaved sought meaning in this immense and unavailing sacrifice. It also saw the end of hopes for a swift end to the war, and of the essential optimism of pre-war Germany. This all became symbolised by the young *kriegsfrei-williger*, especially the idealistic student in the volunteer tradition of the wars against Napoleon. Though not so numerous as later claimed, students were certainly present in numbers disproportionate to their tiny share of the population. The legend of the *Kindermord* (Massacre of the Innocents) focuses on Prussian XXVI. Reserve-Korps at Langemarck, but the Saxons and Württembergers on their left endured a similar ordeal. They too used singing to aid identification as Germans, or nerve themselves for the attack. It is interesting here to compare the 'official' account (p. 28) with that of Vizefeldwebel Penther (p. 191), who emphasises religious consolation when facing death.

In autumn 1914 the Germans were still fighting a traditional war of movement. Officers and NCOs went into action with drawn swords, though brocade belts and sashes had vanished. The regular Saxon infantry took their battalion colours into the field in August, and these were carried in battle for the last time in Flanders; in senior regiments these were the flags of 1870. The campaign also saw the last mounted action in regimental strength for Saxon cavalry in the West.

XIX. AK and IR 105 were already familiar with the reckless aggression of the French and the lethal efficiency of their artillery. The BEF was an unknown quantity, but soon recognised as a highly professional and well-equipped opponent. Accounts by Saxon regulars emphasise their marksmanship, use of ground and *zähig-keit* (tenacity) – a virtue traditionally attributed to the Saxons themselves. According to Unteroffizier Siegfried Brase of RIR 241, the 'eight week soldiers' of XXVII. RK were in awe of their first fallen Tommy at Ledegem on 19 October. This *'strapping English sergeant'* made a deep impression on men unused to death, and acutely aware of being novices facing *'veteran English troops ... some of whom had already served their King for many years in India and other colonies. They gazed on the first dead enemy in reverential silence, and no-one dared take the many English pound notes from the body.'*[1]

It is clear that the Saxons had a reputation on the British side before the Christmas Truce cemented it in popular imagination. As one truce account puts it, '*as soon as we saw they were Saxons I knew it was all right, because they're good fellows on the whole and play the game as far as they know it'.*[2] When accusing IR 143 of mistreating prisoners at Gheluvelt on 31 October, the Official History makes a point of exonerating IR 105. Perhaps more reliably, the published history of the Leinster Regiment describes a brief ceasefire by IR 179 on 20 October, during which both sides rescued their wounded. Each side seemingly came to see the other as a people like themselves, with similar values – stoically resigned to the business of war, but divorced by geographical good fortune from the violent passions of their allies. By focusing on the Prussians, British atrocity propaganda encouraged this perception.

Like other Germans, the Saxons tended to feel linguistic and cultural affinity for the Flemish people, and distrust for French speakers. As Generalmajor Kaden shows (p. 211), social class and fluency in French modified these feelings. The Flemish language was no obstacle for the Saxons, who found it no stranger than some German dialects. Flemish names were easily pronounced, but the common *landser* mangled French ones as thoroughly as any Tommy. For instance Quesnoy became '*Genua*' and Wambrechies '*Warmbierschiss*' ('warm beer shit'), with similar obscenities used for Pérenchies and others with the same suffix.

XXVII. Reserve-Korps (53. and 54. Reserve-Division)

The Calvary of the Saxon-Württemberg *'Kinderkorps'*

53. Reserve-Division
(s.) *Inf. Brig.:* (s.) RIR 241 | (s.) RIR 242
(s.) RIR 243 | (s.) RIR 244 | (s.) RJB 25
(s.) Res. Kav. Abt. 53 | (s.) RFAR 53
(s.) Res. Pi. Komp. 53 | (s). Res. Div. Brückentrain 53
(s.) Res. San. Komp. 53

54. Reserve-Division
(w.) *Inf. Brig.:* (s.) RIR 245 | (w.) RIR 246
(w.) RIR 247 | (w.) RIR 248 | (s.) RJB 26
(w.) Res. Kav. Abt. 54
RFAR 54 [(s.) I. Abt., (w.) II. Abt.]
(s.) Res. Pi. Komp. 54 | (w). Res. Div. Brückentrain 54
(w.) Res. San. Komp. 54

(s.) schw. Res. Feldhaub. Battr. 27
(s.) Res. Scheinwerfer-Zug 27
(s.) Res. Fernsprech-Abt. 27
Additional artillery and *pioniere* (from 4. Armee)

The men of the new regiments formed in late August were an uneven mixture. Young volunteers formed only 37 per cent of RIR 244, but the majority of RIR 242 and the *jäger* battalions. Due to the romantic *jäger* tradition, students from Freiberg formed a small but tightly-knit clique in RJB 26. While in theory at least 18, the published history of RIR 241 admits some *kriegsfreiwilligen* lied about their age. Most of the NCOs and remaining men were older Landwehr reservists with at best four weeks of exercises between the ages of 27 and 32, and none thereafter. Thus their training was outdated – especially in the field artillery, which had introduced a new 10.5cm howitzer (arming three of nine batteries in both RFAR 53 and 54) in 1909. Due to a lack of officers many platoons were led by *offizierstell-vertreters* or *feldwebelleutnants*, and the divisions had only ad-hoc brigade staffs. Most available officers were retired (*außer dienst*) or semi-retired (*zur disposition*), and often fell ill under field conditions. Others had held desk jobs,

Personnel of Reserve-Bäckerei-Kolonne 33 (the corps bakery column) encamped at Dresden. Second right is the unit's *zahlmeister* (paymaster); the man behind him holds a wooden paddle used for moving loaves into and out of the oven. On the back (dated 10 October) Reinhold Schwarzbach informs his parents of his hasty marriage to his Ida and imminent departure for the front the following morning.

The entire 5. Zug / Reserve Fernsprech-Abteilung 27 (one of five platoons of the corps telephone detachment) in Dresden on 11 October. They wear a unit sleeve insignia 'F27' (see also p.235) and the Prussian-style *tschako* worn by Saxon telegraph, balloon and aviation units.

Reserve-Jäger-Bataillon 25 about to leave Dresden aboard a gaily decorated troop train. The graffiti includes the then-popular slogan '*Jeder Stoß ein Franzos*' ('a Frenchman with each bayonet thrust') and lurid warnings that 'the *jägers* are coming' and they 'thirst for French blood'. John Bull also appears in caricature form beside the arms of the *Kgl. Sächs. Staatseisenbahnen* (Saxon state railways).

Crowds of well-wishers gathered to see Reserve-Infanterie-Regiment 245 off from Leipzig. The Saxon and Württemberg elements of 54. Reserve-Division first met up in transit at Luxembourg, only a week before going into battle together.

though Oberstleutnant Pudor of RIR 242 and Major von Wolffersdorff of III. / RIR 241 were from the infantry. The latter had been severely wounded on the Marne, and was soon taken ill. In the field officer casualties crippled the fragile command structure, and from 25 October replacements arrived from other Saxon corps.

Under this uncertain leadership two years of training was squeezed into six weeks, with only a few days of larger-scale exercises. The problem was worse for the artillery (who usually trained for three years) and the corps was plagued by inaccurate barrages and 'friendly fire'. Equipment shortages were acute. Each infantry regiment had only two machine-guns (except RIR 248 with four), and entrenching tools, optics and telephones were all scarce. Field kitchens and other light vehicles were substituted with cumbersome wagons, which could rarely get as far forward as required. In battle the troops were often without hot food for days at a time and forced to forage, to the detriment of discipline, health and morale.

Nonetheless all units were declared 'ready' and entrained on 11–12 October, arriving at Ath and Leuze four days later. On 17 October the cavalry and cyclists reached the Lys at Harelbeke (53. RD) and Kortrijk (54. RD). 53. RD clashed with British cavalry on the 19th at Rollegem-Kapelle and Ledegem,

as did 54. RD at Moorsele. Combat with *Francs-tireurs* was reported, and six armed civilians caught by RIR 241 were shot (c.f. p. 190).

At the morning orders group on 20 October, General von Carlowitz proposed to reconvene that night in Ypres. The stunning unrealism of the Saxon corps commander soon alienated the Württembergers, while the able but ruthless army commander Generaloberst Archduke Albrecht of Württemberg gave a corresponding focus to Saxon criticism of the conduct of the battle.

On the right *Detachement von Criegern* (RIR 241 and 243) took Keibergmolen by 3 pm and dug in on the Becelaere–Broodseinde road under heavy fire. Unsupported on its right flank, it fell back to Keibergmolen at 6 pm. On the left *Detachement von Reinhardt* (RIR 245 and 246) reached Terhand by midday. After meeting serious resistance they stormed Becelaere at 2.40 pm supported by RFAR 54. RIR 245 attacked head-on with Oberst z. D. Baumgarten-Crusius in the lead, losing many killed and wounded. RIR 246 were luckier, entering Molenhoek close behind a retreating enemy and attacking from the north with RIR 244 of *Detachement Bierling* on their right. Becelaere soon fell but repeated attacks on the trenches beyond

Ltn. Hans von Schmieden of RIR 244 fell on 24 October in the assault on Polygon Wood. His father Generalmajor z.D. August von Schmieden commanded 105. Reserve-Infanterie-Brigade from late November.

Jäger Curt Gottschalk from Glauchau was one of six men of 1. Kompanie / Reserve-Jäger-Bataillon 26 (from Freiberg) killed by the same shell in their quarters at Molenhoek on 28 October.

were bloody failures, losing cohesion as units intermingled and leaders fell. According to Baumgarten-Crusius, Oberstltn. z.D. Haeser of I. / RIR 245 was the first to strike up 'Deutschland, Deutschland über alles' in these futile attacks. The survivors dug in after dark under heavy rain and shelling. They were joined by most of RIR 248, under conflicting orders to support them and 3. KD on their left. In this chaotic situation there were many panicked shots in the dark and false reports that Becelaere was lost. At one point men of RJB 26 fled through the lines of II. / RFAR 54 shouting that the British had broken through. In their published history the Württemberg gunners freely admit to plundering the Saxon jägers' abandoned baggage in their absence.

Early on 21 October Detachement von Criegern threw the British back to the Becelaere–Broodseinde road at heavy cost, but were hit by their own barrage. Due to the continued threat on their right they had to stay put under constant British fire, and repelled repeated attacks that night. Meanwhile Detachement von Reinhardt made

ruinous assaults on Reutel and Poezelhoek, to which the fresh RIR 247 was also committed. Again German shells inflicted losses, including Baumgarten-Crusius severely wounded.[3] By evening RIR 242 of Detachement Bierling and RJB 26 had reinforced the left, where RIR 248 was sorely depleted.

Orders for 22 October insisted the enemy was in full retreat and XXVII. RK was to take Ypres that day. Genltn. von Criegern protested that any advance would be enfiladed unless XXVI. RK supported it on the right, but the latter had its own problems and could not help. In the centre RIR 244 advanced on Polygon Wood from Holle Bosch, gaining about 500m on their left and contact with von Criegern's men. Genltn. von Reinhardt reported that his troops were fought out, and that he was establishing reserve positions in case of disaster. He did however commit RIR 247 and elements of RIR 248 to assist 3. KD. For once hot food and a thorough barrage were laid on, plus close support from RFAR 54. The attackers reached the woods north of Oude Hond largely unscathed, but could not advance further.

Einjährig-freiwilliger Soldat Fritz Hüppner of 8./RIR 242 from Cunnersdorf near Löbau fell on 25 October, probably one of many killed at Kruiseik (including his regimental commander Oberstltn. Hammer on the 26th).

Divisional morale fell further that night when Genltn. von Reinhardt was killed by a stray bullet.

Early on 23 October von Criegern attacked again. RJB 25 seized Broodseinde, but due to enfilade fire from the right the advance was discontinued at 2 pm. RIR 245 and 246 also attacked, breaking into Reutel and taking prisoners before being counterattacked. Oberstltn. Haeser was killed in action, and Major von Heygendorff (see p. 55) took over RIR 245 the next day. That night patrols near Zonnebeke identified French IX Corps, and RJB 25 repelled their attack on Broodseinde at 1.30 am. On 24 October the French made progress to the north, but RJB 25 and RIR 241 held their ground. After an intense bombardment RIR 244 and 246 stormed Reutel at 7.30 am, taking over 600 prisoners mainly from 2nd Btn. Wiltshire Regiment. RIR 244 pressed on into Polygon Wood, forcing 7th Division to commit its cavalry and prepare to defend its HQ. Under German shelling in the dense wood the Saxons lost all cohesion, and were driven back by counterattacks into the old British line to the east. RIR 244 and 246 were each reduced to a composite battalion, with RIR 244 down to six officers.

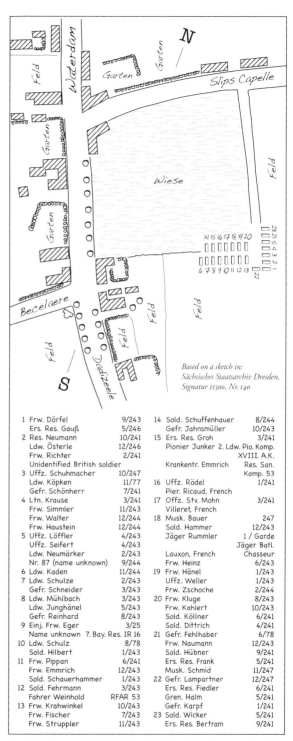

Based on a sketch in:
Sächsisches Staatsarchiv Dresden,
Signatur 11300, Nr. 140

1	Frw. Dörfel	9/243	14	Sold. Schuffenhauer	8/244
	Ers. Res. Gauß	5/246		Gefr. Jahnsmüller	10/243
2	Res. Neumann	10/241	15	Ers. Res. Groh	3/241
	Ldw. Österle	12/246		Pionier Junker 2. Ldw. Pio. Komp.	
	Frw. Richter	2/241			XVIII. A.K.
	Unidentified British soldier			Krankentr. Emmrich	Res. San.
3	Uffz. Schuhmacher	10/247			Komp. 53
	Ldw. Köpken	11/77	16	Uffz. Rödel	1/241
	Gefr. Schönherr	7/241		Pier. Ricaud, French	
4	Ltn. Krause	3/241	17	Offz. Stv. Mohn	3/241
	Frw. Simmler	11/243		Villeret, French	
	Frw. Walter	12/244	18	Musk. Bauer	247
	Frw. Haustein	12/244		Sold. Hammer	12/243
5	Uffz. Löffler	4/243		Jäger Rummler	1 / Garde
	Uffz. Seifert	4/243			Jäger Batl.
	Ldw. Neumärker	2/243		Lauxon, French	Chasseur
	Nr. 87 (name unknown)	9/244		Frw. Heinz	6/243
6	Ldw. Kaden	11/244	19	Frw. Hänel	1/243
7	Ldw. Schulze	2/243		Uffz. Weller	1/243
	Gefr. Schneider	3/243		Frw. Zschoche	2/244
8	Ldw. Mühlbach	3/243	20	Frw. Kluge	8/243
	Ldw. Junghänel	5/243		Frw. Kahlert	10/243
	Gefr. Reinhard	8/243		Sold. Köllner	6/241
9	Einj. Frw. Eger	3/25		Sold. Dittrich	4/241
	Name unknown 7. Bay. Res. IR 16		21	Gefr. Fehlhaber	6/78
10	Ldw. Schulz	8/78		Frw. Naumann	12/243
	Sold. Hilbert	1/243		Sold. Hübner	9/241
11	Frw. Pippan	6/241		Ers. Res. Frank	5/241
	Frw. Emmrich	12/243		Musk. Schmid	11/247
	Sold. Schauerhammer	1/243	22	Gefr. Lampartner	12/247
12	Sold. Fehrmann	5/243		Ers. Res. Fiedler	6/241
	Fahrer Weinhold	RFAR 53		Gren. Halm	5/241
13	Frw. Krahwinkel	10/243		Gefr. Karpf	1/241
	Frw. Fischer	7/243	23	Sold. Wicker	5/241
	Frw. Struppler	11/243		Ers. Res. Bertram	9/241

Map of a field cemetery in Strooiboom, with sixty-seven dead from the October and November fighting. Although nearly all are from XXVII. RK (and the attached 38. Landwehr-Brigade; see p. 30), there are a few exceptions, including one British and three French soldiers. The German dead were all moved to the *Soldatenfriedhof* Langemark after the war.

Card printed for RIR 244 in memory of 'the heroes of Becelaere'. Vfw. Kühn (see pp. 182–185) and Gefr. Conrad (of RIR 245; see pp. 198–203) were among those who received first aid at this church, which was hit by artillery fire on 25 October with horrific results.

Sunday at Becelaere (25 October 1914)

Many warriors lay upon hard straw
Their wounds but roughly bound
The fierce fight had left them there
Outside where they'd been found
In every eye a homeward yearning
Would they ever be returning
    From the church of Becelaere?

And Sunday came. The sunlight shone
Through the windows gently shimmering
In tired eyes whence hope had gone
Showed a faint and hopeful glimmering
And a priest was murmuring a prayer
For one whose end was drawing near
    In the church at Becelaere

A doctor doled some comfort out
'Enjoy your Sunday while you may
The British are all too devout
To dream of shooting on this day!'
He spoke and then they unleashed hell
Shot on shot, shrapnel and shell
    On the church at Becelaere

Then all at once the roof beams broke
With crashing and thumping and groaning
And out there welled a stifling smoke
Then crying and yelling and moaning
And pain and despair were all about
Sunday had come and death strode out
    Through the church of Becelaere

Kriegsfreiw. Karl Möbert, Meißen, RIR 245

Was wir erlebten, *245er Erinnerungen, Nr. 1*

After dark the British probed the entire line of 53. RD, and at 4.45 am on the 25th the French attacked Broodseinde with their support. By 1.30 pm RJB 25 had to retire to avoid encirclement, and *Detachement von Criegern* fell back to the Keiberg heights. RFAR 53 suffered severe losses covering the retreat, and Zahlmeister Bruno Vogel of III. / RIR 241 won the Iron Cross 2nd Class for organising the new line in the absence of officers. Meanwhile 54. RD had supported attacks by 3. KD on Kruseik. After dark RIR 242 surged through the line of 2nd Scots Guards and cleared the village in bitter hand to hand fighting, only to be driven out by repeated counterattacks (c.f. pp. 190–191). Heavy Saxon losses included five officers and 189 men captured. After a huge bombardment they attacked again at 10 am alongside bRIR 1 and dismounted cavalry. Kruseik was taken together with 400 prisoners, and some Saxon wounded liberated.

Further north RIR 247 and 248 gained about 400m, and 53. RD began to advance again.

General von Carlowitz reported sick on 27 October, to universal relief. Meanwhile his corps held off the British at the Keiberg heights and secured Oude Kruiseik. With XV. AK on the way to join the battle, an attack was planned for 6.30 am on 29 October by *Gruppe von Bendler* (RIR 247, 248, and 242, reinforced by I. and III. /bRIR 16 and *Detachement Waxmann* – six companies each of LIR 77 and 78). Heavy fog put paid to the barrage, but helped RIR 247 and 248 get forward with limited losses. 1st Guards Brigade was overwhelmed and the Becelaere–Kruseik road taken, but the Bavarians suffered badly in a further push on Gheluvelt. Attacks the next day made little progress, partly due to poor coordination with XV. AK.

Das Schrapnellhaus.

The 'Schrapnellhaus' lay west of Keibergmolen, overlooking the slope where RIR 241 blindly marched into the devastating fire of the main British position on 20 October. Many more died later that day when it was demolished by British artillery. In November Genltn. von Criegern and his adjutant Oltn. Breithaupt (see photo p. 103) observed the fighting from the ruin, hence the ladders. As shown here, its cellar housed the forward dressing station of RIR 243. When relieved by RIR 247 on 18 November, the surviving two officers and 120 men of RIR 241 buried thirty dead comrades nearby; the regiment had a fighting strength of seventy-two officers and 2717 other ranks when it left Dresden.

The *Nachweisebüro des Kriegsministeriums* in Dresden was responsible for establishing and recording the fate of Saxon casualties and POWs. This card informs the regional *Nachrichtenstelle* in Leipzig (which dealt with public enquiries) that Johann Moritz Rübener of 6./RIR 245, last seen at Becelaere on 29 October 1914, is still missing in April 1915. Later confirmed killed in action, he is buried at Menen (Block N Grave 1353).

After a sharp ten-minute barrage *Gruppe von Bendler* attacked Gheluvelt at 6.40 am on the 31st with 30. ID on the left and *Gruppe Mühry* (RIR 245 and 246, RJB 26 and II. / bRIR 16) on the right. Although the Bavarians briefly broke into the chateau grounds, 54. RD could not make major progress until IR 105 had cleared the high ground to the south (c.f. p. 43). By mid-afternoon masses of intermingled and often leaderless troops drove the British into the southwest corner of the grounds, before being counter-attacked by 2nd Btn. Worcester Regiment and forced to defend the village. Losses were grievous, especially to RIR 247 and bRIR 16. After dark the British withdrew, and patrols reentered the grounds. I. / RJB 26 was sent to clear the chateau, where they found a British dressing station, some German prisoners and finally the wine cellar. The hung-over *jägers* were in reserve on 1 November, while the division consolidated its new line and buried its dead. On 2 and 3 November RFAR 54 supported 30. ID in the drive on Veldhoek. 54. RD could do little more than move its flank to conform, but repelled repeated Anglo-French attacks from Polygon Wood. In a final effort on 4 November RIR 248 took Pottyn Farm, which became the new corps boundary when the Prussian *Garde* were inserted on the 9th.

Though it too was grinding to a bloody halt and fighting strength was only 2,200 men, 53. RD was to attack in support of the last drive on the Menin Road. RIR 242 returned on 11 November, together with RJB 26, RIR 247, *Detachement Waxmann* and the Garde-Jäger-Bataillon. A *Brigade Pudor* of Prussian *ersatz* units was inserted on the right. At 6.30 am on the 12th the division made a silent bayonet charge, seizing high ground west of the road from the French and taking 700 prisoners. Attacks continued daily, and on 14 November Oberst z. D. von Holleben of RIR 243 led the storming of the British-held *Calvairewald*. An adjacent trench was taken on the 18th, but RIR 243 and the Garde Jägers could not advance further; the new corps commander General von Schubert was wounded observing this attack. Between 15 and 17 November the French relieved the British as far as the Menin Road. After receiving thousands of fresh men, 53. RD vainly attacked again on 27 November for a few days in deteriorating weather. From 5 December the flank was extended to Wallemolen, and the haggard survivors struggled to make the new line habitable for the winter. Fraternisation may have occurred near Broodseinde on 12 December, but after a failed French attack on Christmas Eve only a brief tacit truce followed.

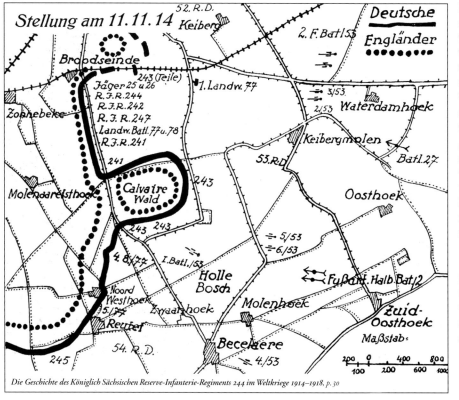

Dispositions of 53. RD and attached units before the attack on 12 November. Written accounts indicate that the line between Broodseinde and *Calvairewald* (Justice Wood) actually lay further east at this time. A British trench called the *Hochländergraben* ran along the road, and was captured on 18 November. As the name (referring to 2nd Btn. Highland Light Infantry of 5 Brigade / 2nd Division) suggests, most of the enemy here were not '*Engländer*'.

East of Zonnebeke the French held the line, and later the whole sector. Units sighted opposite included cuirassiers and Moroccan infantry.

Die Geschichte des Königlich Sächsischen Reserve-Infanterie-Regiments 244 im Weltkriege 1914–1918, p. 30

An officer of XXVII. Reserve-Korps has personalised this field postcard with a drawing of his billet at Rollegem-Kapelle to send home to his family. Although he has omitted his own name, he has included that of his Flemish host Emil Bertheloot.

Gunners and drivers of Reserve-Feldartillerie-Regiment 53 and Reserve-Artillerie-Munitions-Kolonne 73 (a corps ammunition column) in December 1914. Their billets have been decorated with fir twigs and a rather scrawny tree in anticipation of Christmas.

XIX. Armee-Korps (24. and 40. Infanterie-Division)

The storming of Lille and the battle for the Lys front

24. Infanterie-Division
47. Inf. Brig.: IR 139 | IR 179
48. Inf. Brig.: IR 106 | IR 107
UR 18
24. Felda. Brig.: FAR 77 | FAR 78
Div. Brückentrain 24 | San. Komp. XIX/1

40. Infanterie-Division
88. Inf. Brig.: IR 104 | IR 181
89. Inf. Brig.: IR 133 | IR 134
HR 19
40. Felda. Brig.: FAR 32 | FAR 68
Div. Brückentrain 40 | San. Komp. XIX/2

JB 13 | II. Batl. / FußaR 19
Stab I., 1.–3. Komp. & Scheinwerfer-Zug / Pi. Batl. 22
Korps-Brückentrain XIX | Fernsprech-Abt. 19
Flieger-Abt. 24

Saxony's second active corps had crossed the Meuse on 24 August and fought in the Battle of the Marne, losing over 6,000 killed or wounded. In its infantry regiments roughly half the officers and a third of the NCOs and men were casualties. Nevertheless it still displayed a wealth of professionalism and experience at all levels, and was equipped to the highest standards. For example, in the October fighting the battalion staffs of IR 107 were in near-constant telephone contact with their troops and with regimental HQ, which liaised with the artillery. Equally importantly, hot food or coffee regularly reached the front line.

On 3 October the Kaiser addressed the men of XIX. AK at Saint-Souplet-Sur-Py: *'es war gut so, Sachsen. Macht's weiter so!'*[4] ('You have done well, Saxons. Continue to do so!') The next evening most of them began a series of punishing night marches to a secret destination, leaving a 'half-division' based on 48. Infanterie-Brigade in the Champagne

The flowers suggest that these volunteers of Feldartillerie-Regiment 77 are about to leave Leipzig for the front after only a few weeks of training. XIX. Armee-Korps already contained many 'green' replacements in October 1914, but retained a solid core of regular NCOs and officers.

'Farewell to loyal friends' from Ersatz-Bataillon / Infanterie-Regiment 139 in Döbeln. Although these men are certainly going to the front, this card was posted on 2 September by Unteroffizier Wilhelm Bierwage, who remained behind in Döbeln to train recruits.

(see p. 205). From 7 October the baggage went by rail and the pace was more moderate. The troops arrived about 15km south of Lille on the afternoon of 11 October, and received orders for its capture at 3.15 pm.

It had been thought unlikely that the French would defend the old fortified city. The extensive outer works added after 1871 had been rendered obsolete by new explosives, and the fortress downgraded. Commandant Félix de Pardieu had orders from Général Foch to defend Lille as long as possible, but only a weak territorial brigade, some colonial cavalry and one field battery. He had concentrated this force in the walled inner city, and tried to exaggerate their numbers with a great display of firepower whenever Germans were seen.

After the Saxon cavalry had cut the railway lines to the north, the infantry rested a kilometre from the walls while civilians took a formal surrender request to the commandant. This was ignored, and the city was shelled at midnight. Meanwhile in front of 88. Infanterie-Brigade, nine volunteers from 3. Feldkompanie / Pionier-Bataillon 22 cut through the perimeter fence and stealthily crossed four

moats up to six metres deep (one of them heavily wired) to reach the wall undetected. Other *pionier* patrols confirmed that the walls could only be stormed via the strongly barricaded gates and the railway, and that the garrison was numerically weak.

At 7.00 am the Saxons advanced in thick fog. On the left, 89. IB and JB 13 circled the western perimeter toward the citadel to cut off any escape, while 47. IB advanced on the Porte des Postes. On the right, IR 181 was to take the Porte de Douai and IR 104 the Gare de Lille-Saint-Sauveur, a freight station at the southeastern corner of the walls. The Prussian *Detachement Wahnschaffe* was known to be advancing on Hellemmes, and was to make contact on the right. However by 10 am the attack had halted at the walls, which proved impervious to 7.7cm field guns. On the left JB 13 had reached the Canal de la Deule and was lavished with food and drink by the locals, who assumed the unfamiliar Saxon *jäger* uniform to be British – until paid in German currency. A platoon under Oltn. Freiherr von Miltitz reached the citadel and captured two French officers in the grounds, but was denied permission to storm it.

Infanterie-Regiment 181 storms the Porte de Douai at Lille in concert with a *zug* (two-gun section) of Feldartillerie-Regiment 68 led by Leutnant Heinrich Elssner. In the centre gunners bring up 7.7cm ammunition in three-round wicker carriers. Ltn. Elssner was severely wounded in this decisive assault, and died of wounds a week later aged 22; he was awarded a posthumous *Ritterkreuz* of the *Militär-St. Heinrichs-Orden* on 17 November.

After a final ultimatum to the commandant the heavy artillery opened fire at midday, but at first the assault troops remained bogged down at the gates. At the freight station IR 104 was pinned down by flanking fire from Hellemmes, where the Prussians had not appeared. From 2.30 pm the entire corps artillery concentrated on the Porte de Douai. Many buildings were soon ablaze, increasing the pressure on Lille since the *pioniere* had found the main pumping station outside the walls and shut off the water. IR 181 began the final assault at 3.00 pm, supported by demolition parties from Pi. Batl. 22 and two field guns of FAR 68. The outer gate was soon stormed and blown by *pioniere*, and the inner gate breached after a furious firefight, with the field guns in action a mere 100 metres from the enemy. Pushing into the square beyond, the attack was halted by heavy fire from the houses opposite until Ltn. Elssner brought his field guns forward again – at the cost of his own life. Under their concentrated fire all resistance collapsed, and IR 181 advanced triumphantly into the city. Within an hour, Genltn. Götz von Olenhusen reported the formal surrender of Lille. According to 'Sachsen in großer Zeit' the booty included over 4,500 prisoners, an aircraft, a field battery and over 200 old fortress artillery pieces. The Saxon Army would be quick to celebrate

its success, and a commemorative medallion was struck bearing the names of von Laffert, von Olenhusen and the army commander Crown Prince Rupprecht of Bavaria (who moved his HQ to the city on 8 November).

Over the next two days, the corps set up a defensive perimeter among the northern and western outer works. Early on 15 October 40. ID pushed forward its flank to the east bank of the Lys, with IR 181 and IR 104 digging in between Warneton and Frelinghien, in contact with IR 133 on the left. Across the river, Husaren-Regiment 19 sighted British cavalry to the north-west. Meanwhile JB 13 had been alerted and sent to Armentières, where it was ordered to hold the river bank west and north of the town. That evening *jäger* sentries spotted 1st Btn. the Hampshire Regiment approaching the crossing at Pont de Nieppe; one of their supporting machine-guns jammed, but the other cut down a dozen men and scattered the survivors. British 11 Brigade then abandoned its attempt to cross, having received corps orders to wait for daylight. Meanwhile JB 13 was reinforced by a single battery of FAR 77 and by Ulanen-Regiment 18, which clashed with British cavalry at Ploegsteert, Nieppe and Steenwerk the next morning. To the left of JB 13,

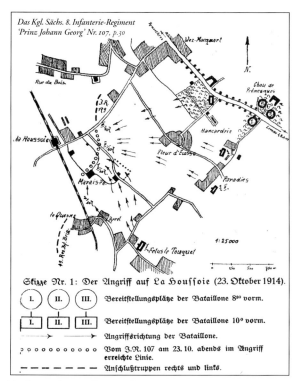

For the attack on 23 October all three battalions of IR 107 were inserted between IR 179 and the Hessian 49. Reserve-Infanterie-Brigade (RIR 116 and 118), reaching the edge of La Houssoie by evening.

'The first English prisoner at La Bleue (1914)' according to the same unknown member of IR 139 as the photos on pp. 60–65. His missing cap badge precludes closer identification

1st Btn. Somerset Light Infantry crossed the Lys unopposed and took Erquinghem by about 1.00 pm. An hour later British artillery bombarded the Armentières–Nieppe road, as Saxon gunners struggled to find targets in the fog. At 5.00 pm the enemy advanced in force on the crossings at Nieppe and Houplines, and a withdrawal was ordered after dark; JB 13 escaped with all of its wounded, losing only three dead and one missing. Meanwhile 88. IB had established bridgeheads on the west bank of the Lys at Pont Rouge and Le Touquet, skirmishing with British cavalry patrols.

The British reached Chapelle d'Armentières and Le Gheer on 17 October, and their 4th Division moved against Frelinghien the next morning. North of the Lys, 12 Brigade took the western end of Le Touquet, with III. / IR 104 still in the eastern end. A few hours later 10 Brigade advanced on the south bank, but soon dug in near Le Ruage under crossfire from IR 133; the following afternoon, 2nd Btn. Seaforth Highlanders of 10 Brigade daringly infiltrated the houses at the edge of Frelinghien by crawling along the river bank under cover of artillery. Meanwhile British 6th Division had reached Prémesques and L'Epinette.

That night XIX. AK redeployed to attack. On the left, JB 13 was inserted at L'Aventure between IR 139 and IR 133. On the right IR 181 was inserted to the left of I. and II. / IR 104. III. / IR 104 remained at Le Touquet, forming an ad-hoc *Regiment Larras* with II. / IR 133 and II. / IR 134 at Frelinghien. This regiment was subordinated to 89. IB, anchoring the centre of a pincer movement toward Armentières. Both flank brigades were to push their start lines forward during the two-hour bombardment and attack simultaneously at 9.00 am.

On the right it was 11 am before all units reached the start line, across the Lys at the railway west of Pont Rouge. The open ground east of Le Gheer was a wide pre-ranged killing field studded with wired obstacles, but IR 104 advanced by bounds in loose order, covered by machine-guns on the embankment. By evening the regiment was entrenched 300 metres from Ploegsteert wood, but on the flanks IR 181 fell behind in boggy going near the Lys, and JB 7 made little progress (see map p. 38). At Frelinghien British 10 Brigade attacked at dawn, taking fifty prisoners from IR 133 and 134 and occupying the massive brick brewery near the Lys. Further south, JB 13 attacked L'Epi-

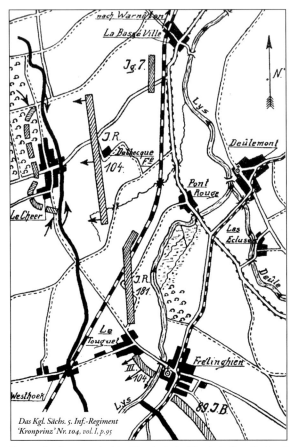

Das Kgl. Sächs. 5. Inf.-Regiment
'Kronprinz' Nr. 104, vol. I, p.95

Successive lines reached by 88. Infanterie-Brigade in the attacks of
20 and 21 October, when Le Gheer was briefly taken. I. and III./IR 134
supported IR 104 and 181, but from 29 October were attached to the
neighbouring 4. Kavallerie-Division. On 31 October IR 106 was inserted
on the right of IR 104.

Kriegsfreiwilliger Erich Freimark was born on 16 February 1895 in Wurzen. He was killed in action on 2 November 1914, when III. Batl. / IR 106
was committed to support I. Batl. / IR 104 in a renewed effort to take
Le Gheer supported by heavy *minenwerfers*. The Saxons launched
three assaults that day, all of which were bloodily repulsed.

nette at 9.00 am supported by IR 139; the advance stalled
in the open east of the town and the battalion withdrew
after dark. Simultaneously IR 179 stormed Prémesques
from the heights overlooking the town, catching 2nd Btn.
the Leinster Regiment in their trap; the Leinsters recorded
217 missing. The British 6th Division had also lost ground
to XIII. AK on the Saxon left, and retired to its second line
after dark.

On 21 October I. and II./IR 104 approached silently at
6.30 am under cover of mist, and overran the trenches of
2nd Btn. Royal Inniskilling Fusiliers by surprise. Carrying
their colours from 1870 into action for the last time, they
stormed Le Gheer and began to dig in. However JB 7 and
IR 181 had again been halted by heavy fire well short of
the British lines. Lacking flank support, I. and II./IR 104
were overwhelmed by parts of four British battalions in

fierce bayonet fighting. Le Gheer was lost, after costing the
regiment 150 killed, 193 wounded and 134 captured. Major
Larras of III./IR 104 was also killed by a shot from Frelinghien brewery that afternoon, his 'regiment' passing to
Hptm. Rühle von Lilienstern of II./IR 134. The other battalions of IR 134 had been sent to reinforce IR 104 and 181,
but it was already too late. Meanwhile on the left, IR 139 and
179 pursued the British to their second line and dug in.
During the night JB 13 infiltrated L'Epinette but lost
cohesion under fire in the dark, finally abandoning the
position as untenable in daylight.

The remaining units of 24. ID now arrived in Lille, and at
10 am on 23 October the division launched a general attack.
JB 13 and IR 139 pushed into the edge of L'Epinette under
heavy fire, forcing the British to abandon Pont Ballot. On
the left IR 107 advanced at La Houssoie, in contact with

IR 179 at Wez-Macquart. Although the Hessians on their left were checked at Le Quesne and a promised armoured train did not appear, the fresh regiment gained ground (see map p. 37). For the next attack at 6.30 am on 25 October, Oberst Löffler of IR 107 had RIR 118, two *pionier* companies and ten assorted batteries at his disposal. After a brief but violent bombardment and the explosion of demolition charges, the Saxons gradually fought their way into La Houssoie and had outposts beyond the railway by evening; the British evacuated Le Quesne that night. On 26 October IR 107 cleared La Houssoie, while Frelinghien brewery was stormed by II. / IR 133 and II. / IR 134 after a heavy *minenwerfer* barrage had driven most of the Seaforths from the buildings. The next day IR 107 launched a dawn attack on Rue du Bois aided by IR 179, but found the new objective strongly fortified and well supported by artillery. II. / IR 107 dug in south of the town, while III. / IR 107 captured its eastern edge. In a renewed attack on 28 October, the regiment briefly took the town and trenches to the south. By now gravely depleted, IR 107 was forced out by weight of numbers and struggled to hold its start line. Its part in the battle was over, with losses of twenty-five officers and 650 other ranks. A fresh assault was planned using heavy *minenwerfers* and three large mine galleries, only to be cancelled due to flooding in late November after multiple postponements.

Despite the disaster of 21 October, smaller-scale dawn and night attacks continued at Le Gheer. The offensive resumed on the evening of 29 October after extensive artillery preparation. The next day 88. IB attacked in the afternoon all along the front, with III. / IR 106 inserted right of IR 104 and IR 134 with the army cavalry on the flank; after heavy losses the Saxons once again dug in facing Ploegsteert Wood. The fighting in November was even bloodier, with the commanders of both IR 104 and 106 among the slain. From 2 November attacks on Le Gheer were supported by heavy *minenwerfers*, but made no progress. However a dawn attack by IR 106 in thick fog on 7 November overran 3rd Btn. the Worcestershire Regiment, breaking into the wood and briefly taking Le Gheer. Despite dreadful losses the resulting salient remained in Saxon hands (see pp. 114–117). A British attack on 19 December retook the outpost line, but made no impression on the main position.

Though corps orders of 8 November demanded continued harassment of the enemy, worsening weather and munitions shortages soon forced all units to concentrate on improving their rudimentary trenches. Somewhat cheered by a visit from the King on 2 December, the corps prepared for its first Christmas in the field.

The sector of IR 106 between *Wassergut* (Factory Farm) and the Le Gheer road on 2 December 1914. On the flanks were IR 104 and *Detachement von der Decken*, comprising I. and III. / IR 134 plus elements of 4. Kavallerie-Division. In the attack of 7 November the regiment advanced from the line marked 'd-d' to the edge of Ploegsteert Wood. As the weather worsened the front line in the wood became untenable, and on 2 December the garrison retired to a new trench (b-b) built behind it by 3. / Pi. Batl. 22. The last outposts in the wood were abandoned on 19 December, but the attack of British 11 Brigade was repulsed at the well-wired strongpoint beyond, known as the *Entenschnabel* (Duck's Bill) or 'Birdcage' to the British. After the departure of IR 106 in March 1915 this sector was held by IR 104 (see pp. 114–117).

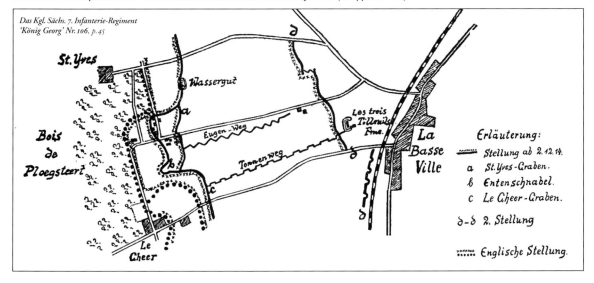

The Christmas Truce on the front of XIX. Armeekorps

For a full account we recommend *Christmas Truce* by Brown and Seaton (1994). We aim merely to clarify the situation on the northern half of the front where mass fraternisation occurred. Many Westphalian regiments of VII. AK also took part, often misidentified as 'Saxons' in British reports. It seems that this misapprehension was created or at least encouraged by the Westphalians, presumably hoping for a warmer reception.

In most sectors contact began on Christmas Eve, marked by the Saxons with singing and the display of candles and trees in the trenches. Most Saxon officers accepted the truce, seeking only to regulate it and to exploit the opportunity for work in the open and burial of the dead. After a strict anti-fraternisation order from OHL was relayed to XIX. AK on 29 December, all units were keen to assert that contact with the enemy had been limited to formal burial truces. British press coverage, often sharply anti-Prussian in tone, was to prove acutely embarrassing (see p. 208).

Detachement von der Decken comprised IR 134 with attached Prussian and Bavarian *jägers*. On the right was JB 10, a Hanoverian unit who wore the 'Gibraltar' cuff title. When

men of 2nd Battalion Seaforth Highlanders left their trenches, Hptm. Richter could not get his men to shoot them; his threats of punishment were quashed by the battalion commander. The neighbouring Bavarians of BJB 1 also fraternised with the Seaforths. Bruce Bairnsfather's famous turnip field lay in front of the adjacent battalion of IR 134, supported by MGK / JB 6 at Damier-Ferme. The truce here survived the relief of JB 10 by JB 13 and bJB 1 by bJB 2 on 28 December; two men of JB 13 were punished for fraternisation with the job of burying a rotting cow in no man's land.

IR 106 held the Ploegsteert Wood sector with one of its own battalions on the right and the attached II. / IR 133 on the left. From 4 am on Christmas Day both sides heard the regimental band playing at La Basse Ville (see p. 208). After unofficial contact that night, a formal burial truce for the whole sector of IR 106 was agreed in the morning. The subsequent fraternisation is recorded in many famous photographs and continued for almost a week, barely interrupted by token machine-gun fire at midnight on 27–28 December. On the 30th the Saxons regretfully informed the enemy of the OHL anti-fraternisation order, but gave 1st Battalion

One of the six *fuhrpark-kolonnen* (supply park columns) of XIX. Armee-Korps celebrates Christmas behind the front. On paper each such unit had five officers (all here on horseback), 109 other ranks, 163 horses and sixty-two vehicles. Like all XIX. AK supply troops they wear the uniform of the peacetime Train-Bataillon 19 with no unit-specific insignia. In 1914 all *train-soldaten* were still issued with swords.

the Rifle Brigade a New Year burial truce proposal approved by XIX. AK and signed by Oberst William Kohl of IR 106. Although terms could not be agreed, peace lingered here until 11 January.

Although **IR 104** only admitted to a formal burial truce, British sources describe fraternisation with both 1st Battalion the East Lancashire Regiment and 1/2nd Battalion the Monmouthshire Regiment. Casualties among the latter may have been due to **IR 181**, who claim to have 'energetically' rejected all British advances; nevertheless men of 10. / IR 181 were identified at the burial truce.

Regiment von Rühle held Frelinghien with III. / IR 104 and II. / IR 134 respectively north and south of the Lys. On the north bank an envoy approaching 2nd Battalion Lancashire Fusiliers was taken prisoner due to a sentry's error. A truce still ensued, during which the Fusiliers claim to have beaten the Saxons 3-2 at football. On Christmas afternoon Captain Stockwell of 2nd Battalion the Royal Welsh Fusiliers met his counterpart (possibly Hptm. Wilhelm Graf Vitzthum von Eckstädt of IR 134) to receive a gift of two casks of beer from the brewery, and gave him a plum pudding. After first contact late on Christmas Eve, company officers of **IR 133** and 2nd Battalion Argyll and Sutherland Highlanders agreed a burial truce in the morning. Fraternisation continued well into the afternoon until broken up by the Saxon battalion commander. Writing in 1969, Ltn. Johannes Niemann described a football match (won 3-2 by the Saxons) and much hilarity when it was discovered that the Scotsmen wore nothing under their kilts!

South of the railway, officers and men of 3rd Battalion the Rifle Brigade and **IR 139** met in no man's land on Christmas Eve and agreed a burial truce; IR 139 claimed that a British chaplain was the instigator. The next morning a working party in the partly flooded sector of 'B' Company / 2nd Battalion the Leinster Regiment (immediately north of the railway) fraternised with a Saxon burial party until about 2 pm. Earlier there was a brief panic when regimental commander Oberst Einert set out to inspect the line. Attempts to hide the situation from him soon failed, but he saw the funny side and the truce continued into January. On the right of 19 Brigade, 1st Battalion the Cameronians did not take part. Attached companies of the regiment's territorial 1/5th Battalion did so, losing Corporal Walter Smith killed in a rash exchange of fire on Christmas Day; Saxon claims that a Prussian was to blame are implausible.

IR 107 had all three battalions in the line. On the right, III. / IR 107 were visited on Christmas Eve by three men of the Queen's Westminster Rifles and by Corporal Thomas Latimer and two men of the 3rd Rifles. All six were

British brigade and Saxon regimental sectors on the XIX. AK front at Christmas 1914.

allegedly drunk, and had to be taken prisoner after seeing the German defences; the British were informed the next day (see p. 208). Meanwhile near Rue du Bois, Captain R.J. Armes of 1st Battalion the North Staffordshire Regiment met Ltn. Horst von Gehe of I. / IR 107 on Christmas Eve and agreed a burial truce until 1 am on Boxing Day. Fraternisation ensued on Christmas Day along the entire regimental front; at Rue du Bois the truce persisted informally well into January 1915. In the last days of 1914 the Saxons freely visited the British lines, in numbers too great to be taken prisoner; according to his memoirs, HRH Prince Ernst Heinrich von Sachsen and a fellow staff officer of XIX. AK were among them. Meanwhile Major Arbuthnot of 24 Battery Royal Field Artillery freely reconnoitred Wez-Macquart disguised as a German.

IR 179 observed trucing in adjacent sectors with interest, but was not directly involved. An account from 9. / IR 179 suggests that the non-arrival of their relief on Christmas Eve put them in a foul mood, after which they switched from songs to cat-calls at the enemy. They were later misidentified as Prussians by 1st Battalion the Leicestershire Regiment.

The Trenches in Flanders

Raised walkway over a flooded area at La Bleue; this solution was taken to extremes north of Ypres (see pp. 123–125).

Slightly exaggerated wall painting from the officers' mess (*offiziers-kasino*) of IR 139 at Château Pérenchies.

The soil in the Flanders region was covered by a thin stratum of clay, with a thickness of 10 to 20 metres and without the slightest admixture of stony elements. Under dry conditions, this clay layer had a great solidity that allowed for the cutting of vertical trench walls several metres in depth without risk of subsequent collapse. However as soon as the sheer torrential rains of this region set in, the clay was inundated with water from above, the upper layers became heavy and pushed in the cleanly cut trench walls, and the loose masses of clay – excavated from the trench to form the parapet – became a viscous slurry, which inexorably flowed back into the trench. The sapper would vigorously set to the task of shovelling out the trench – but already after five or six strokes, he no longer held a spade with an iron blade in his hand. Instead on the end of the shaft there was a lump of clay bigger than his head, which he struggled in vain to shake off – but it was stuck fast!

With the increased rainfall the level of the groundwater naturally rose; depending on the locality one would strike groundwater at 50cm or even sooner, which rose inexorably in spite of any amount of baling with mess tins and tin cans. A trench 50cm in depth with a parapet of liquid clay slurry offered little protection to a fully grown man, and the

opposition delighted in shooting at just such places. Here the wit of the *landsers* came up with the apt phrase: '*better a whole day with a wet arse, than a whole life dead*', and one sat on the soaked trench floor regardless.

The soldiers had been trained to exploit any ditch or deeper hollow in the ground to reduce the effect of enemy fire. In the flat ground over which we attacked at Ploegsteert there were many small knee-deep or hip-deep ditches, which in this well-cultivated land must have served for the drainage of rainwater into the Lys, and formed a well-levelled system by taking advantage of the slight gradient. Wherever some of our troops occupied such a ditch when the attack was called off, it was quite understandable that this ditch was then deepened and developed into a trench. Now the autumn downpours came and turned the deepened part of the trench into a swimming pool, from which the natural outflow was blocked and which received a constant inflow. The same phenomenon occurred if one of these drainage channels was crossed when constructing a new trench during the night – and the new trench immediately and inexplicably filled with water.

Das Kgl. Sächs. 5. Inf.-Regiment 'Kronprinz' Nr. 104, pp. 109–110

Infanterie-Regiment 105 with Prussian 30. Infanterie-Division
Against the British at Gheluvelt and the French north of Hollebeke

In March 1871 the XV. Armee-Korps was established at Strassburg in the newly won *Reichsland Elsass-Lothringen* from existing units. These included 6. Kgl. Sächs. Infanterie-Regiment 'König Wilhelm II. von Württemberg' Nr. 105, and despite continual lobbying by the *Kriegsministerium* in Dresden for its return this was still the case in 1914. However the corps now consisted mainly of nominally local regiments (recruited largely in Westphalia and the Rhineland), forming 30. Infanterie-Division (Strassburg) and 39. Infanterie-Division (Colmar).

The regiment left Strassburg on 8 August. The next day Oberst Allmer was hit by friendly fire at Wittelsheim near Mülhausen, the first of three commanders of IR 105 to die in the war. On 13 August XV. AK marched north, fighting in the Vosges west of Strassburg and then advancing into France via Badonviller. Engaged in the Battle of the Marne until 19 October, it began marching northwards to join *Armeegruppe Fabeck* on the 24th and crossed the Lys east of Bousbecque on the 29th.

Ordered to join the assault on Gheluvelt the next morning, II. and III. / IR 105 deployed south of the Menin Road, with IR 99 to the left and 54. RD to the right. After much delay, IR 105 received an hour's notice to attack at 4 pm together with bRIR 16 and RIR 242. Unable to establish contact with the Bavarians, IR 105 advanced unsupported and was halted 200–300m from the British line by ferocious rifle fire. That night Oberst Martin Freiherr von Oldershausen of IR 105, now in tactical command of his division's drive on Gheluvelt, chaired an orders group at Kruiseik. His corps commander General der Infanterie Berthold von Deimling had ordered a night attack, but this was postponed to 6.30 am on 31 October due to the difficulty of coordination with the depleted units of XXVII. RK. This problem was exacerbated when British artillery hit a concentration of senior officers at the Kruiseik crossroads on the Menin Road (later known as *Deimlings-Eck*). The wounded included von Deimling himself and Oberst von Bendler of RIR 247, commanding the assault troops of 54. RD. These came under Freiherr von Oldershausen's command for the rest of the day, though he too was wounded in the afternoon.

After a brief barrage the two Saxon battalions (with I. / IR 143 in reserve) were again checked by rifle fire at close range, and

three of their four machine-guns knocked out. After a second failed assault, 2. / FAR 84 was deployed in close support to supplement the barrage on the high ground south of the Menin Road. From here 1st Btn. Queen's stubbornly resisted the advance of IR 105 and 54. RD, even after IR 99 broke through toward Gheluvelt on their other flank. Around midday an officer and fifty-three men of the adjacent 2nd Btn. Welsh Regiment surrendered to the Saxons, and a machine-gun was soon enfilading the Queen's from their trench. The final assault went in at 1 pm; within twenty minutes III. / IR 105 had broken into Gheluvelt, and I. / IR 143 moved to roll up the British flank. II. / IR 105 pushed on toward the Veldhoek Heights and overran a battery on the Menin Road, but could not recover or destroy it before a scratch force defending the main gun line drove them back. Nevertheless the regiment had taken about 400 prisoners and two machine-guns. By about 3 pm the village was secured by the capture of the high ground to its southeast. The British counterattack at Gheluvelt Chateau was a less serious threat to the disorganised mass of troops in the village than the heavy

IR 105 fought on both flanks of XV. AK. On 9 November the corps sector was reduced and 30. ID moved to the left of 39. ID, due to the insertion of *Korps Plettenberg* for the final offensive effort.

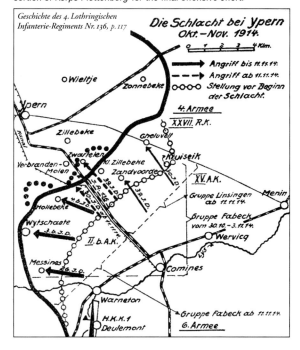

Geschichte des 4. Lothringischen Infanterie-Regiments Nr. 136, p. 117

shelling which did not abate until nightfall; the first field gun deployed by Hptm. Huber of 2. / FAR 84 on the Menin Road to counter it was immediately knocked out.

The remains of II., III. and MGK / IR 105 withdrew to divisional reserve on 1 November, having suffered over 600 casualties in two days. Meanwhile I. / IR 105 was committed piecemeal to reinforce IR 136 south of Gheluvelt, and took part in an attack on the morning of 2 November which established a foothold in Herenthage Wood. Most of the Saxons rejoined their regiment at Tenbrielen on 3 November, but 1. / IR 105 was not relieved until the 5th and 4. / IR 105 until the 10th.

On 6 November IR 105 reinforced 39. ID at the *Kanalknie* north of Hollebeke (see photo p. 127), where it attacked on the 8th and gained about 200m between the canal and Battle Wood; in accordance with corps orders the *Regimentsmusik* played in support behind the railway embankment. XV. AK was now assigned to *Heeresgruppe Linsingen* and IR 105 to 30. ID. With the regimental frontage reduced on the right, the next attack on 10 November overran the canal bank as far as the St. Eloi road bridge; however this had to be partly abandoned due to lack of flank support. The next day

IR 99 cleared Battle Wood. IR 105 got within 150m of the tree-lined St. Eloi–Verbrandenmolen road, and took it on 12 November, but the regiment was down to thirteen officers and 500 men. Artillery preparation on the 13th had to be called off due to premature detonations in the treetops over the road, and the attack failed entirely. The survivors were withdrawn to Tenbrielen, where IR 105 received 900 fresh replacements and reformed as two composite battalions. It reoccupied its former position on 15 November, cut down the troublesome trees by night and attacked on the 17th after heavy artillery and *minenwerfer* preparation. Progress by IR 143 on the right allowed the Saxons to enter Ravine Wood, where they became bogged down facing 'The Bluff'. The next day's attack was a limited line-straightening exercise.

On 7 December the regiment was relieved, reformed with three battalions (each of three companies) and paraded before the King of Saxony. After a week in reserve it relieved IR 132 at Hill 60 on 16 December; the sector was extended to include Hill 59 and Zwarteleen by the 21st. Christmas was quiet, but two local French attacks were beaten off on 27 December. The year concluded with a French mine detonation on the 29th which killed three and wounded twelve, an ominous sign of things to come.

Regimental memorial in Gheluvelt, commemorating the town's capture and marking the grave of an officer and seven men of IR 105.

CHAPTER 4
THE YEAR 1915

Soldat Paul Spreer, working as a bicycle messenger (*radfahrer*) in Lomme near Lille, February 1915. He can be identified as a member of 8. Kgl. Sächs. Infanterie-Regiment 'Prinz Johann Georg' Nr. 107 by the regimental belt buckle with the crowned cypher 'JG' of their honorary colonel-in-chief (*chef*), the King's brother. This regiment and Kgl. Sächs. Schützen-(Füsilier-)Regiment Prinz Georg Nr. 108 were unique among the German armies in displaying their unit (rather than state) identity in this manner. In wartime such distinctions were maintained as long as possible, but inevitably eroded by supply difficulties.

1915 in Flanders

German strategy in 1915 focused on Russia, while the armies in the West were required to hold their existing front with the practical minimum of men and materiel. This situation was popularly caricatured with the saying '*Im Osten kämpft das tapfere Heer, im Westen steht die Feuerwehr*' (In the East the brave army is fighting, in the West the fire brigade is standing by). The sector of **XIX. Armeekorps** east of Armentières certainly exemplified this, gaining a lasting reputation with the enemy as a 'nursery sector' which shaped British perceptions of the Saxons. Further north however, **XXVII. Reservekorps** and **IR 105** saw brutal fighting against the French and British throughout the year. The two Saxon corps in Flanders were also called upon for reinforcements to counter offensives further south. The new **58. Infanterie-Division** and **123. Infanterie-Division** both spent long periods behind the front near Lille as a reserve for such emergencies, with the latter returning to Flanders in October to recuperate from the Autumn battles in Artois.

Although it led to a major defensive crisis for the Entente, the *Zweiter Flandernschlacht* (Second Battle of Ypres) in April and May was in essence a large-scale diversion for operations in the East. It was also a field trial for poison gas, a weapon regarded with widespread disgust and suspicion at all levels of the field army. However the majority were content to stifle their scruples if it reduced German losses in the attack as its advocates promised. Chlorine cylinders arrived in Flanders as early as January, and officers of Pionier-Bataillon 35 (AKA '*Desinfectionstruppe Peterson*') spent weeks surveying locations around the salient. The '*stinkpioniere*' were never popular with the infantry who provided the labour to carry and dig in the cylinders, and could spend many weeks sharing a trench with them while waiting for a rare favourable wind. Since Peterson's unit was small, the gas was often released by regular *pioniere* or seconded infantrymen (some of whom joined the *stinkpioniere* when the battalion became a regiment). While specialists had Dräger breathing apparatus (see p. 65) most troops relied on the *gasschutzpäckchen* (AKA '*riechpäckchen*' – 'stink packet'), a crude cloth pad soaked in hyposulphite solution and carried in a rubberised pouch on the left breast.

Demand for the skills of the regular *pioniere* reached unprecedented levels under trench warfare conditions, as the only troops already familiar with hand grenades and the construction of field fortifications. From early 1915 suitable infantrymen were trained as auxiliary *hilfspioniere* or *infanterie-pioniere*, and a multitude of ad-hoc sub-units soon sprung up among the infantry to tackle tasks such as drainage, electrical engineering and concreting. The infantry also provided crews for the countless crude smoothbore mortars which supplemented the rifled *minenwerfers* of the *pioniere*, and *mineur-kommandos* to aid the *pioniere* in the underground war against French and British tunnelers.

The 'Special Relationship' – Saxons versus Württembergers

Necessity drove the two smallest German armies to join forces in the formation of XXVII. RK as a means of preserving their units from mixture with (and absorption by) the Prussian Army. However tensions between the stereotypically blunt, dour and often Roman Catholic Württembergers and the more relaxed Saxons were never absent. The claim by Oberstltn. Fromm (RIR 120) that '*even Saxon officers often told us openly that the Swabian is a better soldier than the Saxon*'[1] reflects an attitude which Württembergers were never slow to express, to the eventual irritation of the patient Saxons. The disastrous early experiences of XXVII. RK brought the relationship to its nadir, according to the regimental history of RIR 245:

The primitive dugouts [at In de Ster Caberet] *had no sooner been put into some makeshift order, than the best part of the trench had to be handed over to the neighbouring Württemberg regiment. The troops feel that in every respect they are discriminated against in favour of the Württemberg regiments within the 54. RD. The relationship between Saxons and Württembergers is the worst imaginable and dates back to the first days of the fighting here. Each accuses the other of cowardice and mocks them by aping their dialect. At the field kitchen on dark nights everyone is tested on his native accent, and woe betide any Württemberger caught at a Saxon field kitchen or vice versa. Better that the field kitchen should return to the billets half-empty, than a Württemberger should get a spoonful of food from it.*[2]

The experiment was repeated more successfully in 1915–1916 with 58. ID and less so with 204. ID, after which mixed divisions became purely Saxon or Württemberg.

XXVII. Reserve-Korps (53. and 54. Reserve-Division)

Victories and disasters from Broodseinde to Bellewaarde

53. Reserve-Division

(s.) *105. Res. Inf. Brig.:* (s.) RIR 241 | (s.) RIR 243

(s.) *106. Res. Inf. Brig.:* (s.) RIR 242 | (s.) RIR 244

(s.) RJB 25 | (s.) RFAR 53 | (s.) Res. Kav. Abt. 53

(s.) Res. Pi. Komp. 53 | (s.) Res. Div. Brückentrain 53

(s.) Res. San. Komp. 53

54. Reserve-Division

(w.) *107. Res. Inf. Brig.:* (s.) RIR 245 | (w.) RIR 247

(w.) *108. Res. Inf. Brig.:* (w.) RIR 246 | (w.) RIR 248

(s.) RJB 26 | (s./w.) RFAR 54 | (w.) Res. Kav. Abt. 54

(s.) Res. Pi. Komp. 54 | (w.) Res. Div. Brückentrain 54

(w.) Res. San. Komp. 54

38. Ldw. Inf. Brig.: (p.) LIR 77 | (p.) LIR 78

(s.) *Res. Pi. Batl. 27:* (s.) Res. Scheinwerfer-Zug 27

(s./pr.) Res. FußaB 27

(s.) Res. Fernsprech-Abt. 27

Winter brought little relief from shelling in the flooded trenches, but gave the corps time to correct its worst faults. Though rebuilt with thousands of raw recruits, it also gained experienced officers from other Saxon units and numerous returning convalescents. On 25 January RJB 25, RIR 242 and RIR 244 lost at least 280 killed or missing and 200 wounded in a disastrous attack on Broodseinde, despite meticulous planning.[3] Smaller efforts in February and March by RIR 241 and 243 also failed, as did a French attack on 10 April to cover their relief by British 28th Division.

While the '*stinkpioniere*' waited for the wind to be right, RIR 241 sapped toward Broodseinde crossroads. Late on the 16th raiders broke into a gap torn in the British line by *minenwerfers*. Though ejected in a fierce grenade battle, they returned the next night during a relief and could not be dislodged. From 22 April orders to 53. RD were to hold on here at all costs and pin down enemy troops. After days of

An honour guard from Reserve-Infanterie-Regiment 243 presents arms at the open casket of a fallen officer – most likely Leutnant Mantius, shot by a sniper on 7 January 1915 while looking through a loophole. Whenever possible, officers received full military honours in death (c.f. pp. 188–189).

feints, mock attacks and shelling it launched a major ope-ration on the 25th (see p. 52).

While all donor regiments kept a battalion in line to hide its existence, *Sturmbrigade von Schmieden* secretly formed at Moorslede. *Regiment Reußner* (II. and III. / 241, II. / 242) and *Regiment Wilhelmi* (II. and III. / LIR 78, II. / 244) were joined by I. / RFAR 54, two heavy batteries and *pioniere*; *Regiment von Heygendorff* (III. / 245; 3., 4. and 9. / 246, II. / 247) was in reserve. The brigade deployed from Poel-kapelle at 4 am on 24 April with orders to advance once XXVI. RK did so and take Hill 32 (see map p. 51). According to the British chlorine was discharged at 5 am, but Saxon sources claim only tear gas shells were used. In the Canadian trenches a third of 8th Btn. and a quarter of 15th Btn. CEF were affected, and about 6 am wounded and gassed men were seen going back. II. and III. / 241 surged forward un-bidden and overran the opposing front line, taking over 300 prisoners. 13th Btn. CEF found its right flank exposed and retired over Hill 32 under devastating shelling, while Reussner's men tried to roll up 8th Btn. from the flank to aid *Regiment Wilhelmi*. After a fresh barrage they advanced

and dug in on the hill, where they were later reinforced by part of Matrosen-Regiment 5. Early on 25 April the enemy launched a major counterattack, but found 51. RD in St. Julien and the *Sturmbrigade* advancing down Hill 32. The attack collapsed, but blunted the Saxon advance. At 3 pm *Regiment von Heygendorff* left Poelkapelle to expand Reußner's bridgehead eastward, taking about 300 prisoners and forcing the evacuation of the old Canadian front line after dark. On the 26th the *Sturmbrigade* reached the Ypres–Langemarck crossroads. It was relieved over the next two days and dissolved on the 29th.

From 4 pm on 3 May the *Erdwerk* in Berlin Wood was pul-verised by a two-hour barrage. Shattered survivors were seen retiring, and III. / 241 charged after them. By evening they had taken s'Gravenstafel and dug in 50m from Hill 38 (Abraham Heights), with RIR 243 further back on the left. At dawn patrols found the entire line opposite XXVII. RK empty, and a general advance began in which much booty and some stragglers were seized. By afternoon the enemy line on the Frezenberg Ridge was located and heavily shelled while 53. RD dug in. 54. RD was then inserted on the left,

Early patrol or raiding party from Reserve-Infanterie-Regiment 241. Shoulder-straps have been removed, and the *pickelhauben* will probably be left behind. Most are armed with a pistol and a dagger or sharpened spade. The rolled *zeltplane* could be used as a stretcher or to carry booty.

Jäger Erich Wilhelm of Reserve-Jäger-Bataillon 26 was killed in action on 1 February 1915 at Molenaarelsthoek and buried on the spot. Although it was officially worn at all times, the *tschako* on his grave lacks the horsehair plume (c.f. photos pp. 53 and 69).

Uffz. Oberreuter and comrades from Infanterie-Pionier-Kompanie / Reserve-Infanterie-Regiment 243 beside a newly constructed field searchlight dugout in Moorslede. Many regiments on the Western Front formed such a company in 1915 to aid the overstretched *pioniere*.

with two regiments per division in line. The bombardment for the attack on 8 May devastated the British line on the forward slope north of Frezenberg. Retaliation was weak, and by 9.30 am white flags were seen. Some units broke cover to take prisoners, but withdrew under fire from other British units. At 10.30 am RIR 241 stormed through Frezenberg as far as Verlorenhoek (see p. 52) while RIR 242 overran Wilde Wood; a hasty counterattack at 6 pm failed bloodily. To the south RIR 247 and 248 were held at the British support line at appalling cost to the defenders. 54. RD reached *Storchschnabelwäldchen* (Dead Man's Bottom) by 10 May, and the tired corps attacked on 13 May without success. RIR 241 took the British front line, but found it untenable; the next day an informal truce was arranged by medical officers, and the dead and wounded retrieved. A gas attack on 24 May was a disaster for 53. RD (see p. 51), but 54. RD exceeded its objectives, taking *T-Wäldchen* (Y Wood) and *Eierwäldchen* (Railway Wood).

From 7 June 54. RD held the whole corps front. A major attack on the 16th threw RIR 246 back to the lake with grievous losses (see p. 187), but by nightfall the British had

withdrawn to the old German front line under heavy shelling from both sides. They made another attempt on the 22nd, and RIR 248 took revenge with a raid on 5 July. 53. RD was at St. Eloi (see pp. 80–81) from 20 June to 16 July with IR 105 attached; RIR 242 lost nineteen dead and fifty wounded to mines on 6 July. 53. RD relieved 54. RD from 8 July to 17 September and concentrated on improving the line.

After three days of 'drum fire' and a mine explosion at Railway Wood the British broke into the lines of RIR 246 and 248 on 25 September, but were trapped there and destroyed by bombing parties. From 1 October RIR 242 and 244 served with 40. ID at Ploegsteert Wood in place of IR 104 and 134 (see p. 62), while the rest of 53. RD saw extremely heavy fighting against the French Champagne Offensive. From mid-November 53. RD was in reserve providing artillery and working parties to 54. RD, which dominated the enemy by aggressive raiding. After a large German mine explosion near Railway Wood on 14 December (which killed men on both sides) and an unsuccessful gas attack on the 19th their year drew to a bloody close.

A young leutnant of RIR 245 and his men in a typical sandbagged breastwork with rifle loopholes at In de Ster Caberet in early 1915. The excessive length of the G98 rifle under such conditions is obvious; barrels often became damaged by constant collision with trench walls.

These infantrymen are wearing a mixture of enemy uniform items and civilian clothing to play the part of the opposition during a tactical exercise. Uffz. Adolf Höhle of 5./RIR 244 sent this photo home on 23 April, the day before his company attacked as part of *Regiment Wilhelmi*.

(right) Broodseinde crossroads, showing the sap completed on 21 April to connect the trenches taken by RIR 241 on 14–20 April. The regiment held the line south of the Passchendaele road with RJB 25 on its right and RIR 243 on its left. This area was so devastated that a surveyor from the attached 2. / Pi. Regt. 24 was needed to confirm that the crossroads was now inside the Saxon lines.

(below) While I./241 remained at Broodseinde, II. and III./241 attacked south of Poelkapelle on 24–26 April as part of *Regiment Reußner*. On its left was *Regiment Wilhelmi*, leading the advance of 38. Landwehr-Brigade (on the right of 53. RD at Wallemolen since December). The reassembled RIR 241 took over the line south of the s'Gravens-tafel road on the night of 1–2 May, with RIR 243 on the left and *Regiment von Heygendorff* in brigade reserve. On 3–8 May it advanced triumphantly via s'Gravenstafel and Frezenberg to Verlorenhoek. However it suffered a horrific ordeal on 24 May, when it received almost no notice to evacuate before gas was discharged from the second line. 126 infantrymen were hospitalised, as were several of the 'amateur' gas engineers while trying to reseal the cylinders. In the RIR 242 sector many pipe seals failed, filling the front line with gas. Nevertheless the line was advanced a few hundred metres south of Verlorenhoek.

From 7 June the front was held by one division at a time, allocated as follows: RIR 242 or 246 (Bellewaarde), RIR 244 or 248 (Railway Wood), RIR 241 or 245 (Verlorenhoek), RIR 243 or 247 (flank). The *jägers* were used to allow whole regiments to be relieved alternately.

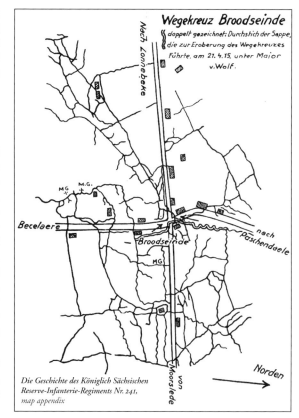

Die Geschichte des Königlich Sächsischen Reserve-Infanterie-Regiments Nr. 241, map appendix

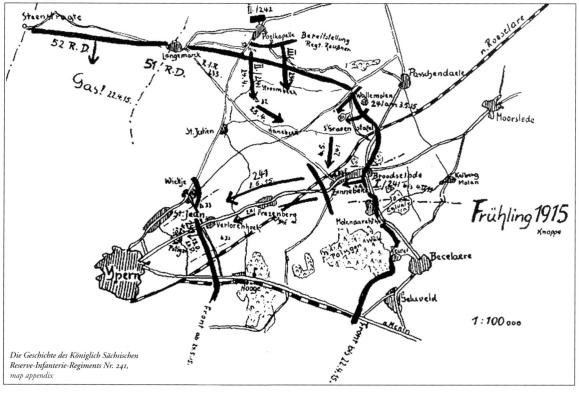

Die Geschichte des Königlich Sächsischen Reserve-Infanterie-Regiments Nr. 241, map appendix

Ersatz-Reservist Arthur Fischer from Dresden was killed in action with 9./RIR 242 on 25 April and is now buried at Langemarck. He fell in a diversionary attack launched by 53. Reserve-Division along a front from south of Broodseinde to the railway line at 2.15 pm, after hours of shelling with high explosive and tear gas shells (*T-Granaten*). Though the Saxons were driven out at two other break-in points, elements of 10., 9. and 4./242 captured part of the line of 2nd Btn. East Surrey Regiment south of the railway and held it against all counterattacks. This force was led by New York born Oltn. Harry Linck, a close comrade of Vfw. Penther and a future storm troop leader with Sturmabteilung der 53. RD and Sturmbataillon 8.

Men of RIR 245 inspect a British motor vehicle destroyed by artillery during the advance. The regimental history of RIR 241 proudly recalls how they overran 83 Brigade (28th Division) at Frezenberg on 8 May: '... *at 10.30 prompt we burst forward, and no other regiment came with us* [in fact RIR 242 also made major progress]. *The assault was bloody, bloodier still for the English. Quite tamely they let the storm pass over them and hurried with raised hands into captivity. No-one hindered the regiment, and no-one would have been able to do so.*'[4] Serious resistance in the support line was overwhelmed by a bayonet charge, and the RAMC dressing station near Verlorenhoek almost overrun before fire from the flanks forced the Saxons to dig in. The streets and fields in the regiment's wake were said to be '*littered with English dead and wounded*'. The next day '*a whole platoon*' in the trench opposite surrendered, and deserters continued to trickle in for days.

From the standing orders of Armee-Oberkommando 4 and Generalkommando XXVII. Reserve-Korps

Carrier Pigeons   10.5.1915

Divisional staffs and *ortskommandanten* are to ensure that the published decree is applied in their districts, and in future to prove to their satisfaction by means of frequent searches that there are no living pigeons in the possession of the inhabitants. The enforcement of this measure can best be achieved by keeping the area around villages under surveillance in favourable flying weather, especially in the early hours of the morning. Sentries and patrols are henceforth most emphatically instructed to search all carts driven by civilians, [their] parcels and baskets – including those of individual travellers – for living pigeons…

In conducting the investigations it should be noted, that pigeons deliberately withheld [from confiscation] are not to be sought after in pigeon lofts, but rather hidden in residential houses inside cupboards adapted for the purpose, in cellars, attics, stables, barns, ricks, in outlying cottages, chapels, sheds, in woods or in fields.

Wherever it is necessary for our own signals staff to keep carrier pigeons, the lofts and birds in question are to be kept under constant military guard.

Photographic Regulations   10.5.1915

On several occasions recently postcards with views of destroyed villages have been sold, which are likely to provoke unrest among the population. With regards to the *etappe*, the Etappen-Inspektion [4] is requested most emphatically to prevent the distribution of these postcards. The rule is that all scenes of destruction which purport to have been carried out by German troops are banned from sale.

Only scenes of destruction caused by enemy armies are permitted. Under such scenes there is to be a caption in large type: 'destroyed by the Belgian, French or English Army' or similar. Because photography is prohibited within the area of operations, cards of destroyed villages in the operational area cannot appear on sale. Should this be the case despite the ban, the cards and [printing] plates are to be seized immediately. The *ortskommandanten* of the operational area must also constantly ensure that no other cards of destroyed villages (from the rear area) are distributed without the caption described above…

Sächsisches Staatsarchiv Dresden, Signatur 11358, Nr. 48

A 10.5cm howitzer crew of Reserve-Feldartillerie-Regiment 53 entertain visitors at their camouflaged gun pit near Passchendaele in May 1915. Guests include a *jäger* of RJB 25 (without his plume), 'the *munitionsunteroffizier*' (of the battery?), 'a man from another gun' and a medical orderly of the *Freiwillige Krankenpflege*. The latter is technically a civilian and should not be present in the gun line (c.f. p. 60).

A working party from Reserve-Jäger-Bataillon 25 sing to keep their spirits up on a field railway train to Hooge. Since the gas attacks in April, all wear the *riechpäckchen* on the left shoulder.

Jäger Kurt Steinborn of 1. / RJB 25 was killed near Hooge on 9 August, the same day as his company commander Hauptmann Krippendorf (see pp. 186–189), and buried in the *Jägerfriedhof* at Broodseinde.

In the summer RJB 25 was used to hold the line in the Railway Wood sector, and to help fortify the *Hooge-Stellung*. Reserve accommodation was provided here, at *Calvairewald* (Justice Wood) east of Molenaarelsthoek (see map on p. 32) These primitive dugouts look like death-traps, but since April this area lay well behind the front. Nevertheless, gas discipline is being maintained.

Card commemorating the first anniversary of RIR 245 and its commander Major Alfred von Heygendorff. Born on 1 March 1868 in Bad Elster, he commanded II. Batl. / IR 177 in peacetime. After taking over RIR 245 on 24 October 1914 (see p. 29), he was awarded the *Ritterkreuz* of the *Militär-St. Heinrichs-Orden* on 17 November and later promoted to oberstleutnant. Much-loved by his men, he was often called 'the soul of the regiment'. In the veterans' newsletter '*Was wir erlebten – 245er Erinnerungen*' (1922) Professor Max Geissler from Leipzig wrote: '*Rarely indeed has a regimental commander been able to describe his regiment as 'his' in such a strict sense as he could. Rarely indeed have those belonging to a regiment regarded their commander as 'theirs' in such a heartfelt sense* [as we could]'.[5]

On 12 September 1916 von Heygendorff was killed in action at Rancourt on the Somme. The regimental history states: '*at 7.15 pm a heavy shell smashed through the vault of the underground observation post and buried the entire regimental staff. Rescue efforts began at once, but only managed to recover the body of the revered commander an hour later. With Oberstleutnant von Heygendorff fell his adjutant Leutnant Müller, the commander of the MGK Leutnant Ramshorn, Leutnant Fischer-Brill and many brave runners.*'[6] Only three days earlier the oberstleutnant's previous HQ cellar in Rancourt had been shelled, and his son Egon (the regimental orderly officer) severely wounded. The young leutnant died in hospital at Manancourt on 10 September, and his father's last letter home was to break the news to his mother. Their other son Ralph also served, but survived the war.

Officers and men of RIR 245 in the line at Verlorenhoek, which mainly consisted of sandbagged and loopholed breastworks due to the high water table. RIR 245 held this sector in July and from September onwards, after RIR 241 had made improvements including concrete dugouts for medical personnel. In late 1915 this quiet sector was praised by General von Schubert as the 'model position' of XXVII. RK.

Surprisingly relaxed men of RIR 248 (and a lone sailor) fortifying the British mine crater of 25 September at Railway Wood. Many of that day's ninety or so dead from 1./248 were buried in this fetid pit, retaken by the regiment 'over mounds of corpses' and soon partly flooded by rainwater.

Stray 'trench cats' often befriended the troops, and were welcome allies against rats and mice. Although their shoulder-straps are covered, the unit here can be identified by the collar and cuff *litzen* on tunics issued by the grenadier regiments who co-founded RIR 241.

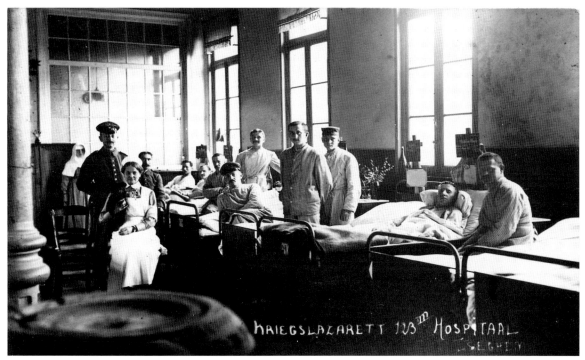

A brightly lit ward of Kriegslazarett 123, based in the corps rear area at Isegem. This hospital was an existing Roman Catholic institution taken over by Etappen-Inspektion 4, and was staffed by a combination of Belgian nuns and German Red Cross personnel.

Commemoration of the fallen of Reserve-Infanterie-Regiment 244 on 11 September 1915, at the regimental cemetery in Moorslede. Fresh garlands have been placed on the graves of the officers and 'acting officers' killed at the First Battle of Ypres in autumn 1914.

The battalion canteen of I. Batl. / Reserve-Infanterie-Regiment 241, evidently doing a roaring trade in 'German beer' ca. summer 1915. The bicycles (and the wearing of ankle boots with puttees or leather gaiters) suggest that many or all of these men are battalion messengers.

'Field comedian' Max Haupt was a frequent source of amusement in Reserve-Infanterie-Regiment 241. Once his battalion commander spotted Haupt on sentry duty and remarked on his facial hair (a serious issue when gasmasks first appeared): 'you could comfortably lose half of that!' Haupt promptly retired to his dugout, cut off the left half of his moustache and right half of his sideburns, and returned to his post.

The *Weihnachtstisch* (Christmas table) of Reserve-Fuhrpark-Kolonne 88, a Saxon supply park column of XXVII. Reserve-Korps (c.f. p. 40). As in 1914, the table is lavishly stocked with *liebesgaben* to share amongst the troops and adorned with a well-decorated tree. Successive war Christmases would be increasingly meagre. On the wall is painted a quotation from Bismarck '*Wir Deutschen fürchten Gott, sonst nichts auf der Welt!*' ('We Germans fear God and nothing else in the world!') Familiar quotations from the Kaiser or Bismarck used as patriotic slogans were a common motif in the rear areas, akin to the decorative use of biblical quotations in German churches (c.f. pp. 77 and 118).

From mid-November to late February Reserve-Infanterie-Regiment 241 was resting at Ingelmunster (III. Bataillon) and in and around Oostrozebeke, where this photo was taken. On Christmas Day the professional singer Fräulein Margarethe zur Nieden performed in Oostrozebeke church – one of the highlights of a period fondly recalled in the regimental history as '*the most beautiful weeks we ever spent in the field*'.

XIX. ARMEE-KORPS (24. AND 40. INFANTERIE-DIVISION)

Holding the line east of Armentières and Ploegsteert Wood

24. Infanterie-Division
89. Inf. Brig.: IR 133 | IR 139 | IR 179
UR 18 (without 4. Esk.)
24. Felda. Brig.: FAR 77 | FAR 78
1. Komp. / Pi. Batl. 22 | Div. Brückentrain 24
San. Komp. XIX/1

40. Infanterie-Division
88. Inf. Brig.: IR 104 | IR 134 | IR 181
HR 19
40. Felda. Brig.: FAR 32 | FAR 68
2. & 3. Komp. / Pi. Batl. 22 | Div. Brückentrain 40
San. Komp. XIX/2

(p.) *38. Ldw. Inf. Brig.:* (p.) LIR 77 | (p.) LIR 78
JB 13 (until 25 August) | II. Batl. / FußaR 19
Stab I. & Scheinwerfer-Zug / Pi. Batl. 22
Fernsprech-Abt. 19 | Flieger-Abt. 24

New Year was marked with drinking and celebratory gunfire on both sides. Hopes of a formal burial truce at Ploegsteert Wood had been quashed by British prevarication, and on paper the fighting resumed. However while Saxon officers enforced the anti-fraternisation order, most accepted or shared their men's disinclination for more than token shooting (of which the enemy were politely forewarned). In most sectors the truce ended by early January, due to British orders to resume shooting and the arrival in Lille of fresh shells for the artillery. At Rue du Bois it persisted until the end of the month, though Wez-Macquart was shelled. In IR 107, regimental policy was that the need to work in the open militarily justified the ceasefire; few in either front line would have disagreed. After a dry spell at Christmas torrential rain was inundating the trenches. By exerting its full manpower, the corps had made its front broadly habi-

Two German Red Cross nurses from Lille on a 'Sunday visit' to the front line, in blatant disregard of both military regulations and social conventions. This remarkable photo and those on pages 61–65 are all taken from the private album of an unidentified junior officer of Infanterie-Regiment 139, suggesting awareness and casual acceptance of this illicit visit up to at least company level.

table by mid-January. By February, electric pumps and lighting were widespread and the troops adequately protected from the rain, if not the increasingly frequent shelling. However due to lack of ammunition and heavy guns, British artillery remained a localised and sporadic threat.

In spring parts of the line were almost idyllic. Lacking any strategic imperative to attack, there was a pragmatic consensus at all ranks to minimise aggression. Many British units played along, and for much of the year 'live and let live' was tacitly in force on most of the corps front. Though armed with scoped rifles as early as December, Saxon snipers killed very few of the Tommies – who suspected *'a tactful blend of constant firing and bad shooting, which while it satisfies the Prussians causes no serious inconvenience to Thomas Atkins'*.[7] Parts of the line became model trenches to show press and VIPs, like the British 'tourist line' in Ploegsteert Wood. On 22 February a neutral military delegation visited the fortified houses in Le Touquet, where a display of American-made shells fired by the British was spoiled by the absence of the US attaché.

In early March 48. Infanterie-Brigade left the corps (see p. 72). In exchange 4,800 new recruits were used to form thirteenth and fourteenth companies of the remaining regiments. After final training at the front these companies were assembled at Lille on 21 May to become IR 183, which left to join a new brigade of the same number. The divisional boundary was now the Lys, and IR 133 part of 24. ID. While the main sector of IR 104 shifted northwards to Ploegsteert Wood, its detached battalion remained at Le Touquet until 20 April.

On 10 March the British opened fire all along the line as a diversion for their attack on VII. AK at Neuve Chapelle. The next day a burning raft was floated down the Lys toward the footbridge at Frelinghien, but ran aground. In the night of 11–12 March, a limited advance at L'Epinette threatened the outpost line of IR 139. None of this hindered the flow of reserves to the adjacent corps, including II./IR 104, a composite battalion from 24. ID and about eight batteries. Simultaneously JB 13 was engaged in nightmarish fighting at Notre Dame de Lorette.

Leutnant d.R. Nauenburg, adjutant of I. Batl./Infanterie-Regiment 139 at the trench telephone. The operator holds a hand-held spool for the line, a simple unshielded wire at this stage of the war.

Vizefeldwebel Erich Schmidt, later killed in action at Warlencourt (Somme) on 20 October 1916 as a leutnant d. R. with 7./IR 139. Note the locker on the left for *patronen* (ammunition).

The weather defeated initial mining attempts by both sides at Rue du Bois in the winter, and the *pioniere* had made limited progress since. Then at 9.30 am on 9 April a mine explosion and barrage partially destroyed the schoolhouse in Le Touquet, killing eighteen and wounding twenty-three from IR 104 – which hastily consolidated the crater. Energetic countermining by 3./Pi. Batl. 22 under Ltn. d. R. Hermann Stock resulted in a break-in to a British gallery near the railway on 20 April, and its destruction by a Saxon *camouflet* after a desperate underground firefight. The Le Touquet road and railway were now intermittent flash-points for the mining war and its attendant barrages and bombing raids. Frelinghien soon became another, followed by the 'Birdcage' at Ploegsteert Wood, and the whole line became dotted with mine shafts.

On 9 May the corps again sent two battalions to defend Neuve Chapelle, plus four field and three heavy batteries (the latter on long-term loan). On 20 May the attached Bavarian and Hanoverian *jägers* (see p. 40) were transferred to the Italian front; JB 13 was excluded only because it was heavily engaged in Artois. An army order to form a reserve of two active regiments led to the relief of IR 133 and 134 by LIR 77 and 78 on 31 May. As a result IR 134 was lying in wait between Givenchy and Festubert to inflict a crushing defeat on the British and Canadian attack of 15 June.

For the autumn offensive the British simulated a gas attack on 25 September, but did not leave their trenches. At Fromelles the Bavarians (6. bRD) were attacked, but only two companies of IR 179 were needed to aid them. By mid-October the corps had sent three infantry regiments (IR 104, 133 and 134), all its brigade staffs plus artillery, *pioniere* and *jägers* to the Vimy Ridge and Arras fronts; near Cuinchy I./IR 104 fought the British at the *Hohenzollernwerk*. From 23 October the battleworn 117. and 123. ID were attached to XIX. AK (see p. 76). Luckily for its overstretched staff, the rest of the year passed quietly on the extended 30km front of the resulting 'Gruppe von Laffert'.

The old sector of Infanterie-Regiment 107; after that regiment left the corps, Infanterie-Regiment 139 extended its flank south of Wez-Macquart. A field railway line ran along the main road parallel to the front (known as the '*Strich*'), defended by a sandbagged second position.

The twin approaches from Wez-Macquart to the front line ran through the houses on either side of the road, and were called the *Linken* and *Rechten Barbarenweg* (Left and Right Barbarian's Way) – a typical sarcastic reference to Entente propaganda.

The crossroads at Wez-Macquart in early summer 1915, still virtually untouched by artillery fire.

The area between La Bleue und L'Epinette, taken looking westwards across the opposing front lines into the British hinterland. This aerial photograph was almost certainly the work of Feld-Flieger-Abteilung (FFA) 24, the corps' organic aerial reconnaissance unit.

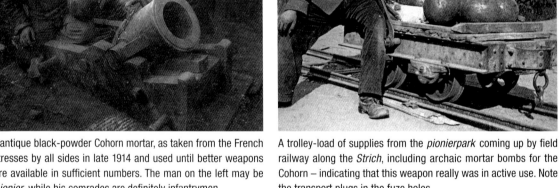

An antique black-powder Cohorn mortar, as taken from the French fortresses by all sides in late 1914 and used until better weapons were available in sufficient numbers. The man on the left may be a *pionier*, while his comrades are definitely infantrymen.

A trolley-load of supplies from the *pionierpark* coming up by field railway along the *Strich*, including archaic mortar bombs for the Cohorn – indicating that this weapon really was in active use. Note the transport plugs in the fuze holes.

A model 1914 rifle grenade 'battery', using typical rack mountings to absorb the heavy recoil. This unpopular rod-type grenade was replaced by a French-style model with a discharger cup in 1917.

Leutnant Wendler and friend in front of a latrine marked 'officers only'. Similar facilities existed for NCOs, while common soldiers used the communal '*donnerbalken*' (see p.137).

A questionably stable early anti-aircraft mounting for the MG 08, complete with four-legged 'sledge'; the weight on the tripod here is almost 70kg. Later the gun (minus its 'sledge') was usually mounted on a simple metal cradle bolted to a pole for this role.

Miners (mostly seconded infantrymen) resting beside a shaft fitted with a heavy pump. Mining in the Infanterie-Regiment 139 sector was mainly concentrated on the right at L'Epinette, but a few shafts existed south of the Lille–Armentières railway and one at Wez-Macquart.

Machine-gunners at their post. Whilst the MG 08 itself remains covered up in reserve for actual attacks, a sniper rifle with telescopic sight is kept ready to hand for targets of opportunity.

Miners with two models of Dräger 'Selbstretter' self-contained oxygen breathing apparatus. Developed for civilian mine rescue before the war, it was later issued to gas units and medical personnel.

An armoured platoon commander's dugout in the IR 139 sector, somewhat later in 1915. Whilst the defences are more solid, the weather is now reducing the neat German trenches to archetypal Great War squalor. Note the use of a tin can to seal the stovepipe when not in use.

A working party from 7. / Infanterie-Regiment 133, constructing a new trench in the sector of Infanterie-Regiment 179 at Rue du Bois. In March 1915 this sector was shifted to the right, to cover part of the former frontage of the departing Infanterie-Regiment 107.

The 6. Gruppe, 3. Zug (6th section, 3rd platoon) of 3./Infanterie-Regiment 134 on 20 February 1915 near St. Yvon, legendary scene of the Christmas football match (see pp. 40–41). Their trench has been heavily built up with sandbags due to the ever-troublesome groundwater.

Men of 11./IR 134 in the reserve line east of St. Yvon in May 1915. On the back Gotthilf Lippold writes to his brother (with IR 96, a Prussian regiment from the tiny states of Reuss and Schwarzburg-Rudolstadt) that he is in a telephone troop and his dugout is marked with an 'x'.

From 31 May the Prussian 38. Landwehr-Brigade was attached to the corps, while IR 133 and 134 went into army reserve at Haubourdin. Here men of Landwehr-Infanterie-Regiment 77 (formed in Osnabrück) are occupying the usual sector of IR 134 north of Ploegsteert Wood.

Landwehr-Infanterie-Regiment 78 (formed at Braunschweig and Celle in Hanover) buries another comrade in October 1915; after a year in Flanders their cemetery already contains 132 crosses. This regiment took over the former IR 133 sector on the south bank of the Lys.

When JB 13 took over at Frelinghien on 19 June the underground war had begun in earnest. In a typical measure for the period, the battalion therefore formed this ad-hoc *miniertrupp* under Vfw. Sauermann to assist the overstretched army *pioniere* (Res. Pi. Komp. 90) in the tunnels.

An unteroffizier of Jäger-Bataillon 13, his section and their friends somewhere near Verlinghem. Five of them (including the NCO) wear the *Königsabzeichen* on their right sleeve, an annual company marksmanship prize won by the 4. Kompanie in the last pre-war contest.

Four friends from Infanterie-Regiment 104 pose with a crude mortar bomb in February 1915, either an unexploded enemy projectile (*blindgänger*) or a German 'present' for the British.

From left: Ltn. Erdmannsdorf, Ltn. Ander and Fwltn. Grünewald of Jäger-Bataillon 13 at Frélinghien brewery. Ander fell on 25 September 1915 at Beaurains, Grünewald on 10 August 1916 in Galicia.

Artillerymen of I. Abteilung / Feldartillerie-Regiment 32 in Lille ca. March 1915, armed with the old single-action *Reichsrevolver*.

Gunners of 5. Batterie / FAR 68 (a 10.5cm howitzer battery) outside their dugout somewhere between Warneton and Deulemont.

The 'Lichtsignalabteilung des XIX. AK', drawn from the Saxon infantry and *pioniere* plus an unknown Prussian unit (with the *litzen*). Electric signal lamp units were first formed for the *Alpenkorps* in May 1915, then throughout the German armies in August. In April 1917 they were designated *blinkertrupps*, and incorporated into *divisions-fernsprech-abteilungen* as a back-up system for the telephones.

A supply unit of the corps *train* passes through a rear-area town. Their vehicles seem to be of irregular design, and may be civilian farm wagons pressed into military service.

58. INFANTERIE-DIVISION

In OHL reserve at Roubaix and Ingelmunster

58. INFANTERIE-DIVISION (4.1915)

(s.) *116. Inf. Brig.:* (s.) IR 106 | (s.) IR 107 | (w.) RIR 120

(s.) 4. Esk. / UR 18 | (s.) Radfahr-Komp. 58

(w.) *58. Felda. Brig.:* (s.) FAR 115 | (w.) FAR 116

(s./p.) FußaB 58

(s.) Pi. Komp. 115 | (w.) Pi. Komp. 116

(s.) Scheinwerfer-Zug 115

(s.) Div. Brückentrain 58

(s.) Fernsprech-Doppelzug 58

(s.) San. Komp. 58

58. Infanterie-Division was officially formed at Cambrai on 5 March 1915, but it took another week to assemble all of its units. On 10 March Genmaj. Kaden's renumbered brigade (see pp. 204–211) was joined by Württemberg Reserve-Infanterie-Regiment 120, formerly with 26. Reserve-Division on the Somme since September 1914. Their commander's dis-

armingly frank regimental history suggests that this second 'joint venture' was more successful than XXVII. RK, but never ideal. While certain of his men's military superiority, he credits the Saxons with a courtesy and flexibility lacking in his own army.

'However a close relationship never developed between Swabians and Saxons. The active Saxon regiments had men who were years younger than our reserve regiment, but above all the national characters are very different.' [8]

Württemberg also provided one of the two field artillery regiments and their brigade commander, Genltn. von Fritsch. In addition his command boasted an organic 15cm howitzer battalion with one Saxon and one Prussian battery. The new 'independent' division also possessed other traditional corps assets such as half a battalion of *pioniere*, a telephone unit (see

Cavalrymen of 4. Esk. / Ulanen-Regiment 18 enjoy a quiet drink with a friend from Infanterie-Regiment 107 (and a fiercely scowling young civilian). The next wave of new divisions (including 123. ID) mostly had two squadrons each, but divisional cavalry was reduced to one squadron as standard from August 1916. In trench warfare they served as despatch riders and escorts for prisoners, but also as a final battle reserve of trained riflemen.

The newly formed Mittlerer Minenwerfer-Zug 161 in 1915. This mortar platoon was armed with the 17cm mMW and became part of Minenwerfer-Kompanie 58 when the latter was formed (probably in spring 1916). All personnel wear the uniform of Pionier-Bataillon 12 with no unit distinctions – in 1915 oval sleeve badges (see photo p. 235) were widely adopted, later replaced by shoulder-straps with 'MW' and the company number.

pp. 235–240) and an extensive supply train. However there were also some shortages. Most seriously, both Saxon infantry regiments (who had left their Mausers with XIX. AK) had to rearm with the obsolescent *Gewehr 88*; this was not rectified until June. The division was also thought to lack cavalry; Radfahrer-Kompanie 58 (a *jäger* cyclist unit) was intended as a substitute.

For RIR 120 the early days at Cambrai offered a rest from their exertions at La Boiselle. However IR 106 and 107 were busy, with numerous new recruits to be integrated and trained with the 'new' rifle. Welcome breaks were provided by visits from HRH Prince Friedrich Christian on 14 March, and the King himself on 23 March. His Majesty was accompanied by his youngest son HRH Prince Ernst Heinrich, who would later serve with FAR 115.

The next day the division set out on a staggered series of night marches, intended to conceal its movement from the enemy. Reassembled at Roubaix on 27 March, it now spent over a month in this area at the disposal of OHL. Training in this period realistically concentrated on attack and defence of fortified positions, to which end each infantry regiment spent four days a week building a trench system

at Sailly-lez-Lannoy. These were complete by mid-April, and were then used for battalion and company-level battle exercises, sometimes together with the artillery. Away from the training field, the two main contingents led separate social lives. For the Württembergers the highlights were the *regimentsfest* of RIR 120 on 12 April and a visit from their own King (the confusingly-named Wilhelm II) on the 14th, both at Chateau Hem. Meanwhile IR 107 was visited by regimental patron HRH Prince Johann Georg on 16 April.

On 9 May the division was rushed south by railway to oppose the French offensive between Givenchy-en-Gohelle and Neuville-Saint-Vaast. Its units were committed piecemeal and embroiled in heavy fighting in various sectors north and south of Lens for over a month; losses were enormous (see p. 211). The elements of the division were gradually withdrawn between 19 and 27 June, and transferred to 4. Armee in Flanders. Based from 28 June at Ingelmunster and then from 13 July in Roubaix, the division was rapidly rebuilt with fresh recruits. In between exercises and working parties behind the front of XXVII. RK, there were also battalion trips to the seaside at Ostend – and even home leave for a lucky few. On 20 July the division entrained for the Eastern Front.

Artillery drivers of 1. leichte Munitions-Kolonne / Feldartillerie-Regiment 115, the ammunition column of the regiment's I. Abteilung. In spring 1917 these columns were independently numbered and integrated into the army-level supply system, until mobile warfare resumed in 1918.

Drivers at work – Württembergers of 3. Batterie / Feldartillerie-Regiment 116 with harnessed team and 7.7cm field gun limber (*protze*) in early July 1916. I. Abt. / FAR 116 returned from the Arras front on 24 June and spent the next three weeks on exercises and anti-aircraft duty.

123. Infanterie-Division

As a *'fliegende Division'* at Lille and in the Wytschaete Salient

123. Infanterie-Division was assembled around Rozoy-sur-Serre in early April 1915 under Generalmajor Karl Lucius, almost entirely from existing elements of XII. AK and XII. RK. As with 58. ID, rifle shortages forced the division to arm its infantry with the *Gewehr 88*; the vulnerability of its Mannlicher-type action to dirt proved a handicap in Artois that autumn. The division was also short of field artillery, with one regiment of six four-gun 7.7cm batteries. It had only one battery of four 15cm howitzers as organic heavy artillery, and a single *pionier* company. These deficiencies were largely rectified by the end of 1915 – the order of battle on p. 91 was achieved by October, and the old rifles replaced with Mausers in December.

The division was initially deployed on the left of XII. AK near Reims. On 18–19 May it was transported to Lille as a *'fliegende division'* in OHL reserve, available for reinforcements and reliefs on the Flanders and Artois fronts. The following weeks saw numerous railway embarkation exercises leading to 'day trips' for training in the countryside. As a show of strength for Entente spies, there were frequent parades through Lille with regimental bands playing and battalion flags flying. This period concluded on 12 June with the division's first visit from the King of Saxony, when the traditional pageantry was supplemented with an aerobatic display by leading Saxon aviator and future ace Ltn. Max Immelmann. The photos on pages 75–79 were all taken in May and June for the regimental album of Infanterie-Regiment 178, quartered in the eastern suburb of Hellemmes. Compiled with their commander's approval, it contains over 200 photos from autumn 1914 to early 1916. Apart from 15 censored images (depicting the front line, POWs, aircraft and artillery) the remainder were printed for sale as postcards.

1. Kompanie / Infanterie-Regiment 178 drawn up for inspection in the Place de la République at Hellemmes on the morning of the King's birthday (25 May 1915). The photo was taken from an upper window of the old *Mairie*.

123. ID spent the next month mainly in Artois, relieving Prussian regiments exhausted by the fighting at Vimy Ridge. After regrouping at Lille it took over the St. Eloi sector from 53. RD over the nights of 13–16 July, but was relieved within a week by Bavarians; this tour was chiefly notable for a German mine detonation on 17 July. The rest of the summer was spent in OHL reserve at Lille and Roubaix, with opportunities for open-air bathing and sightseeing. For the first time, home leave was granted to those who had been longest in the field. However the troops were also kept busy with tactical exercises or detached on working parties, sometimes as far away as Arras. To enhance the infantry's capacity for construction work and reduce dependence on the *pioniere*, each regiment sent a group (from Infanterie-Regiment 178, three officers and 125 ORs) to Hem for a three-week course organised by Pionier-Kompanie 245; upon their return each group formed a supernumerary *infanterie-pionier-kompanie.*

In the second half of August the division returned to Artois. Here they held the vital Souchez salient, a narrow bulge in the German line overlooked on multiple sides by Notre Dame de Lorette and Vimy Ridge, where con-

ditions were nothing short of hellish. When the Entente offensive opened on 25 September it had to defend itself simultaneously against a massive French frontal assault and a British threat to its rear in Lens. By the time the last of its infantry were relieved on 29 September the regiments had lost a combined total of twenty-three officers and 595 men dead, thirty-five officers and 2,029 men wounded and 1,525 men missing. RIR 106 lost another fifty-six dead, 298 wounded and eighty-four missing in an attempt to retake Loos on 8 October.

The division returned to the St. Eloi sector to recuperate on 15–16 October. Here they faced the British 24th Division, a New Army formation which had suffered even higher losses in its first action at Loos. Initially under Bavarian command (II. bAK), the 123. ID and adjacent 117. ID (itself nearly obliterated at Loos) were subordinated to XIX. AK from 23 October. The Saxons noted major improvements since July – in addition to an expanded trench system (see p. 81) these included numerous observation posts, sniper plates and periscopes. However most of the dugouts (in the '1B' trench behind the front line) were insufficiently deep due to the high water table, and could

H.M. Friedrich August III reviewing a detachment of machine-gunners from Infanterie-Regiment 178 on 12 June 1915. To the King's right (with drawn sword) is their regimental commander, Oberstleutnant Theodor Pilling.

Generalmajor Max Morgenstern-Döring (11 May 1858–12 August 1931) as commander of 245. Infanterie-Brigade in summer 1915. He later commanded 24. Reserve-Division (from April 1916) and 212. Infanterie-Division (from January 1918).

Oberstleutnant Pilling (right) and his adjutant visiting Fort MacDonald in Mons-en-Barœul (an eastern suburb of Lille). In 1917 Australian P.O.W.s were detained here in notoriously overcrowded conditions, but in summer 1915 the fort housed German labourers.

not be considered shell-proof. Constant pumping was needed to prevent flooding, and each regiment was obliged to form an *entwässerungsabteilung* (drainage detachment) and *betonbauabteilung* (concreting detachment). Working parties were also required to assist the *pioniere* in the mine galleries, of which over twenty existed in the IR 178 sub-sector. On 25 October the *pioniere* detonated a counter-mine to destroy a shallow British gallery near St. Eloi, producing a crater 15m across by 6m deep. Its edge was immediately occupied by IR 178, leading to tit-for-tat bombing and raiding in this area where advanced posts lay only 8–15m apart. The British occupied the edge of an older crater several days later, but were ejected on the night of 31 October.

In reserve at Wervik facilities included canteens, a cinema and numerous estaminets. Occasionally, leave was granted to Menin or Lille. On 13 November the King of Saxony visited Wervik and personally decorated the most distinguished veterans of the autumn battles. A lavish expenditure of British shells the next day was believed to be

a late response to this parade. However troops out of the line were mainly kept busy with roll-calls and instruction. Large batches of replacements began to arrive even before the division reached Flanders, mostly new recruits unfamiliar with such staples of trench warfare as gas defence and grenade throwing. Early ad-hoc field training was superseded from 20 December by the formation of *Infanterie-Feldrekrutendepot der 123. Infanterie-Division* at Halluin with a fixed cadre of instructors, to which IR 178 gave three officers, eleven NCOs and thirteen men.

The beginning of November brought heavy rain, and both sides spent the rest of the year battling mainly with the weather. Part of *Bayernwald* was flooded, allegedly due to the British damming a small brook downstream, and had to be abandoned in favour of an improvised sandbag line. Many trenches became nearly impassable, and carrying parties routinely approached the front line by night over open ground. In these grim conditions the sick list mounted. Because of fears that the state of the defences would invite trench raids IR 178 went on heightened alert, but it

The divisional *feldschlachterei* (butchery column) at work in Roubaix. Like the *feldbäckerei-kolonne* (below) this would usually be a corps asset in 1915; the new 'independent' divisions were intended to be self-sufficient at all levels.

A civilian bakery in Roubaix manned by the divisional *feldbäckerei-kolonne*; under normal circumstances the column would use their horse-drawn mobile ovens. Although butchers and bakers were officially drawn from the *train*, the mixed uniforms in both of these photos show that men from other arms were also assigned to these units in the field.

The staff baggage wagon of Infanterie-Regiment 178 departing from rest quarters in Lille. In 1914 an infantry regimental staff had two horse-drawn vehicles, and each battalion a further nineteen. Of these, the field kitchens and ammunition wagons (one per company) plus the ambulances (one per battalion) formed the combat echelon baggage (*gefechtsbagage*) and the remainder the rear echelon (*große bagage*).

was soon clear that this was unnecessary. The state of the British positions on the lower ground opposite is vividly described by 2nd Lieutenant F.C. Hitchcock of 2nd Battalion, the Leinster Regiment (regulars transferred to 24th Division after Loos). Entering the line at St. Eloi on 2 November, he found *'practically no trench at all. We seemed to have been in one continuous nightmare of mud… Practically the whole company front was under water.'*[9] At the flash point near the craters Hitchcock expected trouble, but was surprised to see Saxons *'walking about in the mist, swinging coke braziers to and fro to keep them alight! Like us, they were caked in mud. We did not fire as they, being on the brow of the ridge, had the advantage over us.'*[10] Once the ice was broken, both sides often worked in the open to drain their respective trenches. The unofficial truce soon escalated to fraternisation. On 5 November, Leinster officers struck up a conversation with Saxon sentries, throwing over a flask of whisky in the hope of gaining information. Hitchcock *'had a good look into their advanced post'*[11] but misread '178' on their muddy shoulder-straps as '129'. The next day he found one of his bombers chatting with a Saxon unteroffizier in a crater.

Early signs of 'live and let live' in the Reserve-Infanterie-Regiment 106 sector (where the lines were further apart)

soon fizzled out, and for Infanterie-Regiment 182 (facing the Canadians) no such signs appeared. At St. Eloi, only snipers and artillery continued to fight – but the artillery too was impeded by flooded gun-pits, dugouts and munitions lockers. It was also sometimes called on by the infantry for 'punishment fire' to suppress bombing or machine-gunning, thus helping to 'keep the peace'. However increased shelling by both sides later in November caused significant losses and drove working parties under cover. The truce did not end when the largely regular 3rd Division took over at St. Eloi. Upon relieving an advanced post at the craters on 22 November, Pte. Edmund Herd of the Liverpool Scottish learned that a system of whistle signals had been agreed for fraternisation. His party met the Saxons several times, trading tobacco, alcohol and small souvenirs. A former waiter at Hotel Cecil in London even gave him a letter for his English girlfriend, but Herd was unwilling to risk posting it!

High command on both sides was emphatic that there should be no Christmas Truce. Thus for the troops in the line Christmas was marred by a heavy bombardment, while those in reserve at Wervik were able to celebrate in peace.

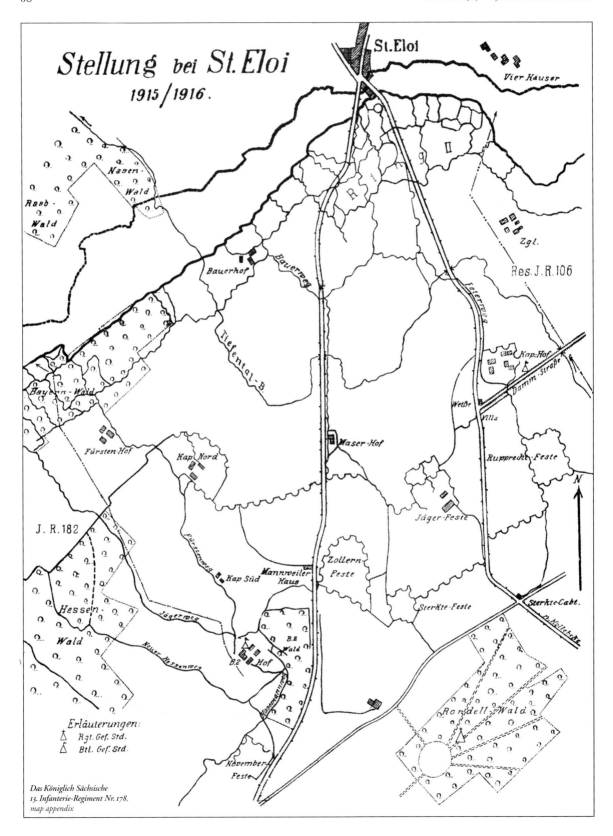

*Das Königlich Sächsische
13. Infanterie-Regiment Nr. 178,
map appendix*

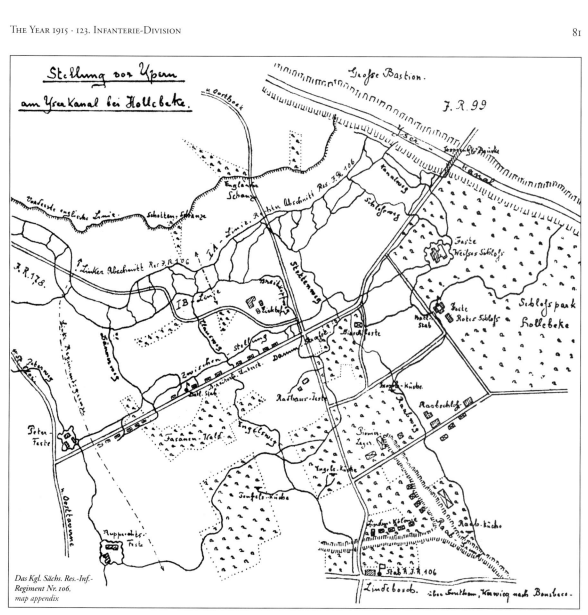

Das Kgl. Sächs. Res.-Inf.-
Regiment Nr. 106,
map appendix

(above) The division's right flank sector at the Ypres-Comines Canal, held by Reserve-Infanterie-Regiment 106. Their regimental history notes that the Bavarians had made substantial progress since the division's first visit in July – including the '1B' line immediately behind the front line ('1A'), the intermediate line (*zwischenstellung*) on the *Dammstrasse* and numerous strongpoints (*festen*) in varying degrees of completion. The right-hand battalion held the 1A and 1B line with three companies, plus a reserve company with the battalion staff at *Feste Rotes Schloss*; the left-hand battalion only had two companies forward, and two with the battalion staff on the *Dammstrasse*. From 29 October onwards, a company of the third ('resting') battalion was deployed as entrenching company in the *Raabgrund* between *Raabschloss* and *Lindebosch*. (see photo p.94). The *regimentsgefechtsstand* was initially at *Lindebosch*, later relocating to the *Clauß-Ferme* (see map pp. 96–97).

(left) Trench map from the regimental history of Infanterie-Regiment 178. In winter 1915–1916 all three regiments held the same sectors they had occupied on their first visit in July. Each sector was held by two battalions abreast, each with three companies in line; battalions were relieved after six days in line for a three-day 'rest' in the rear. The small triangles at *B2-Hof* and *Kap-Hof* denote a battalion battle HQ (*bataillonsgefechtsstand*). Reserve companies were stationed at *B2-Hof, Sterkte-Feste* and (provided by Reserve-Infanterie-Regiment 106) *Dammstrasse*. A total of nine machine-guns were deployed forward, with another four further back in support. The large triangle in *Rondellwald* (Oosttaverne Wood) is the *regimentsgefechtsstand*; this was gradually developed into a sturdy nine-room concrete fortress known as the *Sachsenfeste* and equipped with heating, electricity, telephones and a carrier pigeon station. The most notable feature of this sector for visitors is *Bayernwald* (Bois Quarante) where original trenches from 1915–1916 have been restored – complete with the fascine revetting described by Infanterie-Regiment 178.

Street view in Belgian Wervik with the church of St. Medardus in the background.

Divisional *pionierpark* at the church in Belgian Comines. Until April 1916 the town was considered safe from long-range shelling.

Oberst Pilling and his adjutant aboard their (decidedly unofficial) regimental coach outside the headquarters of Infanterie-Regiment 178 in Bousbecque, prior to visiting the division's newly formed *infanterie-feldrekrutendepot* at Halluin in December 1915.

The partially destroyed town of Wytschaete, at the boundary with the Prussian 117. Infanterie-Division. Already only a kilometre from the front in 1915, 'White Sheet' was virtually obliterated in summer 1917.

Gunners of Feldartillerie-Regiment 245 posing in front of their self-built accommodation. A few trees have been spared from the axe in the hope of providing cover from aerial observation.

Reserve quarters in *Rondell-Wald* (see map on p. 80). British maps show a group of three buildings in the south-western corner of the wood and a single building on the southern edge, within 200 metres of regimental HQ (the *Sachsenfeste*, AKA *Rondell-Hof*).

One of the buildings in *Rondell-Wald*, showing reinforcement with early improvised sandbags (made from multi-coloured civilian cloth) and conversion of the cellar into a dugout. Marked 'not for publication' in the regimental album of Infanterie-Regiment 178.

4.5 INFANTERIE-REGIMENT 105 WITH PRUSSIAN 30. INFANTERIE-DIVISION

The Battle of Hill 60 and Defence of Hooge

As of 12 January IR 105 held both Hill 59 and 60, plus a slightly extended line on the right in dire need of drainage and repair. French bombardments and raids grew increasingly frequent, and on the 27th they blew a mine under a sap at Zwarteleen. Expecting an attack, the Saxons were surprised to see Tommies opposite on 3 February. A lull ensued while British 28th Division improved its new trenches, and IR 105 was in reserve from 10–16 February. Oberst Freiherr von Oldershausen left to head the staff of VIII. RK, and Oberst Max von Hopffgarten of JB 13 took command of IR 105 on 8 March. From the 14th it ceded Hill 59 to IR 143, but took it back in early April when XV. AK was triangularised. After its sectors were redrawn IR 143 was on the right of IR 105, and IR 99 on its left.

At 6.15 am on 17 February the *pioniere* blew a mine under houses at Zwarteleen to deny them to miners and snipers. A volunteer *sturmabteilung* occupied the crater under growing pressure from bombers, but had to withdraw carrying its wounded leader Ltn. d.L. Rudolf Kanis when the British launched a counter-attack. 2nd Btn. East Yorkshire Regiment lost thirty-five killed or missing to the mine and raid, and took six prisoners. On 12 March a further 1200kg mine was blown to obliterate the ruined houses. The 100m wide crater was not occupied but bombarded to keep the enemy out, while a covering sap was dug to the rim. The same day the last gas cylinders were emplaced on Hill 59 and 60. The infantry had received the *gasschutzpäckchen* and purely theoretical emergency drill for gas leaks. From 22 March they were repeatedly alerted for gas attacks, invariably cancelled when the wind changed.

The regimental history claims that high command and sector *pioniere* had long downplayed its fears of hostile mining. At 8.05 pm on 17 April 171st Tunneling Company RE blew a series of huge mines beneath Hill 60, annihilating the front platoon of 2./105 in a yellow-black mushroom cloud. At once the British guns opened up, and 13 Brigade stormed the hill to bayonet

One in a series of at least six humorous postcards depicting the 'night work' of a Saxon labour company at Hill 60 – here, bringing up mining supplies. The British Very lights in the distance suggest that they may have been spotted. Leutnant d. R. Lachmann was with 6. / IR 105 in August 1914, and held temporary command of the combined 9. and 10. / IR 105 in November. He then seemingly disappears from the regimental history.

Sachsen-Arbeitskomp. „Lachmann" 30. J. D.

Nachtarbeit auf Höhe 60. (№ 2.)
Rauf geht's hier nach Höhe 60.,   Gerne sonst wohin verkriechen,
Weh' da pfeift's und jeder möcht sich,   Wenn die bösen Kugeln fliegen.

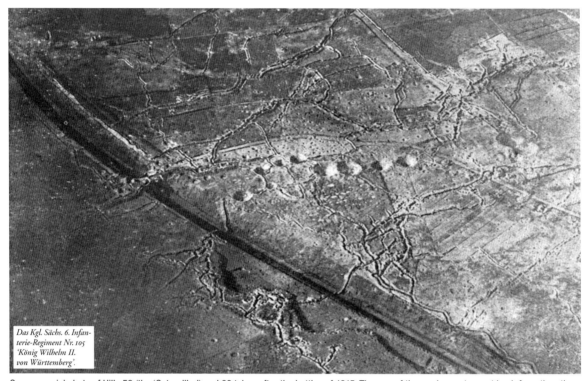

Das Kgl. Sächs. 6. Infanterie-Regiment Nr. 105 'König Wilhelm II. von Württemberg'.

German aerial photo of Hills 59 (the 'Caterpillar') and 60 taken after the battles of 1915. The row of three mine craters set back from the others and the two large ones to their right are those blown on 17 April; two 1200kg, two 910kg and two 230kg black powder charges were fired in pairs at 10 second intervals. Beyond the curved road lie the ruins of Zwarteleen and the German mine craters of February and March.

the survivors. Ltn. d. R. Steinmann (a 'borrowed' Prussian *train* officer) of 2./105 led an immediate counterattack, but the loss of Hill 60 had torn the sector in half, exposing all approaches to heavy fire and preventing coordination with the attacks of 1. and 3./105. Steinmann was wounded and many of his men fled in panic, convinced that the gas was escaping. They were rallied at the railway embankment by Oberstltn. Fürstenau of III./105, and returned to the front led by Fähnrich Freiherr von Feilitsch of 12./105. The reserve companies were now reinforcing the defenders, while the British consolidated under heavy shelling. During the afternoon Oberst von Hopffgarten returned from brigade with orders to retake the hill at any cost, and the use of Feld-MG-Zug 106 plus four companies of IR 99 and 143. At 11.10 pm six companies of IR 99 and 105 launched simultaneous frontal and flank attacks on Hill 60, but were soon forced back into cover under fire from multiple machine-guns. On the right 8./105 and some *pioniere* crossed the barricade held by 1./105 on the lower slope, and bombed their way almost to the craters. Here they were hit by shells from both sides, and every officer killed or wounded. Fahnenjunker-Unteroffizier Müller took command and the survivors dug in. The Germans now held Hill 59, the communication trench to within 30m of the old front line, and the front line from Zwarteleen to 30m

short of the craters. The attack resumed at 3.15 am on the 18th. Bombers from 2./Pi. Batl. 15 eventually broke into the left crater, but being too few to hold it were all but wiped out. After a British counterattack at 7 pm all the day's gains were lost. The battle had now cost the regiment four officers killed, one captured and seven wounded; about 300 NCOs and men were dead, wounded or missing.

On 19 April the artillery hammered Hill 60, where the British were being relieved. The next attack at 7.30 pm on the 20th was preceded by two and a half hours of intense 'annihilation fire', but still ground to a halt under machine-gun fire. A jumping-off line (*sturmausgangstellung*) and parallel 'stop line' were now slowly dug across the fragmented front, while the artillery worked to prevent enemy interference. British retaliation was weakening as batteries moved to the battle further north. By the end of April fresh gas cylinders were ready in the IR 105 and 143 sectors. After a heavy barrage the gas was released at 8 pm on 1 May. In the IR 105 sector the 90m wide cloud struck 10./105 as they waited to attack, gassing three officers and forty men and forcing a company relief. Opposite them 15 Brigade (protected merely by wet rags) suffered appallingly, but enough survived to hold off the Saxons until reinforced. It was be-

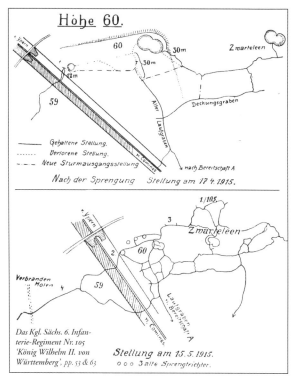

Hills 59 and 60 late on 17 April (showing lost trenches and planned *sturmausgangstellung*) and in mid-May (with company subsectors).

Prussian infantrymen of Unter-Elsässisches Infanterie-Regiment 143 and their (ex-cavalry) officer, in the former Saxon positions on Hill 60 in late June or July 1915.

lieved that the cloud had been too narrow, letting the enemy 'side-step' its effects. When gas was next released at 9.30 am on 5 May cylinders had been added in the IR 99 line, but here and on Hill 59 the piping broke off the cylinders and the trenches had to be cleared. At Hill 60 the gas swept the whole British line, forcing the survivors to flee or perish. IR 105 quickly seized Hill 60 and part of the original British line, taking five machine-guns and a mortar but only eight prisoners. Counterattacks that night and early on 7 May broke up under fire from the hills, and IR 105 left that morning for 24 hours out of the line. From 8 May the regiment steadily fortified Hill 60, under constant threat from artillery and mines. It was visited by the King on 10 June, and moved to Hollebeke on the 20th for a month with 53. Reserve-Division (see p. 49). Oberst von Hopffgarten fell ill, and was replaced on 1 July by Major von Schmalz of Etappen-Inspektion 3. The regiment was relieved by RIR 106 on the 16th and went into reserve.

On 10 August IR 105 took over from the exhausted IR 126 at Hooge, a ghastly cratered wasteland strewn with blackening corpses that could not be safely buried. Much of the front line, wire and drainage system was wrecked, and IR 105 struggled daily to repair it under incessant heavy shelling and bombing

attacks. From 19–24 September the shelling escalated to furious drum fire, and on the last night the British were seen cutting lanes in their wire. When they attacked at 5.20 am few got past the regiment's wire, but a party of 2nd Btn. Royal Irish Rifles got in on their right. Here they were cut off and overwhelmed, and twenty-four taken prisoner. Aided by mine detonations the British had broken into both adjacent sectors (RIR 246 and IR 172) and tried to roll up the Saxons from the flanks, but were held at bay until those regiments successfully counterattacked at 10 am. IR 105 was relieved on the 11th and congratulated on its victory at a cost of fifty dead and 153 wounded. Many Saxon, Württemberg and Prussian decorations were awarded at a series of parades and royal visits.

From 10 November IR 105 replaced IR 172 at Sanctuary Wood, where relative peace was punctuated by violent artillery duels when a mine went off. On 1 December the *pioniere* fought an underground grenade battle with British tunnelers, followed by a heavy barrage to catch them at the surface. When XXVII. RK attacked with gas on 19 December, IR 105 'stood to' in their new masks, laying down rapid fire and preparing for a possible advance. They were relieved by IR 125 late on the 29th, and left Flanders for Verdun in January.

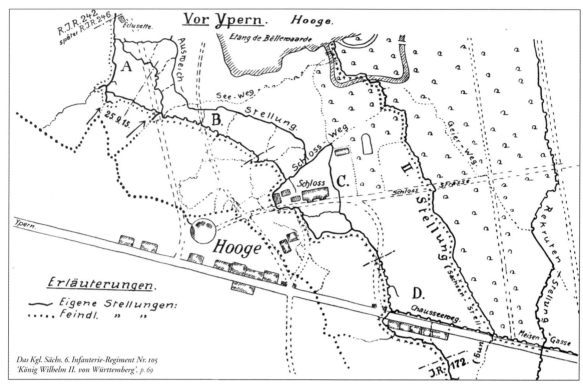

Das Kgl. Sächs. 6. Infanterie-Regiment Nr. 105
'König Wilhelm II. von Württemberg', p. 69

The IR 105 sector at Hooge, showing the point in company subsectors 'A' and 'B' (7. and 5. / 105) where 2nd Royal Irish Rifles broke in as far as the *ausweichstellung* on 25 September 1915. MGK / 105 was relieved the night before, and the front line and *II. stellung* bristled with seven German and four British machine-guns of MGK / 126, plus three guns of Feld-MG-Zug 108 or 134 and six *minenwerfers*.

Officers of 6. / 105, from left to right: Ltn. Albrecht Freiherr von Fei-litzsch (see p. 86; KIA at Hooge 20.8.1915), Ltn. Fiedler and company commander Oltn. d. R. Richard Kröber (KIA at Verdun 5.5.1916).

Transport personnel of 6. / 105 with the company's small arms am-munition wagon (*patronenwagen*) in front of its orderly room (*schreib-stube*) at a farm in Polderhoek in October 1915.

Leutnant der Reserve Alfred Pache of 16. Kgl. Sächs. Infanterie-Regiment Nr. 182, a senior secondary school teacher from Steinigtwolmsdorf near Bautzen. He was mobilised in August 1914 and took command of 8./Infanterie-Regiment 182 in Lens on 29 September 1915 after the death of his predecessor. Serving in this role (save for periods on the regimental and brigade staffs) until the regiment's demobilisation in Freiberg in January 1919, he was promoted to oberleutnant in July 1917. Leutnant Pache was wounded twice (at Souchez in September 1915, then seriously in Rumania in November 1916) and was awarded the *Ritterkreuz* of the *Militär-St. Heinrichs-Orden* for his courageous leadership in the fighting for Trônes Wood on the Somme in July 1916, during which he survived being buried alive.

1916 in Flanders

The German offensive at Verdun ensured that Flanders remained a secondary front throughout the year, forcing the British to make their own offensive further south to relieve the pressure on the French. **XIX. Armee-Korps**, **XXVII. Reserve-Korps** and **123. Infanterie-Division** all held their established sectors in January, but in late March 123. ID went into reserve and XXVII. RK moved to French Flanders. Both corps were subjected to diversionary attacks for the Somme offensive in July and XXVII. RK to artillery preparation for the major attack at Fromelles, during which it lent its weight to the defensive bombardment. All existing Saxon divisions in Flanders were soon transferred to the Somme, while the novice **204. Infanterie-Division** arrived to release more experienced troops for the battle. In the autumn both **58. Infanterie-Division** and XIX. AK returned to the front in between tours on the Somme.

Nevertheless the fighting in Flanders grew in intensity, with gas attacks by both sides and increasingly large mine explosions. Aggressive forward patrolling was supplemented by larger-scale trench raids with thorough artillery preparation; one such operation is described in detail on pages 114–117. As a result it rarely became quiet enough for 'live and let live' to take a firm hold. In October at Vimy Ridge, Second Lieutenant Hitchcock of the 2nd Leinsters (a unit which had repeatedly fraternised with Saxons in Flanders; see pp. 41 and 79) approvingly noted the treacherous shooting of men of RIR 101 who approached one of his sentries. However one curious incident near Givenchy on 9 August was recorded by the poet Edmund Blunden, then serving as a subaltern with 11th Btn. Royal Sussex (39th Division).

By good luck, I escaped a piece of trouble in this sector. Had I come on trench watch two hours later, not young C. but myself would have been puzzled by the appearance of a German officer and perhaps twenty of his men, who with friendly cries of 'Good morning, Tommy, have you any biscuits?' and the like, got out of their trench and invited our men to do the same. What their object was, beyond simple fraternizing, I cannot guess; it was afterwards argued that they wished to obtain an identification of the unit opposite them. And yet I heard they had already addressed us as the 'bastard Sussek', in any case, our men were told not to fire on them, both by C. and the other

company's officer on watch; there was some exchange of shouted remarks, and after a time both sides returned to the secrecy of their parapets.[1]

Second Lieutenants Cassels and Redway were both placed under open arrest, but suffered no serious repercussions. While the history of RIR 241 has nothing to say on the matter, 'Sachsen in großer Zeit' describes the vigorous rebuffing of British attempts to fraternise with forward posts in this sector, as well as the aerial scattering of propaganda leaflets with incentives to desertion. Reading between the lines, it seems likely that both sides tried to use fraternisation to gain information as Hitchcock had done at St. Eloi.

The year brought major changes in organisation and equipment, some of them due to the replacement in August of von Falkenhayn at OHL by von Hindenburg and Ludendorff. Steel helmets were trialled at Verdun in February, issued as trench stores in the worst sectors in March and universal by the end of 1916. By the summer the steady growth in the infantry's machine-gun strength (via extra guns and attached independent platoons) reached a point where the formation of a second and third MG company per regiment could be ordered, and a second for each *jäger* battalion. By the end of the year each company had doubled in strength to twelve guns. From summer onwards the development of assault tactics led to the establishment of 'permanent' *sturmtrupps* at regimental level, notionally combined to form a divisional *sturmabteilung* or *sturmkompanie* for major operations. Less glamorously, each division also now had a *feldrekrutendepot* to complete the training of new arrivals under field conditions before they were assigned to regiments; in emergencies this could be committed as a battle reserve. Meanwhile each division gained a *minenwerfer* company, divisional cavalry was reduced to one squadron and the allocation of field artillery standardised (see p. 175).

Numerous letters and diaries show that the Kaiser's published peace proposal on 12 December made a deep impression on the men in the trenches, and many dared to believe that a negotiated settlement was possible. However with so much blood and treasure committed on all sides, none could really afford anything less than total victory. The worst was yet to come.

5.1 123. INFANTERIE-DIVISION

In the Wytschaete Salient and in reserve

245. Inf. Brig.: RIR 106 | IR 178 | IR 182
1. Esk. / UR 18 | 5. Esk. / HR 20
123. Felda. Brig.: FAR 245 | FAR 246
Fußa.Battr. 123
Pi. Komp. 245 | Pi. Komp. 264
Scheinwerfer-Zug 245 | Fernsprech-Doppelzug 123
San. Komp. 123

At St. Eloi both sides greeted the New Year with heavy fire; there would be no unofficial truce here in 1916. A few days earlier XV. AK (to the right of 123. ID) had been relieved by XIII. AK; as the only active corps of the Royal Württemberg Army, it had already earned a fearsome fighting reputation. On 9 January the British artillery became increasingly active. The next day an intensive bombardment cost IR 178 alone six dead and twenty-seven wounded. This provoked a furious response from the Saxons, whose firepower had

now been enhanced by the addition of crude smoothbore mortars (including the 9.14cm *Lanz behelfsminenwerfer*) and grenade launchers, though the division still lacked an official *minenwerfer-kompanie* armed with rifled weapons. The weather remained the main enemy, but with the aid of attached working parties from other units (including the prestigious 5. Garde-Regiment zu Fuss and an unarmed labour company) the regimental *entwässerungstrupps* were now gaining the upper hand. Significant progress was also being made on the rearward defences.

On 8 February, British 3rd Division was relieved by 17th (Northern) Division between St. Eloi and Hill 60. This was almost immediately discovered, due to a small patrol from 12th Btn. Manchester Regiment of 52 Brigade falling into Saxon hands. On the afternoon of 14 February the Württembergers seized the '*Große Bastion*' ('The Bluff') north of

Infantrymen of Infanterie-Regiment 178 in a 'fighting trench' between *Bayernwald* and St. Eloi, notably lacking the fascines described in the sources. Pumps and duckboards could overcome groundwater, but not heavy rain or the dammed-off stream which flooded the *Bayernwald*.

the Ypres-Comines Canal from 51 Brigade after a mine detonation, with Saxon artillery firing in support. A series of British counter-attacks followed, culminating in their recapture of 'The Bluff' on 2 March. South of the canal, IR 178 captured an officer of 7th Btn. the Yorkshire Regiment (50 Brigade) on 23 February. The regiment soon noticed the departure of 17th Division after the retaking of 'The Bluff', although unclear on the boundary between the British and neighbouring Canadians. According to their regimental history, the advanced posts at the St. Eloi craters were so close that cap badges and shoulder titles could sometimes be read; from this, the Saxons deduced a British company relief cycle of two days in the first line, two in the second and four in reserve. Meanwhile the British artillery fire was still gaining in intensity, and a heavy bombardment on 25 February inflicted serious damage. Another on 1 March cost IR 178 twenty-seven killed and fifty-seven wounded. Divisional artillery could not retaliate effectively, due to strict limits on ammunition expenditure imposed by the demands of the Verdun Offensive.

From 28 February the 117. and 123. ID came under the temporary command of XIII. AK, and rejoined 4. Armee.

On 9 March XXIII. RK took control of both divisional sectors, and began the gradual relief of the garrison with its own units. The infantry of 123. ID were withdrawn between 16 and 18 March. According to the regimental histories of the relieving units from 46. RD, the British and Canadians noticed and regretted the change. Signboards seen on the enemy parapet included the friendly, almost wistful 'Adieu Sachsen'[2] and improbably fluent 'Lebt wohl, liebe Sachsen, jetzt kommen die Preussen, denen werden wir was sch[eissen].'[3] ('Farewell dear Saxons, now the Prussians are coming, whom we shit upon').

The Saxon infantry had a narrow escape. For many months 172 Tunnelling Company RE had been purposefully distracting the *pioniere* with shallow mines and counter-mines, whilst patiently excavating major galleries through the blue Ypres clay beneath at unprecedented depth. On the morning of 27 March 1916 they detonated five charges (totalling 82,300 pounds of explosive) beneath the former positions of IR 178. These were now occupied by Reserve-Jäger-Bataillon 18, which had lost 270 officers and men killed, fatally wounded or missing (and legally declared dead) by the end of the day. The artillery and *pioniere* of 123. ID

The *Jäger-Feste* (see map on p. 80), a strongpoint of the *zwischenstellung* (intermediate line) in the Infanterie-Regiment 178 sector.

195. Jäger Feste

In de Sterkte Cabaret (see map on p. 80), the regimental *pionierpark* of Infanterie-Regiment 178 where mining, wiring and construction supplies were stockpiled for transport to the front line. Carrying parties would also meet the field kitchens here to collect rations.

had not yet been relieved and took part in the subsequent fighting for the resulting craters. Hptm. Curt Otho and Ltn. d. R. Albert Kroitsch of FAR 246 were both subsequently awarded the MStHO(R) for directing the Saxon guns from exposed positions in the devastated forward zone, helping to render British gains untenable. Meanwhile the infantry regiments of 123. ID were in quarters south of Bruges in 4. Armee reserve; due to the attack their rifle companies were placed at the disposal of 46. Reserve-Division on 3 April and returned to their previous rear area. Here they were mainly employed for several weeks in constructing new defenses behind the '1B' line, and incurred significant losses from artillery fire. II. / IR 182 however was put back into the front line from 3 to 9 April; their commander Hptm. Max Bunde was awarded the MStHO(R) on 12 May, having remained at his post throughout although wounded. After the successful counter-attack at the craters on 6 April by RIR 216, RIR 106 was used to relieve RIR 215 in the left flank sector (8–25 April) and did not rejoin 123. ID until 22 May.

Meanwhile the division's regimental machine-gun companies had spent most of April providing air defence for rear-area railway stations. On 20 May, 4. Armee decreed

that XXIII. RK would have the continued use of one battalion from the division (II. / IR 182, then I. and II. / RIR 106) on a fortnightly relief cycle. From 25 May a further battalion (II. / IR 178 until 5 June, then III. / RIR 106 until 24 June) served in the front line with 4. Ersatz-Division, facing the inundations near Woumen south of Diksmuide (see map on p. 124). IR 178 was reunited at Kortrijk on 5 June at the disposal of XIII. AK, leading to dangerous working parties on the Menin Road. During this period the elements in reserve south of Bruges were fully occupied with tactical exercises and the training of newly arrived replacements. On 1 June elements of IR 178 were inspected at Hertsberghe by the army commander, Generaloberst Duke Albrecht of Württemberg. The division's presence near the border was also intended as a precaution against potential amphibious attack on the Dutch or Belgian coast. Thus there were also familiarisation visits to naval installations, where the *landsers* marvelled at submarines and torpedo boats.

On 27 June the reassembled division was placed on alert to entrain at six hours' notice. The fateful order came on 5 July, and the division departed for Cambrai to take part in the Battle of the Somme.

A *Baukommando* (construction party) from 11. / RIR 106 in the *Raabgrund* area (Ravine Wood) in early February. As the map on p. 81 shows, the structures hidden by the wood included a *pionier-lager* at the northern tip of the ravine – hence the *sanitäter* here from Pionier-Kompanie 245.

The '*divisionswurst*' – observation balloons near Wervik. Marked 'not for publication' in the regimental album of Infanterie-Regiment 178.

The *Müllerhof* (Maize Farm) northwest of Houthem, *regimentsgefechtsstand* of Feldartillerie-Regiment 245 (see map p. 97).

Major Paul Mueller (centre), commander of I. Abt./Feldartillerie-Regiment 245, with his staff in front of their *abteilungsgefechtsstand* at *Caleute-Ferme* (c.f. map p. 97). It is unclear whether the words 'MAJ. MUELLER' on the ground here serve a practical or merely decorative purpose.

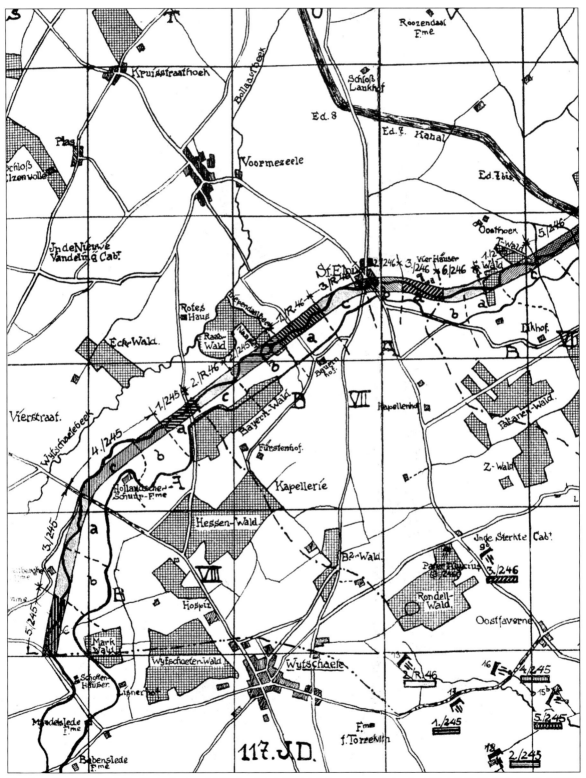

Map from the history of Feldartillerie-Regiment 246 showing defensive barrage zones (*sperrfeuerräume*) in the Wytschaete Salient. At the signal for *sperrfeuer* each battery would fire on its allocated section of the enemy line to suppress any infantry advance.

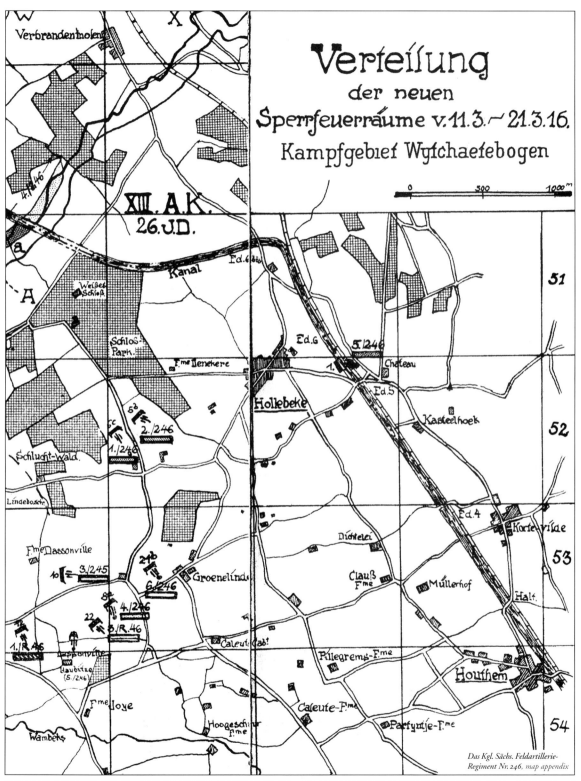

In the period depicted, 123. ID was in the process of relief by 46. RD – hence the presence of batteries from RFAR 46 as well as FAR 245 and 246. Note the different symbols for batteries of 10.5cm lFH (4.–5./245, 4.–6./246) and of 7.7cm FK (all others).

Infantrymen of 7. Komp. / Infanterie-Regiment 178 toasting the King's birthday on 25 May 1916.

Gunners of 2. Batterie / Feldartillerie-Regiment 245 at the battery's *gulaschkanone* ca. May 1916. Note the use of white fatigue clothing both in its original form and dyed in the interests of camouflage – exemplified by the jacket and trousers of the man on the right.

A group of friends from Infanterie-Regiment 182 and an unidentified non-Saxon unit celebrate Whitsun, which fell on 11 June in 1916.

'The pride of 12./RIR 106' in Kortemark on 14 May 1916. After working on the *Sonne-* and *Breisig-Stellung* in *Wytschaetewald*, the regiment occupied rest quarters in Aertrycke, Torhout and Kortemark from 11 to 22 May.

5.2 XXVII. Reserve-Korps (53. and 54. Reserve-Division)

On the old front and in the mining zone at La Bassée

53. Reserve-Division

(s.) *105. Res. Inf. Brig.:* (s.) RIR 241 | (s.) RIR 243
(s.) *106. Res. Inf. Brig.:* (s.) RIR 242 | (s.) RIR 244
(s.) RJB 25 | (s.) RFAR 53 | (s.) Res. Kav. Abt. 53
(s.) Res. Pi. Komp. 53 | (s.) Mw. Komp. 253
(s.) Res. Div. Brückentrain 53
(s.) Res. San. Komp. 53

54. Reserve-Division

(w.) *107. Res. Inf. Brig.:* (s.) RIR 245 | (w.) RIR 247
(w.) *108. Res. Inf. Brig.:* (w.) RIR 246 | (w.) RIR 248
(s.) RJB 26 | (s./w.) RFAR 54 | (w.) Res. Kav. Abt. 54
(s.) Res. Pi. Komp. 54 | (w.) Mw. Komp. 254
(w.) Res. Div. Brückentrain 54
(w.) Res. San. Komp. 54

(s.) *Res. Pi. Batl. 27:* (s.) Res. Scheinwerfer-Zug 27
(p.) Pi. (Min.) Komp. 295–300 & 309
(s.) Res. Fernsprech-Abt. 27

By 1916 the former '*Kinderkorps*' was a battle-hardened formation equipped almost to 'active' standards, and a tough opponent for less experienced troops. On the nights of 26–28 January Second Lieutenants Richard Marchant and Frederick Handford of 9th Btn. East Surrey Regiment were both killed on forward patrol, respectively by a rival patrol under Vfw. Zimmer of RIR 246 and sentries from RJB 26. In 1916 volunteers like Zimmer and Vfw. Penther (see p. 190) would develop patrolling and raiding to a fine art.

At the end of January the whole corps went into reserve. From 25 February RIR 242 spent a month with 117. ID between Wytschaete and the Douve, enduring a gas attack and heavy flooding. Meanwhile the rest of 53. RD was transported to Hasselt for tactical exercises on the Belgian training ground near Beverlo. On 8 March 54. RD arrived at Hasselt, and most of 53. RD returned to the old front. At Railway Wood the enemy was now only 40m away, and just 8m at the densely wired *Roschmannsappe* crater (see photo p. 56 and map p. 187).

Mobile company field kitchen ('*gulaschkanone*') of RIR 242 at Meulebeke. The clumsy wagon-mounted *kochkisten* were a thing of the past by 1916.

The officers of III. Batl. / Reserve-Infanterie-Regiment 241 on the Kaiser's birthday (27 January 1916) in Isegem. In the centre is their commander Major Erich Seeck; at the outbreak of war he was supervising ammunition manufacture at the *Munitionsfabrik Dresden*.

Reserve-Jäger-Bataillon 25 drawn up for inspection in Pitthem (west of Tielt) at the parade marking the Kaiser's birthday.

Troop trains carrying RIR 241 through ruined Leuven (Louvain) – either heading to Hasselt on 29 February for training at Beverlo, or else returning on 8 March.

Officers (and an unteroffizier) of III. Batl. / Reserve-Infanterie-Regiment 241 and Reserve-Feldartillerie-Regiment 53 with German railway officials at Hasselt. Like the picture above (from the same album) this photo could have been taken on either the outward or the return journey.

Hauptmann Hans Breithaupt (centre) was born at Ulm in Württemberg, but in Saxon service as adjutant of Fussartillerie-Regiment 19 in August 1914. As adjutant of 105. Reserve-Infanterie-Brigade he received the MStHO(R) on 30 July 1915. While visiting the front line near the *Eierwäldchen* (Railway Wood) on 22 March 1916 he was shot by a sniper, and is buried at Soldatenfriedhof Menen (Block H Grave 2290).

H.M. the King of Saxony visits corps HQ at Dadizele. Château and church (visible behind it) both survived the war and are clearly recognisable today.

In March regiments of XXVII. Reserve-Korps were attached to other units both on their old front and as far south as Messines. Although there was some frontline duty they mainly worked on the rear defences. Here Reserve-Infanterie-Regiment 241 helps construct concrete pillboxes at Zonnebeke railway station.

NCOs and men of Reserve-Infanterie-Regiment 244 pose casually with their Flemish hosts in the garden. Seated left is the company's feldwebel (recognisable by the double row of braid on his cuffs). Also note the pipe-smoking unteroffizier wearing slippers – a highly unofficial privilege of rank!

From the end of March XXVII. RK lay astride the La Bassée Canal from Fosse 8 to Rue d'Enfer at Aubers. From mid-April RIR 242 held Auchy and RIR 244 the Brickstacks south of the canal. RIR 241 held the north bank, with RIR 243 on its right (see map p. 106). RIR 246 was on the left of 54. RD, while RIR 248 faced Richebourg and RIR 247 Neuve Chapelle, with RIR 245 on the right at Mauquissart. South of the canal, at Givenchy and north of Neuve Chapelle the front was studded with mine craters. Below lay 10km of German tunnels worked by seven *pionier-(mineur-)kompanien*, later joined by Saxon Pi. (Min.) Komp. 313 and 324 (see p. 177).

The corps arrived in heavy rain to find flooding even in the rear areas and many defences in ruins. During April *infanterie-pioniere*, labour units and companies of the *Korps-Feld-rekrutendepot* toiled to recreate continuous defensible lines. On the 53. RD front alone five British and seven German mines were blown, followed by bombing duels at the craters. April cost 53. RD almost 500 casualties, and losses rose steadily until August. Patrolling began in late April and escalated to raids in May, while each side blew nine mines on the 53. RD front and others in the RIR 245 sector. British shelling greatly increased, including many 'dud' gas shells. Where no man's land was narrow, the rebuilt German lines were often hit by heavy trench mortars; by summer some affected areas were partly abandoned to reduce losses. Concerned that an attack could be brewing, 54. RD ordered a raid to gain intelligence. From 9 pm on 30 May artillery and *minenwerfers* pounded the breastworks facing RIR 248 and its neighbours, with pauses to lure the enemy out of cover. At 10.46 pm three patrols advanced close behind the barrage, met little resistance and left a 'Made in Germany' sign in the ruins. RIR 248 had no fatal casualties and took thirty prisoners, maps and a Lewis Gun.

In June raiding increased and mining peaked at twelve British and twenty-eight German detonations in the 53. RD sector alone. RIR 241 now conceived a major raid codenamed Chemnitz in support of a mine of unprecedented size at Givenchy. Defensive detonations on both sides and two British raids on RIR 241 in the night of 4–5 June and early on the 18th did not disrupt the plan. At 3 am on 22 June, Pi. (Min.) Komp. 295 blew a 16,000kg charge below the lines of 2nd Btn Royal Welsh Fusiliers, creating the 60m wide Red Dragon Crater (*Chem-nitzer Trichter*).[4] In quarter of an hour over 15,000 shells and 300 heavy *wurfminen* fell on the target, before it was attacked by three patrols totalling nearly 200 officers and men including *pioniere* and artillery observers. On the right Ltn. d. R. Zängel's group found only corpses as far as the third line, and were then forced back. On the left Ltn. Schumann was killed clearing a dugout, but his men brought prisoners when the patrols returned at 3.40 am. The raiders lost eleven dead, thirty-six

wounded and four missing, and the enemy at least fifty-seven dead and seven captured. On the afternoon of 29 June RIR 248 was severely shelled left of the La Bassée road, and the Boar's Head salient at Richebourg wrecked by heavy mortars. The regiment was well prepared when 12th and 13th Btn Royal Sussex attacked there at 4.05 am. After taking this salient, the Sussex were pounded by German artillery and cleared out by bombing parties, losing over 360 dead, 1,000 wounded and fifty-four captured. RIR 248 lost over 100 dead, 200 wounded and four captured.

In July losses rose to sixteen officers and 1100 men in 53. RD alone. On the 1st the British blew the first of July's many mines opposite RIR 245, and launched a major raid on RIR 242 supported by gas and three more mines. Although they got in they were caught at the wire by bombers and machine-guns, and lost heavily. The same night RIR 245 entered the British lines near Mauquissart after artillery had crushed all resistance; the explosives store of 3rd Australian Tunnelling Company and one mineshaft were destroyed, and a second damaged. Minor raids by both sides were now constant, especially on the 53. RD front. RIR 241 suffered a revenge raid by 2nd Royal Welsh Fusiliers on the night of 4–5 July after prolonged drum fire, losing fifteen dead, forty-nine wounded and forty-three missing. On 12 July the British discharged gas north of the canal and raided RJB 26 after blowing a mine. A week later the corps helped both its neighbours to repel heavy attacks. Late on the 27th RIR 247 and 248 went on a long-rehearsed '*Ausflug nach London*' ('Trip to London') south of Neuve Chapelle. In places they were delayed and diverted by unbroken wire and by drop-shorts as they advanced behind the barrage; two groups from RIR 248 briefly attacked each other, and one was pinned for three hours in no man's land on its return. RIR 248 had lost fourteen dead and forty-two wounded, but taken thirty-two prisoners and two machine-guns.

A demolition raid by RIR 244 at the Cambrin road on the night of 29–30 July took five prisoners and blew up a mining party, but cost the lives of Ltn. Wolf and Ltn. Jungnickel. On the 31st RIR 241 and 243 were heavily shelled all day, and four mines blown in half an hour in the RIR 241 sector before both were attacked after midnight. Three successive assaults were broken up by heavy fire and counter-charges with bomb and bayonet, costing RIR 241 five dead and twenty-eight wounded. After this a 'quiet' August saw 53. RD lose only seven officers and 627 men, though mine explosions and small-scale raids continued (see p. 197). Two large patrols from RIR 243 made a final foray on the 20th after the British lines had been levelled by artillery. On 1 September the relief by XIX. AK began, and XXVII. RK was committed to the Somme.

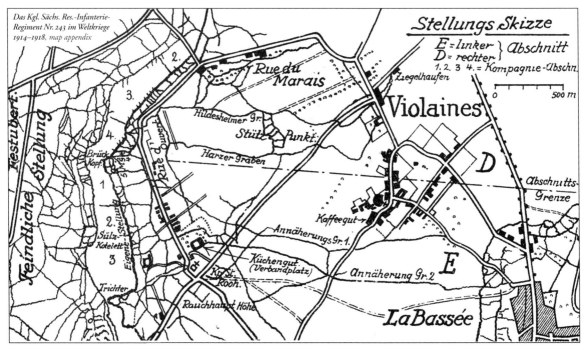

Battalion sectors 'D' and 'E' (Violaines / Festubert) and their company sub-sectors on the right flank of 53. RD. From mid-April RIR 243 took over 'D' and 'E' from RIR 241, with RJB 25 intermittently holding 'D' and RJB 26 the flank sector of RIR 246 on their right.

Grave of Hans Leistner, who died of wounds at Moorsele on 16 March 1916. He is now buried at Menen (Block M Grave 230).

Grave of Arno Hessel (6. / 242), killed in action at La Bassée on 31 May 1916 and buried at Salomé, where he still rests today.

Kriegstrauung!

An unteroffizier and men of RIR 242 celebrate a mock 'war wedding' at the brewery in La Bassée, ca. April–May 1916. The man reclining right in shirtsleeves is wearing his *halsbinde* (separate collar), a standard but rarely photographed piece of equipment.

Saxon trench raiders, stripped of insignia and extraneous kit and armed mainly with pistols (P08 Luger). Numerous grenades and sharpened entrenching tools would also be carried. All have the new steel helmet and latest gasmask in its handy 'readiness can' (*bereitschaftsbüchse*).

Frontline post of RIR 245 near Mauquissart. Note the sentry's *pickelhaube* placed nearby; like grenades, the steel helmets are 'trench stores' and would be left here for the relief. Steel helmets were issued on the old front by March, but only reached La Bassée in May.

RIR 245 set up a forward *pionierdepot* under Vizefeldwebel Otto in the reserve line at '*Weißes Haus*'. The '*Werkzeugausgabe*' sign beside the shovels indicates that tools are issued here to working parties. Another sign points the way to the '*Piss-Rinne*' ('piss ditch').

60cm gauge field tramways (*förderbahn*) for unpowered trolleys ran almost up to the front line, as seen here in the RIR 245 sector.

Starkstromabteilung ('high-voltage detachment') of XXVII. Reserve-Korps at the generator building in La Bassée. The demand for power was huge, especially in mining areas where underground lighting and ventilation were vital. Electrical units were first improvised in 1915 with qualified personnel taken from all arms of service, but only gained an official organisation (at army level) in spring 1917.

Pionier NCOs with an infantry wiring party at the divisional *pionierpark* of 53. RD behind the La Bassée front on the King's birthday (25 May 1916). The object in the foreground is a cylinder of concertina wire (*drahtwalze*).

The newly formed Pionier-Kompanie 279 joined Reserve-Pionier-Bataillon 27 on 17 January, and lost two men seized by raiders at the *Entenschnabel* in the RIR 245 sector on 20 July. The fouled anchor traditionally symbolises the use by *pioniere* of pontoon bridges.

A sanitäts-unteroffizier of Reserve-Infanterie-Regiment 242 and his subordinates posing with a monstrous British 15" dud (*blindgänger*) at La Bassée in April 1916. Other photos reveal that this shell was still standing in the street attracting 'tourists' a month later. Note the large belt pouches for medical orderlies, containing first-aid supplies.

Card commemorating the second anniversary of 53. Reserve-Division and listing its battle honours to date.

A later card from Reserve-Infanterie-Regiment 241, also recalling their actions on the Somme (1916) and in Galicia (1917).

5.3 XIX. Armee-Korps (24. and 40. Infanterie-Division)

On the old front, at La Bassée and in the Wytschaete Salient

24. Infanterie-Division
89. Inf. Brig.: IR 133 | IR 139 | IR 179
1. & 4. Esk. / HR 19
24. Felda. Brig.: FAR 77 | FAR 78
1. Komp. / Pi. Batl. 22 | Mw. Komp. 24
Div. Brückentrain 24
San. Komp. XIX/1

40. Infanterie-Division
88. Inf. Brig.: IR 104 | IR 134 | IR 181
Stab, 2. & 5. Esk. / HR 19
40. Felda. Brig.: FAR 32 | FAR 68
2. & 3. Komp. / Pi. Batl. 22 | Mw. Komp. 40
Div. Brückentrain 40
San. Komp. XIX/2

38. Ldw. Inf. Brig.: (p.) LIR 77 | (p.) LIR 78
JB 13 | II. Batl. / FußaR 19
Stab I. & Scheinwerfer-Zug / Pi. Batl. 22
Fernsprech-Abt. 19 | Flieger-Abt. 24

In early 1916 British shelling became a constant nuisance, increasingly supplemented by trench mortars. Due to the demands of Verdun retaliation was limited. January also saw the first British gas attacks on this front, to little effect against troops with the new *gummimaske*. A more worrying innovation was the large-scale trench raid, following initial ventures by the Canadians in 1915. On 19 January over 200 men of 2nd Btn. Royal Irish Rifles stormed Le Touquet after an intense barrage, inflicting heavy losses on IR 181 and taking a dozen prisoners; smaller raids south of the Lys were far less successful. At the end of February LIR 77 and 78 were withdrawn and the frontage of 40. ID reduced. IR 179 was inserted on the right at Frelinghien, where they soon faced flooding when the Lys burst its banks.

In early April regimental *patrouillenkommandos* of volunteer raiders were formed, and developed into divisional *sturmabteilungen* in July. IR 179 made a successful demolition raid on the shallow Trench 88 mine system on 23 April; a similar raid by IR 104 (see pp. 114–117) was the only one in May

A 7.7cm field gun battery of FAR 77 at rest. On the right is the observation trailer (*beobachtungsanhänger*) with sections of its armoured shield on the back; this was used with a folding ladder and scissors periscope (*scherenfernrohr*) under mobile warfare conditions.

not cancelled to conserve ammunition. In a bombing skirmish with IR 133 on 13 June the newly arrived New Zealand Division took their first German prisoner (possibly Soldat Karl Scheer).

A major gas attack against both divisions on 30 June had been expected, and IR 104 beat off three raiding parties from the novice 41st Division. In July such raids grew more frequent, as diversions for the attack at Fromelles (during which corps reserves were not needed) and to hinder the transfer of XIX. AK to the Somme. Most of the British raids failed, with bombers ambushing the raiders in or in front of a pre-evacuated front line; the New Zealanders were more successful. On the nights of 3–4 and 8–9 July IR 139 launched major raids at L'Epinette and the *Giftpilz* salient ('The Mushroom'). In both cases the New Zealanders lost 140–150 men, many buried by the bombardment; the raiders faced fierce resistance and suffered losses, but identified the enemy and the presence of gas cylinders. A few nights later IR 181 seized four prisoners near Le Touquet. After more minor raids, the British launched a major assault by two companies on the night of 26–27 July; IR 104 suffered heavy losses when the line near Le Gheer was pulverised by heavy mortars and siege guns. Raiders of 10th Btn. Queen's (Royal West Surrey Regiment) overran a forward patrol but could not get beyond the first line. Simultaneously IR 181 beat off an attack by 20th Btn. Durham Light Infantry.

Nevertheless XIX. AK left the Armentières front at the end of July. Only JB 13 was spared the Somme, as it became independent and left for Galicia. From 9 to 27 August the corps held High Wood and the line near Pozières, under constant attack in unspeakable conditions. September was spent rebuilding on the La Bassée front, where British aggression was mainly limited to constant mortar barrages, gas and aerial bombing. The Saxons soon dominated no man's land, taking numerous prisoners and repelling several raids.

The corps again defended the road to Bapaume from 6 October to 5 November, with 40. ID at the Butte de Warlencourt. Though losses were less than in August, they faced the new horror of tank attacks. After this ordeal XIX. AK occupied the *Wytschaetebogen* (Wytschaete salient) between the Douve and the Ypres-Comines Canal. For the rest of 1916 they mainly battled with the elements, hampered by British batteries with aerial observation and copious ammunition. The Saxons knew this critical salient would not be easy to hold. They were however blissfully unaware of the plans for 1917 taking shape opposite and beneath them.

The new *Regimentsfriedhof* of IR 179 in Lomme, replacing the original cemetery at La Vallée (south of La Houssoie) which was increasingly disturbed by enemy artillery fire. In 1921–1922 over 1,000 German dead buried at Lomme were moved to the new *Soldatenfriedhof* Lambersart.

'Unternehmen Kratzbürste' – the Raid on Hampshire Trench, 13 May 1916

The main flashpoint in the Ploegsteert Wood sector was a salient around the hamlet of Le Pelerin known as the *Entenschnabel* ('Duck's Bill'). Tommies knew it as 'the Birdcage', due to the belts of wire strung around it by 3./Pi. Batl. 22 after its capture on 7 November 1914. IR 106 had abandoned its outposts in the wood under attack from three battalions of 11 Brigade on 19 December 1914, but held the main position. British casualties were 150 wounded or missing and seventy-four dead, some of whom were buried that Christmas.

Although no further attempts were made to take the *Entenschnabel*, it was a focus for sniping and minor raids. Mining began in earnest in spring 1915, and between June and August both sides blew many small mines and camouflets near its northern and southern faces. IR 104 made some minor raids that winter but could not locate the enemy mineshafts. In spring 1916 underground listening posts confirmed that British tunnelers were still at work. Painstaking analysis of listening reports and aerial photos suggested they were tunnelling toward the southern face from the *Erdwerk*, where they had incorporated two craters into an extended sap known as Hampshire Trench. In fact the *Entenschnabel* had been undermined from the northwest by 171st Tunnelling Company, who finished laying four charges containing a total of over 100,000 lb of explosives in April. By May only limited maintenance was needed on these mines, and the British later surmised that the lack of active tunnelling had led the *pioniere* to misinterpret work on concrete dugouts. Thus the aims of *'Unternehmen Kratzbürste'* (meaning a back scratcher or a coarse and prickly woman – so roughly 'Operation Scrubber') were misconceived from the outset.

The raiders were to seek and destroy mineshafts in *Ostgraben I* and *II* (the front line and support trench south of the *Erdwerk*, British designations T116 and ST116). Secondary objectives were to destroy concrete dugouts, and to take prisoners and booty. For this mission, Oltn. Schmidt of IR 104 was allocated four other officers, twelve NCOs and twenty-eight men of his regiment plus two officers, four NCOs and twenty-seven men of 1./Pi. Batl. 22. These formed seven small *stoßtrupps* or *sturmabteilungen* (in this case, assault parties) under infantry officers or NCOs and two *sprengtrupps* (demolition parties) under *pionier* officers. Three *stoßtrupps* were to block the approaches to the raided area, while others cleared it and located targets for *sprengtrupps* to

destroy with 15kg charges. All of this would have to be done to a precise timetable, on unfamiliar ground and in the dark. The raid was therefore rehearsed in a copy of the British trench system at the divisional training ground near Wambréchies under the direction of Hptm. Max Koch (see photo p. 21). The division was temporarily reinforced with 15cm howitzer batteries, plus numerous grenade launchers and *minenwerfers* (including the deadly 25cm heavies). On either flank additional machine-guns were emplaced in the front line to cover the advance.

The trenches to be attacked were held by 'B' Coy. of 11th Btn. Royal Scots (27 Brigade / 9th Division) under Lieutenant-Colonel William Denman Croft. This veteran 'Kitchener' battalion was reinforced by ten officers and forty other ranks of 15th Btn. Hampshire Regiment (2nd Portsmouth Pals). This belonged to the 41st Division, which had only been in France a week and was being introduced to the trenches as small parties attached to experienced units before taking over the Ploegsteert sector.

Uffz. Walter Junghanns of IR 104, born on 23 October 1886 in Taura and seen here on 1 March 1915 at Le Touquet. Assigned to *Stoßtrupp 6*, he was recorded missing during *'Kratzbürste'* and later confirmed dead.

Sketch of the British front line at Le Gheer, printed for IR 104 as a postcard in 1915. On 14 May 1916 Lt.-Col. Croft reported Picket House (centre) '*finally demolished with the exception of a wall nearest the parapet*' by the bombardment for '*Kratzbürste*'.

On 10 May the Royal Scots noted that German artillery "*appeared to be registering on our front line.*"[5] Fifteen men were wounded by shrapnel over the next two days, while others were saved by the new steel helmets. On 12 May the guns were "*seen to have been registering all important points in our line – such as new C[communication] T[renche]s, S[upport] T[renche]s etc*". During the night *pioniere* cut discrete gaps in the German wire. The next morning the howitzers ranged in on the objective. "*The trenches in the HAMPSHIRE locality just east of PLOEGSTEERT WOOD were subjected to a fairly heavy artillery fire from 4.2" [10.5cm] & 5.9" [15cm], necessitating constant breakdown gangs to repair.*" That afternoon 9th Division's field artillery retaliated energetically, allowing Saxon observers to identify targets for counter-battery fire.

From 8.35 to 9.35 pm the reinforced artillery of 40. ID 'fired for effect' on British positions from the Le Gheer road to the northern edge of Ploegsteert Wood. Support and reserve lines were shelled by heavy howitzers. The raid objective was pounded by heavy *minenwerfers*, blasting away the British wire and reducing the *Nordgraben* and *Erdwerk* to a mass of craters. Given their short range these weapons must have been emplaced in the *Entenschnabel*, where their huge muzzle flashes attracted heavy retaliation. "*Although the enemy smothered the minenwerfers [with shells] the dutiful crewmen kept on firing, emulating their fearless leader. Under heavy shelling [Ltn. d. R. Alfred Wilhelmi of 1. / Pi. Batl. 22] hurried from one* minenwerfer *to another, spurring them on to stick it out and thus making possible the bombardment of the break-in point with about 1,000 minenwerfer bombs.*"[6] The *Erdwerk* was also targeted with rifle grenades, and the whole British line swept by machine-guns.

In the southern part of T116 Lt.-Col. Croft observed "*a constant rain of explosives, which fortunately for us just missed the parapet for the most part.*"[7] However he also saw 2nd Lieutenant William Meek Falconer killed a mere

two traverses away while approaching from Gap 'G'. Parts of the line were blocked, dislocating the defence: "*it was found impossible to clear the trenches and movement was out of the question*". As soon as this bombardment ended, Lieutenant John Allen Henry "*saw that all men able to stand were ready to resist a raid, though we both thought a raid was unlikely owing to the fact that we had been observing the enemy's wire just before & all the gaps we could discover had been made by our guns in the afternoon*". Convinced that the situation was "*well in hand*", Lt.-Col. Croft proceeded down ST116 toward Gap 'G' and was not present for the raid. From 9.45 to 10.45 pm the artillery focused on the approaches to the objective, forming a *feuerglocke* (literally a 'bell of fire') to prevent escape or reinforcement of the garrison. Lt.-Col. Croft noted that "*it was even more intensive than the 1st bombardment & it was noticeable that much more fire was directed against the support lines and CTs, though the front line came in for a good share.*"

The raiders had deployed to jump-off positions at 10.10 pm, and went over the top after a systematic five-minute

Pionier Jantscher's darkly whimsical Easter card for Minenwerfer-Kompanie 24. Both divisions are believed to have formed a company with two heavy, four medium and six light weapons at the end of 1915. It is likely that both companies supported '*Kratzbürste*'.

machine-gun barrage. They were not fired on while approaching and found the British wire obliterated, though it had been up to 10m deep. As planned the garrison was now isolated: *"those on the right of CT116 junction with T116 had no idea that there had been a raid as we were cut off by a bad block, and there was such a noise going on that one didn't distinguish rifle shots."* [8]

Stoßtrupp 1 (Vfw. Georgi) advanced via the old craters, *Erdwerk* and points A and J to point K. At point J they took three unwounded prisoners after a brief struggle. The party established a trench block at point K, and fought off seven opponents approaching via the communication trench (CT117) with hand grenades.

Stoßtrupp 2 (Ltn. d. R. Emil Leichsenring) followed close behind to search section A-J. Seven British soldiers were found in the dugouts, four of whom were killed and three captured. Section K-C was quickly found to be clear. In the western half of section K-J dugouts were found and bombed.

Stoßtrupp 3 (Ltn. d. R. Wilhelm Flehmig) crossed the old craters to the devastated *Erdwerk*. Several survivors resisted here and were wiped out with hand grenades, Flehmig himself apparently killing two of them. The party found two concrete structures in the *Erdwerk* and searched section B-C, where they identified a supposed mineshaft and some dugouts. Two rough shelters were found to be occupied and accordingly bombed.

Meanwhile **Sprengtrupp 1** (Ltn. Nowotnik) set concentrated charges on the two concrete dugouts in the *Erdwerk*. In section B-C two 'wooden' dugouts were prepared for demolition, and a 30kg charge buried in the 4m deep 'mineshaft'.

The other parties attacked from the east. **Stoßtrupp 6** (Vfw. Weigert) rushed overground to point 'F' to set up a block. They were placing signboards on the parapet to mark progress for observers when they met the enemy. *"Surprise in each case seems to have been mutual, as the fire had barely lifted when Lieut. Henry saw the Germans on the parapet. To use Lieut. Henry's own words 'I shot them down like rats, and none got in.'"* [9] The whole party was killed. Unaware of the timetable, the Royal Scots saw the other raiders return to the German lines and believed Henry had chased them off. *"The remainder bolted as hard as they could back to their trenches with our fire to help them."*

Stoßtrupp 4 (Ltn. Stülpnagel) was searching *Ostgraben II* when they were rushed from *Ostgraben I* by four of the enemy with pistols, three of whom were captured after a brief melee. Shortly before withdrawing the party was attacked by a group with pistols and bombs, possibly led by Lieut. Henry. Vfw. Matern und Sold. Müller were killed, and Ltn. Stülpnagel severely wounded.

Stoßtrupp 7 (Sergt. Louis Möller) set up a block at point E and defended it with hand grenades. Eight of the enemy got close enough for hand-to-hand fighting, in which Sergt. Möller, Gefr. Hanft and Sold. Röder were all wounded, and Sold. Jung went missing. The party was hard pressed while withdrawing, and all of its wounded continued to fight.

Stoßtrupp 5 (Ltn. d. R. Adalbert Thum) searched section E-C. Several dugouts were found to be occupied, and were bombed when the occupants refused to surrender. A supposed mineshaft and booty including a Lewis Gun 'with accessories' were found.

Following the assault parties, **Sprengtrupp 2** (Ltn. Otto Richter) split into two groups to tackle *Ostgraben I* and *II*. The latter was under counterattack and held only 'wooden' dugouts, so the party regrouped in *Ostgraben I*. Three 45kg charges were buried in the 6.5m deep 'mineshaft', a fourth behind it to shatter its metal frame and a fifth in a nearby dugout. Charges were also set on a metal machine-gun post and in a 'funk hole' to bring down the parapet. The party finished work in nine minutes and also took a prisoner (who had perhaps been hiding in one of these structures).

At 10:25 pm Oltn. Schmidt gave the scheduled whistle signal for withdrawal from his observation post. As soon as all were clear the *pioniere* hit the detonators. Blasts were clearly heard from the German lines, though two unexploded charges were later found and examined by 171st Tunneling Company. Patrols immediately went forward as planned to search for the missing, but were soon forced back under heavy fire.

IR 104 had lost one NCO and one man dead, Ltn. Stülpnagel severely wounded, two NCOs and four men lightly wounded; Pi. Batl. 22 had two men wounded. Another three NCOs and five men were missing and later confirmed dead by the British, who had struggled to identify them. The dead raiders carried no ID and wore no shoulder straps, though buttons for these were present and bore the company numbers '1', '4', '11' and '12'. As a recognition sign all of them had *"a strip of white cotton about 1/2" wide sewn on the collar"*.[8] The regiment was finally identified by the armourer's marking '104.R' on a pistol. It took longer to assess British casualties, many of whom lay buried in the wreckage. By the time the Royal Scots' regimental history was written, their losses were given as sixteen killed, sixty-one wounded (mainly by the bombardment) and eight missing. Of these, at least two (Acting Quartermaster-Sergeant Sydney Thomas Rew and Private John Davanna) were definitely captured. The Hampshires recorded unspecific losses of two officers, five NCOs and four men; one of the officers was among those believed buried.

IR 104 judged the results of this operation as "extremely positive". In addition to taking prisoners (of whom the regimental history sadly gives no details) British mining operations had apparently been halted, since no further underground work was detected. In reality, the shafts destroyed must have been underground listening posts or deep dugouts. This misapprehension certainly affected the decision to award the Iron Cross 1st Class to Sergt. Möller and the *Ritterkreuz* of the *Militär-St. Heinrichs-Orden* to Flehmig, Leichsenring, Richter, Thum and Wilhelmi. Ltn. d. R. Leichsenring (from Siegmar near

Chemnitz) and Ltn. d. R. Wilhelmi (from Neustadt in Thuringia) were both killed in the fighting for the Butte de Warlencourt in October 1916 at the age of 24. Ltn. d. R. Flehmig (a teacher from Leunitz near Werdau) was wounded at the same time and later transferred to IR 474, where he became leader of the Sturmabteilung of 241. ID. His death from Spanish Flu on 14 October 1918 at the age of 25 was a further heavy blow for a regiment and division already shattered by massive losses. On the British side Lieut. Henry was awarded the Military Cross. He too was killed on the Somme, on 14 July 1916. Pte. Alfred Holland received the Distinguished Conduct Medal, while Cpl. Guthrie, L./Cpl. Andrew Wigton and Pte. Thomson all received the Military Medal.

Main sources: Das Kgl. Sächs. 5. Inf.-Regiment 'Kronprinz' Nr. 104 (vol. I, pp. 212–218); Im Weltkrieg unter dem Sachsenbanner (pp. 82–84); war diaries of 27 Brigade (WO 95/1769/4), 11th Royal Scots (WO 95/1773/1) and 15th Hampshires (WO 95/2634/5).

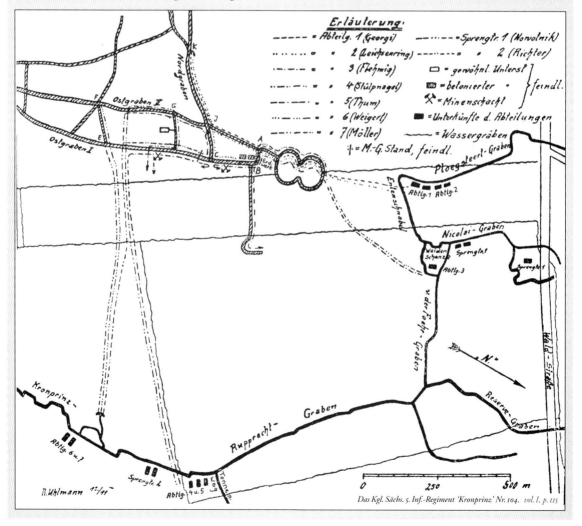

Das Kgl. Sächs. 5. Inf.-Regiment 'Kronprinz' Nr. 104, vol. I, p. 115

From 10 March 1916 rest quarters were established at Fort Carnot (AKA 'Fort du Vert Galant') near Wambrechies for the corps reserve – here, men of Infanterie-Regiment 181 in April 1916. As at Fort MacDonald (see p. 77) the 'refurbishment' included prominent patriotic slogans.

Farewell to Flanders! A *vorkommando* from IR 139 sets out for the Somme front to arrange quarters for their regiment at the end of July 1916.

XIX. AK returned from its first tour on the Somme to occupy the La Bassée sector from 1–30 September 1916, freeing up XXVII. RK to take part in the battle. After a four-week 'rest' on this relatively quiet front, the rebuilt corps was relieved by Bavarian III. bAK and returned to the Somme.

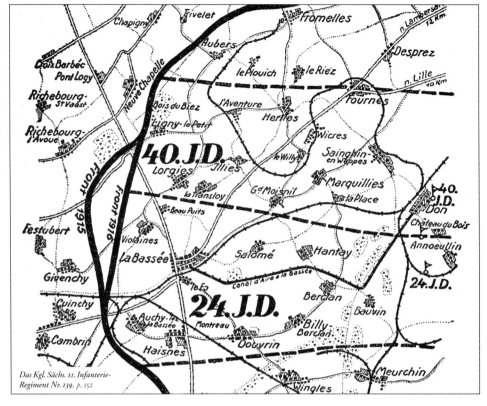

Das Kgl. Sächs. 11. Infanterie-Regiment Nr. 139, p. 152

After its second tour XIX. AK took over the *Wytschaetebogen* from Württemberg XIII. AK on 14 November. Whereas a year before 123. ID had held its half of this front with two battalions per regiment abreast, each regimental sector was now held by a single battalion (with a second in reserve and the third in rest quarters). Note the successive defensive lines – in June 1917, the Messines offensive would force the Germans back to the *III. stellung*.

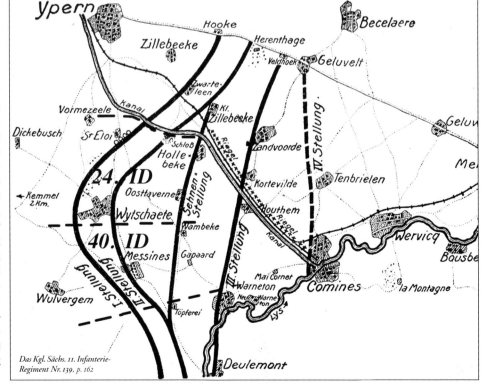

Das Kgl. Sächs. 11. Infanterie-Regiment Nr. 139, p. 162

Forward positions of Infanterie-Regiment 139 near St. Eloi at the end of 1916. Since 27 March this sector was dominated by four huge mine craters (see pp. 92–93), which had since been incorporated into the defences. **Top left:** staircase leading to the front line on the rim of *Trichter 2*. **Top right:** *kompanieführerstand* (company HQ dugout) in *Trichter 2*. **Bottom:** a view across *Trichter 1* from the rim.

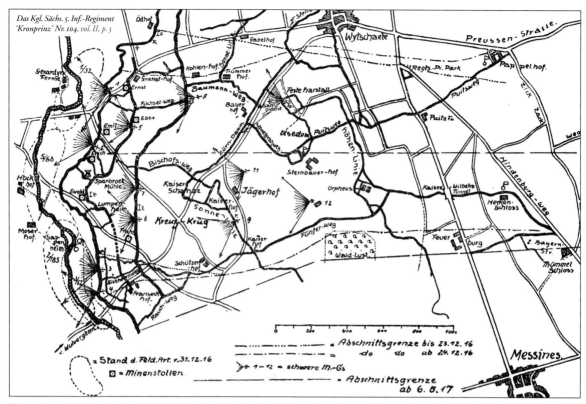

Das Kgl. Sächs. 5. Inf.-Regiment 'Kronprinz' Nr. 104, vol. II, p. 3

The northern (IR 104) subsector of 40. ID at Spanbroekmolen, showing boundary changes between November 1916 and May 1917. Also marked are field artillery defensive fire zones (including an attached battery from FAR 185), mineshafts and fields of fire for heavy machine-guns.

From the *Grabenbuch* (trench diary) of IR 134, pp. 134–135 *Sächsisches Staatsarchiv Dresden; Signatur 11359, Nr. 3868*

18.12.16
All quiet in the morning hours. Isolated shrapnel shells in the afternoon on area to rear of [sector] IIa. Quiet in the evening. Weak rifle and machine-gun fire throughout the night. Weather: wet and cloudy.

19.12.16
Calm at dawn and in the morning hours. Isolated [H.E.] shells in the afternoon on area to rear of [sector] VIa, and mortar bombs on left flank. Complete calm during the night. Weather: wet with snowfall.

20.12.16
Calm in the morning hours. Isolated [H.E.] shells at midday and in the afternoon on the *Klostergraben* and area to rear of sector VIa. Weak rifle and machine-gun fire throughout the night. Weather: clear and cold.

21.12.16
Weak rifle and machine-gun fire in the morning hours. In the morning and afternoon a few shrapnel shells on sector VIa. 1 man lightly wounded as result. Calm throughout the night. Weather: clear and rainy.

Inventory of equipment and munitions
8 water scoops, 12 pickaxes, 27 spades, 7 shovels, 3 water jugs, 3 wooden mallets, 1 two-man saw, 3 handsaws, 1 crosscut saw, 3 pairs of wire cutters, 3 hatchets, 1 hammer, 1 measuring plate, 1 suction hose, 1 drainage hose, 5 pairs of gloves, 1 pair of waders.

VIa Line:
200 hand grenades, 1 large alarm bell, 10 alarm rails[10], 1 alarm air horn, 2 small alarm hooters, 10 trench periscopes

VIb Line
5 alarm rails, 3 trench periscopes, 400 hand grenades
Flare cartridges: 300 white
Signal cartridges: red 30 rounds, green-white 10 rounds, yellow-yellow 10 rounds
K-Munition:[11] 320 rounds in company commander's dugout
S-Munition:[12] 12,040 rounds

At the field watch post there is a path cut through the wire entanglement for patrols, this must be closed up again without delay.

Tegeln, Ltn. d. R.

Nr. 3 gun (a standard 7.7cm FK 96 n.A.) of *'Feldartillerie-Kursus des XIX.AK'* at Christmas 1916, evidently in one of the rear area towns. The purpose of the course is unknown, as is the regiment to which these gunners belong (their shoulder-strap numbers are masked). Note the long shovels stored on the back of the gun shield and the panoramic sight (*rundblickfernrohr*) mounted to the left of the breech.

Corps telephonists of Fernsprech-Abteilung 19 at Christmas 1916, outside their station in Oosttaverne. The rhetorical question *'gediegen, nicht wahr?'* ('sound, isn't it?') suggests that the writer is pleased with his relatively 'cushy' and solidly constructed post.

5.4 204. INFANTERIE-DIVISION

Facing the flooded zone south of Diksmuide and the Ypres Salient

204. INFANTERIE-DIVISION
(30.7.1916.)

(w.) 407. Inf. Brig.: (w.) IR 413 | (w.) IR 414
(s.) 408. Inf. Brig.: (s.) IR 415 | (s.) IR 416
(s.) Radfahr-Komp. 204
(w./p.) Ldst. IR v. Schellerer
(s.) FAR 408 | (w.) Felda. Abt. 407
(s.) FußaB. 404
(s.) Pi. Komp. 404 | (s.) Scheinwerfer-Zug 404
(w.) Div. Brückentrain 404 | (s.) San. Komp. 404
(s.) Fernsprech-Doppelzug 404

On 8 June the Saxon and Württemberg war ministries each agreed to form an all-arms brigade, and the latter a divisional staff. Since the division was intended for static defence on the German and Flemish coast, its units were designated in Landsturm style by corps and garrison town and its personnel merely '*garnisonsdienstverwendungsfähig*' (fit for garrison duty). Most officers were convalescent or old and retired, including some veterans of 1870. Convalescents formed most of Infanterie-Regiment 'Stuttgart XIII' (IR 413) and 'Ulm XIII' (IR 414), and about a quarter of 'Dresden XII' (IR 415). The remainder, including most of Infanterie-Regiment 'Leipzig XIX'

(IR 416), were untrained Landsturm with an average age of 45. Machine-gun companies were an exception, raised separately with much younger and fitter men. Due to events on the Somme the regiments were redesignated as mobile units for front service while still training in July. By then IR 413 and 414 had lost their fitter men to other units in exchange for teenage recruits. The most unfit were to remain behind, but replacements were scarce and none of the officers was willing to leave.

The division reached Flanders in late July and relieved 4. Ersatz-Division between Chateau Heernisse (1km south of Diksmuide) and Langewaede on the 31st. The Saxons were on the left, with IR 416 at Poesele and Withuis and IR 415 at Luigem (see map p. 124). To their right was Landsturm-Infanterie-Regiment von Schellerer, left behind by 4. ED at Woumen. IR 413 held the right flank, with IR 414 in reserve. Ironically their new role was coastal defence of a kind. As units of 123. ID (earlier in 1916) and of XXVII. RK (August–September 1915) had already found, this picturesque sector was firmly secured by the floodwaters released by the Belgian Army in 1914. Defences consisted of sandbag and log breastworks, with numerous con-

'Trenches' on the fringe of the inundated area. All movement here relied on an extensive network of raised plank walkways.

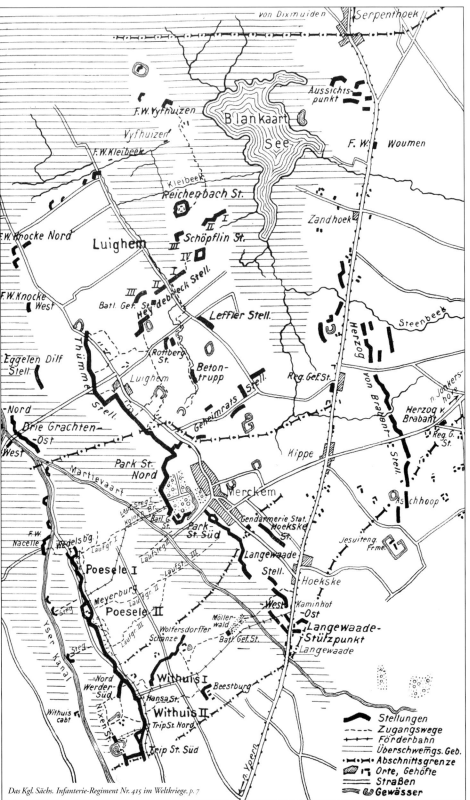

Southern half of the 204. ID front, unevenly divided into the Luigem, Poesele and Withuis sectors. In *Abschnitt Luighem* the area inundated by the Belgians in 1914 (*Überschwemmungs-Gebiet*) was up to 1.4km across, and contact was maintained with the adjacent *Abschnitt Woumen* by boat under cover of the dense reedbeds. The 'coast' was guarded by a tenuous network of advanced posts (*Feldwachen*) reached by narrow paths and vulnerable plank walkways (the dotted lines) which were often targeted by machineguns and rifle batteries.

In *Abschnitt Poesele* and *Withuis* the enemy lay as little as 200m away. Though connected to the field tramway system (*Förderbahn*) the front line on the Yser Canal also relied on screened walkways across the Martjevaart. The massively fortified island at Drie Grachten (500m² in total area) was 600m from the enemy with isolated forward posts. Note that there is only one regimental HQ for these two sectors, which were usually held by two battalions of the same regiment.

I. Batl. / Infanterie-Regiment 415 was formerly II. Ers.-Batl. / Grenadier-Reserve-Regiment 100, and arrived at the front wearing *grenadierlitzen* on their collars and cuffs. The bicycle and despatch cases suggest that this group in the *Löffler-Stellung* are runners.

Section II of the *Heydebreck-Stellung*, seen from the other side of the flooded road; the sign behind the two officers of Infanterie-Regiment 415 indicates that *Feldwache Kleibeek* is to the right. For this new regiment in a quiet sector gasmasks are merely a source of amusement.

Young machine-gunners of IR 415 at Drie Grachten with their MG 08 stowed under concrete. Until November the regiment only had one MG company.

crete blockhouses slowly sinking into the boggy ground. Concreting of trench walls had soon been abandoned because any damage blocked the way with rubble. Though many of the enemy's sporadic bombs and shells were swallowed by mud and water, a steady stream of casualties was incurred. Accidents with grenades and rifles also took a toll on the novice troops.

On the night of 11–12 August thirteen men of IR 416 went missing from a forward post in the Poesele sector. At 1am on the 14th a relief party found that a five-man listening post of IR 415 in front of Drie Grachten West had been raided after heavy shelling, and only the dying Sold. Kreuzmann remained. The alarmed divisional staff asserted that the Saxon brigade lacked skill and caution. Its popular commander Genmaj. z.D. Alfons de Vaux was sent home, to die in humiliated retirement in October 1918. In his regimental history Oberst Friedel of IR 416 bitterly notes that these isolated forward posts had already cost 4. ED many men, and sector commanders had long argued for their abandonment. Relations with the Württembergers grew strained, and both Friedel and his successor Oberstltn. Binkau would soon follow de Vaux.

By divisional order the brigades swapped places on 18 August. IR 413 took over Luigem, IR 414 Poesele / Withuis and IR 415 Chateau Heernisse, with IR 416 in reserve. In the second half of August frequent shelling near the Chateau inflicted damage but few casualties. Air raids on Zarren killed a sentry, three civilians and some livestock, and levelled the divisional gas-

mask depot. While patrols were active on the flanks, no serious clashes occurred. 204. ID was triangularised on 29 August and IR 416 relieved IR 413, which joined 207. ID on the Somme. IR 414, 415 and 416 now began to form fourth battalions, using their own officers and NCOs plus older men from Prussian depots. These battalions combined in September under Saxon Major von Mandelsloh as LIR 388, and took over Poesele / Withuis on the 27th. Like the Landsturm regiment it was left behind when 19. LD relieved 204. ID two days later.

On 3 October 204. ID relieved 5. ED and was subordinated to 58. ID on its right. Its new sector (see map p. 128) extended from south of the Ypres-Comines Canal to the edge of Sanctuary Wood, including the *Grosse Bastion* (The Bluff), Hills 59 and 60 and *Doppelhöhe 60* (Hill 62). I. ANZAC Corps opposite was resting from the Somme, and both sides focused on improving their positions for the winter. Due to the demands of the battle the artillery was relatively inactive and partially replaced on both sides by trench mortars and rifle grenades. On 6 October Australian patrols were repelled by IR 414 at the wire, but seized a man in no man's land and identified 204. ID. Serious raids on the 12th inflicted losses on both IR 414 and IR 106 of 58. ID, but another east of Armagh Wood on the 14th was fatally delayed, allowing the Saxons to repair their wire and ambush the raiders.

The newly arrived 47th (London) Division fell victim to a major defensive detonation by Saxon Pi. (Min.) Komp. 324 on

22 October. At 7 am three 1,250kg charges were blown under the eastern slope of the Bluff, adding a fifth crater and burying many men. Rescue operations were interrupted by a machine-gun team from IR 416, which dominated the craters until retiring after dark. The staff of 204. ID believed the mining threat under control, but still made it their priority upon assuming corps responsibilities from 27 November as the *verstärkte* ('reinforced') 204. ID. On 11 December two galleries under the Bluff were cut off by a large camouflet, burying three *mineure*. The British blew a mine at the railway embankment near Hill 60 on the 19th and a camouflet at *Waldgreuth* on the 21st, raising fears that they were at work below the German tunnels. The trench garrison was reduced as a precaution, while artillery attacked suspected mineshafts and aircraft searched for blue clay spoil from deep mining. Meanwhile increasingly confident night patrols from 204. ID had identified British 23rd and 47th Divisions from prisoners. On 15 December IR 415 launched a successful raid codenamed *Star* (Starling) against mineshafts south of Hill 62 (see p. 128).

Since 204. ID was now to become purely Württemberg and 58. ID purely Saxon, RIR 120 relieved IR 415 on 21 December. IR 416 had to wait until 3 January for IR 413, and fiercely resisted a raid by the Civil Service Rifles on 22 December. The two Saxon regiments joined 212. ID in Champagne, and went to Rumania in March 1917. It was a lucky escape; 204. ID was still present when the Hill 60 and Caterpillar mines were blown on 7 June, obliterating hundreds of men from IR 413 and RIR 120.

Bat. K. S. Jnf. Regt. 415

verleiht dem
für bewiesenen Schneid als Patrouille
gegen den Feind einen Ehrendolch.

im Felde

Das Kgl. Sächs. Infanterie-Regiment Nr. 415 im Weltkriege

Blank certificate for an "honour dagger", awarded at battalion level for "proven courage" on forward patrol.

Immediate reserve position (*bereitschaftsstellung*) of Infanterie-Regiment 416 at the so-called *Kanalknie* (the sharp bend in the canal north of Hollebeke).

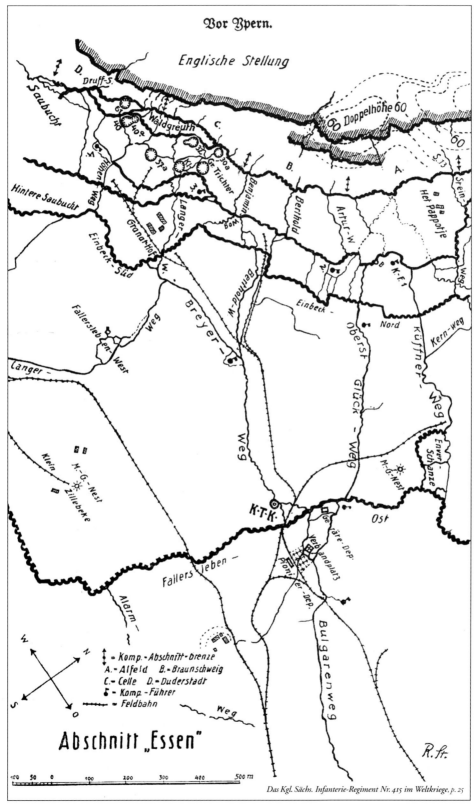

Das Kgl. Sächs. Infanterie-Regiment Nr. 415 im Weltkriege, p. 25

Abschnitt Essen opposite *Doppelhöhe 60* (Hill 62) was held by IR 415 from 3 October to 21 December 1916. The double arrows mark the boundaries of company sectors *Alfeld*, *Braunschweig*, *Celle* and *Duderstadt*. South of *Essen* was *Abschnitt Frankfurt* (IR 414), including Hills 59 and 60. *Abschnitt Goslar* (IR 416) faced the *Grosse Bastion* (The Bluff) and extended 700m beyond the Ypres-Comines Canal.

For '*Streifunternehmen Star*' on 15 December the garrison of *Celle* and *Duderstadt* withdrew to the *III. stellung* (*Hintere Saubucht/Einbeck-Süd*), with a forward observation post at the *Saubucht*. Shelling began slowly at 5 am, provoking a response to disguise preparations as an artillery duel. While the whole front facing 204. ID was hit, the actual target area was devastated and its wire cleared by *minenwerfers*. After a hurricane barrage Ltn. d. R. Coccius and his men attacked at 5.22 pm from the saps at *Waldgreuth*, supported by a telephone and aid post in the *Höhenweg* near crater 37a. The first and second British lines were found empty. After *pioniere* had blown up three suspected mineshafts the raiders returned in twenty minutes laden with booty, losing two dead and two wounded to artillery fire.

Concrete pillboxes in the second line near the boundary of *Alfeld* and *Braunschweig*, possibly at the location marked 'B' near 'KF 1' (the company HQ for *Alfeld*) on the map opposite. The naked autumn trees belong to the wood named Clonmel Copse by the British.

Maintenance on a second line trench somewhere in *Essen*.

Advanced post in the 'B' sap directly opposite *Doppelhöhe 60*.

5.5 58. INFANTERIE-DIVISION

At Bellewaarde, Hooge and Sanctuary Wood

58. INFANTERIE-DIVISION

116. Inf. Brig.: (s.) IR 106 | (s.) IR 107 | (w.) RIR 120
(s.) 4. Esk. / UR 18
(w.) *58. Felda. Brig.:* (s.) FAR 115 | (w.) FAR 116 *
(s.) Pi. Komp. 115 | (w.) Pi. Komp. 116
(s.) Mw. Komp. 58 | (s.) Scheinwerfer-Zug 115
(s.) Div. Brückentrain 58 | (s.) Fernsprech-Doppelzug 58
(s.) San. Komp. 58

* The heavy artillery remained on the Somme

After a grievous ordeal on the Somme the division relieved
4. Ersatz-Division from north of the Ypres–Roulers railway to
Het Pappotje on 29–30 September, with 204. ID attached from
3 October. IR 106 at Sanctuary Wood and RIR 120 at Hooge
each had one battalion sector, while IR 107 held two with
help from the detached IV. / IR 362. The regimental history of
IR 107 roundly criticises the departing regiment, alleging that
IR 362 took all of the maps and the fixed telephone system, gave
minimal briefings and even evacuated the front line at Railway
Wood before the arrival of the relief! It describes the trenches
as neglected and unimproved since the departure of XXVII.
RK, and the old concrete dugouts as too small and too light.
IR 106 however was fairly content, and RIR 120 (who had never
served at the front in Flanders or against the BEF) greatly impressed with the solidly constructed *Hooge-Stellung* and its
electric lighting.

Enemy patrols were rarely seen and easily driven off, and the division largely dominated no man's land. There was far greater
concern at groundless reports that plague had broken out opposite, after which shooting at rats with rifles (usually banned to avoid
accidents) was permitted. However artillery, mortars, machine-
guns and aircraft all reacted swiftly to any movement in daylight.
German retaliation was limited, as shells had to be spared for the
Somme. The main enemy was the autumn rain. IR 106 suffered
serious flooding, and in all sectors electric pumps were in constant
use. IR 107 suffered 'friendly flooding' early on 3 October when
pioniere blew a camouflet and broke a drainage pipe, swamping
other mineshafts; in the trenches at Railway Wood many sleeping men barely escaped drowning. On the 19th the dam at Bellewaarde Lake burst, submerging IR 107's left sector; simultaneously part of the right flank flooded to a depth of 60cm.

Meanwhile the division was rebuilding, forming one MG company per battalion and a company-strength divisional *sturmabteilung*. On 20 October representatives of its units were
reviewed and decorated by the Kaiser. The next day 4. Ersatz-
Division began to arrive, and the relief was completed late on
the 22nd. Opposite IR 107 it was greeted with a siren from the
British lines and heavy shelling. This tour had cost 58. ID seventy
dead, but worse was to come. As almost everyone had guessed,
they were returning to the Somme.

Tough Swabian reservists of
RIR 120 at a *feldschlachterei* or company cookhouse.
In September the regiment
had suffered over half of the
division's 1,700 casualties
against the French at Barleux
south of Péronne; it was a
source of both pride and resentment to the Württembergers that they were entrusted
with the most dangerous and
difficult tasks. However according to Oberst Fromm his
regiment would later miss
their special status as 'guests'
of the Saxons, whom he
credits for their politeness,
practicality and the unfussy
efficiency of their logistics.

Grenadier Robert Winkler of Grenadier-Reserve-Regiment 100. This unit was raised in Dresden from reservists of both active grenadier regiments and wore the same uniform, but with numerals instead of a royal cypher on the shoulder-straps. Apart from two regiments of the Prussian *Garde*, GRR 100 was the only such unit to have a title other than 'Reserve-Infanterie-Regiment' and to wear the *litzen* on collar and cuffs. Grenadier-Landwehr-Regiment 100 also bore the 'grenadier' title, but not the *litzen*.

1917 in Flanders

Long-developed British plans for an offensive in Flanders were finally realised in the summer of 1917. The result was the *Dritte Flandernschlacht* (Third Battle of Ypres AKA Passchendaele), an apocalyptic bloodbath which devoured hundreds of thousands of lives and dragged on into November in conditions of inconceivable squalor. While defined by concentrations of artillery that stunned even veterans of the Somme and Verdun, it introduced other horrors. On Messines Ridge in June mining warfare reached its zenith with the largest man-made explosions the world had yet seen, killing thousands and traumatising thousands more. It also saw the first use of tanks in Flanders, though their effectiveness declined as the weather worsened. The chemical war escalated that summer, with the Germans introducing mustard gas and the British the Livens projector; emplaced in their thousands these disposable mortars could instantly inundate a wide area with gas or burning oil. The misery increased when strategic rubber shortages forced the introduction of the *lederschutzmaske*. Though it included some improvements over older models, prolonged wear of this chrome-tanned leather mask in warm weather was a ghastly ordeal.

During 1917 corps staffs were separated from their organic divisions and became interchangeable command teams for geographical *gruppen*. Each *gruppe* shuffled its varying cast of divisions between the front and the *eingreif* ('intervention') role, held behind the line to counterattack or reinforce threatened sectors. **XIX. AK** was designated *Gruppe Wytschaete* on 7 January, with its organic **24. ID** and **40. ID** still under its control until June. After the disastrous Battle of Messines the corps staff was relieved and took over *Gruppe Aubers* for the remainder of the year. General von Laffert died of a heart attack on 20 July and was replaced by Genltn. von Carlowitz, whose reputation had recovered since 1914. 24. ID and **32. ID** served with *Gruppe Wytschaete* from August to October, when 32. ID moved to *Gruppe Lille*. The recently formed **219. ID** served under XIX. AK with *Gruppe Aubers* from July to September. East of the dead city **XII. RK** became *Gruppe Ypern* on 2 April with its organic **23. RD** and **24. RD** under its command. From 15 June to August its staff controlled *Gruppe Gent*, responsible for coastal and border defence. While 24. RD soon left, 23. RD served multiple tours with *Gruppe*

Ypern until September. On the northern face of the salient 40. ID was with *Gruppe Dixmuide* between July and October, and **58. ID** with the new *Gruppe Staden* from October onwards. **LIR 388** (see p. 126) served mainly with Prussian 19. LD in the inundated area, becoming fully Saxon in April by absorbing the supernumerary IV./Grenadier-Landwehr-Regiment 100. Available sources suggest that I./388 was with 40. ID in March and the whole regiment with 23. RD in April, then back with 19. LD when it was mauled by the Franco-Belgian offensive in October.

From winter 1916–1917 all divisions were 'triangular' and 'independent', with an infantry brigade of three regiments plus a *feldrekrutendepot* and a *sturmabteilung* (both of which were often dissolved and reformed as manpower allowed, and are thus omitted in orders of battle). The ArKo (*Artillerie-Kommandeur*) controlled a field artillery regiment of nine batteries (see p. 175) plus a varying allocation of attached units, and its *pionierbataillon* at least two field companies and a *minenwerfer* company with 17cm and 25cm weapons. Each infantry battalion had up to twelve heavy machine-guns, four 7.58cm *minenwerfers* and eight small grenade launchers. Rifle companies typically gained two light machine-guns (Maxim MG08/15) each in the spring, increasing to six by 1918. This was reflected in a tactical emphasis on firepower over manpower which greatly reduced losses. The forward zone of a regimental sector was now typically held in depth by one battalion, whose commander served as KTK (*Kampftruppen-Kommandeur*), with tactical authority over all units entering his zone regardless of rank. Further back the commander of the battalion in the immediate support (*bereitschaft*) zone exercised a similar role as BTK (*Bereitschaftstruppen-Kommandeur*), while regimental HQ managed the allocation of reserves.

Though regular reliefs kept morale relatively high during the battle, by 1917 the strain of the war and the shortages caused by the naval blockade were biting hard. Lavish *liebesgaben* were long gone, rations within Germany and behind the lines dwindled and shoddy *ersatz* materials proliferated. As the spartan *feldbluse* steadily displaced older uniform tunics, the depressed and hungry Saxon *soldaten* became increasingly indistinguishable amid the homogenous field-grey masses.

6.1 24. Infanterie-Division

At Wytschaete, Houthem and south of Gheluvelt

24. Infanterie-Division (6.1917)

89. Inf. Brig.: IR 133 | IR 139 | IR 179

1. Esk. HR 19

ArKo 24: FAR 77 (plus attached units)

Pi. Batl. 22: 2. & 5. Komp. / Pi. Batl. 22

    Mw. Komp. 24 | Scheinwerfer-Zug 22

Div. Fernsprech-Abteilung. 24

San. Komp. 47

Since November 1916 the division had occupied the northern half of the *Wytschaetebogen* (see map p. 119), with IR 133 on the left at Wytschaete, IR 179 in the centre and IR 139 on the right at St. Eloi. Though fears of a British attack during the winter proved unfounded, the garrison often endured extravagantly heavy shelling which the German guns could rarely match. Aggressive patrolling and raiding continued on both sides, with the Germans keen to identify enemy units and disrupt mining activity. The greatest success was achieved when IR 133 captured thirty men from 16th (Irish) Division on 8 March.

During April the staff of 4. Armee proposed a local withdrawal before the predicted offensive, but *Gruppe Wytschaete* successfully argued that the forward slope of Messines Ridge remained more tenable than the lines behind it. Deceived by the reduced noise of British mine workings largely completed even before the arrival of XIX. AK, the *mineure* supported this belief. After relief in the last week of April, 24. ID received orders on 1 May to occupy a narrower front, shifted to the right to insert 2. ID between the two Saxon divisions. Over the following nights IR 139 returned to a reduced St. Eloi sector with IR 133 on its right, and IR 179 took over *Abschnitt Goslar* from 204. ID (see p. 128).

While the British did not disrupt this deployment, it was soon clear that they too were reinforcing their line. After a slow build-up the bombardment began in earnest on 21 May. Major raids to secure prisoners on 21 and 23 May found the British trenches evacuated to frustrate them. Nevertheless 41st Division and numerous fresh bat-

Landsers queuing at a delousing station run by *Gruppe Wytschaete* in March 1917. Although well behind the front many still carry their gasmasks.

teries were identified on 26 May, by which time the German forward and depth positions were being systematically pulverised under aerial observation. The 'shell-proof' concrete shelters attracted such overwhelming fire that in the daytime much of the garrison took refuge in shell holes, where they endured shelling even worse than the Somme and intermittent probing attacks. Despite frequent battalion re-

liefs 24. ID was so exhausted by 31 May that its withdrawal was ordered. The next day the bombardment grew even heavier, as the massed artillery of British 2nd Army attacked the salient from three sides. Hindered by nightly machine-gun barrages on approach routes, the infantry of 24. ID was relieved by 6 June, while its artillery endured devastating counter-battery fire.

The zone of the fighting troops was policed primarily by the sixty-man *feldgendarmerie-trupp* at each corps HQ, recruited from cavalry NCOs and civil police. Larger units were attached to the *etappen-inspektionen*. The plainclothes *Geheime Feldpolizei* attached at higher level acted as 'detectives' against both espionage and ordinary criminality. *Geheime Feldpolizei Armeeoberkommando 4* in Flanders ultimately comprised three senior *kommissaren*, eighty *beamten* and numerous support personnel divided among its regional offices (*nebenstellen*).

Geh. Feldpolizei AOK4 Nebenstelle Wervicq Nr. 699v. 17.1.17   *Sächsisches Staatsarchiv Dresden, Signatur 11358, Nr. 1432*

To *Gruppe Wytschaete* Abtlg. IB[1]

I consider it my duty to inform the *gruppe* that thefts of all kinds are becoming increasingly common in the billeting areas.

With the weak police forces available, it is in most cases difficult to apprehend the perpetrators; indeed it only allows us to say with certainty in a minority of cases whether the thief is one of the local inhabitants or a serviceman. Naturally the cases where soldiers are the culprits become generalised by the population, and it must be noted that in this climate the reputation of the German Army among the civil population has suffered.

It has already been suggested that the units and *ortskommandanturen* should be instructed to apply the severest punishments upon the arrest and conviction of soldiers, to be announced via the order of the day as a deterrent.

The following cases were brought to the attention of this office in the last two months, partly via official channels and partly via private communication:

1) Menen: a) Two unidentified soldiers (artillerymen) asked in two shops to see wool to the value of several hundred marks, and ran off with it without paying.

b) A soldier of the *Sturmabteilung* [der 24. ID] formerly quartered in Bousbecque took a 20-mark note from a till in Menen and ran away, but was detected by the woman there and reported to his unit by *Ortskommandantur Menen*. The money was returned to the woman.

c) Several soldiers were buying cigars at the Franco Belge tobacconist's shop on Brueggestraße in Menen, and while doing so pocketed a box of cigars. The proprietor spotted this and got the box returned.

d) In Menen there are widespread complaints of theft of chickens and rabbits, in several cases the prints of soldiers' boots have been detected.

2) Bousbecque: tough measures have been taken by the *ortskommandantur* against the reduction of poultry stocks, threatening heavy punishment for anyone caught in possession of missing chickens. On two occasions a couple of artillerymen (from Flakzug Wenzel and [Feld-] Artl. Regt. 68) were caught stealing by farmers in Bousbecque, confined overnight and brought to *Ortskommandantur Bousbecque*.

3) Werwicq: a) A cow was stolen from a woman in Basse Flandre. The Gendarmerie in Werwicq have identified as the perpetrators two *pioniere*, who have been remanded in custody.

b) The same artillerymen who committed the mischief described in 1 (Menen) case 'a' have cheated a shopkeeper in Werwicq of ca. 120,– marks in the same manner, and struck a young woman on the chest when she tried to prevent one of them from escaping.

c) In a single street (Cominer Str.) in Belgian Werwicq over the past month virtually the entire stock of rabbits and chickens has been cleared out by night. An informer attests that he has clearly recognised local residents and soldiers taking part.

4) Comines (Belgian): a) A woman was robbed in her presence of till money with a value of ca. 200,- francs by a soldier of IR 179. The perpetrator has been identified.

b) A cow was stolen by two *pioniere* of Prussian Pi. Komp. 24, both men are in custody.

c) It was learned through an informer, that a woman had been knocked down in the street one evening by soldiers, and her handbag taken. The matter was however not reported to the *ortskommandantur*.

The list of cases above only considers incidents in which property has been stolen from the inhabitants. Quite frequently of late, the property of the military treasury has also been made away with.

signed Wolff, F[eld] P[olizei] H[aupt] B[eamter]

The massive artificial earthquake of 7 June could be heard and felt far to the rear, and the weary Saxons were instantly aware just how narrow their escape had been. While fresh troops struggled forward to stabilise the front, 24. ID spent a tense and confusing day of order and counter-order. 3. MGK / IR 133 were among the first to be recalled, followed by I./179, III./139 and I./133 in the evening. From 8–10 June these three battalions reinforced the heterogeneous garrison of the *sehnenstellung* and *III. stellung* in the former 40. ID sector, while their parent regiments were stationed behind in reserve. The division was then regrouped and inserted into the front line on the night of 13–14 June. Initially its main position was the *III. stellung* west of Houthem, with a thin outpost line at Hollebeke anchored on the right by 8./179 at the canal embankment. During the day this weak line was subjected to drum fire, before an attack by two battalions of 41st Division at 8.30 pm. The British quickly secured their limited objectives despite stubborn resistance and dug in, seeing off a small counterattack on 15 June. After this the front unexpectedly stabilised, the divisional sector was reduced and the outposts were developed into the main line of resistance. 24. ID was finally relieved at the end of June and sent for its long-delayed rest.

The division spent six weeks resting and rebuilding as an *eingreifdivision* with *Gruppe Aubers* before returning to the front west of Houthem on 11 August. By this time the town and the many nearby farms the Saxons had known in the spring were all but obliterated, leaving only the concrete bunkers once hidden inside them. The front line consisted of partly roofed and often flooded shell holes, devoid of wire. Although this sector now lay outside the main battle area, artillery and aircraft remained highly active.

After settling in 24. ID resumed its aggressive raiding policy. On the night of 19–20 August IR 179 captured a Lewis gun and identified British 37th Division, followed by 30th Division a week later. On 1 September 32. ID arrived on the left of 24. ID, and the truncated *Wytschaetebogen* again became a Saxon front. That night two groups from IR 133 conducted a major raid, creeping to within 60m of the British line before the barrage. Complete surprise was achieved and eleven prisoners taken, with only two raiders missing and seventeen wounded. IR 139 was even more successful on 9 September, but on the 21st raiders from IR 179 found the British front line evacuated. The intelligence from these raids won the raiders numerous decorations and the division high praise from corps and army staff. By the end of the month its artillery was heavily engaged against major attacks further north. 24. ID was relieved on the night of 7–8 October and immediately recommitted between Zandvoorde and Gheluvelt. In eight weeks it had lost twenty-one officers and 907 other ranks, many of them taken ill in the foul conditions. However the worst was yet to come.

The new sector was a feculent swamp littered with the dead of previous attacks, in which the infantry were steadily ground down by foul weather, unspeakable squalor and relentless shelling. To preserve their guns from the mud, machine-gun teams were crammed into the few surviving pillboxes, at constant risk of being overturned by super-

Lothar Blankenburg's striking Gothic tribute to the Saxon *minenwerfer-pioniere*, printed in 1917 for the newly formed Minenwerfer-Ersatz-Bataillon 8 in Königsbrück. This combination of grim realism and morbid symbolism (with its triptych form and 'dance of Death' motif from medieval ecclesiastical tradition) typifies the apocalyptic 'spirit of 1917' in German war art.

heavy shells. The British launched major attacks on 9 and 22 October after heavy drum fire, both bloodily obliterated in no man's land. The tired and depleted division then endured three days of artillery preparation for the Second Battle of Passchendaele, and on the night of 25–26 October enemy troops were observed struggling into position. After ten minutes of devastating drum fire the survivors faced the assault of 7th Division at 6.40 am. Along most of the front the British were butchered by machine-guns as they waded through the mud, but on the right they broke through the neighbouring IR 69 into Gheluvelt to threaten the flank of IR 179. Observing from the roof of his KTK bunker in the absence of reports from the front, Hptm. Paul Selle directed 10, 11. and 12./179 to counter-attack. Despite intense shelling, they forced their way forward through the mud and pouring rain to storm Gheluvelt at 11.30 am. The British were driven back to their start line with appalling losses, and over eighty prisoners taken. This victory had bled the division white, especially IR 179 (see p. 225). It was relieved during the nights of 27–29 October, having lost fifty officers and 1,900 other ranks during the month, and never returned to Flanders.

The southern half of the 24. ID front before the attack of 26 October. North of IR 133 was IR 179, with its right flank on the Menin Road covering Gheluvelt. Each sector was divided into an A-Zone (front line), B-Zone (*bereitschaft*) and C-Zone (reserve area, not shown).

Certificate of honour awarded to Uffz. Kurt Richter of I. Batl. / Infanterie-Regiment 139 on the Kaiser's birthday (27 January 1918), in recognition of his 'courage, bravery, excellent performance and decisiveness' during the fighting at Gheluvelt in October 1917.

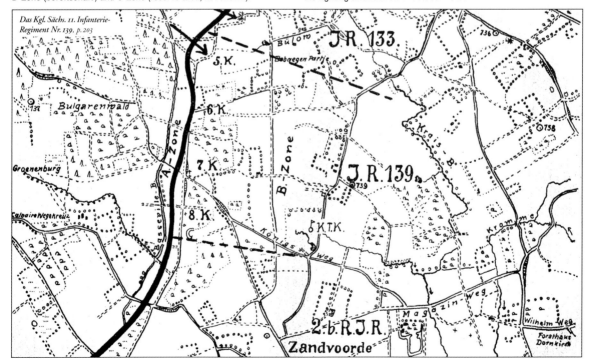

6.2 40. INFANTERIE-DIVISION

At Messines and northwest of Houthulst Forest

40. INFANTERIE-DIVISION (6.1917)

88. Inf. Brig.: IR 104 | IR 134 | IR 181

2. Esk. HR 19

ArKo 40: FAR 32 (plus attached units)

Pi. Batl. 141: 1. & 3. Komp. / Pi. Batl. 22

    Mw. Komp. 40 | Scheinwerfer-Zug 310

Div. Fernsprech-Abteilung. 40

San. Komp. 48

Since November 1916 the division held the southern half of the *Wytschaetebogen* with IR 134 on the left at Messines and IR 181 in the centre. The IR 104 sector at Spanbroek-molen was its greatest concern due to the mining threat, which an intensive *minenwerfer* barrage and major raid on 8–9 March failed to eliminate. As in 1915–1916, IR 104 spent many months with colossal explosive charges below its front line and escaped unscathed.

40. ID was relieved at the end of March and returned on 21 April. Its frontage was reduced on 6 May, ceding half of the old IR 104 sector to 2. ID. As signs of an offensive multiplied

the Saxons made determined efforts to gain intelligence, but major raids by IR 104 and 134 early on 20 May failed to enter the lines of the highly alert enemy. On the 25th however IR 181 took two prisoners when a British raid was beaten off. A final effort by IR 104 on 29 May failed at once due to drop-shorts from the *minenwerfers*. Nevertheless by June *Gruppe Wytschaete* had identified most of the attacking units.

The artillery preparation had taken an appalling toll, 40. ID having lost 1,300 men since 21 April. Bavarians from 3. bID began to arrive on 4 June, the same day Messines was pulverised by super-heavy guns and flooded with gas. When the battle began on 7 June, each regiment still had a machine-gun company in the combat zone. I./134 and I./181 had been relieved during the night and the staff of I./181 was finalising the handover at the *Thümmelschloss* (Fanny's Farm), which housed both the BTK and KTK. I./104 was waiting near the *Heckenschloss* (Lumm Farm) for relief by III./bIR 23, which had been delayed by shelling. FAR 32 was still in action, and suffered grievous losses that day including most of its guns.

Men of Infanterie-Regiment 104 using a typical *donnerbalken* ('thunder beam'). Privacy on the lavatory was a privilege of rank (see p. 64).

Orders for the patrol operation on the morning of 9 March 1917 *Sächsisches Staatsarchiv Dresden, Signatur 11358, Nr. 1432*

1. Patrol Wehmeyer [IR] **104** is to break into the English trenches directly north of *Blaupunkt* 559, penetrate as far as the 2nd line, assess the damage to the English mineshafts located there from the *minenwerfer* barrage on 8 March and complete their destruction, destroy enemy facilities and take prisoners and booty.

Patrouille Fiedler [IR] **181** is to enter the enemy's 1st line north of the Wulverghem–Wytschaete road, penetrate as far as the 2nd line, destroy enemy facilities and take prisoners and booty. Both patrols will remain in the enemy trenches for [no more than] 10 minutes. Upon the approach of superior enemy forces both [patrol] leaders are to give the signal to abandon the enemy trenches.

2. Overall command: Oberstltn. von Berger[2] at the *Thümmelschloss*. More specific instructions on the disposition of patrols in parties and practice for same have been and will be issued for Patrol Wehmeyer by Hptm. Thomas[3] [IR] 104, for Patrol Fiedler by Major Hanson[4] [IR] 181.

3. Strength of patrols:
Patrol Wehmeyer: 1 officer, 1 vizefeldwebel, 5 unteroffiziere, 4 *pioniere*, 34 men
Patrol Fiedler: 1 officer, 1 sergeant, 4 unteroffiziere, 4 *pioniere*, 30 men

4. Dress: field cap, woollen uniform with white band 5cm in width on each arm, ankle boots, trousers with legs tied up at the bottom or puttees. Insignia and shoulder-straps removed, no name labels, unit stamps rendered illegible, no papers or items to be carried which could betray unit affiliation to the enemy. For each man one man is to be assigned by name in our own trenches, who is to hand him his gasmask immediately upon return …
Equipment for blocking and assault party: belt equipment with dagger (without bayonet), pistol, hand grenades. Selected men as per more specific orders of Hptm. Thomas and Major Hanson: cudgels, wire cutters, electric torches, ropes for restraining prisoners who offer resistance or dragging the dead, in order to identify English units.
For security and contact parties: rifle, belt equipment with short bayonet, hand grenades, *zeltbahn*.
For *pioniere*: belt equipment with dagger, hand grenades, explosives.

5. Conduct of operation: more detailed instructions for movement of patrols from *Barbarahof* to the trenches and for creation of gaps in our wire will be issued by Major Hanson and Hptm. Thomas.

4.55 am – patrols will stand ready at the exit points. Hptm. Pflugbeil[5] will issue instructions for MGs to be directed from this time onward against enemy MGs enfilading the break-in points, and to silence them by means of precision fire.
5.00–5.05 am – 2 heavy and 2 medium MW will open up suddenly on the projecting 'nose' east of *Gerardyn-Ferme*, 1 heavy and 2 medium MW north and south of the break-in point near the *Fransecky-Nase*[6]. For the purpose of putting out of action any MG that may have been dug in again during the night, at least long enough for the patrol to rush forward, 5 light MW on the break-in points.
5.05 am – sudden onset of artillery fire as a screen: 3 [10.5cm] light howitzer batteries (5./68, 1 and 2./185); 2 field gun batteries (2 and 5./32) covering the break-in point at the *Fransecky-Nase*.
5.05–5.15 am – continued heavy fire by the artillery.
5.05 am – patrols will break cover.
5.15 am – return of patrols.
5.20 am – slackening of artillery fire.
5.25 am – cessation of artillery fire.

6. The artillery will be requested to place heavy batteries on standby to combat any enemy artillery intervention and to keep the artillery liaison officer posted at the *Thümmelschloss* until the morning of 9 March.

7. Instructions for escort of prisoners and transport of booty, and for the assembly of the patrols and deployment of men to flash electric lanterns at the passages through our own wire, will be issued by Major Hanson and Hptm. Thomas. …

8. Timetable will be issued on 8 March 9 pm at the *Thümmelschloss*.

9. Discussion of the operation by telephone is prohibited.

10. Password for the operation, 'Chemnitz', must be known to all participants.

11. *Regts.-Ärzte* of [IR] 104 and 181 will put medical officers and stretcher bearers on standby. [Regts.-Ärzt of IR] 181 in *Ansbach*[7].

12. Maj. Hanson and Hptm. Thomas are to hand me their individual operational orders by midday on 8 March at the *Thümmelschloss*. The location of both officers and manner of reporting [during the operation] must be apparent from these [orders].

13. III. [Batl. / IR 104] must arrange for increased sniper activity, and the MG officer on the [regimental] staff for MG fire against enemy targets in the damaged portions of the enemy trench system, on the morning of 9 March.

signed von Berger

Report on the patrol operation on the morning of 9 March (see map p. 121)   *Das Kgl. Sächs. 5. Inf.-Regiment 'Kronprinz' Nr. 104, vol. 2, pp. 29/30*

... The break-in point was at the *Gerardyn-Ferme*. Simultaneously with the onset of preparatory artillery, *minenwerfer* and MG fire at 5.00 am the patrol left the 1a line. When the heavy weapons established the fire screen on the break-in point at 5.05, the break-in to the enemy trench followed. During the crossing of the last wire obstacle, an English Lewis MG suddenly emerged above the parapet and opened fire. Soldat Taube immediately noticed the threat, and put paid to the brave and vigilant defender with a well-aimed pistol shot. The MG and the rest of the crew fell into German hands soon afterwards. Further prisoners were taken during the rolling-up of the trench. No mine gallery was found on this occasion. A foray as far as the second English trench was not attempted in view of strong English MG fire and insufficient destruction of obstacles by the artillery preparation. After ten minutes and the demolition of a dugout Ltn. Wehmeyer gave the signal to go back, and reached our trenches with all of his men and without loss. About 10 am the victorious *sturmtrupp*, who had made their presence felt from afar via the wail of a captured signal siren, made their entry into Comines. With them they brought ten prisoners from 6th Connaught Rangers of 16th (Irish) Division[8] and assorted booty, including an MG and thirteen rifles. A patrol from IR 181, which pushed forward at the same time west of *Fransecky-Ferme*, was unable to complete its task due to fire from enemy artillery and enfilading MGs.

At 4.10 am four huge mines (Spanbroekmolen, Kruisstraat I–III) were blown in the northern and one (Ontario Farm) in the central sector, followed by a devastating creeping barrage. By 5 am news reached the KTKs that the forward zone was lost and its garrison wiped out. Major Ferdinand Koch of I./104 occupied the *Höhenlinie* (see map p. 121) with his battalion and the newly arrived 9./bIR 23, while at least four guns of 2. MGK/181 deployed with I./bIR 17 west of the *Thümmelschloss*. Another three gun teams of IR 104 and 181 under Vfw. Landgraf went down fighting at *Waldlust* (L'Enfer Wood), while others from IR 134 and 181 aided II./bIR 18 in the doomed defence of Messines. By 6 am Major Koch's force had fallen back toward the *Heckenschloss*, while the regimental staff of bIR 23 broke out to the rear to report to 88. Infanterie-Brigade. The British now halted for two hours to mop up resistance, and the *Thümmelschloss* again came under drum fire. Having lost his battalion Major Ritter von Kohlmüller of III./bIR 17 refused to retreat, and his dwindling band of Saxons and Bavarians beat off repeated assaults in brutal hand-to-hand fighting. When the major was killed by a shell at 7.30 am Hptm. d. R. Emil Wildenhain of I./181 assumed command.

At 8 am the British advance resumed supported by tanks, cutting off and overwhelming the defenders of the *Heckenschloss*; Major Koch survived in captivity to collect his MStHO(R) in 1920. New Zealanders stormed the *Thümmelschloss* to find it full of the dead and wounded, a group led by Hptm. d. R. Wildenhain having broken out to join the Bavarian reserves in the *sehnenstellung*. At 9.40 am the enemy paused again to face the expected counterattack, launched by three fresh battalions of Garde-Reserve-Regiment 1 and bRIR 5 at 2.45 pm. After seventy per cent losses

from machine-guns and artillery they reinforced the *sehnenstellung*, and later fought the Australians to a standstill. All remaining units of 40. ID were now subordinated to 1. Garde-Reserve-Division, primarily in the defence of the *III. stellung*, which soon became the front line in the southern half of their old sector. Further north III./181 beat off an attack on the *sehnenstellung* late on the 9th, and was then relieved by I./179. This line was abandoned the following night and the remaining Saxons withdrawn.

After a month rebuilding near Bruges the division relieved 19. LD of *Gruppe Dixmuide* north of Steenstraat on 17–19 July. IR 134 took over *Abschnitt Luighem-Poesele* (the entire area shown on p. 124) with two battalions abreast, and IR 181 the *Jägerabschnitt* west of Draaibank. Initially in reserve, IR 104 later briefly held the adjacent *Abschnitt Bixschoote*. While the right flank remained quiet, the rest of the new sector suffered increasingly intense and destructive shelling as far back as Kortemark. No longer judged shellproof, the concrete fort at Drie Grachten was now evacuated during heavy bombardments. Early on 31 July the shelling reached its peak, including overwhelming quantities of gas. The half-choked survivors bloodily repulsed the French assault, but 111. ID was driven back from Bikschote and the flank of IR 181 briefly threatened until reserves arrived from IR 134. With frequent battalion reliefs the depleted 40. ID survived two more weeks of constant shelling and minor attacks. By 4 August it had lost forty-one officers and over 1,600 men (many of them irreplaceable veterans), and Genmaj. Meister pleaded for relief of his division. A major operation to relieve the pressure was disrupted when the French broke into the front line of IR 134 on the Yser Canal late on 9 August. After they had been ejected, IR 104 and the *sturmabteilung* attacked in the

The *Regimentsmusik* of IR 134 plays at a mass funeral for the division's dead in Comines after the Battle of Messines.

Jägerabschnitt at 3 am and gained 200m against weak opposition. The relief began on 14 August, and 40. ID was transferred to a quiet sector south of St. Quentin.

When it relieved 119. ID between Langewaede and Houthulst Forest on the night of 18–19 October with 58. ID on its left (see map p. 142) 40. ID found a scene of unspeakable devastation. Despite dense fog and heavy shelling the infantry reached the front line almost unscathed. The next day saw a massive German gas bombardment, to which the enemy replied in kind on the 20th. Shelling was relentless, and communications hopelessly disrupted as troops changed position to escape the worst of it. French assaults were bloodily repulsed on 21, 22 and 25 October, but the division's ability to withstand a major attack was now in serious doubt. On the 26th the French waded the St. Jean Steenbeek after two hours of drum fire to take Draaibank, where they were halted by determined counterattacks. The next morning they attacked in overwhelming force covered by fog and drum fire, breaking in frontally and from the right through the adjacent 20. LD. Neither fierce resistance led by the *sturmabteilung* at *Jesuitengut* and Klostermolen, nor artillery firing over open sights could stop the French from forcing the Saxons back to the Brabant and Bultehoek lines. The enemy's attention then moved north, facilitating the relief of 40. ID over the next two nights and its transfer to the Eastern Front.

Vfw. Bernhard Rössler from Wülknitz near Großenhain, killed in action with 6./Infanterie-Regiment 104 at Draaibank on 26 October 1917.

6.3 58. INFANTERIE-DIVISION

Against the French and British at Houthulst Forest

116. Inf. Brig.: IR 106 | IR 107 | RIR 103

4. Esk. UR 18

ArKo 57: FAR 115 (plus attached units)

Pi. Batl. 142: 2. Res. Komp. / Pi. Batl. 22 |
   Pi. Komp. 115 | Pi. Komp. 404

Mw. Komp. 58 | Scheinwerfer-Zug 115

Divkonach 58: Div. Ferna. 58

San. Komp. 58

The first units of 58. ID arrived from the Eastern Front on 10 October. Others were still en route when IR 106 struggled through Houthulst Forest under fire to reinforce 119. ID on the 13th. While the rest of the division was in reserve IR 106 endured severe shelling, gassing and local attacks, and FAR 115 began to deploy in support. On the night of 18–19 October IR 107 and RIR 103 were inserted left of IR 106, and 58. ID assigned to *Gruppe Staden*. The next day shelling focused on the *bereitschaft* and artillery

zones, and two traumatised survivors trapped in an overturned bunker since the 15th could finally be rescued.

Days of heavy bombardment heralded a fresh offensive, and the forest was repeatedly flooded with gas. Losses were severe, and conditions almost unendurable. On 21 October troops massing opposite were pounded by the German artillery. After intense shelling the French and British attacked the next morning through smoke and mist. Wearing gasmasks under heavy fire, 3. / FAR 115 alone fired 2,600 rounds in defence. On most of the 58. ID front French objectives lay at the edge of the outpost zone, and the attack thus seemed to have failed. North of Veldhoek the French and British pushed into the forest, but were thrown back by IR 107 and RIR 103 early on 23 October.

The infantry were then gradually relieved, only to be alerted almost daily so that rest was impossible. Late on 31 Octo-

Men of Reserve-Infanterie-Regiment 103 before deployment at Houthulst Forest. On the back (dated 20 October) a soldier writes: '...*we are no longer in the forest, since there was no position left to hold there, but instead directly behind it. It's a bit better here, but not pleasant either. Have you read about the latest fighting at Langemarck and Draaibank? It was simply horrific. Now 181, 106, 107, 104 and 134 are deployed here, all Saxons.*'

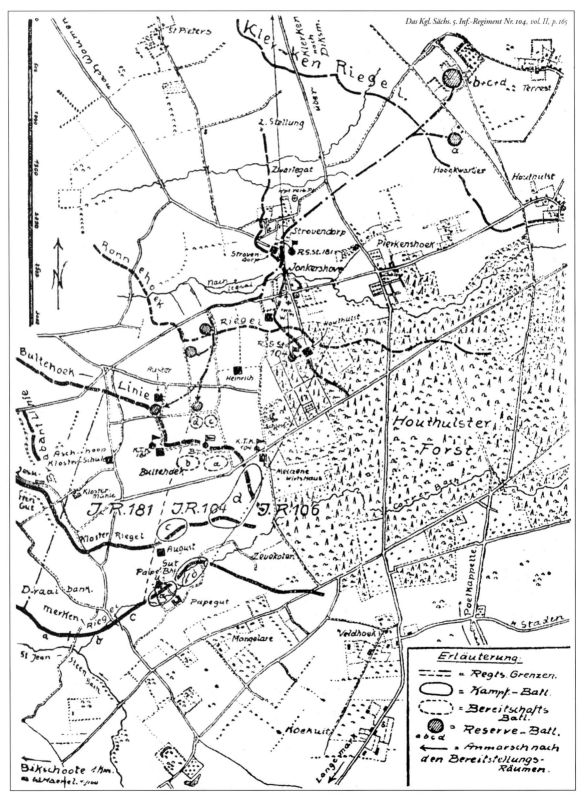

Das Kgl. Sächs. 5. Inf.-Regiment Nr. 104, vol. II, p.165

Sectors held by IR 134 (partly visible), 181, 104 and 106 on 19 October. IR 107 lay beside IR 106, and RIR 103 on the flank north of Veldhoek.

A battle-scarred KTK bunker in Houthulst Forest during the winter of 1917–1918; note the size of the shell holes in the foreground.

The defence of Houthulst Forest by '*Leipziger Infanterie*', as depicted by Saxon soldier-artist Fritz Buchholz for '*Sachsen in großer Zeit*'.

Sachsen in großer Zeit,
vol. III, p. 203

ber they returned to the sector, now with IR 107 on the right and 106 in the centre. The Entente offensive had halted here, and both sides were busy wiring and reinforcing their lines under intermittent shelling. Meanwhile Saxon patrols waded through the mire to locate and harass the enemy, using flares to simulate the presence of forward posts. The infantry regiments were relieved again late on 8 November, all now at half strength. 58. ID held the sector for the last time from 19–28 November, concentrating on drainage and salvage of abandoned equipment. On 23–25 November

patrols from IR 107 crept forward as far as Draaibank and clashed with the French. Enemy artillery was growing more active, but a predicted raid did not occur before the division was relieved at the end of the month. It now spent a month recovering near Torhout where FAR 115 was joined by Prince Ernst Heinrich, now trained as an artillery officer. Late on Christmas Day 58. ID took over a sector east of Poelkapelle with *Gruppe Staden*. By New Year the swamp in front had frozen over, and the ghastly wasteland became eerily beautiful.

6.4 219. INFANTERIE-DIVISION

Facing the Portuguese at Aubers Ridge

219. INFANTERIE-DIVISION (7.1917)

47. Ersatz Inf. Brig.: RIR 101 | IR 391 | IR 431

4. Esk. / HR 19

ArKo 219: EFAR 45 (plus attached units)

Pi. Batl. 219: Pi. Komp. 254 | Res. Pi. Komp. 54
　　Mw. Komp. 416

Divkonach 219: Div. Ferna. 219

San. Komp. 404

The division was formed with elements mainly from 19. Ersatz-Division and XII. Reserve-Korps in January 1917 on the Vosges front. It was transferred to 6. Armee at the end of June, and assigned to *Gruppe Aubers* (XIX. Armee-Korps) on 8 July. Four days later the division assumed control of *Abschnitt Fromelles*.

Sadly neither IR 391 nor IR 431 produced a published history. RIR 101 held its sector with two battalions abreast –

Abschnitt Aubers on 1 August 1917. The artillery *untergruppen* for sub-sectors *Freiburg* (IR 431), *Erfurt* (IR 391) and *Düsseldorf* (RIR 101) include all nine batteries of EFAR 45 and one of obsolete 9cm guns.

A few of the division's many dead. Soldat Burkhardt (RIR 101, KIA on 23 July) und Gefr. Franz Möbius (IR 391, KIA on 27 July) are now buried at the *Soldatenfriedhof* Fournes-en-Weppes.

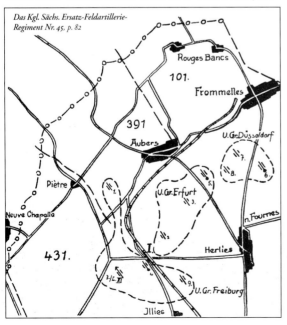

Victorious trench raiders pose with some of the sixty-one Portuguese prisoners (including one officer) taken on 14 August. Ltn. d. L. Arthur Vorwerg (whose company led the assault) and Ltn. Otto Hamann (whose platoon secured the right flank) of IR 431 were both awarded the MStHO(R).

each with two companies forward, one in support and one in reserve at Fromelles. The first line (about 300m from the enemy) was mostly derelict and held only by posts and patrols. Another 600–800m behind was the main defensive line or *Kistenstellung* ('crate position'), built up with piles of wooden crates full of earth due to the high water table. Ruined houses reinforced with concrete provided this well-wired line with dugouts and MG posts, and further strongpoints studded the open ground beyond. The *II. stellung* immediately north of the Fromelles–Aubers road was in better shape and equipped with deep concreted dugouts. Approach routes to the *II. stellung* were good, while those to the *Kistenstellung* were dilapidated and dangerously exposed. The sector possessed well-developed field telephone, field railway and provisioning systems.

Along most of its front the division faced the increasingly homesick and demoralised Corpo Expedicionário Português (Portuguese Expeditionary Corps), with British 57th Division to their north. The entire Saxon sector and immediate rear were frequently harassed by aircraft and 'nuisance' artillery fire, with mortar fire and nocturnal machine-gun fire in the forward area. Patrolling and bombing exchanges were frequent. Shortly after midnight on 29 July a patrol codenamed *Fallobst* (windfall) from

RIR 101 waylaid a group from 2/4th Battalion the Loyal North Lancashire Regt in no man's land. Four prisoners were taken, and a total of four 1st Class and four 2nd Class Iron Crosses awarded. A major raid was launched on 14 August in cooperation with the neighbouring Bavarians (1. bRD). Several companies from IR 391 and 431 temporarily occupied Portuguese trenches over an area 500m wide by 200m deep, while accompanying *pioniere* planted demolition charges. It appears that IR 431 in particular encountered some serious localised resistance, and overcame it after heavy hand grenade fighting. On the Portuguese side Alferes (ensign) Hernâni Cidade of Batalhão de Infantaria 35 distinguished himself by taking several prisoners, supposedly including an officer. Nevertheless the operation was judged a great success, and mentioned in OHL's order of the day. The Saxons felt that they had shown their clear superiority to the enemy, and morale soared in the 219. ID while it continued to sink in the CEP.

Despite these distractions the division was able to spare battalions from RIR 101 as reinforcements at La Bassée in late July, and again at Hulluch from 15 August (when a battery of EFAR 45 was also provided). On the night of 29–30 September units of 50. Reserve-Division began to relieve the Saxons. The relief was completed on 3 October, and the division transferred to the Baltic front.

6.5 23. RESERVE-DIVISION

Defending Langemarck and Passchendaele

46. Res. Inf. Brig.: GRR 100 | RIR 102 | IR 392

2. Esk./s. Res. HR

ArKo 118: RFAR 23 (plus attached units)

Pi. Batl. 323:
 4. Komp., 2. & 5. Res. Komp. / Pi. Batl. 12
 Mw. Komp. 223 | Scheinwerfer-Zug 309

Divkonach 423: Div. Ferna. 423

San. Komp. 270

The division arrived near Bruges at the end of March. On 10 April it began to relieve 208. ID in *Abschnitt Langemarck*, with IR 392 at Struyve and RIR 102 at Pilkem. The right flank was extended on the 17th, with LIR 388 (loaned from the adjacent 19. LD) at Het Sas and GRR 100 at Bikschote. At first the peace was disturbed only by occasional barrages and brief sightings of the enemy. While the French facing GRR 100 and LIR 388 remained quiet, the British were more active by late April, raiding a machine-gun post of IR 392 on the 30th. Artillery exchanges grew heavier in May, with long-range shelling and air raids on the rear. Early on 6 May raiders from RIR 102 took three prisoners without loss. This attracted severe artillery retaliation, as did a raid by IR 392 on the 14th. Another by RIR 102 on the 27th failed due to an increasingly alert enemy.

23. RD was relieved at the end of May, but alerted on 12 June as reserve to *Gruppe Dixmuide*. On the 23rd it reoccupied the Struyve (IR 392) and Pilkem (GRR 100) sectors with RIR 102 in reserve. British patrolling increased from early July, and RIR 102 was repeatedly alerted before

relieving GRR 100 on the 10th. The enemy now had aerial dominance and their reinforced artillery systematically devastated the sector; on the night of 14–15 July the Saxons endured a massive gas barrage from Livens projectors. The front line was now a scorched moonscape shrouded in dust and gas, and the defenders suffered agonising thirst. RIR 102 lost at least one man snatched by raiders on the 18th, but killed four when they returned on the 20th. GRR 100 relieved RIR 102 on the night of 23–24 July, and faced daily probing attacks which were only repelled after protracted grenade battles. On the 28th the British took part of the front line, and RIR 102 was sent to eject them that night. The shelling was so severe and the going so bad that only III./102 could get forward, and not all the ground was retaken. After a final attack on 29 July the relief by 3. Garde-Infanterie-Division began. Despite the devastating bombardment most of the infantry escaped before the offensive of 31 July, though RFAR 23 remained in action. Relief of III./392 by I./Lehr-Infanterie-Regiment was incomplete when the British broke into *Abschnitt Struyve* from the front and left flank. Both battalions resolutely defended the KTK, and Major Johannes Schäffer of III./392 was killed. By 10 am the ammunition was spent. Breakouts were led by Ltn. Braun and the badly wounded Ltn. d. R. Arthur Prager of IR 392, who received the MStHO(R).

23. RD spent August recovering east of Bruges, and much of September as *eingreifdivision* to *Gruppe Dixmuide*. On the 20th it was rushed to *Gruppe Ypern* east of Passchendaele, losing thirty-nine men of RIR 102 killed or injured in a train crash. On the nights of 22–24 September it re-

The Pilkem sector (divided into company subsectors 'a' to 'd'), as occupied alternately by GRR 100 and RIR 102 from 23 June to 30 July 1917.

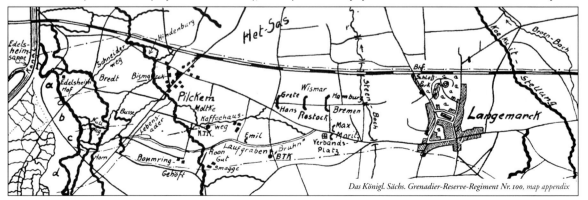

Das Königl. Sächs. Grenadier-Reserve-Regiment Nr. 100, map appendix

A 'beer evening' for the men of Reserve-Infanterie-Regiment 102 at the windmill in Maldegem in April 1917.

A section of *Reserve-Grenadiere* posing behind the front with the long-range 'dud' which nearly killed them on 7 May 1917.

Surviving comrades attend a mass burial for the fallen of Infanterie-Regiment 392 at Westrozebeke on 4 May 1917.

lieved 2. Garde-Reserve-Division in *Abschnitt C* (see map p. 150), a cratered wasteland with few concrete bunkers. Each regiment had three companies in line and one near the KTK, with the other battalions deployed in depth. Losses were grave from the outset, due to constant heavy shelling that peaked at evening. On the 24th a raid on IR 392 was beaten off. The next day the bombardment raged all night and rose to drum fire at 5.30 am on the 26th, while the artillery was gassed and a dense smokescreen obscured all signal flares. At 5.50 am British 58th and 59th Division attacked with tank support, breaking into the IR 392 sector and rolling up I. / 100 and II. / 102 from the flank. Unable to retreat through the mire, 5. / 102 was wiped out. The badly wounded Oltn. d. R. Johannes Gelfert of 3. / 100 (awarded the MStHO(R) for heroism on 28 July) led a counterattack from the right while 7. / 100 met the British drive on s'Gravenstafel head on. The enemy were halted at Aviatik Farm and driven back, and a rough front line formed with III. / 100 in support. Meanwhile the *regimentsgefechtsstand* of GRR 100 had been destroyed by a direct hit, killing twenty-three; the survivors moved to the BTK. Further south the depleted IR 392 defended its KTK, while elements of II. / 102 held out around *Rote Haus* (Judah House). About 2 pm the first elements of 4. bID got through the withering barrage to Mosselmarkt, and

joined the ongoing counterattacks after 5 pm. A renewed British assault on the extreme left at 6 pm was pre-empted and driven back by 9. and 10. / 102 together with the adjacent FR 34. By evening the line had stabilised despite relentless shelling, which escalated again early on 27 September. The heterogeneous garrison beat off a renewed assault on the left at 6.40 pm, after which the Bavarians took over more of the front. After the recapture of the *Almenhof* (Otto Farm) by IR 392 and the divisional *Sturmkompagnie* on the evening of the 28th, the survivors of 23. RD were finally withdrawn and sent to the Eastern Front.

---

23. Res. Div. Abt. IIa Nr. 3649; Div. Stabsquartier 25 July 1917 *Sächsisches Staatsarchiv Dresden, Signatur 13187, Nr. 1791*

As a result of the shortage of coffins, burial of the fallen in the *zeltbahn* will now be adopted. This is to be expressly noted on the muster roll excerpt for the graves registration authority. In addition a note is to be attached to every corpse in a well-sealed bottle, on which the name and unit of the deceased are recorded in large and clear letters.

If desired, funerals can take place in the cemetery near Reserve-Feldlazarett 8 in Hooglede.

signed Frhr. v. Leukert[9]

Minenwerfer observation post in the forward positions of IR 392 at *Struyve-Hof* (Hindenburg Farm, 1 km south of Pilkem) in spring 1917. Note the lucky horseshoe and the helmetless spectators in the background, indicating that this is the quiet period of April or early May.

Canteen of '*Pionierkompanie Biesold*' at Spriet (east of Poelkapelle) in summer 1917. Hauptmann der Landwehr Johannes Biesold was awarded the MStHO(R) for his leadership of elements of Pionier-Bataillon 323 west of Passchendaele from 23 to 30 September. Despite multiple wounds, he continued to direct the supply of ammunition and food to the front line from reserve positions west of the *Pottegemsgut*.

Survivors of Infanterie-Regiment 392 enjoy a well-earned 'seaside holiday' during the division's assignment to *Gruppe Gent* in August 1917.

The Passchendaele sector (*Abschnitt C* of *Gruppe Ypern*) held by 23. RD on 26 September, showing command posts and machine-gun positions of RIR 102 (plus the attached MGSSA 71). *Rote Haus* is the westernmost of the small cross-hatched blobs in the RIR 102 subsector.

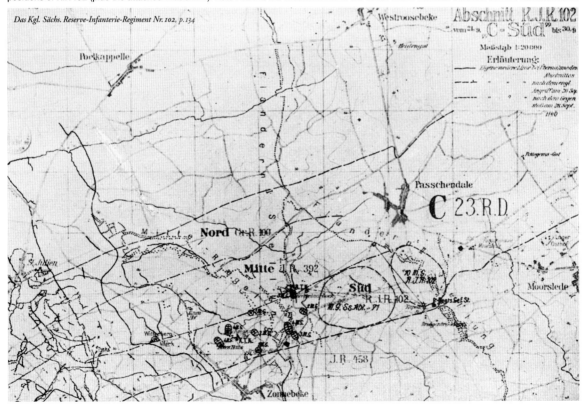

Pre-deployment group picture of 4. Kompagnie / Grenadier-Reserve-Regiment 100 at Bruges in April 1917. Of these men thirteen would be killed or go missing (and later be declared officially dead) at Pilkem. A further forty-six would be lost at Passchendaele, where this company was overrun in the front line on 26 September together with 2. / 100. Taking into account those invalided out due to wounds or captured, virtually no-one in this photo would be left by October. The brief deployment at Passchendaele cost 23. Reserve-Division as a whole an estimated 255 killed (including fourteen officers), 1302 wounded (including thirty-seven officers) and 721 missing (including twelve officers), the great majority of them from its three infantry regiments.

6.6 24. Reserve-Division

Quiet days at Passchendaele

24. Reserve-Division (4.1917)

48. Res. Inf. Brig.: RIR 104 | RIR 107 | RIR 133
3. Esk. / s. Res. HR
ArKo 120: RFAR 40 (plus attached units)
Pi. Batl. 324:
  1, 4. & 6. Res. Komp. / Pi. Batl. 12
  Mw. Komp. 224 | Res. Scheinwerfer-Zug 12
Divkonach 424: Div. Ferna. 424
San. Komp. 271

24. RD arrived in the Gent area from the Arras front at the end of March. On 10 April it began to relieve 185. ID in *Abschnitt Passchendaele* on the left of 23. RD, with its southern flank on the Ypres–Roulers railway. RIR 104 had fought off a British trench raid mere hours before its trans-

port to Flanders, and found its new sector at Verlorenhoek a pleasant change. Shelling was intermittent and aerial activity lively when the weather allowed, but little was seen of the enemy even by the nightly forward patrols. After an uneventful tour the division was relieved on 25–27 April and transported to the Eastern Front.

After major victories in Galicia the division headed west again. On 4 November it was assembled southwest of Bruges and assigned to *Gruppe Dixmuide* but not deployed. From the 24th it occupied new billets near Staden as *eingreif-division* to *Gruppe Staden*, providing working parties to 41. ID in the Houthulst Forest sector. Four days later it was suddenly ordered to leave for the Cambrai front, and left Flanders for good at the end of November.

6.7 32. INFANTERIE-DIVISION

In the battle for Herenthage Park and at Warneton

32. INFANTERIE-DIVISION (8.1917)

63. Inf. Brig.: IR 102 | IR 103 | IR 177

3. Esk. / HR 20

ArKo 32: FAR 64 (plus attached units)

Pi. Batl. 140:

    2. & 5. Komp., 3. Res. Komp. / Pi. Batl. 12

    Mw. Komp. 32 | Scheinwerfer-Zug 12

Divkonach 32: Div. Ferna. 32

San. Komp. 28

On arrival at the beginning of August the division was assigned as *eingreifdivision* to *Gruppe Wytschaete* and FAR 64 committed piecemeal to its front-line divisions. Though 32. ID was new to Flanders, its commander Generalmajor Gustav von der Decken[10] had already distinguished himself with 106. Reserve-Infanterie-Brigade (53. RD) in 1915. From 10 August the infantry was often alerted to take up reserve positions, suffering some losses to artillery (see pp. 228–229). On 18 August III. / 177 was sent to support 34. ID in its sector on the Menin Road, and by the 20th the entire IR 103 was near Dadizele as counterattack reserve to that division.

On 22 August British 14th Division pushed forward to the edge of Herenthage Park in an assault spearheaded by tanks. Most of 32. ID now lay behind the 34. ID sector on high alert, and by nightfall I. and II. / 177 held the *Wilhelmstellung*. Early next day I. / 177 supported IR 67 in a counterattack which met three advancing tanks, and fell back into the park with severe losses. For the next attempt on 24 August IR 67 and I. / 177 were joined by elite stormtroops[11], including flamethrower

teams from 9. / Garde-Reserve-Pionier-Regiment. At 6 am this assault force surged through the park bombing, burning and bayoneting anyone in their path. Simultaneously 5. / IR 30 thrust southwards from *Abschnitt Hooge* to the Menin Road and dug in. This position grew increasingly tenuous, since the attackers in *Abschnitt Becelaere* had taken so many casualties to machine-gun fire and artillery drop-shorts (including all the Saxon company commanders) that they could not hold the western edge of the park against British counterattacks. A new ad-hoc line within the park was reinforced by II. / 177, and the assault renewed at 12.45 pm. Much of the lost ground was retaken and held despite counterattacks and heavy shelling. By evening the lines stabilised with the British holding the dry lakes west of Herenthage Chateau and the western end of Inverness Copse. During the night the assault troops were relieved, including the shattered I. / 177. II. / 177 took over the front line in *Abschnitt Becelaere* and III. / 102 in *Abschnitt Gheluvelt*, though 34. ID remained in overall command.

Throughout 25 August the defenders were relentlessly shelled. After the explosion of a nearby munitions dump the BTK bunker in *Abschnitt Hooge* attracted such intense shelling that it had to be abandoned. When I. / 103 struggled through clouds of gas to relieve I. / 30 that night they were warned that the KTK bunker too was untenable, and it was empty when finally destroyed the next morning. Further assaults on the park had been beaten off in the evening, while another at 4 am after a heavy barrage was wiped out by army stormtroops and flamethrower teams, who had been preparing to attack with III. / 177 in support. The relief

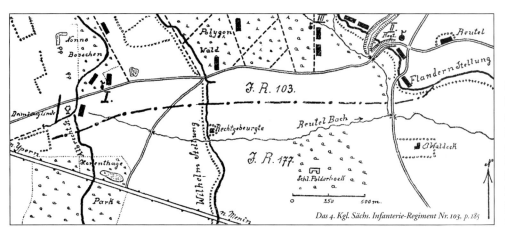

Main trench lines held by IR 103 (*Abschnitt Hooge*) and IR 177 (*Abschnitt Becelaere*) on the Menin Road from 26 August. IR 102 held the left flank (*Abschnitt Gheluvelt*).

Das 4. Kgl. Sächs. Infanterie-Regiment Nr. 103, p. 185

Sectors held by IR 103 and 177 from September 1917, on the south and north banks of the Lys respectively; IR 102 held the right flank. The *weberei* (weaving mill) near La Basse Ville is Carlin Mill, target of '*Unternehmen Näher heran*' on 16 September. This raid established that 32. ID was again facing 14th Division, and earned Ltn. Achim Wittrow of the divisional *sturmabteilung* the MStHO(R).

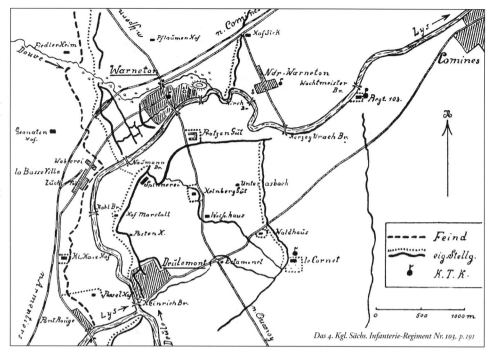

Das 4. Kgl. Sächs. Infanterie-Regiment Nr. 103, p. 191

The *Wachtmeisterbrücke*, with the *regimentsgefechtsstand* of Infanterie-Regiment 103 beyond on the right (see map above)

The *Betonturm* (concrete tower) in Warneton was originally hidden inside a multistoried house, but grew increasingly exposed as this and all of the surrounding houses were destroyed. Although a major target, it survived everything the enemy artillery could throw at it while IR 103 was in residence.

Infantrymen of IR 102 in the divisional rear area in autumn 1917, posing with one of their regiment's twelve 7.58cm light *minenwerfers*.

of 34. ID was completed during the day and 32. ID took command. The next British attack about 6 am on 26 August was supported by tanks, nearly all of which were soon knocked out or hopelessly mired. Further attacks in the afternoon and evening were also bloodily repulsed in increasingly heavy rain. At 9 pm a taskforce from IR 177 with divisional and army stormtroops tried to clear Inverness Copse with flamethrower, artillery, *minenwerfer* and air support. This too failed in the appalling conditions and no more attempts were made.

Over the nights of 29–31 August 32. ID was transferred to the Warneton sector, beating off further attacks during its relief. Although out of the battle, it continued to endure severe shelling, air raids and frequent Livens projector attacks; by the end of the year Warneton would be completely levelled. At 5.30 pm on 16 September a party from 5. and 6./177 and the divisional *sturmabteilung* raided Carlin Mill, blowing up a concrete dugout and taking one prisoner and a machine-gun. IR 102 was equally successful on the 17th and IR 103 on the 18th, while IR 177 beat off a raid on the 20th. The Saxons continued to raid and take prisoners from the fought-out units opposite throughout the year. From the end of November shelling intensified and IR 103 fought off two strong night attacks. No offensive ensued, but the year ended bitterly when the revered commander of IR 177 Major Lucas Kirsten was killed by a sniper on 10 December.

'Our dear comrade' Gefr. Hermann Hanke of 8./ Feldartillerie-Regiment 64 was killed in action on 18 November 1917, and is now buried at the *Soldatenfriedhof* Bousbeque.

Private soldier (*soldat*) of Reserve-Infanterie-Regiment 243 in the typical field
uniform of 1917–1918 – steel helmet, gasmask in its 'readiness canister' (*bereitschaftsbüchse*), ankle boots with puttees
(*wickelgamaschen*) and a baggy all-arms
feldbluse made of poor-quality fabric.
By 1918 uniform wool was routinely eked
out with a variety of questionable *ersatz*
materials such as nettle fibres, producing a variety of shades when dyed (and
more so after exposure to the elements
in the field).

1918 in Flanders
....

It was clear that the war must end in 1918, due to the crippling shortages caused by the British blockade. Troops released by victory in the east gave Germany a temporary numerical advantage in the west, which would be steadily negated by the arrival of the Americans. OHL therefore planned to force the Entente to negotiate on acceptable terms via a massive offensive effort in the spring. Privately, the King of Saxony was deeply sceptical of this desperate strategy. Acutely aware of growing unrest among his subjects, he also received candid accounts from his youngest son of conditions at the front in Flanders. In March he backed the City of Hamburg's peace proposal, based on evacuation of France and Belgium plus a plebiscite in the *Reichsland*. Lacking the support of almost all other German states, the proposal was never published.[1]

As the year opened **32. ID** held the line on the Lys and **58. ID** facing Poelkapelle. **53. RD** was at Houthulst Forest, but left in mid-February. In April 32. ID spearheaded the *Georgette* Offensive at Armentières and supported the attack on Bailleul, while 58. ID pursued the British as they retired from Langemarck. Subsequently 32. ID held new sectors at Bailleul and opposite Nieppe Forest (May–June), **23. RD** at Calonne-sur-la-Lys (June–August) and the partly-Saxon **IR 354** with 216. ID east of Bailleul (May–June). 58. ID held the Kemmelberg (May–August) and was slated to take part in the cancelled *Hagen* Offensive. From September onwards **23. ID**, 23. RD and **40. ID** were almost constantly engaged in a desperate fighting retreat.

In early 1918 a distinction was drawn between *angriffs-divisionen* (for use in the attack) and *stellungsdivisionen* (for use only in holding ground). Of those discussed in this chapter, all but 40. ID and 216. ID were rated as 'attack divisions'. The downgrading of the 'active' 40. ID is striking; '*Sachsen in großer Zeit*' laments that 1917 took a disproportionate toll of its combat veterans and junior leaders, and that the teenage replacements were no substitute. Divisional organisation was modified in early 1918 by the return of heavy artillery as an organic asset. The major effort however was to restore the *angriffsdivisionen* to full mobility after years of trench warfare; even in 32. ID during *Georgette* two field batteries (5. and 7./FAR 64) lacked horses and were initially left behind. The main changes in the infantry

occurred later, dictated by a growing lack of replacements. By OHL order of 18 August 1918 regiments were to dissolve one company per battalion (often the 4., 8. and 12. Komp.) if average battalion fighting strength fell below 650 men, and by the armistice this was almost universal. Shortages of *pioniere* prompted the dissolution of divisional *minenwerfer* companies in September, and the grouping of their 17cm mMW into regimental companies with the infantry's existing 7.58cm lMW. From early 1918 this had a new mount for flat-trajectory fire and was the main infantry anti-tank weapon, even after the 13mm *Tankgewehr* was issued in the summer.

The enemy observed that in 1918 "*it was soon noticed that practically all Saxon troops were not fighting as well as before*".[2] This opinion was reflected in their downgrading of *all* Saxon divisions by one on a four-point scale. It may be surmised that with no threat of occupation or annexation to motivate them and a relatively urbanised population infused with left-wing politics, Saxon morale never recovered from the failure of the offensives. Left holding rudimentary trenches on recent battlefields, the men had ample time to ponder both the grim strategic situation and the gulf between their dismal rations and peacetime-quality supplies found in British stockpiles. The decay was aggravated by air-dropped enemy propaganda. In May a mysterious epidemic broke out in the Kemmelberg sector – this '*Kemmelfieber*' was the first (and less lethal) wave of the 'Spanish flu' pandemic which ravaged the army and home front alike.

During the retreat battles all divisions were irreversibly depleted by casualties and desertion, though in many regiments the residual hard core fought with exceptional tenacity. As the end neared there was civil unrest behind the lines, and even those sympathetic to the Germans were understandably aloof. After the armistice the new regime introduced the system of democratic soldier's councils (*soldatenräte*) which had wrecked the Russian Army. Most rear-area formations fell into anarchy, and combat units struggled to get home. As per the Russian example, volunteer *freikorps* formed to do the work of the paralysed regular units, guarding Saxony's border with the new Czechoslovak state and helping to defeat attempts to establish communist rule in the ruined kingdom.

7.1 32. Infanterie-Division

In the *Georgette* Offensive at Armentières and Bailleul, and the disaster at Nieppe Forest

32. Infanterie-Division (4.1918)

63. Inf. Brig.: IR 102 | IR 103 | IR 177
4. Esk. / HR 20
ArKo 32: FAR 64 | (p.) Fußa. Batl. 80
(plus attached units)
Pi. Batl. 140:
    2. & 5. Komp., 3. Res. Komp. / Pi. Batl. 12
    Mw. Komp. 32 | Scheinwerfer-Zug 12
Divkonach 32: Div. Ferna. 32 | Div. Funka. 20
San. Komp. 28

The division was withdrawn in early January to train for mobile warfare, and took over the front between Deulemont and Frelinghien on 15 February. It began regular raiding on 11 March with '*Münchner Fest*' in the IR 102 sector on the left, taking two prisoners from British 38th Division. On 25 March IR 177 and 103 were moved south, with IR 103 now on the left at Wez-Macquart.

The eighty-eight batteries assigned to ArKo 32 were in place by 4 April, and pounded towns and gun lines around Armentières with over 15,000 mustard gas shells on the 7th.

The infantry moved southwest of Lille that night, and into no man's land north of Rouges Bancs on the night of 8–9 April. Each regiment had an escort battery of FAR 64 plus *pioniere*, 17cm *minenwerfers* and (at least with IR 177) flamethrowers. Several British Mk IV tanks assigned to support IR 103 broke down behind the lines, aggravating traffic jams that hindered the division's deployment.

The bombardment opened at 4.15 am against British artillery and communications. From 6.45 am the infantry lines were pounded and the Portuguese (see p. 145) began to flee. In the confusion IR 103 overran outposts on the British flank and reached their line *before* the creeping barrage advanced. At 8.45 am IR 103 and 177 stormed the first position, hindered only by a few machine-gun nests and boggy ground. When the barrage ended at 9.55 am, IR 103 was into the second position and IR 177 attacking Croix Maréchal. While IR 102 and 177 turned right IR 103 drove towards Erquinghem. However resistance was stiffening and fire support limited as FAR 64 relocated, and the advance stalled at Fleurbaix–Delettrée–Bois Grenier. Reinforced by I. / IR 102 and III. / IR 177, attacks on Erquinghem resumed at 5.30 am

Dishevelled infantrymen of 10. / Infanterie-Regiment 177 (many of them decorated veterans) in the winter of 1917–1918.

on 10 April, and the northeastward push at 8 am. By 5 pm the British were retiring over the Lys at Erquinghem with the Saxons in hot pursuit, but progress to Armentières was slowed by German shelling on the railway line. An advance party from 2./IR 103 was unable to prevent demolition of the railway bridge at 6.45 pm, and the British held off the fresh IR 94 (38. ID) long enough to blow the bridge at Pont de Nieppe at 10.40 pm (see p. 177). That night patrols crossed the Lys from Erquinghem to Houplines by raft, while *pioniere* built new bridges. Over 2,300 prisoners and thirty-eight guns had been taken (including a 12" railway gun by I./IR 102 at Dormoire) and morale was high. The main attack by IR 94 on 11 April bogged down before Nieppe, and it was relieved by IR 103. Next day the Saxons took the town unopposed but were halted by machine-gun nests on the Steenwerk road, which were cleared by evening with close support from FAR 64 and MwK 32.

After a brief rest 32. ID joined the attack on Bailleul on 15 April. Following an hour's bombardment IR 102 assaulted the Mont de Lille at 4 pm under murderous shelling and machine-gun fire, and took it by 7 pm. Having secured the town, attacks on the hills north and east of Bailleul on 16–17 April failed bloodily under intense artillery fire. The offensive was called off, and the demoralised Saxons counted the cost (see pp. 233–234) while consolidating their line under relentless shelling. After crushing a major French attack on 4 May they were relieved a week later.

At the end of May 32. ID relieved 48. RD opposite Nieppe Forest. Incessantly harassed by artillery and aircraft, the division was ravaged by influenza in late June. On the 28th the Saxons were thrown back to the Plate Becque by a massive British assault, with over 700 missing and many dead. The relief began next day and the shattered division went to the Verdun front.

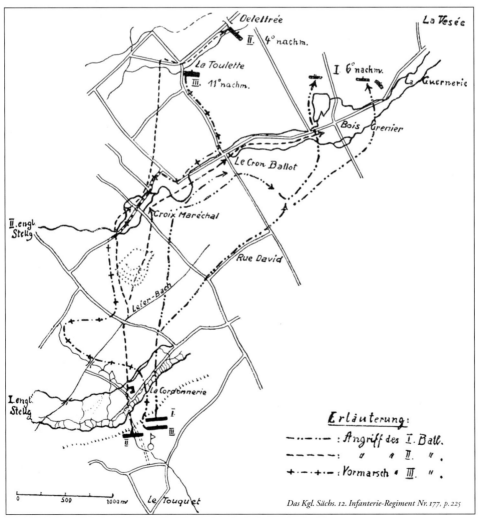

Das Kgl. Sächs. 12. Infanterie-Regiment Nr. 177, p. 225

The advance of IR 177 through the flank of British 40th Division on 9 April 1918. IR 103 attacked left of IR 177 (III./IR 103 left, I./IR 103 right, II./IR 103 reserve) with II./IR 369 of 10. Ersatz-Division attached on its left. Following IR 177, II. and III./IR 102 plus the *sturmabteilung* rolled up the British front line as far as Bois Grenier.

I./IR 102 followed IR 103, which took the British line between Fleurbaix and Delettrée by mid-afternoon before the advance stalled in the absence of promised close fire support and tanks.

One of the eight 17cm mMW of Minenwerfer-Kompanie 32 on the march in April 1918. The unit also possessed four 25cm sMW, but only the 17cm was mobile enough to follow the infantry. Even so, it was a challenge to move the 483kg weapons and their ammunition across the swampy wasteland (made worse by recent heavy rain), and they did not reach the infantry until evening on 9 April.

The sector opposite Nieppe Forest held by IR 103 from 27 May to 1 July 1918, alongside IR 29 (16. ID); IR 102 was on the right of IR 177. The *Pankebach* (Plate Becque) lay further east along most of the divisional frontage, anchoring the *artillerieschutzstellung* (artillery security line). British attackers on 28 June found the rudimentary trenches barely wired and the shelters not even shrapnel-proof.

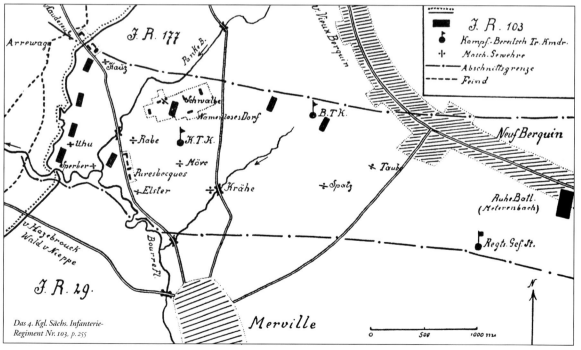

7.2 58. INFANTERIE-DIVISION

The pursuit to the Steenbeek and defence of the Kemmelberg

58. INFANTERIE-DIVISION (5.1918)

116. Inf. Brig.: IR 106 | IR 107 | RIR 103
4. Esk. / UR 18
ArKo 57: FAR 115 (plus attached units)
Pi. Batl. 142: 2. Res. Komp. / Pi. Batl. 22 |
Pi. Komp. 115 | Pi. Komp. 404
Mw. Komp. 58 | Handscheinwerfer-Trupp 127
Divkonach 58: Div. Ferna. 58 | Div. Funka. 135
San. Komp. 58

The line facing Poelkapelle was held from left by IR 107, IR 106 and RIR 103, each deployed six companies deep. The line facing Poelkapelle was held from left by IR 107, IR 106 and RIR 103, each deployed six companies deep. Initially neither the outpost line nor the *hauptwiderstandslinie* (the Schaap-Balie–Wallemolen road) was wired, and some men went astray before a fence was put up. Luckily the British did not attack before the thaw on 13 January and onset of rain made much of the area impassable. While shelling and air raids were sometimes severe, Saxon patrols went unchallenged. On 24 January a party from I. / IR 103 seized two prisoners. Relief by 204. ID began the next day, and 58. ID

returned on 25 February with Prince Ernst Heinrich commanding 9. / FAR 115. Until late March the enemy was jumpy and shelling heavier. 5. / IR 107 lost fifteen dead to a direct hit at Westrozebeke on the 9th, and the town was abandoned. Saxon trench raids repeatedly failed, twice due to artillery drop-shorts. *Gruppe Staden* was reduced from three to two divisions on the night of 23–24 March, and IR 107 moved to Houthulst Forest with IR 106 on its left.

From 3 April 58. ID held the whole 7km front of the dissolved group with two battalions each of (from left) IR 107, RIR 103 and IR 106. The expected enemy retirement due to the *Georgette* Offensive (contingency *Blücher*) began on the 16th and was spotted by IR 107, which reached the Steenbeek that night. Due to delays issuing the *Blücher* orders and appalling terrain the others were still advancing next day. Under heavy fire RIR 103 took Langemarck and IR 106 the Broenbeek. An attack on 18 April was cancelled due to the strength of the enemy line, and the tired and near-mutinous state of the supporting 83. ID. The evacuated zone was now plundered of supplies and strategic materials.

Verbandsplatz 'Wilder Mann', a 58. ID dressing station at the junction of the Westrozebeke–Hooglede and Oostnieuwkerke roads in March 1918.

The Saxons were disgusted to find that (probably due to rapid unit rotation) the enemy had neither dug latrines nor buried even their own dead from the autumn, hundreds of whom were interred over the following weeks. The enemy now grew more aggressive, snatching five men of 12./IR 107 early on 23 April. A failed Belgian raid on the 26th revealed that their front now extended to the IR 107 sector, and a slight withdrawal on the left was spotted the next day. Patrols from II./IR 107 crossed the Steenbeek and saw serious fighting, losing some men cut off by the enemy before the bunker line 300m beyond was secured. RIR 103 also advanced two days later. After defeating minor raids the division was relieved on 12–15 May. A royal parade at Roeselare on the 16th was disturbed by an air raid, forcing the King to take cover with his troops. Prince Ernst Heinrich now left FAR 115 for the Garde-Reiter in the east.

Late on 20 May 58. ID began to take over the dreaded Kemmel sector. North of the Kemmelberg II./IR 106 was forced to eject the French before occupying its new front line, and soon suffered from severe shelling and the outbreak of 'Kemmelfieber'. RIR 103 on the right was luckier. On 27 May the division took part in a major attack. Followed by III./IR 107, IR 106 took the French front line but was weakly supported on the flanks. Falsely believing that they had been relieved most of them withdrew after dark, and a counterattack drove III./IR 107 back to the old front line. IR 107 took over the sector on the 29th and was likewise heavily shelled and ravaged by influenza, though few man died. Prisoners were taken in morning raids by RIR 103 on 4 June and IR 106 on 13 June, having relieved IR 107 late on the 7th.

From 14–29 June 58. ID rested at Menen and Kortrijk. On returning its sector was extended left with RIR 103, IR 106, IR 107 (Kemmelberg) and the borrowed bRIR 21 (Kemmel village) in line. On the 30th the regimentsgefechtsstand of IR 107 was targeted by a railway gun (described as 38cm) which scored three direct hits after over a hundred shots. Rescue efforts by MwK 58 were abandoned that night, as the last six buried men were believed dead. After cries were heard a survivor was dug out on 3 July and another on the 4th. Major preparations for the Hagen Offensive provoked increasingly severe shelling by the enemy, identified as British 41st Division when Soldat Friedrich Stemmler (3./IR 107) took three prisoners in a solo daylight raid on the 2nd. A similar raid by Vfw. Lehmann and two men took seven more on the 21st, while multiple British raids were beaten off. After colossal artillery battles from 19–23 July the tension eased. From 27 July IR 107 traded places with IR 106, while RIR 103 replaced bRIR 21. Tired and demoralised by the cancelled offensive, 58. ID was withdrawn on 4–7 August.

Vfw. Emil Thomas, born at Mügeln near Oschatz on 6 January 1880, was acting as *ordonnanzoffizier* (company orderly officer) of 10./IR 106 in spring 1918. Seen here with his *bursche* (batman) at their concrete dugout south of Houthulst Forest, Vfw. Thomas was killed in the advance north of Langemarck on 17 April.

Positions held by IR 107 on the Kemmelberg from 29 May, with RIR 103 to the right and bRIR 21 (16.bID) to the left.

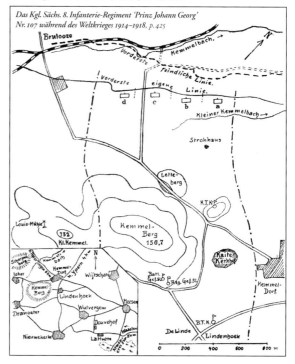

An unidentified unit of 58. Infanterie-Division in reserve positions behind the Kemmelberg in early June. On the back is a message dated 13 June: '*In the night of 14 to 15 June we'll be off again from here, we still don't know where to yet.*' While the divisional artillery remained in the sector, the infantry were sent to Basse-Flandre, Gullegem and Halluin for rest and training.

Reserve positions of I. Batl. / IR 107 in late June 1918, on the reverse slope of the *Nachtigallhöhe* (Hill 63) at Ploegsteert Wood. A poster on a tree (left) warns of the undiminished threat of aerial observation: 'enemy aircraft can see you here; vehicles must not stop here!'

7.3 53. RESERVE-DIVISION

A bleak winter at Houthulst Forest

53. RESERVE-DIVISION (1.1918)

105. Res. Inf. Brig.: RIR 241 | RIR 242 | RIR 243

Res. Kav. Abt. 53

ArKo 155: RFAR 32 (plus attached units)

Pi. Batl. 353:

    4. Res. Komp. / Pi. Batl. 12 | Res. Pi. Komp. 53

    Mw. Komp. 253 | Res. Scheinwerfer-Zug 27

Divkonach 453: Div. Ferna. 453

San. Komp. 535

The division detrained at Bruges just before Christmas after a gruelling six-day journey from Galicia. Unusually cold weather failed to dampen morale, and the veterans were glad to see Flanders again. While billeted east of Bruges to guard the coast and Dutch border, the infantry were re-trained and rearmed with the MG 08/15. On 23–25 January they took over the Houthulst Forest sector. Conditions in the waterlogged trenches and shell holes were ghastly, aggravated by frequent heavy shelling. The artillery too suffered severely under counter-battery fire directed from the air. To minimise casualties each subsector was lightly held in depth by a 'half-regiment', with two companies

each in the front line and in 'near' and 'far' *bereitschaft* (immediate reserve). Companies rotated every two and 'half-regiments' every six days.

On the afternoon of 9 February raiders led by Ltn. Marx of RIR 241 and Ltn. Zeissig of RIR 242 set out with blackened faces to attack a listening post near Mangelare before the arrival of the stronger 'night shift'. Approaching in daylight, they found the position unexpectedly strongly held but escaped with a wounded prisoner (from 2nd Btn. Manchester Regiment / 32nd Division) leaving two of their own dead behind.

53. RD was relieved on 14–15 February and sent to the Cambrai front. After months of intense fighting, the depleted division and its infantry regiments were dissolved in late September. II. and III. / IR 241 arrived in Lichtervelde on the 27th as a draft for 23. ID, then in mid-relief (see p. 168). Moved up in reserve during the next day's disaster, they were in the front line on the 29th. Reduced at first to a composite battalion, they formed two companies of the rebuilt LGR 100 at Gent in late October and RIR 241 finally ceased to exist.

Positions held by RIR 241 around Houthulst Forest in 1918. From 23 January to 15 February the regiment was on the left flank of 53. RD south of the forest, with RIR 242 in the centre and RIR 243 on the right; see the map on p. 142 for more detail of this sector.

Following the disbandment of their division and regiment the 'orphaned' II. and III. / RIR 241 held a rough defensive line east of the forest on 29 September, attached respectively to GR 101 and LGR 100 of the depleted 23. ID.

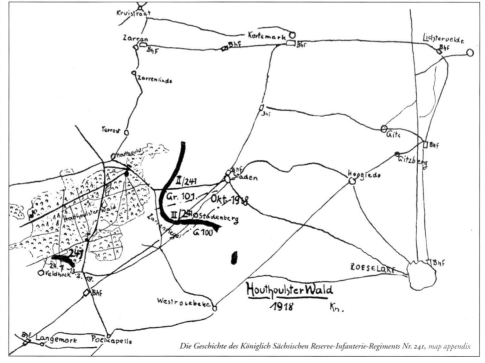

Die Geschichte des Königlich Sächsischen Reserve-Infanterie-Regiments Nr. 241, map appendix

7.4 INFANTERIE-REGIMENT 354 WITH PRUSSIAN 216. INFANTERIE-DIVISION

Between Bailleul and the Kemmelberg

The supernumerary Landwehr-Brigade-Ersatz-Bataillon 48 was raised in August 1914 and sent to the fortress of Breslau in Silesia. Mobilised together with much of the garrison as '*Division Menges*' (later 88. ID) in November, it saw heavy fighting against the Russians during 1915. In August it became the III. Bataillon of the mixed IR 354, which was transferred to 216. ID in September 1916 (together with IR 182) and sent to Transylvania. By 1918 it was the only Saxon element in the division and the only Saxon battalion still with a mixed regiment. Nevertheless it retained its distinct identity, and its officers also served at times as regimental adjutant and commander of II. / IR 354.

216. ID left Rumania in April 1918. During a brief stop in Leipzig, about thirty Saxons went AWOL; while some returned freely, others had to be hunted down. Upon arrival at Orchies and St. Amand on 14 April, IR 354 was deloused and quarantined due to endemic typhus in the Balkans. After retraining and reorganisation to western standards, 216. ID was ordered to relieve 117. ID west of Bailleul. Despite the protests of some Alsatians at fighting the French,

IR 354 took over the shell-torn Ravetsberg on the nights of 7–9 May. Initially in reserve at Pont de Nieppe, III. / IR 354 saw no action until the regiment moved to a subsector between Koudekot and Loker on the 22nd. This ghastly wasteland of roughly wired shell holes lay only 3km west of the Kemmelberg, and the battalion endured increasingly frequent gas shelling and aerial bombing.

On 27 May 9. / IR 354 took part in a local attack by the neighbouring 16. bID near Loker. Though initially successful, the captured ground could not be held against the overwhelming firepower of the French artillery. A second attempt the next day also failed, and III. / IR 354 was relieved on 30 May. Initially in *bereitschaft* it returned to Pont de Nieppe on 6 June, where it was so badly hit by influenza as to be rendered unserviceable. After the division was relieved and IR 354 moved to Meulebeke on the 19th the epidemic spread to the whole regiment, subsiding by mid-July with few deaths. After further training (and issue of the *Tankgewehr*), 216. ID entrained for Laon on 28 July to join the fighting southeast of Soissons.

The Saxon element of the regimental band, which played daily at the marketplace in Meulebeke while the regiment was quartered there. The Saxon battalion and MG companies were billeted 3km away at Marialoop. On the back (dated 16 July) one of the bandsmen writes of a different kind of 'conquest': "*Our regiment was on the Kemmelberg, but for three weeks now we've been here at rest. An offensive should shortly be taking place here near Ypres – on the daughter of mine hosts. This sort of offensive is more to my taste.*"

7.5 23. Reserve-Division
Resisting to the bitter end from Calonne-sur-Lys to Anzegem

46. Res. Inf. Brig.: GRR 100 | RIR 102 | IR 392
2. Esk. / (s.) s. Res. HR
ArKo 118: RFAR 23 | I. Batl. / (p.) Res. Fußa. Regt. 15
Pi. Batl. 323:
> 4. Komp. / Pi. Batl. 12 | 4. Res. Komp. / Pi. Batl. 22
> Mw. Komp. 223 | Handscheinwerfer-Trupp 133
Divkonach 423: Div. Ferna. 423 | Div. Funka. 143
San. Komp. 270

[margin: 23. Reserve-Division (6.1918)]

At the end of June 23. RD moved from Vimy Ridge to *Abschnitt Calonne*, where (from left) GRR 100, RIR 102 and IR 392 held the line from Quentin to south of Merville. The outpost zone was thinly wired, the non-continuous front line only 1m deep and other lines barely extant, all overlooked by balloons so that any daylight movement was fired upon. Its crude dugouts gave little protection and its squalid billets were blamed for the outbreak of Spanish flu. The Saxons began improvements at once, harassed day and night by artillery and aircraft. A major attack was expected, and there were many false alarms. After a failed daylight raid on 25 July, Vfw. Noack of 1. / RIR 102 approached the British lines with four men under a Red Cross flag. Two Tommies helped retrieve his casualties. Amused by his refusal to say whether his unit was Saxon, they invited him to desert and expressed deep war-weariness.

Work on the old line was halted at the end of July and the new *Grüne Stellung* east of Calonne occupied on 4–5 August, screened by rearguards which fell back slowly to the new outpost zone. On the 8th the pursuit reached the *Grüne Stellung*. The British were repeatedly beaten off in close combat, but after dark pushed back the left of IR 392 and right of RIR 102. Losses had been significant, and the *sturmkompagnie* was dissolved on the 11th to replenish the regiments. During the night of 12–13 August the British advanced on the right flank near Regnier le Clerc, but were routed while deploying in a bombing attack led by Ltn. d. R. Weber[3] of 8. / IR 392.

23. RD fell back to the *Karlstellung* on the night of 15–16 August, but in expectation of an offensive the phased retirement was accelerated and this line abandoned for the *Friedrichstellung* on the Lawe three nights later. The British advanced cautiously, attacking at 9.15 am on 22 August after a prolonged artillery exchange. Initially pushed back on the right, by midday the Saxons had counterattacked taking thirty-two prisoners. Demolitions began on the 26th for the next withdrawal, and I. and II. / RIR 102 extended the division's left flank. On the 29th I. / IR 392, III. / RIR 102 and III. / GRR 100 under Oberst Fürstenau of RIR 102 occupied the *Wotanstellung* in the Aubers-Fromelles area, to which the division retired after heavy rearguard fighting on the Lawe on 29–30 August and south of Laventie on 3 September.

GRR 100 fought off a probe west of Aubers on the 12th, after which the new front was held by two regiments. RIR 102 went into reserve on 15 September and returned late on the 26th, aiding a counterattack by GRR 100 which reversed a minor breakthrough and took several prisoners. A further screened withdrawal followed on the night of 28–29 September.

Next day GRR 100 (now in reserve) was sent north by truck to plug a gap north of Menin, on the right of the intermingled 39. ID and 40. ID. Unaware of friendly or enemy dispositions, II. and I. / GRR 100 dug in facing north and west on the line Artoishoek–Vijfwegen–Hill 41–Kezelberg. Four guns of RFAR 23 joined them during the night, and contact was made with adjacent units. The enemy were located at Zuidhoek and in the northern part of Vijfwegen, where an attempt to eject them at dawn failed with severe losses. From midday GRR 100 beat off three attacks by 36th (Ulster) Division on Hill 41, each preceded by sharp bombardments including smoke and incendiaries. About 4.30 pm the Irish drove the depleted Saxons from the hill, but were thrown back an hour later in a furious charge led by Ltn. d. R. Landgraf and the regimental snipers. Now backed by the artillery of 39. ID, GRR 100 smashed two more attacks before nightfall and another twelve on 1 October, during which Hill 41 was again lost and retaken. After further attacks on the 2nd, GRR 100 was relieved north of the Kezelberg road by bRIR 1 (1. bRD) that night. Its achievement was commended in the *amtliche Heeresbericht*[4] and its commander Oberstltn. Ralph von Egidy awarded the *Pour le Mérite*.

Meanwhile 23. RD retired to the *Englos-Stellung* southwest of Lille on the night of 1–2 October, and 47th Division dug in opposite on the 5th. After beating off raiders early on the 4th and capturing four, GRR 100 also enjoyed a lull. From 7 October it endured systematic shelling, bombing and strafing from the air, while the *Englos-Stellung* too was heavily shelled from the 9th. The British attacked Hill 41 again in force on 11 October behind a powerful creeping barrage, driving back bRIR 1 and encircling a flank post of GRR 100. The Bavarians retook the hill that afternoon, but the Saxon advance was stalled by machine-gun fire on the road to Vijfwegen. On the 13th the British smashed through the left flank of bRIR 1 at 6 pm and secured the hill, since GRR 100 was now too weak to eject them. The next morning the regiment was hit by a colossal bombardment and an encircling attack from north and south in dense smoke and fog. The reserve companies were ambushed as they rushed to assist, and the guns of 7./RFAR 23 and FAR 80 spiked by their crews before they were overrun. On 15 October GRR 100 regrouped at Bissegem as a nominal battalion only 120 strong, and Obersltn. von Egidy and his adjutant Ltn. d.R. Oehmig were both wounded by a shell.

23. RD was now falling back toward the Scheldt. On 16 October the last Saxons abandoned Lille. Daringly, rearguards of RIR 102 raided Fort Englos and snatched two prisoners before escaping over the Canal de la Deule and blowing the bridges. Regrouping east of Tournai, the division was rejoined by the few survivors of GRR 100. On the night of 23–24 October it went into line near Anzegem, with RIR 102 on the right alongside 40. ID. After drum fire heavily laced with gas and smoke the British attacked in force on the 25th. The bombardment had carved bloody holes in the line, reducing 2./RIR 102 to an officer and eight men, but somehow the depleted regiments held out. After driving off weak patrols on 28–29 October, they faced another massive assault supported by tanks on the 31st. On the right II./RIR 102 beat off the attack, claiming four tank kills. III./RIR 102 was overrun, but I./RIR 102 filled the gap and artillery and *minenwerfers* stopped the tanks. 23. ID crossed the Scheldt that night at Oudenaarde, and was inspected by the Kaiser on 4 November before retreating to the *Antwerp-Maas-Stellung*. As the American assessment states, it had shown "*considerable power of resistance*".[5]

Leutnant Hans Rohde was born on 11 May 1895 in Bautzen. He joined Grenadier-Regiment 101 in the field as a *fahnenjunker* in August 1915 and was commissioned that November. Over the next two years he fought at La Ville aux Bois, on the south bank of the Somme, and against the Nivelle Offensive in the Champagne. In January 1918 he fell ill. After treatment in Saxony, he was assigned to Grenadier-Reserve-Regiment 100 and took over the 4. Kompanie. He was killed in action on 1 October 1918 in the defensive fighting north of Menin – according to the regimental history, on his feet and firing his rifle. He was buried at the *Ehrenfriedhof* in Lauwe near Kortrijk, and reinterred at the *Soldatenfriedhof* Menen (Block I Grave 2726).

„Ich bleibe euch treu, Kameraden!"

Instructions for German Prisoners

You fought desperately to the last round of ammunition before you were taken prisoner. Now you stand under French or English interrogation. In the fighting you were a hero. And now before the eyes of the enemy – for whom you were and are always the dirty Boche, the bestial Hun, who lurk maliciously nearby just to see you act the coward – will you be slack or foolish? Do you not see the enemy's secret contempt for the wretch who betrays his Fatherland: 'Look how the cowardly pig talks his comrades to their doom!' and their scornful sneer at the idiot, who chatters like a washerwoman: 'They really are the greatest asses, these stupid Boches!'

Who would care to earn a reputation as one or the other of these? Remember how you once stood at the advanced post before many a heavy attack. What would you have said if you had known that a comrade had betrayed everything to the enemy? You are a captive now certainly, but you will never lose your honour! 'I remain loyal to you comrades!', so you should say in captivity also.

You know what they want to get out of you.

They will ask you:	Your answer will be:
'What is your division? Your corps?' –	I do not know. I have only been out of hospital and with the regiment for the past eight days.
'Where are the German artillery positions?' –	I came up into the line for the first time last night. I was thinking of things other than batteries at the time.
'Do you have letters with you? Papers?' –	I never take such things with me to the front. What I received I tore up immediately after I had read it.
'How is your own line?' –	I had neither the time nor the inclination to go for a walk, I just knew the sector of my platoon.
'When do your reliefs take place?' –	They are supposed to vary. I have not had any yet.
'Which units are further back?' –	I have no idea about that. The numbers are always concealed.
'How are your rations?' –	We have enough.
'And your morale?' –	We would rather die, than be dependent on England all our lives and labour only for the benefit of others.
'And your replacements?' –	Young and old. But all healthy.
'What do you think about the victory of the Entente?' –	None of us believes in that.
'But surely Germany wants peace?' –	An honourable peace, yes. Because each of us knows what he is fighting for.
'Surely there are a lot of strikes in Germany?' –	I know nothing about that.

In this way you are to answer the enemy interrogator, If you do not prefer to declare from the outset 'I will say nothing. I will not betray my Fatherland!' And if the other party then throws aside his friendly mask and threatens or even ill-treats you, you are to draw yourself up with redoubled pride as a German man before the stranger who berates you, and look him in the eyes: 'If one of your soldiers made such disclosures, would you not consider him a dishonourable wretch?'

Das Königl. Sächs. Reserve-Infanterie-Regiment Nr. 102, p. 177

Translation of a leaflet from 1918 on correct behaviour under enemy interrogation, entitled '*I remain loyal to you, comrades!*'

7.6 23. INFANTERIE-DIVISION

A bloody fighting retreat from Houthulst Forest to the Scheldt

45. Inf. Brig.: LGR 100 | GR 101 | SR 108
1. Esk. / HR 20
ArKo 23: FAR 12 | I. Batl. / Fußa. Regt. 19
(plus attached units)
Pi. Batl. 12: 1 . & 3. Komp. / Pi. Batl. 12 |
    Handscheinwerfer-Trupp 125
Divkonach 23: Div. Ferna. 23 | Div. Funka. 12
San. Komp. 30

[sidebar:] 23. INFANTERIE-DIVISION (21.9.1918)

Since March Saxony's 'guards' division had fought in four major battles. It arrived at Orchies on 6 September within days of bloody fighting against tanks near Bapaume which cost it 117 dead, 653 wounded and 1,064 missing. For lack of replacements one company per battalion was dissolved, while MwK 23 was absorbed by regimental *minenwerfer* companies.

23. ID began to relieve units of 13. RD and 11. bID from Langemarck to the Corverbeek late on 26 September (from left: SR 108, LGR 100, GR 101). Unusually all arms were relieved at once, and the last guns were hauled into Hout-hulst Forest the next night. The forward battalions were still struggling through unfamiliar wasteland in the dark at 2.30 when devastating drum fire erupted. The slaughter was dreadful and confusion total, and the Belgian assault at 5.30 am behind a creeping barrage swiftly overran the survivors. The remaining infantry lost heavily in counter-attacks and attempts to hold successive lines as the flanks collapsed, while the stranded artillery threw their breech-blocks into the mire. By evening the front was at the *Zarren-riegel* (Zarren–Stadenberg–Westrozebeke). On the left the first line was now held mainly by III. / bIR 11, while II. and III. / RIR 241 reinforced the grenadiers. The Belgians attacked without artillery support early on the 29th and were cut down; when the shelling did begin it had little effect on the thin and ill-defined German lines. However threats to their flank forced the Bavarians and SR 108 to bend back (see map p. 163), and 4. / LGR 100 was cut off and destroyed before III. / RIR 241 counterattacked.

The division retired to Gits that night, having lost eighty-nine confirmed dead, 622 wounded and 1,795 missing plus

Two days before their departure for Roulers on 22 September, Generalfeldmarschall von Hindenburg visited the division at Orchies. Here the *'Ersatz-Kaiser'* inspects Schützen-Regiment 108; the traditional *tschako* has now disappeared from the field even as parade-wear.

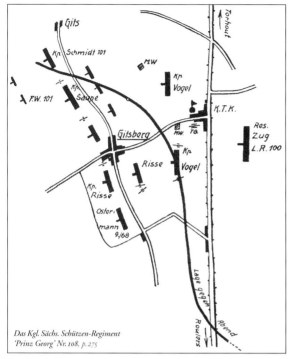

Das Kgl. Sächs. Schützen-Regiment
'Prinz Georg' Nr. 108, p. 275

Positions held by *Bataillon Kirchner* (SR 108) alongside *Bataillon Panse*
(LGR 100) from 2.45 pm on 14 October with reinforcements from
GR 101 and remnants of RIR 68 (16. RD). The battalion withdrew to the
thick black line by evening after 16. RD had fallen back.

most of its guns. Each infantry regiment (including RIR 241) reformed as one battalion of one MG and three rifle companies plus a *minenwerfer* platoon. Early on 14 October '*Regiment Watzdorf*' (*Bataillon Panse*/LGR 100 and *Bataillon Kirchner*/SR 108) deployed behind 16. RD east of Hooglede, enduring drum fire and gas shelling from 6.15 am. When sent to occupy the town it found the enemy there. In desperate fighting the *artillerieschutzstellung* north and east of Hooglede was held until 1 pm against French infantry and tanks as well as German drop-shorts. The Saxons then fought near Gitsberg until evening, destroying several tanks with *minenwerfers*. However too few survived the next morning's drum fire to prevent a French breakthrough at Gits, and upon withdrawing to the next line LGR 100 was only seventy strong. Now comprising all the divisional infantry, '*Regiment Watzdorf*' withstood a major attack east of Lichtervelde on 16 October and minor rear-guard actions before reaching Gent on the 19th.

All three regiments were now rebuilt with men from the baggage, RIR 241 and other remnants, and relieved 2. GRD at the bend in the Scheldt around Semmerzake on 3–5 November. The French won a small bridgehead at Eeke on the 8th with massive artillery support, but were held at bay there until 23. ID retired to the *Antwerp-Maas Stellung* on the last night of the war.

After a long and exhausting journey hindered by mutinous *etappenschweine*, the survivors of Schützen-Regiment 108 reached Dresden-Reick on 15 December 1918, where they were deloused and housed in civil quarters in the southeast of the city. Demobilisation began four days later.

7.7 40. INFANTERIE-DIVISION

Desperate defensive fighting from the Wytschaete Salient to the Scheldt

88. Inf. Brig.: IR 104 | IR 134 | IR 181

2. Esk. / HR 19

ArKo 40: FAR 32 | (p) Fußa. Batl. 403

Pi. Batl. 141: 3. Komp. / Pi. Batl. 22

    Res. Pi. Komp. 54 | Mw. Komp. 40

    Handscheinwerfer-Trupp 131

Divkonach 40: Div. Ferna. 40 | Div. Funka. 171

San. Komp. 48

40. ID arrived in Roubaix on 1 September following severe fighting alongside 23. ID near Bapaume, and began to relieve 236. ID in the deceptively quiet sector between Zillebeke and the *Bayernwald* a week later. After three hours of drum fire, the British attacked in heavy rain behind a creeping barrage early on 28 September. Having broken through the adjacent 12. bID, they encircled *Doppelhöhe 60* and the Saxon front collapsed. On the left, IR 134 held out on the *Dammstrasse* (see map p. 81) until all units fell back to join 39. ID on a new front between Becelaere and Houthem. 40. ID retired behind 39. ID that

night to the *Flandern-I-Stellung* north of Wervik. The next day 39. ID was thrown back to this line, where GRR 100 plugged the open flank right of IR 172 (see p. 165). The attacks ended on 2 October and 40. ID was relieved a week later.

The division halted the breakthrough of 14 October between Wevelgem and Gullegem, partly by counterattack. Joined by the depleted GRR 100 it held out until nightfall on the 15th, then retired over the Lys to the line Marcke–Harelbeke. Its right flank was almost turned next day before 6. and 7. Kavallerie-Schützen-Division counterattacked. By 18 October it had cleared the east bank of the enemy and thwarted all attempts to cross. Briefly relieved, it rejoined the battle near Vichte on the 20th. With 23. RD now on its left it held its line east of the Waregem–Anzegem railway against the full weight of the offensive on the 25th. Greatly depleted, it was relieved that night and crossed the Scheldt near Oudenaarde. From the night of 1–2 November it defended the riverbank southwest of the city for six days before retiring toward Brussels.

The IR 104 sector in mid-September; bIR 28 (12. bID) was on the right and IR 181 on the left. IR 134 held the division's southern flank.

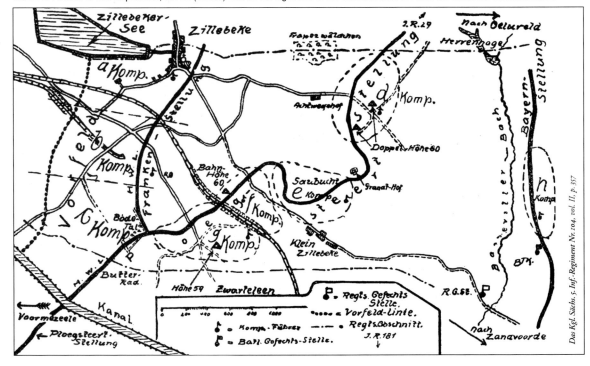

Das Kgl. Sächs. 5. Inf.–Regiment Nr. 104, vol. II, p. 357

CHAPTER 8
INDEPENDENT UNITS

A young signaller in training with Nach-richten-Ersatz-Abteilung 12 at Dresden in 1918, wearing the uniform of the peacetime Telegraphen-Bataillon 7 (re-markably for the date, in peacetime quality). Apart from the tiny Festungs-Fernsprech-Kompanie 7 in Mainz, this was the only signals unit in the Saxon Army at the outbreak of war. In August 1914 it mobilised telephone units for the Saxon corps staffs, and telephone and radio units for the staffs of 3. Armee and 8. Kavallerie-Division. By the end of 1917 a new signals (*nachrichten*) service encompassed telephone, radio, signal lamp (see p. 71), messenger dog and carrier pigeon troops. The number of field units had been greatly increased, and Nachrichten-Ersatz-Abteilung 12 and 19 set up respectively at Dresden and Zeithain. All wore the uniform of the peacetime battalion, with sleeve in-signia to identify individual units; these patches began to disappear in 1916.

In addition to its corps and divisional units (and 'permanent' elements of 3. Armee and the *Südarmee*) the Royal Saxon Army fielded a bewildering array of smaller formations, operating under the control of non-Saxon higher authorities or of OHL itself. These eventually included many former corps assets such as heavy artillery and telephone units, which became permanently detached from their parent staffs when left in place after a corps relief. Even divisional units could become OHL assets – such as several regiments of field artillery in late 1916, some *minenwerfer* companies and various units of the dissolved 53. RD in autumn 1918.

In this chapter we offer a brief survey of some of these units, where enough information exists on deployments in Flanders. For many entire classes of unit this proved unfeasible, notably rear-area troops and the plethora of signals formations (which even lacked individual insignia for most of the war). Some idea of the complexity of the latter subject can be gleaned from the fact that

Divisions-Funker-Abteilung 15 (the only Saxon radio unit with a published history) served with six different divisions when attached to 4. Armee in Flanders between 23 August and 11 October 1917. We have also not attempted a survey of the plethora of anti-aircraft units, beginning with the *ballon-abwehr-kanonen-züge* ('anti-balloon-gun sections') improvised at divisional level in spring 1915 and soon brought under army control. Like aviation units these ultimately came under the control of an entirely new imperial armed force, the *Luftstreitkräfte*, which forms a huge and distinct field of study in its own right.

All of these formations were ultimately administered by the *Kgl. Sächs. Kriegsministerium* in Dresden. The ministry devoted considerable energy to keeping track of and retrieving even individual Saxon servicemen (defined by enlistment in the Saxon Army rather than citizenship) temporarily incorporated by military necessity into non-Saxon units.

The first Saxon **Fußartillerie-Batterien** arrived in Flanders with XIX. AK (**II. / FußaR 19**) and XXVII. RK (**schwere Reserve-Feldhaubitze-Batterie 27**), followed in 1915 by the organic heavy batteries of 58. and 123. ID. All were armed with the 15cm sFH 02 howitzer. In early 1915 the depot of FußaR 12 at Metz formed two batteries with the obsolete 21cm *mörser* of 1899, which lacked the recoil cylinder and shield of the modern gun. From at least June 1915 to March 1916 **Mörser-Batterie 202** supported the Marinekorps on the coast, firing from the *Tempelhofstellung* south of Slijpe (site of a ruined Templar preceptory) toward Nieuwport and Ramskapelle. By June 1916 **Mörser-Batterie 201** was attached to XIII. AK south of the Menin Road. Both batteries probably remained in Flanders during the Battle of the Somme, as did **Fußa. Battr. 123** (formerly **3. / RFußaR 19**), which remained in the XXIII. RK sector before leaving for the Eastern Front with 123. ID at the end of July 1916.

In spring 1917 a 'standard' mix of high-trajectory and flat-trajectory armament was devised for the *fußartillerie*. Previously FußaR 12 had formed pure 21cm *mörser* battalions and FußaR 19 pure 15cm howitzer battalions (some separately numbered). Both had also raised independent batteries with other weapons, including obsolete and captured types. Under the new scheme most battalions consisted by 1918 of either two batteries of 15cm howitzers and one of 10cm cannon, or two of 21cm *mörser* and one of heavier (13cm or 15cm) cannon. By this time FußaR 12 had gained some 15cm and FußaR 19

some 21cm batteries, making both regiments quite heterogeneous. Saxony's biggest gun was a railway-mounted 38cm '*Langer Max*' (the only one not under naval control) acquired from the unfinished super-dreadnought *SMS Sachsen* early in 1917; its battery (Nr. 1015) never served in Flanders.

Thus the exact composition of the eleven battalions engaged in the Third Battle of Ypres is unclear, but it was undoubtedly the greatest concentration of Saxon firepower ever achieved in Flanders. **II., III.** and **IV. / FußaR 12**, **I. / RFußaR 12** and **Fußa. Batl. 72** were chiefly armed with the *mörser*, whereas **III. / FußaR 19**, **II. / RFußaR 19**, and **Fußa. Batl. 58**, **96** and **404** all had some type of 15cm howitzer as their main weapon. Since **I. / FußaR 19** has a published history, we know that from June 1917 it had two batteries of 15cm *lange* (long-barrelled) sFH 13 and one of 10cm K 14.

Seven battalions supported the *Georgette* Offensive of April 1918 and the attacks on the Kemmelberg. Of these **III.** and **IV. / FußaR 12**, **II. / FußaR 19**, **Fußa. Batl. 72** and **Fußa. Batl. 105** were armed primarily with the fearsome 21cm *lange* Ms. 16, **I. / RFußaR 12** and **IV. / FußaR 19** with the 15cm *lange* sFH 13. In June 1918 the staff of **FußaR 19** under Major Max Schmidt conducted reconnaissance for the projected *Hagen* Offensive. In July **II., III.** and **IV. / FußaR 19** formed a 'field regiment' at Wervik under Major Schmidt's command, which left Flanders when the operation was cancelled.

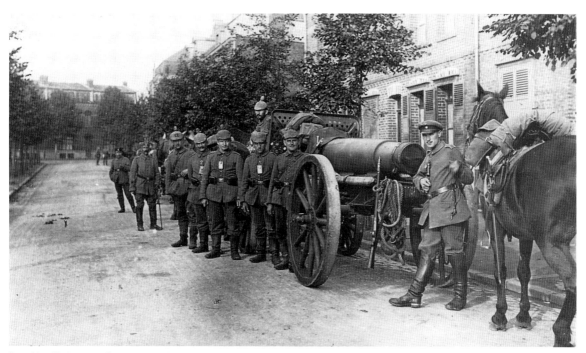

An unidentified 21cm *mörser* battery of Fußartillerie-Regiment 12 at Douai in July 1915, awaiting transport to Flanders. Until 1917 the whole regiment was armed with this gun, which had to be transported in two loads due to its weight; this is merely the *rohrwagen* (barrel wagon).

The precursor to the gun above: Mörser-Batterie 202 with 'thunderous greetings' from Slijpe for the British in Nieuwport. On the back (dated 27 August 1915) a gunner writes '*We've had quite a lazy time for the past three weeks. We had a munitions embargo, and the time really drags when you've nothing to do. Yesterday we fired again, and straight away we had one man killed and one severely wounded.*'

On 22 September 1917 Gefreiter Tetzner of 3. Batterie / Fußartillerie-Bataillon 404 wrote home: '*We are between Ostend and Bruges on the North Sea coast in Flanders. I'm seeing ever more of the world, and in such filthy holes… We have to filch hard potatoes, so that we have something to fill our stomachs.*' His 15cm howitzer battalion had been deployed at Houthulst Forest since early August.

Part of a *parkkompanie* (munitions depot unit) of Fußartillerie-Regiment 12, commanded by a former *train* officer.

Saxon telephonists outside their workplace at the *fernsprechvermittlung* (telephone switchboard) in Kortewilde in May 1917.

The new divisional standard of one **Feldartillerie-Regiment** (of one 10.5cm howitzer and two 7.7cm field gun battalions, each of three four-gun batteries) led to the transfer of many 'surplus' regiments to OHL control from late 1916. **FAR 68** left 40. ID when the division went to the Somme, and its II. Abteilung remained deployed at La Bassée until the middle of October 1916. II./68 then fought at Messines from November to mid-May 1917 (with a short rest in early April). From June to August the entire regiment, now with three battalions, was attached to 16. bID southeast of Messines. **FAR 78** (formerly of 24. ID) returned to Flanders in summer 1917 – from 7 June I./78 fought at Becelaere and III./78 at Langemarck. Initially II./78 (the howitzer battalion) was in corps reserve, but was committed west of Passchendaele on 22 July. The exhausted regiment was relieved at the beginning of August and rearmed with long-barrelled guns (7.7cm FK 16 and 10.5cm lFH 16). On 10 September FAR 78 returned to the battle, mainly between Zandvoorde and Tenbrielen with II./78 further north. It was relieved on 5–6 October and did not return to Flanders. **RFAR 24** was attached to 18. RD as *'sturmartillerie'* in close support of the offensive west of Neuve Chapelle in April 1918. Its I. Abteilung fought at St. Eloi from late May to 2 July, and the others in two divisional sectors near Bailleul in the period 9 May–3 June.

Artillerymen of Feldartillerie-Regiment 78 at the 'Sächsisches Feldartillerie-Rekrutendepot bei der 4. Armee', probably near army HQ in Tielt. Such units were established at army level in February 1917. Like the divisional *feldrekrutendepots* of the infantry, they provided final training for novice gunners (and refresher training for convalescents) under field conditions. A small number of *fußartillerie-ersatzdepots* were formed from November 1916, and a *feld-pionier-rekrutendepot* for each army HQ from June 1917.

Sappers of 3. Reserve-Kompanie / Pionier-Bataillon 22 near Koekelare at Whitsun (23 May) 1915, including two recent recipients of the Iron Cross 2nd Class. This unit was attached to Prussian XXIII. Reserve-Korps north of Ypres from late March or early April 1915, and fought in the offensive toward Het Sas from 22 April. It apparently accompanied the corps to its new sector between the Ypres-Comines Canal and the Douve in March 1916 (see p. 92), and stayed there until at least early August. The company joined Pionier-Bataillon 212 (212. ID) in the Champagne in February 1917 and left for Rumania in March.

Veteran Saxon machine-gunners formed eight **MG-Scharf-schützen-Trupps** in spring 1916, which were merged into four **MG-Scharfschützen-Abteilungen** of the OHL reserve that autumn. The élite 'MG-sharpshooters' were typically deployed in defence of the artillery zone. **MGSSA 51** was heavily engaged from 20 September 1917 near Zonnebeke. The companies of Ltn. Hans Freiherr von Falkenstein and Ltn. d. R. Ernst Kaiser were down to two guns each before the battle of 4 October, in which Kaiser was severely wounded in the head; both officers received the MStHO(R). **MGSSA 52** fought at Terhand that November.

In August 1914 each of the two peacetime **Pionier-Bataillonen** mobilised two battalion staffs ('Stab I' and 'Stab II'), four field and two reserve companies. From these units one field battalion each was formed for XII. AK, XIX. AK and XII. RK, plus a fourth in OHL reserve. This **II. / Pi. Batl. 22** (4. Feldkompanie, 1. and 2. Reserve-Kompanie) under Major Karl von Kobyletzki initially served at Metz and on the Verdun front. It arrived in Flanders on 8 November 1914 and was attached to XV. AK throughout 1915. On 19 February Hptm. Theodor Guericke led bombers from 4. Feldkompanie in the assault on Herenthage Chateau, and was awarded the MStI IO(R) on 16 March. 2. Reserve-Kompanie saw heavy action at Hill 60, notably destroying a dangerous British mine gallery in the night of 28–29 April. Its commander

Hptm. Ernst Schaefer was likewise awarded the MStHO(R). Due to a shortage of specialist '*stinkpioniere*', the battalion helped Pi. Batl. 35 to make a gas attack in the XV. AK sector on 5 May 1915 (see p. 87). It later fought at Verdun in 1916 and was split up in January 1917. 2. Reserve-Kompanie returned to Flanders with 58. ID in October, and with **Pi. Batl. 44** in April 1918. This OHL bridging and road-building battalion was formed for the 1918 offensives from existing units including **Pi. Komp. 254**, which may have served independently in Flanders in 1917.

The Bavarians formed Germany's first **Pionier-(Mineur-) Kompanien** at Vimy Ridge in autumn 1915, but such specialist tunnelling units only appeared in large numbers following the lethal success of British deep mining at St. Eloi on 27 March 1916 (see p. 92). Like the British tunnelers, the *mineure* were also employed in the construction of deep dugouts, demolitions and other hazardous engineering tasks above ground – especially after mobile warfare put an end to mining operations. Casualty lists suggest that **Pi. (Min.) Komp. 311** left the Houplines area for the Somme in September 1916, and was active between the Menin Road and Ypres-Comines Canal from January 1917 until leaving Flanders in May or June. **Pi. (Min.) Komp. 312** lost a man killed near St. Yvon in August 1916, and was then on the Somme and in the Artois mining sectors. It took further losses at

Terhand, Dadizele and Becelaere between September and November 1917, and may have returned to Flanders in 1918.

Pi. (Min.)Komp. 313 and **324** were probably formed by XXVII. RK (see p. 105); the former mined in the Cuinchy/Auchy area from at least May 1916 to late July 1917, and was at Gheluwe in late September and early October. **Pi. (Min.) Komp. 324** was attached to 28. RD on the Somme (La Boiselle/Fricourt) in June 1916, then returned to La Bassée (with a brief excursion to Vimy Ridge). From September it was active near the Ypres-Comines Canal, mainly at Hill 60 and the Bluff (see pp. 126–127). Ltn. d. R. Karl Weihmann received the MStHO(R) and Vfw. Max Puklitsch the MStHM in Gold after they won a deadly race to detonate their gallery ahead of the enemy on 19 March. Ltn. d. R. Heinrich Hülsenberg was awarded the company's second MStHO(R) on 9 August for his daring demolition of two howitzers stranded near enemy lines west of Hollebeke on 11 June. The unit was transferred to the Chemins des Dames in July.

Pi. (Min.) Komp. 414 was formed in Flanders as *Mineur-Kommando Rontz*, then became 'sächs. Infanterie-Mineur-Kompanie B' in April 1917 while attached to 24. RD.

Numbered before July, it was active mainly near Langemark as late as 18 August, then at Houthulst Forest in September and October. It may have remained in Flanders for the duration, and was certainly at Kemmel in August 1918.

In early 1915 a plethora of small *minenwerfer* units were formed, from which divisional companies (each with two 25cm, four 17cm and six 7.58cm weapons) began to be formed in the autumn. **Schwere Minenwerfer-Abteilung 42** is the only such Saxon unit known to have served independently in Flanders, with XXIII. RK west of Bikschote in January 1916; its equipment (though probably not its personnel) was absorbed by Prussian Minenwerfer-Kompanie 245 (45. RD) in April. **Minenwerfer-Bataillon VIII** was briefly deployed to Flanders from OHL reserve for the abortive offensive of August 1918.

Casualty lists indicate that two of the six Saxon **Landsturm-Pionier-Kompanien** served in Flanders. **Ldst. Pi. Komp. XII.1** was at Armentières in May-June 1918. **Ldst. Pi. Komp. XIX.3** was on the Western Front as early as June 1917, and at Houthem in late July. It may have stayed in Flanders into 1918, but was with 2. Armee by August when it was caught up in the Battle of Amiens.

A rebuilding team from Pionier-Bataillon 44 on 24 April 1918 at the Nieppe-Armentières Bridge, recently blown up by the BEF (see p.158).

Tunnellers of Pionier-(Mineur-)Kompanie 311, south of the Menin Road in May 1917. The fresh graves hold reinterred dead of IR 171 (39. ID / XV. AK), dating from 1915 or even 1914.

Grave of Paul Lorenz from Oberplanitz, killed in action with Pionier-(Mineur-)Kompanie 312 at Dadizele on 4 September 1917. Originally buried at Klephoek, he now rests at Menen (Block D Grave 83).

All male Germans aged 17–45 and not otherwise serving were liable for the Landsturm. While trained reservists over 38 formed a few cavalry, artillery and *pionier* units at mobilisation, this militia consisted mainly of **Landsturm-Infanterie-Bataillonen**. Though intended for duties in Germany and the rear areas, some battalions served in the trenches, especially in the East. During the war the Landsturm infantry was stripped of its fitter men, and received convalescents no longer fit for the front (see pp. 182–185). For instance Ldst. Inf. Batl. XII.20 was formed in November 1916 at Aussonce from 1,200 older and less physically fit infantrymen of 53. RD. At least thirteen Saxon battalions were with *Generalgouvernement Belgien* or *Etappen-Inspektion 4* at some point, of which eight were definitely in Flanders. **2. Ldst. Inf. Batl. Chemnitz (XIX.11)** served from 13 September 1914 in Brussels and later in Gent, remaining in Belgium until at least June 1915. **2. Ldst. Inf. Batl. Dresden (XII.2)** was in the Brussels area from 22 September 1914 until sent to the Eastern Front in July 1916. **2. Ldst. Inf. Batl. Leipzig (XIX.2)** was south of Charleroi in October 1915, but later moved to Antwerp. **5. Landsturm-Infanterie-Bataillon Leipzig (XIX.5)** served with 6. Armee at Lille in summer 1916. **Ldst. Inf. Batl. Wurzen (XIX.9)** was deployed initially near Sedan (September–October 1914), then behind the lines in Flanders until transferred to the

Argonne in September 1916. Its duties included railway defence, in which capacity it shot down the famed French aviator Roland Garros at Lendelede in April 1915 (see p. 211). However its main task was to guard the Dutch border, where it lost several men to accidents with the high-voltage electric fence. It was probably a member of this unit whom the American journalist Frederick Palmer encountered at the border on the Roosendaal–Antwerp road in late December 1914: *'One of the conquerors, the sentry representing the majesty of German authority in Belgium, examined the pass. The conqueror was a good deal larger around the middle than when he was young, but not so large as when he went to war. He had a scarf tied over his ears under a cracked old patent-leather helmet, which the Saxon landsturm must have taken from their garrets when the Kaiser sent the old fellows to keep the Belgians in order so that the young men could be spared to get rheumatism in the trenches if they escaped death. You could see that the conqueror missed his wife's cooking and Sunday afternoon in the beer garden with his family. However much he loved the Kaiser, it did not make him love home any the less. His nod admitted us into German-ruled Belgium. He looked so lonely that as our car started I sent him a smile. Surprise broke on his face. Somebody not a German in uniform had actually smiled at him in Belgium! My last glimpse of him was of a grin spreading under the scarf toward his ears.'*[1]

A 'watch party' of 3. Landsturm-Infanterie-Bataillon Chemnitz (XIX.12) in summer 1916 at Oud Fort Spinola near Antwerp, former site of a Spanish fort from 1595. In September the battalion was trained for trench warfare and deployed in a quiet sector of the Argonne front.

Ageing reservists of Landsturm-Infanterie-Bataillon Wurzen (XIX.9) with young Dutch soldiers at a non-electrified stretch of the border fence in 1915.

A standard 7.7cm FK96 n.A. mounted for the 'anti-balloon' role on an elevated turntable and manned by gunners from Reserve-Feld-artillerie-Regiment 53 or 54, ca. 1915.

Sergeant Ernst Postel of Ortsfeste Flak-Scheinwerfer-Zug 697, a stationary anti-aircraft searchlight platoon based with other AA and aviation units near Lille in December 1917.

3. Ldst. Inf. Batl. Chemnitz (XIX.12) was in Belgium from 18 December 1914 to mid-September 1916, latterly around Antwerp. At times it provided guards for French and Italian P.O.W. labourers. **Ldst. Inf. Batl. Zwickau (XIX.18)** served on the Franco-Belgian border from autumn 1914 to at least 1916, with posts at Willems, Cahos, Mouscron and Templeuve. Its HQ was probably at Tournai, where General-major Kaden (cf. pp. 204–211) met its commander Oberst - ltn. a. D. Alfred Schuster (an old friend) on 15 April 1915. **Ldst. Inf. Batl. Pirna (XII.5)** arrived from Russia some-time after February 1916, serving around Antwerp before returning to the Eastern Front by February 1918.

The Landsturm also raised dedicated guard units for P.O.W. and civilian labour such as **Bewachungs-Kompa-nie 69** (at La Bassée in April 1917). Landsturm recruits judged fit for work but not to bear arms (such as the notorious communist Karl Liebknecht) were formed into uniformed but unarmed **Armierungs-Bataillonen** for labour behind the lines.

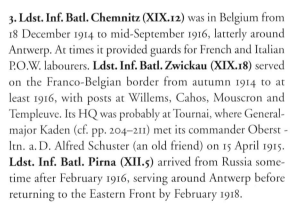

A vizefeldwebel named Herrmann (right) of an unidentified Saxon telephone unit sent this photo home from Beitem in April 1915.

CHAPTER 9
SAXON LIVES AND DEATHS IN FLANDERS

Here we present the war as experienced by individual soldiers, movingly revealed through their photo albums, personal diaries and correspondence with friends and family back home. Many men wrote incessantly while in the line, scrawling postcards in barely legible handwriting on the knee or trench wall, or else by candlelight in a dugout. Although keen to reassure their loved ones, they could often be disarmingly frank. These documents, most of them intended for and seen by only a handful of people, offer vivid and authentic personal perspectives on life and death at and behind the Saxon front in Flanders.

Erich Kühn, Vizefeldwebel

Severely wounded in the First Battle of Ypres. Died in 1918.

Erich Kühn was born in Chemnitz on 22 May 1892, the son of a train driver. By 1913 he had established a career as a bank official, and took the costly but prestigious option of performing his peacetime military service as an *einjährig-freiwilliger* with his local regiment, Infanterie-Regiment 181. As such he was training to become a reserve officer when the war broke out, and in October 1914 was sent to the front as a vizefeldwebel and *offiziersstellvertreter* (acting platoon commander) with **Reserve-Infanterie-Regiment 244**. On the 24th the regiment attacked west of Becelaere, overrunning elements of 2nd Btn. Wiltshire Regt. and 2nd Btn. Royal Scots Fusiliers at the cost of catastrophic losses (see p. 29). Among them was Erich Kühn, severely wounded leading his company in the assault after all of their officers had fallen. His departure from Flanders by hospital train on 2 November was followed by a lengthy period of treatment in Germany, initially in Dessau and later at other institutions including the famous *Berliner Charité*.

We cannot reconstruct his long convalescence or his continuing military career in detail; however after at least a partial recovery Kühn was commissioned as a leutnant der reserve, and served in 1918 as adjutant of Landsturm-Infanterie-Bataillon Döbeln (XIX.8) on the 'home front'. He died at Reservelazarett Döbeln on 26 October 1918 at the aged of 26, probably due at least in part to his severe wounds.

Erich Kühn (sitting behind the table on the right) as an *einjährig-freiwilliger,* during his peacetime training with 2. Kompanie / Infanterie-Regiment 181 at the regiment's barracks in Chemnitz.

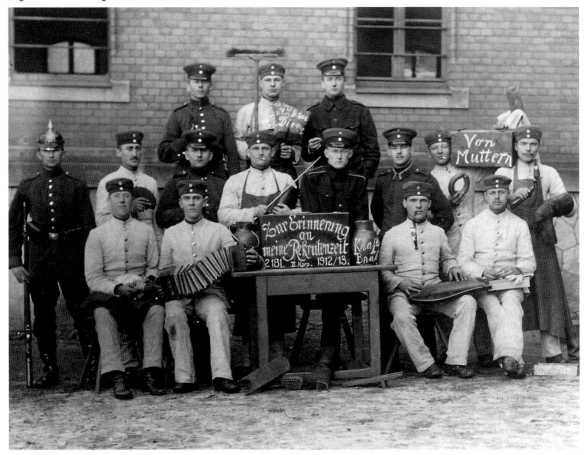

Letter from Erich Kühn to his parents

....

Dessau, 7/11/1914

My dears!

Now at last I have the time to write to you at greater length. I will start again from the beginning. We were marched for a few days after the railway journey. On the 21st we got into a battle, which continued for the whole day. On the 22nd we heard that Duderstädt and Leutnant Lankau had been wounded on the previous day. The fighting continued, then suddenly the hauptmann was wounded and I was acting company commander. Soon after that the *etatsmässige* feldwebel was also wounded. We lay in the trenches all night, then for all of the following day and night. On the 24th we advanced, and first a shot went straight through the full length of my backpack without hitting me. However it came so close that I felt the heat of it on my back.

As I ran further forwards, I received a dreadful blow in the face. After that I was unconscious, but not for long. I was then carried behind a house, and it was not long before the stretcher bearers brought me to the church in Becelaere where there was a dressing station. Our Unterarzt Dr Kolberg bandaged me at once, which was very nice of the fellow, and ensured that I was taken onward to a field hospital. I have much to be thankful to the man for. In the field hospital from which I wrote to you before I was more thoroughly bandaged. But it wasn't cosy there. There was only straw and a sack of chaff for a pillow, besides which the shells kept landing disturbingly close by. On the 30th we went on by motor to Roulers, and then by train to Gent where they removed the splinter, which hurt abominably. But other than that it was really pleasant in Gent.

I haven't described before what I have by way of a wound. It seems that the bullet went in somewhere near the nose and came out at the neck under the ear. I was really lucky – thank God, because if it had hit the carotid artery that would have been it. Anyhow it's all progressing well, I'm not in much pain. I'm only unable to bite, but I'm managing well with food. On 2nd November we set out on the hospital train. First it was supposed to go on to Stettin, then Halle and finally we remained in Dessau. Here I am being extremely well looked after. I share a room with another *offiziersstellvertreter*. We have good beds and very good food. Only, I don't know when I will be able to come home again. As far as my kit is concerned I haven't a thing left. They took the backpack off me when they carried me back and my service belt with pistol, map case and bread bag when they loaded me onto the stretcher. The binoculars and glasses were broken when I fell. My helmet was completely crushed. I handed my sword in a few days before to the company transport, and probably won't see that again either. However they will probably send my trunk to Chemnitz – maybe you'll get it. I can't think of much else to write for the moment. I haven't written to anyone else, back then I had so little time and now I can't because I've lost the addresses. Do write to me soon at greater length, I am curious. But it'll be no use sending me anything if I don't write for it. I hope you are all doing well, for now warmest regards

Erich

Erich Kühn as a vizefeldwebel in Chemnitz shortly before his departure for the front, holding the sword and *portepee* that denote his rank.

From the published history of Reserve-Infanterie-Regiment 244, p. 24. (See also p. 30)

On 25 October the church, although bearing a Red Cross flag visible at great distances, received several direct hits from heavy artillery. The shells punched through the roof into the central hall, which was closely packed with Saxon and Württemberg casualties, and wrought fearful devastation. Under the leadership of the medical officers, all present sprung into action to save the helpless heavily injured cases. But the stretchers were not enough. Under the most intense artillery fire, wagons raced onto the especially vulnerable square in front of the church and were loaded with the severely wounded, while everyone who could still walk clung on to these wagons in order to escape the Hell of Becelaere. Likewise opposite the church at the white house, also densely filled with casualties, shells had penetrated the roof.

Stabsarzt Dr Lohrisch, covered from head to toe in lime and dust, personally hauled the wounded from the burning house. From the rubble of the Church Unterarzt Kolberg managed to rescue Offiziersstellvertreter Kühn, who had been severely wounded on 24 October by five shots to the head. The rescue operation cost the stretcher bearers two dead and three wounded.

The battle front of RIR 244 west of Becelaere, as depicted in the regimental history.

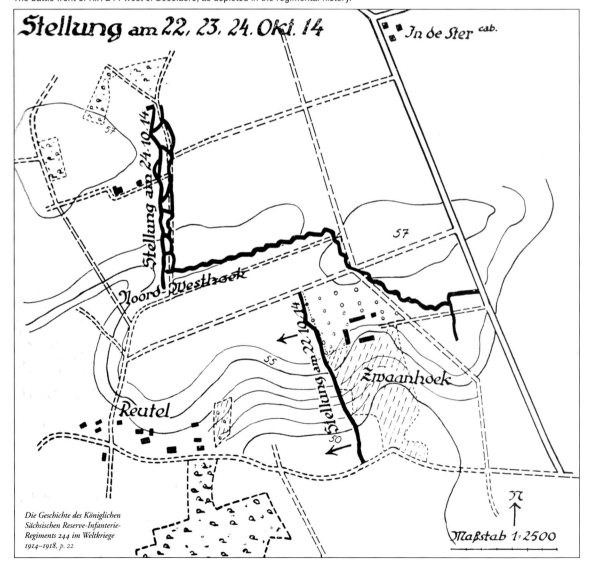

Die Geschichte des Königlichen Sächsischen Reserve-Infanterie-Regiments 244 im Weltkriege 1914–1918, p. 22

Letter from Erich Kühn at the *Berliner Charité* to his parents and sister; the second part of the letter has been added by the doctor in charge of his case, Professor Klein

Berlin, 3/2/15

My dears!

When my Herr Professor Beyer here passed on sister Käthe's greeting, I did not know for the time being what was actually going on. Anyhow your enormous concern is totally groundless, the clouds have cleared. If there had really been any serious grounds for concern, I would already have informed you. As an old soldier proven in battle I counsel you 'don't fret and take your time'.

So for today, finest and warmest regards

Your Erich

Dear Fräulein Käthe!

Well as you can see, your Herr brother is doing quite well. I was unfortunately forced to explore the wound again, because there were still two to three small fragments which had to be removed. After that a fever set in, which however has now passed. Your Herr brother is lying in bed right now rosy as a young girl, his delicate skin tone gives him an interesting complexion. He reads, writes, drinks coffee with enthusiasm, no longer swears and should be on his feet in the next few days. Warmest greetings although (alas, my dear *Fräulein*!) unknown to you

Professor Klein

Erich Kühn as a leutnant d. R. in Döbeln in 1918, after his discharge from hospital. On his new officer's tunic he wears the ribbon of the Iron Cross 2nd Class he won in Flanders.

Erich Kühn's death certificate, recording that he died around 8:30 pm on 26 October 1918 at Reservelazarett Döbeln in Kleinbauchlitz (part of Döbeln since 1922). This document does not indicate the cause of death.

Ernst Krippendorf, Hauptmann der Reserve

A much-loved company commander killed by a stray shell

Ernst Krippendorf was born on 18 November 1875 at Annaberg, a lawyer by profession and a long-serving *jäger* reserve officer. On 9 August 1915 his **1. Kompanie / Reserve-Jäger-Bataillon 25** had just taken over part of the *Eierwäldchen* (Railway Wood) sector, when he fell victim to diversionary operations for the attack of British 6th Division at Hooge (then held by IR 126 / 39. ID). He died of his wounds at Isegem on the 21st, is buried at *Soldatenfriedhof Menen* (Block M Grave 1438) and is commemorated at the *Johannisfriedhof* in Dresden. 106. Reserve-Infanterie-Brigade lost a total of five dead, eighty-nine wounded and four missing in the course of the day's fighting (see Bruckner's account from RIR 242 on p. 218).

From the history of Reserve-Jäger-Bataillon 25, pp. 60–63

From 1 to 6 August the companies saw increasing use as carrying and entrenching parties in the lines of the brigade. Then the whole battalion was deployed to help relieve RIR 242 and 244, and on 8 August took over the latter regiment's sector astride the Ypres–Roulers railway at the so-called *Eierwäldchen*. The scorching August sun parched their bodies, whilst the English artillery incessantly dropped impact-fuzed shells on every significant point in the trench system. The air was abuzz with speculation and rumour of an imminent enemy attack. A tense day fraught with the din of battle was followed at dusk by a dead calm, and an oppressively warm and humid night that brought no relief. By walking his rounds of the sector – easing the tension here and there with his delightful sense of humour – the commander of 1. Kompanie, Hauptmann d. R. Krippendorf, reassured himself of the *jägers'* stubborn determination to hold their line. The sentries and platoon commanders peered deep into the gloom, straining their ears. Nothing. Dead calm. They're not coming! Or could it be the calm before the storm? After midnight a leaden fatigue seized the *jägers* in their barely crate-sized funk holes, dragging down their eyelids to a sleep heavy with dreams. Someone groaned out 'Come with me man, attack in section column!' Who didn't hate the lice at Hooge and Bellewarde Farm! Then suddenly at dawn on 9 August the enemy artillery fire broke out in furious surges like a wild hurricane. The sleepers sprang awake with a start. On the reverse slope they were somewhat sheltered from the devastating effect of the huge amount of ammunition used by the enemy, but swarms of iron greetings careered madly close above their heads. So it continued for an entire hour. By degrees we grew accustomed to the muck and iron. The machine-gunners cleaned their buried guns. The losses had been light, incredibly light in view of the roaring fury of the barrage. Leaning on the parapet Hauptmann Krippendorf listened to the rhythm of the fire. 'When will they come?' There – the explosions erupted in no man's land. The heads of the *jägers* sprang up. It was on. Their well-aimed fire struck the dense waves of attackers with annihilating effect and

brought the enemy attack to a bloody standstill. But this brought no real joy. Hauptmann Krippendorf sprawled pallid on the edge of the trench. A splinter must have gone right into his head, it was serious. His eyes stared wide and questioning in his increasingly pale face. They would never gleam with merriment again at a cheeky *jäger* song! Feldwebelleutnant Seerig was the first to reach the hauptmann. One of his loyal men carried him piggy-back to the nearest dressing station. From there he was taken to the hospital in Isegem, where he died a few days later without regaining consciousness. His company brooded in silence, railing against fate. Why just him, and the rest of the company barely touched! Why just him?

Hauptmann Krippendorf emerging from a pristine dug-out entrance, probably in the reserve trenches at Hollebeke. The pouch on his left shoulder for the early pad-type 'gasmask' dates this photo to the last few months of his life. Most unusually he is wearing an enlisted man's cap possibly to avoid being spotted as an officer by enemy snipers.

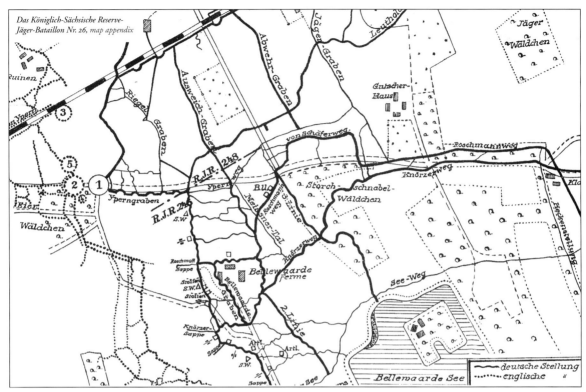

Das Königlich-Sächsische Reserve-Jäger-Bataillon Nr. 26, map appendix

From June 1915 sectors *Bellewaarde Nord* and *Bellewaarde Süd* were usually held (as shown above) by RIR 248 and 246 or by RIR 244 and 242, depending on which division was in residence. The photo below depicts Saxon *jägers* in the third line at *Storchschnabelwäldchen* by the *Schwabengrab*, a mass grave for the dead of RIR 246 from the fighting of 16 June. The German-held crater marked '1' was the result of a British detonation on 25 September 1915 (see p. 56). When RIR 241 held *Nord* and RIR 243 *Süd* in March 1916 this *Trichterstellung* was a deadly flashpoint, where the brigade adjutant Hptm. Breithaupt was shot dead on 22 March 1916 (see p. 103).

Hauptmann Krippendorf in the *Dammstellung* near St. Eloi (see maps pp. 80–81), late June 1915. On the right he is seen with his subordinates Leutnant Schmidt, Feldwebelleutnant Seerig and Feldwebelleutnant Zimmermann, possibly just prior to or after a car excursion (going by the goggles). Although wearing no other equipment in this reserve line, each officer still has his gas pouch at the ready.

The body of Hauptmann Krippendorf laid out in Isegem for his comrades to pay their respects. When circumstances permitted, German dead of all ranks were often displayed in this manner to provide a final photograph for the family.

The hauptmann's coffin is saluted by officers from his battalion and higher staff formations. The group with their backs to the camera include at least one Württemberger (second left). The civilian on the right is probably the mayor of Isegem.

The funeral procession passes through Isegem, flanked by *feldgendarmerie* in their dark green uniforms and gorgets. The pall bearers almost certainly belong to the hauptmann's own company, as perhaps do the large formation of *jägers* near the rear of the column. In addition to the honour guards lining the road, numerous curious civilians observe the procession.

Curt Penther, Vizefeldwebel

Selected letters from the field to his sweetheart and parents

Curt Penther, born on 4 June 1892 at Löbau in eastern Saxony, had pursued a mercantile career. At the outbreak of war he signed up as an *einjährig-freiwilliger* at the barracks of Infanterie-Regiment 103 in Bautzen, and left for the front in October with **II. Bataillon / Reserve-Infanterie-Regiment 242**. Having survived his regiment's disastrous baptism of fire with relatively light wounds, he was sent on an officers' training course and promoted to vizefeldwebel. After rejoining his regiment at the front in 1915 he soon established a formidable reputation as a fearless leader of trench raids and forward patrols, and was commissioned at the end of 1916. Having already won the enlisted man's *Militär-St. Heinrichs-Medaille* in silver and both classes of Iron Cross, he was awarded the officer's *Ritterkreuz* of the *Militär-St. Heinrichs-Orden* in August 1918. He was still with II. / RIR 242 when 53. Reserve-Division and its infantry regiments were disbanded in late September, and spent the final weeks of the war with Reserve-Infanterie-Regiment 103. After the Armistice he returned to civilian life in Löbau. In 1940 he was called up as a hauptmann with Infanterie-Regiment 455, and was again awarded the Iron Cross.

In the trenches before Becelaere, 24 October 1914
My dear Fräulein!

For 5 days now we've been here under the heaviest fire, locked in struggle with a combined French and English opposition. Only those who have taken part in it can really understand what it means to be in such a battle. If I should return, I'll have a lot more to tell you. However for the moment since time is short I will just sketch out a few scenes. First I would just like you to know that we haven't had our boots off since leaving Bautzen, and that I haven't washed for 12 days, sport a handsome beard and can scarcely walk owing to pulled tendons. Furthermore, we have had no *feldpost* to date. Already on the first day of the battle, I took part in the storming of a village. It was reported that the village was occupied; the 6. Kompanie was ordered to advance. At first everything went well. However when we had got within about 100 metres, a murderous fire was let loose. Everyone threw themselves flat and the cavalry retired. Soon we realised that the house opposite us was not held by regular troops, but by *Franc-tireurs*. At this, our rage knew no bounds. With cries of 'Hurra' we charged at the building, which was immediately surrounded and set ablaze. After that, it got too hot for comfort for the gang in there. One after the other – there were three men – they rushed out of the house and tried to flee. However it did them no good – all three were shot. The losses we Germans have taken from these treacherous ambushes are unbelievable. In my own company we've already had five men wounded by these fellows. Even now as I write this, we lie here waiting for the assault on the last enemy positions. Hopefully here too the Lord will shield us with His hand. Above all we are suffering from lack of food. For two whole days there's been a modest cup of coffee, about 100 grams of meat and often no bread. Our physical condition steadily gets worse and worse. My personal food supply is almost

exhausted. Whenever a comrade has to return to the homeland with light wounds, he is envied. All the chickens and pigs in the area have already been requisitioned. Hopefully soon there will be an honourable peace, because we have all had our fill of this. Farewell my darling, dearest wishes and kisses
Your Curt

Reservelazarett II. Abteilung 3 Groß-Auheim,
near Hanau am Main, 10 November 1914
My dear Martha!

You would scarcely believe how hard it is for me to write. I can't hold the paper still, my left hand is abominably painful. The day before yesterday the doctor made an incision from the little finger almost halfway along the back of the hand. It hurt something rotten, but I have comrades here who endure far worse. The pus oozed right out and the doctor washed it all off with hydrogen peroxide. Hopefully it will be better soon.

You've probably already heard about the fighting our regiment was involved in. I will never forget Kruseik, Gheluwe etc. The *Bautzner Nachrichten* has published a pretty account of it, 'How our 242 went into battle'. It concerns our storming of Kruseik on the 25 October, where from 240 men at roll call only 93 returned. Those were the losses from my company alone, just think of the losses for the whole regiment. On 1 November, the day I was wounded, there were only about 200 men left out of 3,000. It is truly heart-wrenching to walk across the battlefield after an attack, and see so many comrades with broken eyes or dreadful mutilations. This demands nerves of steel, but it's possible to get used to anything. I will describe to you one episode which shows how a man's thoughts turn to his God out there. It was on the evening of the 25th. We were all still in our trench, ready for the signal from our leader to advance to the assault. Then suddenly someone, I don't know who, struck up the hymn *'Harre meine Seele'* [Trust Patiently, My Soul]. We all began to sing softly and earnestly, then louder and finally the chorus thundered up to the Almighty *'Harre des Herrn'* [Trust in the Lord]. With this song we stormed forwards into combat, to death but also to victory.

And now farewell my darling, do send my love to your good lady mother too, with best wishes for her recovery. With another heartfelt kiss
Your Curt

Quesnoy, 12 November 1915

Dear parents!

Yesterday I wrote to you that we are now back with the regiment. The recruits are with us here. The regiment left the line on the 14th to march further north. We then went to the depot in Audenarde[1] with the recruits. It is simply marvellous here.

One is entitled to officers' quarters as a feldwebel. We are staying in a merchant's house, and I even have a bed shared with Mikut (that amazed you!). Our batman sleeps on a mat beside us. So it's hardly like being at war at all. I do not need to go into the trenches for now, Mikut and Bräuer will probably go this evening. The sector is quite quiet though, hardly any casualties although the English are only 30 metres away. The villains did chuck six heavies into Quesnoy the night before last, but only managed to kill three civilians. Considering the conditions here the rations are princely. This morning we received half a pound of cervelat and bread. In addition we often get rum and cigars. Duties for the feldwebel here are minimal. I am glad though that I know French, as our hosts are much more forthcoming; the time of shooting from the windows is definitely over. We are even permitted to go out without weapons. This morning we drank coffee with our hosts and had a delightful time. It is quite clean here too, unlike most French houses. The lady of the house has two children, her husband is in the field. One sweet little girl Simone, five years old, is just too cute and silly when she talks. This morning I read with her from a French ABC. She can even write her own name. She will sign this letter with me.

I have one other request. Dear parents, please buy me a pair of leather gaiters and send them on to me. Naturally in tan. The address is 19. Armee-Korps, 40. Res. Div. [sic.][2], RIR 242, II. Batl., 6. Komp., Western Front.

It's been raining like mad all day here. So like I said, it is silly to worry for me at the moment. I'm having it as easy here as on garrison duty. So, do please send me the desired items and pass on greetings to everyone we know from Your Curt

Quesnoy, 13 November 1915

Dear parents!

Hopefully you received my letter from yesterday. At 8 o'clock this morning the company set out. We did not know what was going on. After we had marched off, we were informed that H.M. the King of Saxony was coming. We were then lined up in a farm courtyard. It was all Saxon troops, RIR 242, 244, IR 181 and artillery, a few companies from each regiment. When everyone was in position, bayonets were fixed and His Excellency General von der Decken[3] wished each company good morning. At about 10 o'clock we were called to attention and H.M. appeared. He strolled along the line and spoke with many *landsers* who happened to catch his eye. I was standing on the right flank of the 1. Zug and to the man beside me, an old fellow who had taken part in all of 242's battles, he said: 'I suppose there is less water in the trenches here than further up near Ypres?'. 'Yes your Majesty' he said, 'But there is still enough that it gets into one's boots sometimes.' Then H.M. laughed and walked on. The whole occasion was all very comfortably Saxon. H.M. looked like he doesn't just drink limeflower tea every day.[4] At the end he gave out some medals to the *landsers*, then he drove off again and we marched back to Quesnoy. Other than that, I have nothing new to report. Best wishes,
Your Curt

Meulebeke, 16 November 1915

Dear parents!

As you can see from the place name, we have gone from northern France back to Belgium. Currently we are staying here in rest quarters. Meulebeke is about 30km behind the front. The rumble of the guns cannot be heard here. The regiment had stayed here once before, so the residents already knew the regimental number. Our reception here was just like at home. All along the way into the village there stood a great crowd of people waving to us. We marched as far as the marketplace, where the accomodation chits and instructions were given out. I am staying at a merchant's house and have a lovely bed. My batman is alongside me on a mattress. Bräuer is right next door and Mikut too not far away. The rations here have up to now been consistently very good. Only this evening they were a bit meagre, because the ration wagon hasn't turned up yet. In any case, the soldier out here definitely lives better than many citizens at home. At noon today my batman cooked a fine chop. It cost 35 centimes – so about 30 pfennigs – and it was marvellously large. One can buy all sorts of things here. So, dear parents, please send me 10 marks in cash. I still have some, but while we are staying here in rest quarters a bit more will be required. I have still had no post from the homeland, have you written to me?

I enclose a 5 centime piece from the city of Lille. Silver and nickel are in tremendously short supply here, so the towns now issue money like this. It is only legal tender within that town though. I received it in our last quarters at Quesnoy and can no longer use it. From now on my address is: 27. Res. Korps, 53. Res. Div., RIR 242, II. Batl., 6. Komp. Best wishes
Your Curt

                                    Meulebeke, 26 November 1915
Dear mother!

There is really no need to worry about me, as I am perfectly well off. We have enough to eat and drink, no worries, German beer and the minimal danger to which we have grown so accustomed. We no longer hear the thunder of the guns, we are that far behind the front. We drill now almost like recruits. I don't entirely see eye to eye with my Belgian hosts though, since they are miserable German-haters. I was allotted a room on the first floor, but without a stove. In the room is a bunk bed. My batman sleeps beside me on a mattress on the ground. At night I was always miserably cold, as the houses here are very drafty. If we ever wanted coffee, the old woman pulled a dumb face, because she'd been pinching the coal. I had already asked her a couple of times for a stove, each time in vain. Then I turned to my company, and got an iron stove from the regiment complete with stovepipe and fuel. Now the chimney passes through my room but there was no hole there to stick the pipe through, so we asked the old woman if she would let us make a hole. She messed me around for three days, but today I decided she'd made quite enough of a fool of me. So my batman hacked a hole in the chimney with a pickaxe, and we stuck the pipe through it. Naturally the old woman pulled a really sour face at that. But I told her it was her own fault, and anyway there was a war on. At that point she shut up. It's a good thing I know a bit of French, or else we would be in a fix here. This afternoon I reported the matter to our oberleutnant, who said I should have had the whole hovel hacked to pieces. Now our stove is burning just fine, and I've just cooked a bit of mince. That's what the locals are like round here, where my host has six houses.

Promotion prospects are poor at the moment, we have too few losses, but if the war continues for another year, maybe it will still happen. Write to me again soon, with best wishes
Your Curt

                                    In Meulebeke again, 5 December 1915
Dear parents,

Yesterday evening at 7 o'clock we marched back into this place, after leaving our rest quarters on Wednesday evening to be employed as reserves and to cover the artillery. On Wednesday afternoon there was an alert, but packs were to be left behind, only assault kit and 120 rounds each to be taken. About 10 o'clock we set out once more by railway via Ingelmunster, Iseghem, Roulers and Moorslede–Passchendaele, and from there on a patched-up line to Kerselaerhoek. Here we were unloaded on an open stretch of track and marched along the railway line to Zonnebeke. The hamlet appears to have been a pretty one once. Everything has been shot to ruins. The church is one great pile of rubble. Along the railway and in Zonnebeke, there are small mounds with simple white crosses everywhere, in little gardens amid the fields. Here rest many warriors from RJB 25, RIR 241, 242, 247 and 248. Gradually, all of them are to be dug up and reburied in common cemeteries. Right now the first of them, the *Jägerfriedhof*, is under construction. From Zonnebeke we went one kilometre further on, until we came level with the heavy artillery. Here we were to remain as reserves and cover for the guns. Everyone had their mask with them, as a gas attack was to be expected. At the same time we had to dig trenches every day, to establish a reserve position. A hundred metres to our left a 21cm *mörser* battery was firing. They blazed away incessantly, with a report so powerful it could knock you off your feet. You could even see the shells flying through the air. There were aircraft constantly overhead, which of course soon made us disappear. Half an hour later it kicked off, and the first 'siruptopp'[5] came tearing over. However it went clean overhead toward Zonnebeke. The situation grew increasingly ridiculous. With each shot the shells crept closer to us. Finally the gentlemen[6] called it a day after blazing away for an hour. On the following day they fired again for an hour with shrapnel, and then yet again on Sunday. They never landed anywhere near us – so in the end, we grew so accustomed to it that we no longer paid them any heed. Our fellows are so cheeky now, that they go out looking for driving bands from shells when the fire has stopped. There is scarcely any infantry fire, because we are so far back. Today is a rest day, and tomorrow we will go forward again from Wednesday to Thursday, after which it'll be another battalion's turn. With the artillery I was able to buy some pretty photos, which I will send to you with this letter. I will write on the back of each one what it is.

When I got home yesterday, I met two postmen at once with your card and the parcel with the bacon. Heartfelt thanks for everything. Witte had also sent me the newspaper from the 30th. I now have quite enough bacon. However I had reckoned on some sausage *(knoblauchwurst)* or canned fish, or perhaps some eel or something. You could also send me my stock cubes, which I brought back from Lockstedt[7]. Have you sent any money? I would

The approach route used by reliefs, along the Ypres–Roulers railway line near Kerselaerhoek. Note the dug-outs at the sides of this sunken cutting, which gave localised cover from enemy observation.

The *Sammelfriedhof* (gathering cemetery) of XXVII.RK was established in spring 1915 at the southwest corner of Broodseinde crossroads, for those killed in the fighting at Zonnebeke and further west. The *Jägerfriedhof* of RJB 25 lay opposite at the northwest corner (see photo p. 54). Both also held members of other units and enemy soldiers. The German graves have since been moved to *Soldatenfriedhof Menen*.

like to pay Gretschel back. A pocket torch battery is also needed.

There's not much to say about the weather here. When we got in yesterday we were so wet, that my trousers stood up by themselves when I took them off. What else have I ever seen in this place – nothing but water and more water. My batman wrapped me in blankets straight away and brewed up coffee so strong, that at home Mother would have fainted just from the smell. Every day we get a lot of rum, but it is the purest 90 per cent spirit and gets you as drunk as a sow. How about a bottle of *Stonsdorfer*[8]? Bräuer, together with half the company, has a miserable cold. I am fine. Please write again soon. Bräuer sends his greetings. Best wishes and thanks

Your Curt

Meulebeke, 8 December 1915

Dear parents!

I received Father's letter of 3 December yesterday evening, at the same time as the money that you sent by postal order. My hearty thanks for both. Father's letter was again delightfully long, so I have some idea now of what's happening in the homeland. I always read Father's letters with particular pleasure, since I invariably find some bit of news there which especially interests me. I have read in the paper that you had a lot of snow at home. Here we still have warm weather most

of the time, like in springtime. I have little need of my winter gear, and my batman, who had already overwintered here, laughed when he saw my knee warmers. I'll hang onto the things for a little while longer, then I'll send them home. Mother really shouldn't spend so much money on such stuff, just something good to eat and a little bottle of schnapps is always much better. Woollen things are no use here, only waterproofs, because our greatest enemy is the water. Once woollen things are wet through, all one can do is hang them out to dry. Just send something to nibble instead, only not tinned meat because it's available by the pound here. Bräuer recently got sent a fine *bäbe*[9]. Naturally it was shared out. So you could send me something like that some time. Generally speaking the sending of *liebesgaben* definitely alleviates the misery out here. I don't really need it myself though.

It's hardly amazing that I have clothes lice, since everyone has the little beasts here. We are all lousy, from the oberleutnant downwards. We've already been given something to use for it. In addition, we've been to the *lausoleum* in Iseghem. If you want to send me something for it you can, but it isn't necessary. Maybe I could send you a couple of little lice some time, since you don't have any there. Head lice are only occasionally found here, almost none at all. I haven't a single one. Why don't you want to go to Klemm's wedding then? Are you fearful of not staying at home? Current

Saxon infantry (probably from Reserve-Infanterie-Regiment 242) amid the ruins of Zonnebeke in late 1915.

events should not concern you, they are just for us out here to worry about. Do still go and write to me how it went. I'd like to congratulate them. Send my greetings to *Herren* Geier and Menzel, and also to Mütze's Kathi. Can you say to her that we have a vacancy in the trenches here for a cook, special cooking skills are not required. The only condition is that she can cook hot water. Otherwise, everything here is still much the same. On Monday and Tuesday we were forward again. Today we are in rest quarters, tomorrow we go out there again until Sunday. Yesterday we had one man seriously wounded by aircraft shrapnel. A percussion-fuzed shrapnel bomb hit him right in the left thigh, then the thing exploded and tore away the fleshy parts completely. The bone was still whole though. These aerial shrapnel bombs are devilish little tubes, which the fellows overhead chuck out by the dozen. They go off on impact like a firecracker. As these things were being dropped Bräuer was standing right next to me. We threw ourselves prone straight away and immediately the call rang out, *'sanitäter'*. The man was immediately bandaged up, and has been admitted to hospital. Do write again soon. Did you get the postcard of Zonnebeke?
Best wishes
Your Curt

Meulebeke, 12 December 1915

Dear parents!
Yesterday was our last day of sapping. On Thursday and Friday everything went well, then yesterday the rogues hit us with overwhelmingly heavy shrapnel fire. About 10 shrapnel shells landed right in the trenches, and a further 15 to 20 detonated in front or behind. Although we are 2–3km behind the front, the swine had still got our range exactly. I was developing the so-called *Mittelwerk* with my platoon, to which Bräuer also belonged, when it kicked off. First we laughed because the brethren hadn't got the range, then suddenly one of the devilish things landed in our midst, and tore off the left leg of one of our attached *pioniere*. I whistled at once for a *sanitäter* just as shell number two landed harmlessly nearby. A shrapnel ball whizzed past my skull and embedded itself in the parapet of the trench. I dug the thing out and let it cool off as it was still really hot – I have it still. The *Mittelwerk* was spared after that, instead it was the turn of the *Südwerk* (Mikut). After the first two shrapnel shells he too was whistling for *sanitäters* – he had three wounded, all infantrymen. In the evening we were relieved and will probably be here in rest quarters now for another ten days. Today our company commander sent Mikut and myself a bottle of wine each for sticking it out yesterday. He had not been there with us at the time, but had it recounted to him later. Altogether we have received a really colossal quantity

of liquor since the minor battle. Yesterday ¾ of a Litre of rum each, and today the same again. Here on rest days one gets systematically drunk.
Today I also got the parcel with the writing things. I enclose two more postcards. Have the *stammtisch*[10] seen the previous ones yet? I am sure they must have done. Why was there no letter in the parcel, did Mother not have the time?
Best wishes
Your Curt

Meulebeke, 27 December 1915

Dear parents!
Yesterday I received Father's letter with the 10 marks. Thank you very much for that. However Christmas here has already cost 10 marks, since – as you probably knew already – I also went to Ostend. So I must once again ask you to send 10 or 15 marks after the 1st. While we are here at rest a bit of money is always necessary – when we go into the line, it's different. But now I want to tell you how I spent Christmas under Belgian skies. On Christmas Eve and the preceding day the guns could be heard thundering away heavily along the entire Belgian front, so we were really afraid that we would have to go out there. However they died down again. In the afternoon of Christmas Eve the Christmas table for the companies was laid out in a disused factory. Mikut and I helped with it. A whole box of *liebesgaben* had arrived from the Red Cross and there was something for everyone, above all loads of cigars and cigarettes. Besides these there were also shirts, pocket torches, knives etc. This was all sorted into piles for one man each, with an individual number attached. At 5 o'clock there was a service in the tiny little church of Meulebeke. There everyone's thoughts turned to home. After the end of the service the company fell in and went off singing to get our presents. Everyone drew a raffle ticket to find his place. I got a pocket handkerchief, sweets, cigarettes, a mirror and other odds and ends, plus two little pieces of soap. Then the lovely old Christmas carols were sung. For the chaps who weren't expecting anything from home, there was an extra present. They received a lot more, including 5 marks per man from the officers of the company. After the official part, for which we 'vizes' were seated among the officers, the atmosphere grew convivial. There was beer and sausage with potato salad, and the *landsers* staged comic turns. It concluded around half past eleven. On the first day of the holiday I slept until midday, then in the afternoon there was a party at Mikut's, where we made merry again. One has to spend the holidays out here in merry company, or else fall prey to foolish thoughts. On the second day Mikut and I (Bräuer didn't have leave) drove to Ostende. We arrived there at 10 o'clock. Naturally we went straight to the beach.

Vfw. Curt Penther (right) and his comrades in the trenches near Auchy in late spring or summer 1916; Reserve-Infanterie-Regiment 242 was first provided with steel helmets in May, and left for the Somme with the rest of 53. RD at the end of August. Apart from a relative lull in the last few weeks, this entire period was a bloody one punctuated by mine detonations, bitter crater-fighting and trench raids in which Vfw. Penther actively participated. The gasmasks worn at the alert here recall the unsuccessful British chlorine discharge reported by 53. RD on 12 July; the flare pistol held by the unteroffizier here would be used to call down a pre-targeted defensive artillery barrage (*sperrfeuer*) in the event of an infantry attack.

The grandeur of the place is undeniably unique. Almost everything is made of marble. The hotels, which are right on the beach, all stand empty now – though in peacetime there was real splendour here. Now barbed wire obstacles run along the beach, and German artillery stands on the beachside road. It looks prettiest in the *kursaal*, formerly the exclusive haunt of American millionaires. It is all furnished with fairytale magnificence, but now lanterns stand in the splendid rooms and German soldiers sleep on the ornate carpets. Rifles hang on the famous organ in the concert hall and hob-nailed boots tread all over the marble tiles. The view of the North Sea is magnificent, when one stands there one has to remind oneself that England is on the other side of the Channel. We ate very cheaply at the *marineheim*[11], besides that nothing of note happened on the trip. At 6.34 we went back to Meulebeke. So that's how I spent Christmas, it was quite nice. I also want to let you know that I received the *Stonsdorfer*. Other than that I'm still well. I will return the bottle. Best wishes
Your Curt

On the evening of 5 April, Penther's platoon began their first tour in the trenches opposite Givenchy. Just before they set out he learned that his brother Georg (in Prussian service with the Silesian infantry) had been killed in action. As a platoon leader Penther often had to write to bereaved families, but his duty this time was immeasurably harder.

In the trenches, 6 April 1916

Dear parents!
You will certainly already have received the tragic tidings of the heroic death of our dear Georg. I received a letter yesterday evening, shortly before we marched out, from a certain Musketier Uhlmann, a comrade of Georg's. He informed me in quite dispassionate words, that at half past nine on the evening of 30 March, Georg had died a hero's death for the Fatherland, killed by the detonator of a shell which hit him in the chest. I can't describe my thoughts at that moment. Imagine – I had to go back into the trenches, and on top of that this message. Although I have already seen so much horror, and misery and death surround me daily, all the same such a thing has a direct numbing effect. As far as I can tell, he did not experience much suffering. He is gone from us in the lustre of his heroism, his sacrifice for us all. We will not let the picture that we have of him be tarnished. That must be our example, to emulate him in his quiet heroism. Of course Mother will cry and Father will again try to stifle his pain, but to me out here there falls the precious task of avenging his dear blood. And he shall be avenged, that I swear to you. Although I was prepared for

the worst when I realised that Georg was at Verdun, his death still struck me by surprise.
It is at least a consolation that Georg died straight away, because to see this vigorous man as a cripple would have been too terrible. So we will always have the memory of him as he stood before us in the strength of his youth. We too must now pay our own tribute to the Fatherland, like so many thousands of others whom the Lord has bade take up this cross. I have often prayed, that He might let us both return to you. Yet God has willed it otherwise and we must submit. His counsel is wondrous, he alone knows the good of it. Just grant me this favour – be strong for me, because now I must rely entirely on you. Mother should not fret. Twine a laurel wreath around the picture of the hero. Thus we pay him his due. Mikut and our oberleutnant have expressed their condolences, quietly and seriously, as is the custom among warriors. I will write at once to the kompanie-feldwebel. Perhaps I can get a picture of his resting place. Best wishes to you in deepest suffering, but proud of our hero,
Your Curt

At 7.15 pm on 27 August 1916 patrols of 5. and 6./RIR 242 raided a sap held by 2nd Btn. Royal Inniskilling Fusiliers[12] near the Vermelles road. Penther reported as follows:

After a bombardment by artillery and *minenwerfers* of the enemy positions, especially at *Punkt 819*, the patrol of 6. Komp. – comprising Vfw. Penther as leader, Gefr. Weiß, Sold. Eckert, Sold. Kühn, Gefr. Richter and Sold. Eulenberger – set out from our trenches via the *Gutmannsappe* for the enemy lines. At the same time the patrol of 5. Komp. sprung out of the *Eiersappe* and met up with the patrol of 6. Komp. in the cratered area. After crossing the craters the patrol came across an enemy sap, at the head of which sat four men in a shelter. When ordered to raise their hands, one Englishman reached for his rifle and was shot by Vfw. Penther. The other three gave themselves up after a fierce melee and were hauled out over the saphead. During the struggle two Englishmen who had remained further back in a dugout near the main front line rushed to the aid of their comrades and were likewise cut down. Meanwhile two men of the patrol with an unteroffizier of 5. Komp. rushed toward the enemy's main front line to block it off. After all hostile personnel had been cut down or captured the patrol withdrew. At this point Gefr. Weiß was lightly wounded. It was established that the front line had incurred only minor damage from the bombardment. All members of the patrol acted impeccably and did their duty in all respects. All entered the enemy trench and gave their utmost for the success of the operation.

Max Conrad, Gefreiter

Wounded in battle and discharged due to illness

Max Conrad from Podelwitz near Leipzig fought in the First Battle of Ypres, and survived to be discharged later due to chronic ill health. Unfortunately we have no details of his pre-war life and career, except that he was already a married man with two children. As such he was probably one of the many older reservists who formed the backbone of the so-called '*Kinderkorps*' when it was rushed to the Western Front in October 1914. His first postcard (below) describes his arrival in Flanders with **12. Kompanie / Reserve-Infanterie-Regiment 245**. When he next wrote to his family it was from hospital in Koblenz. Like many others including Kühn and Penther (qq.v.), Conrad had been wounded in the initial fighting at Becelaere. Although shot in the head, it appears that the bullet had glanced off his skull – fortunately without inflicting serious damage. After a relatively brief convalescence he rejoined his regiment at the front in Flanders. His subsequent correspondence with his family indicates that (like many middle-aged infantrymen that winter) his health soon began to deteriorate under the harsh conditions of life in the trenches. For instance he complains of rheumatism in his left leg brought on by the climate, and of nervous trembling in his hand as he tries to write. As a result of these increasingly serious afflictions, he was admitted in May 1915 to the *leichtkrankenabteilung* (light cases ward) of a hospital in Gent.

After a partial recovery he was assessed as no longer fit for frontline duty, and served until spring 1916 in an administrative role with the *Meldeamt* of **Etappen-Kommandantur Gent**. By June 1916 Conrad was back in Germany, rather surprisingly with the Ersatz-Bataillon of Prussian Infanterie-Regiment 24 at Neuruppin in Brandenburg. Writing to his wife Martha, he complains of acute boredom but correctly anticipates that he will soon be returning home as a civilian. Upon his return he took up a post as a teacher in Leipzig.

On this card Conrad writes to his wife: '*Dear Martha! After three enormously long marches, I am now here with my comrades in the Belgian town shown overleaf. Already yesterday evening we had to bivouac. So far the people are friendly. There are however said to be a lot of Frenchmen*[1] *in this town. We have already heard the thunder of the artillery. Our opponents are the English. We have not yet been in battle. Maybe tomorrow or the day after we will get to see the enemy, if they don't fall back. Best wishes, your Max. With us over here it's like being on manouvres. Courtrai, 18/10/1914*'

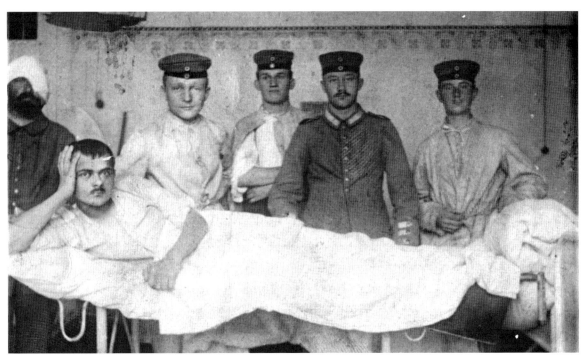

Conrad (furthest left) with bandaged head, posing with fellow-patients at Festungslazarett Coblenz (now Koblenz). Like the unfortunate Vfw. Kühn (see p. 182), he had been shot in the head during the fighting at Becelaere, and received first aid at the church (see p. 30). Fortunately for Conrad it was only a glancing blow, and its treatment relatively straightforward. He sent this photo as a postcard to his wife on 1 November 1914.

Sadly we do not know whether this fine sketch of Conrad is a self-portrait or the work of a comrade.

Max Conrad relaxing off-duty after rejoining 12. / RIR 245 in the field; his wound appears to have left him with a visible scar below his left eye.

Conrad (seated left) with his *korporalschaft* in a Flemish photographer's studio. As the gefreiter, Conrad would have acted as right-hand man to the unteroffizier (traditionally and colloquially, the *'korporal'*) seated alongside him. On 10 April 1915 at Waterdamhoek, Conrad used this card to write to his wife in part as follows: *'If only we never had to go into the trenches again and the war was over. Hopefully this, my dearest wish, will be granted pretty soon.'* At least so far as his own time in the trenches was concerned, his wish would soon be granted.

From the book 'Kriegsalbum von Gent', published by the photographic department of Etappen-Kommandantur Gent in 1916

The Kommandantur conducts its monitoring of the population, most especially those liable for military service, via the *Meldeamt*. Those required to report comprise all Belgians liable for military service between the age of 17 and the end of their 35th year, plus all members of the former Belgian *'Garde Civique'*[2], all enemy aliens of either sex from the end of their 15th year, and all persons who have been placed on any other grounds under heightened surveillance. They are required to present themselves in alphabetical order on certain days of the month. Any such person going on a journey needs to obtain a travel warrant for it, and to report prior to departure and upon return. Changes of residence must also be approved by the *Meldeamt*.

The clientele of the individual departments are infallibly recognisable as such. Elegantly dressed gentlemen proceed confidently to the *'Garde Civique'* department, Flemish peasants clack along in their poplar-wood clogs to the

'Gent Land' department, and labourers and boatmen with hats and neckerchiefs plegmatically attend the two *'Gent Stadt'* departments. All too often when a signature is requested from a peasant, labourer or boatman one hears *'Ik ben niet geleerd, mijnheer'*, that is to say 'I have not learned the hard arts of reading and writing'. The reporting day of the aliens department presents the most colourful scene.

The *'Belgian Bezirkskommando'* monitors nearly 31,000 persons required to report, apart from those liable for German military service[3]. Adjacent to it is a department where all those travelling to or through the area have to report and receive their accomodation chits. On the peak travel days one can observe here all types of the Belgian, and especially the Flemish, people – from the posh, elegant Brussels lady to the thick-boned, heavy-set Flemish peasant woman.

Anyone who misses his control day will be brought before the *strafabteilung* of the *etappen-kommandantur*. This passes judgement on offences of a less serious nature, roughly corresponding to *ordnungsvergehen* and *polizeivergehen* in peacetime[4].

The *Meldeamt* of *Kommandantur Gent*, Conrad's post from May 1915. In the background local men (evidently of military age) queue to have their presence formally recorded, under the casual supervision of two provosts of the *feldgendarmerie*, recognisable as such by their dark green civil police (*landgendarmerie*) uniforms. Like all of the other Germans here they appear to be unarmed.

Conrad at his desk in Gent (fourth from right). The man furthest right appears to be a veteran of Reserve-Infanterie-Regiment 233 (51. Reserve-Division / XXVI. Reserve-Korps), one of many hastily raised Prussian units which shared the bloody fate of Conrad's regiment in autumn 1914. The alphabetic registration system for the 'clientele' can be clearly seen in the background.

Souvenir photo of a military theatrical production in Gent, signed by several of Conrad's colleagues and sent to him on 14 November 1915, while he was on leave at home and celebrating his birthday.

Christmas 1915 at the *Meldeamt*. Gefreiter Conrad is standing in the back row directly in front of the Christmas tree. In the festive spirit of the occasion, the attached *feldgendarme* has put on his sabre and brightly polished duty gorget *(ringkragen)*.

The 'crew' of the *Meldeamt*, including Conrad seventh from left in the first standing row, to the left of the Flemish 'no smoking' sign. The majority of the front row have the 'Brandenburg' cuff worn in all the German armies except that of Saxony, and are probably convalescent infantrymen. The minority wearing smarter *train* uniform (such as the man standing on Conrad's right) are probably professional military clerks of the *intendantur*.

A selection of different postmarks *(briefstempel)* charting Gefreiter Conrad's military service.

Richard Kaden, Generalmajor

Personal reflections of a brigade commander

Richard Kaden was born on 7 March 1862 in Dresden, apparently into a military family. He began his career on 1 December 1879 as an *avantageur* with **Grenadier-Regiment 101**, and was commissioned as a leutnant in 1881. Over the following decades he steadily rose up the ranks, serving with various Saxon infantry regiments and at the *Kriegsministerium* in Dresden. On 23 September 1911 he was promoted to oberst and appointed commander of **Infanterie-Regiment 139** in Döbeln; he would always have a special affection for this regiment, though he never commanded it in battle. Kaden was elevated to the *generalität* on 20 April 1914, with promotion to the rank of generalmajor and command of **48. Infanterie-Brigade** (comprising Infanterie-Regiment 106 and 107), which he led off to war as part of 24. Infanterie-Division on 2 August.

On 5 March 1915 his command was reorganised and renumbered as **116. Infanterie-Brigade**, receiving (Württemberg) Reserve-Infanterie-Regiment 120 as its third regiment (see pp. 72–74). As part of the new 58. Infanterie-Division, Kaden's brigade spent the next two months held in strategic reserve, mainly in the vicinity of Lille. Committed to the Second Battle of Artois in May–June 1915, it briefly returned to Lille in the Summer, before transferring to the Eastern Front to participate in the German offensive in August-September. Kaden's last campaign was Verdun in March–April 1916. For three hellish weeks, his brigade struggled to hold and advance the front through the blockhouse-studded *Caillettewald* (Bois de la Caillette) towards Fleury, in the teeth of the heaviest artillery fire the French Army could muster and a relentless series of counter-attacks. According to '*Sachsen in großer Zeit*' this ordeal cost the division an estimated total of 507 dead (including nineteen officers), 2,391 wounded (including fifty-five officers) and 165 missing (including one officer); a further 2,648 were reported sick. On the very first day, Kaden's brigade HQ dugout was partially demolished by a direct hit from heavy artillery, killing or maiming some of his closest colleagues. He was thus in no mood to be diplomatic in criticising the use made of his brigade (or the wider conduct of the battle), and evidently made some enemies among the Falkenhayn faction, who had staked everything on the Verdun campaign.

Writing in 1933 Kaden declined to name his opponents, but made it clear that he was 'pushed' out of his post. Privately informed that he could not expect to become a divisional commander, he took the implied offer of an honourable retirement and tendered his resignation. This was sweetened on 27 April 1916 by the award of the *Komturkreuz 2. Klasse* of the *Militär-St. Heinrichs-Orden*, with a citation praising his leadership of the brigade in battle under exceptionally difficult conditions. His resignation was accepted on 11 August, with full pension and the (socially vital) right to wear general's uniform. Initially however he was placed on the semi-retired *(zur disposition)* list, and on 24 November 1916 appointed commander of the **Stellvertretende 89. Infanterie-Brigade**. Based in Zwickau, this administered the 'home front' elements of Infanterie-Regiments 105, 133 and 134 and of Reserve-Infanterie-Regiment 133. On 17 June 1918 he was '*charakterisiert*' (granted an honorary promotion) to the rank of generalleutnant. In 1920 he finally left what was now the *Reichswehr* of the Weimar Republic, after over forty years of military service.

All three of Kaden's sons served as junior officers in the war, and only one of them survived. Ltn. Hellmuth Kaden was cut down by French machine-guns at La Salle on 7 September 1914, while serving as adjutant and acting battery commander with the Mobile Ersatz-Abteilung / Feldartillerie-Regiment 77 (a provisional battalion-sized unit belonging to 19. Ersatz-Division). In a particularly harsh blow Ltn. d. R. Hans Kaden (see here the entry for 30 November 1914) was serving with his father's beloved Infanterie-Regiment 139 when he too was killed in action at L'Epinette in June 1916. The fate of the general's third son, Ltn. Gert Kaden, was not so tragic but nevertheless a source of great anxiety for his family. In peacetime a subaltern with the MGK / Infanterie-Regiment 103, Gert was serving in the field with Ersatz-Infanterie-Regiment 23 (again, with 19. Ersatz-Division) when in late 1915 he attempted to arrange a transfer to the cavalry – evidently without consulting his father first. For reasons that remain unclear, this highly unusual request resulted in a protracted and complex case before the military courts, and Gert's eventual discharge from the Royal Saxon officers' corps.

The following excerpts are all translated from the hand-annotated typescript of GM Kaden's journal. Occasional comments (notably in the entry for 25 December 1914) suggest later revision with the benefit of hindsight, the extent of which can only be guessed at. Portions of the journal were included in Kaden's autobiography '*In der Alten Armee*' (1933), but as a rule stripped of all references to family matters and (potentially libellous) criticisms of specific officers.

While most of XIX. Armee-Korps headed westwards on 4 October 1914, a reserve force – comprising Generalmajor Kaden's 48. Infanterie-Brigade together with FAR 78, JB 12, several smaller technical units and attached Prussian troops – was held back in the Champagne under Genltn. Krug von Nidda, commander of the 24. Infanterie-Division. These reserves arrived in Lille on the morning of 22nd October, by which time the rest of XIX. Armee-Korps had already been fighting on this new front for a week – against an unfamiliar opponent, III Corps of the BEF. On the morning of 23 October, Generalmajor Kaden's brigade would take part in the next major attack.

Friday 23 October 1914

Car trip to divisional headquarters in Pérenchies. At the briefing on the attack planned for 10 o'clock this morning, I met my brother Alfred[1] who congratulated me on the *Heinrichsorden*[2]. With some trembling of the heart I think of Hans, who took part in the attack as company commander of 5./139. IR 139 suffered great losses, yesterday they lost a further 200 men. It is said that the English put up a very good fight, did not waver or give ground and were mostly bayonetted in their trenches[3].

Sunday 25 October 1914

Today IR 107 forced their way into La Hausserie [sic.] step by step, against one of England's elite brigades[4], and in doing so earned themselves a bounty of 300 marks from the 'England Fund' offered by Geheimrat Vogel of Chemnitz.

Friday 30 October 1914

Today we learned that the Saxon war minister General von Carlowitz, commander of the XXVII. Reserve-Korps, has resigned his office[5], and has already left together with his chief of staff Reichardt. The Saxon reserve corps under his command must have suffered a serious reverse at Langemark. The corps has got the Prussian General von Schubert now, chief of staff is Fortmüller.

Sunday 1 November 1914

I made an early visit to Genltn. von Krug[6], and heard precisely how Carlowitz had come to grief. Under the impression of seeing the troops rushing back, he had telephoned from the front to the *oberkommando* 'the English are breaking through'. At this there naturally ensued a great deal of confusion and a fatal relocation of the reserves, whilst in reality the English never left their trenches.

A typical page from the original typescript of Generalmajor Kaden's journal, complete with his handwritten corrections and additions.

The portrait of Generalmajor Kaden which appears in his book '*In der Alten Armee*' (1933).

Monday 2 November 1914

In Lille I met many of the English prisoners, who have been crammed tightly together in the Citadel. The beautiful greatcoats of the Englishmen are frequently taken off them and worn by our own fellows. The Bavarians should just have summarily drowned a load of the captured Hindus and the other rabble in the Ypres Canal.

Wednesday 4 November 1914

Today at brigade HQ we took delivery of 15 pigeons from a French carrier pigeon station, at which about 400 birds were picked up. These birds had certainly never imagined, that they would end up one day as welcome roasts in German stomachs.

Thursday 5 November 1915

Reported to divisional HQ. I always get the impression that there is an uncomfortable atmosphere here. Krug absolutely cannot see eye to eye with Laffert[7]. So Krug is nervous, looks pale and exhausted, und won't let himself be cheered up in the slightest by his staff. Kretzschmar is stone-deaf (so entirely calm!) and not on the best of terms with Zeschau, who is bilious, thin-skinned and irascible[8]. While an unhappy, pessimistic atmosphere thus prevails here, I am always cheered by the confident, battle-happy mood among the troops at the front.

Generalmajor Kaden (at the top of the stairs) waiting to receive H.M. King Wilhelm II of Württemberg.

Tuesday 10 November 1914

Again today an officer reported to me, that he had overheard a conversation between two women, one of whom said *'demain les allemands seront coupés'* ['tomorrow the Germans are for the chop']. I reported it to the division, who however did not set much store by it. There seems to be something in the air. Mirus now intends to emplace *minenwerfers*[9] in the IR 107 sector for an assault on the Rue du Bois. These throw 50 kilos of dynamite out to 500–600 metres with great precision. The effect is colossal! Recently the English were driven out of a factory with two shots. Just one wounded prisoner, all the others were dead. The war grows ever more brutal.

Friday 13 November 1914

Today Major v. Bodenhausen of III. Batl. / IR 107 had to go back in a nervous condition, completely broken and scarcely able to walk[10]. Also among the mentally destroyed are Unterarzt Dr Bennecke and Leutnant d. R. Netto (the writer), who shouted at Hauptmann Schreiber that he should order the enemy artillery to cease firing.

Sunday 15 November 1914

Today the first snow fell, something rare in Flanders. How will the Indians and blacks cope with this filthy weather! I am already worrying about infectious diseases among our own fellows.

Saturday 21 November 1914

The Battle of the Canals must come to a standstill here – there is no way forward. In the sector of XIX. Armee-Korps, as the *armee-oberkommando* has now expressly ordered, we must remain on the defensive. I am pleased that this will put a stop to the pressure from Laffert for local attacks and useless losses. A very amusing story is reported from Valenciennes: Here during a visit by a certain Saxon royal personage a precious Gobelin tapestry was identified, which had apparently once belonged to the House of Wettin. Hauptmann von Schweinitz[11] was now obliged to ask the city to explain how it had come into their possession. They were evidently unable to do this, and it was unceremoniously decreed that the tapestry should be cut down and sent to Dresden. At this there was an appeal by the city to the *Reichskanzler* and a ruling: the tapestry is to be sent back again.

Wednesday 25 November 1914

An early visit from General von Krug as always left behind an atmosphere of pessimism. It is true, our situation here is not a pleasant one: in this cold wet weather typhoid fever runs riot, the trenches in which our poor fighters stand are constantly filling with water, and since equally strong forces stand opposite us we simply cannot advance. Anywhere an attempt is made to force a decision, it results in savage losses. Thus for example from the Gardekorps a single Garde-Division of only 6,000 men remains. Furthermore Krug told me some hair-raising things about the assault of the XXVII. Reserve-Korps and its failure, which General von Watzdorf[12] had related to him when he visited. The corps is shattered. By evening one of the regiments was only one officer and eighty men strong. Naturally the enemy is also suffering heavily. And then, I always console myself with the thought: God will see that all is well. A whole people is praying for our cause! Be calm and hopeful, and do not lose courage!

Friday 27 November 1914

In the afternoon I drove to AOK 6 (Crown Prince of Bavaria) in Lille and tried to establish a telephone connection to Leipzig, but could hear absolutely nothing and finally had to give up the attempt.

In the Citadel at Lille I saw 75 captured Indians being interviewed by a professor summoned especially from the oriental seminary in Berlin[13], who has mastered their Hindu dialect. Their diet is very troublesome, because they won't touch anything that an unbeliever has prepared for them.

Monday 30 November 1914

I met Hans in very comfortable quarters in Pérenchies, where he is very snugly and comfortably accommodated together with Ltn. Brandt, adjutant of II. Batl. / IR 139, at the home of a most lovely young woman who has a friend of the same age living with her. Both ladies (one can certainly call them that) have their husbands in the field and have of course had no news since September. How lucky our own wives are. One has to admire the courage of the women who have stayed behind here. For example the lady's friend recently came under shrapnel fire whilst walking in the street, and was wounded in the back and foot. Pérenchies is damned uncomfortable at times . ...

By the way one must say this for the French: everything is clean, complaints of vermin, fleas and bedbugs are few and far between. In any case, I left Hans late in the evening in the sure knowledge that he is being looked after famously on his rest days. He was otherwise healthy and cheerful. What the lads are putting up with is tremendous. Several times today he had personally shot at individual Englishmen and even put a bullet through a small English embrasure, at which there instantly ensued such a ferocious rapid fire from the Englishmen that he knew he had got his opponent.

The jolly mood out there is still in evidence, e.g. today someone took a horse's head from a saddler's workshop and stuck it on a stick so that it stuck out above the parapet, then galloped along the trench with it. A bugler added to it by blowing the signal for 'trot and gallop'. The Englishmen blazed away like mad.

Wednesday 2 December 1914

Once again IR 106 had their usual hard luck. They were in the western part of La Basse-Ville, and IR 134 in the eastern part. Because enemy shells were constantly landing in the western part of the town, an exchange of quarters was arranged to give 106 a rest. 106 had scarcely arrived in the eastern part when the enemy redirected their fire onto it.

Friday 11 December 1914

Made a visit to the regimental HQ of IR 139 in Pérenchies. Today 300 civilian labourers arrived in Lomme for work on the defences. It was also discovered today that the English, on the slightly lower ground opposite IR 139, had prepared an unpleasant surprise for them: using a dam they have forced the water back into the trenches of the 139ers. Now the dam will have to be destroyed with the '*Dicke Minna*'[14].

Saturday 19 December 1914

Again this afternoon furious enemy fire, this time on our right wing. While I was at divisional HQ I witnessed something remarkable. An unteroffizier of Sanitäts-Kompanie [XIX.1] had accused a 62 year old farmer from Lomme of signalling with a light to the enemy. The farmer had denied it, but was condemned to death on the basis of the sworn statement of the unteroffizier. Tomorrow morning he was to be shot. When his protestations of innocence failed, the old farmer asked only to be buried in the local cemetery. Then today the unteroffizier suddenly confessed that he had made it all up. What could the motive have been for this disgraceful act? Krug was thoroughly incensed. He made a present of two bottles of wine to the farmer, whose freedom was immediately restored, and personally assured him that he would be informed of the judgement against the perjurer, who was immediately taken into custody and will get at least three years in jail.

Friday 25 December 1914

Woollens in abundance! Instead of the usual punishments for minor disciplinary infractions, Demmering should have ordered the wearing of two to four pairs of muffs, balaclava helmets etc. depending on the severity of the offence. In IR 139 even the horses are already wearing muffs. The homeland has produced an endless profusion of *liebesgaben*. Who would have thought that the war would last so long and that later such a shortage would arise of those materials which were now all but wasted? The 107ers told me that on Christmas Eve outright contact between Englishmen and Germans had developed in between the trenches. A ceasefire was in force and the dead could be buried. At first an English captain accompanied by six men without weapons made an approach to Leutnant von Gehe[15]. This officer rebuffed the six escorts

An unidentified Saxon unit preparing their first wartime Christmas feast behind the lines in Flanders. Several men have already adopted the typically Flemish wooden clogs, which proved to be convenient and practical rear-area wear in wet weather.

and met the English officer halfway by himself. An amicable agreement was reached: until 1 o'clock on the night of the 25th–26th peace would reign, but no-one was to enter the opposing trenches. Nevertheless two rather inebriated Englishmen – including a corporal with 14 years' service who had fought against the Boers, and a young man who had previously studied in Heidelberg and, so he said, had a particular longing for a German Christmas – still found their way into the German trenches and were immediately detained there[16]. On Christmas Eve they stood at the door as a pair of Krampuses[17] for the distribution of gifts to IR 107! Hptm. Schreiber, who took the Englishmen for 107ers in fancy dress, said: 'how splendid, which company are you from then?'

Sunday 27 December 1914

Hptm. Schröder of IR 106 [18] reported on the ceasefire, which has also been agreed with the English on 106's regimental front. A few of our fellows had very cautiously put up a candle on the edge of the trench, then, when this was not shot at, even a small lighted tree – to applause and cheers from the English! 1.2km behind the trenches in Basse-Ville, Musikmeister Capitän played Christmas songs, also including 'Home, sweet Home'. The English responded with rapturous applause. Here too the dead lying between the lines were buried. It was even possible to take photographs.

Monday 4 January 1915

In Lille I met General Bärensprung[19]. He is looking well, but has had his fill of the war – and run out of champagne! I sent him two bottles in the afternoon by way of consolation.

Thursday 7 January 1915

Major Böhme informs me that – at last – ammunition trains with artillery shells are arriving in Lille again. We have been careless concerning artillery munitions and the issue of rifles, contrary to our customary German thoroughness. Among the new recruits who have arrived here so far, there are still some without a rifle.

Friday 8 January 1915

The *Times* has published an article concerning the fraternisation of the English with the Saxons on Christmas Eve. The Saxons were 'such nice chaps' and the English soldiers were reluctant to shoot at them. What cheek! We are glad of their enmity and want none of their sympathy, so it is quite in order if OHL has indeed begun an investigation into these goings-on.

Monday 11 January 1915

Tümmler told me a really charming story from II. Batl. / IR 139. For recreational purposes Major Bach took his battalion for a route march from Pérenchies to Lille. One can imagine what a relief and a pleasure it must have been, for the lads to see a bit of culture and human life again. With the Regimentsmusik in the lead the II. Batl. / IR 139 marched through the beautiful city to a square, where the field kitchen was emptied and the band played some jolly tunes. Suddenly during a waltz, our Saxons got hold of the local girls and danced with them. It must been a splendid sight.

Tuesday 26 January 1915
Since Crown Prince Rupprecht wishes to personally convey his congratulations to the Kaiser in Charleville tomorrow[20], the *Kaiserparade* took place today instead. The following units took part: a composite battalion of the Gardekorps (from 'Elisabeth'[21] and the Gardefüsiliere), a composite battalion of the XIV. AK, one battalion each of Prussian (Nr. 10) and Bavarian *jägers*, two Landsturm battalions (Aurich and Hamburg), 2. Esk. / HR 19, 2. Esk. / UR 18 und I. Abt. / FAR 77. Because of an order from the *generalkommando* that all higher ranks must remain at their posts in their battle HQs, I was apart from the corps commander the only Saxon general present for this memorable ceremony in northern France. It was moving to see the depleted platoons marching past, some in muddied grey greatcoats, as they had just come from the trenches. Reserve officers as company commanders, very young leutnants with the Iron Cross, stalwart and keen at the head of their platoons. The Landsturm made an excellent impression as they passed. The approach march of the Hessian battalion to the sound of '*Die Wacht am Rhein*' was wonderful.

The parade took place on the square in front of the Citadel. At 10 o'clock sharp the elegant Crown Prince Rupprecht of Bavaria appeared and gave a speech ... it is absolutely tremendous what German thoroughness, order and organisational efficiency have achieved here, so close to the enemy, and how the conquered territory is being brought back into an orderly condition. How marvellously everyone has pitched in. All supplies of copper, rubber, flax, wool etc. are being shipped to Germany, insofar as they can be used for military purposes. All businesses are being encouraged to re-open, and all communities compelled to till their fields. Shower-baths for the troops are being established in the towns. All of us: officers, *beamte*, doctors and civilian experts are striving together in the interest of the troops, for the Fatherland and for the industries at home.

Sunday 31 January 1915
Kohl's Adjutant Olbricht[22] talked most divertingly about the intelligentsia we have accumulated in the trenches. There are e.g. three professors. The first, from a polytechnic, has set up an electrical generator which both pumps the water out of the trenches and provides electric light for all the dugouts. The second, a visiting lecturer from Berlin, was recently hit at a listening post (70 paces from the English) while reviewing the printed version of his new work on Egyptian

excavations. And the third, tenured Professor Dr. jur. Peters from the University of Frankfurt am Main, is an expert on constitutional questions, in particular questions concerning trusts. Recently a letter arrived from very senior quarters, stating that Peters must not be exposed to danger, as he is a real authority in certain areas which will come under discussion at the peace settlement, and the only one with a complete understanding of the matter. Peters' doctoral thesis was of such significance, that the requirement for a professorial dissertation was waived for him. Now at the age of 28 he is a tenured professor and *kriegsfreiwilliger* gefreiter. He serves as Olbricht's orderly and right-hand man.

Wednesday 3 February 1915
The poor French women of the area are living in boundless misery. They beg a great deal from our fellows, by which our good nature is apparent. They may now send money to their husbands in captivity. However the practically minded Pillement only accepts gold or silver from them, no paper money, and it is extraordinary how many small pieces of gold are still coming to light there. The gold reserves of our own *Reichsbank* are now considerable, in excess of 2.1 billion! To punish those wrongdoers who are incredibly still hoarding gold, the *Reich* now intends to restrike all gold currency. After the peace any coin that doesn't bear the new markings will be withdrawn.

Monday 8 February 1915
The massive consumption of coal and paraffin on the part of the troops is striking. It has been discovered that there is a regular trade going on between the soldiers and the French girls. The market price: one bucket of coal to enjoy their favours once, one liter of paraffin for three times.

Thursday 4 March 1915
Today there was a small revolution of the womenfolk in Lille. Everyone was dreadfully agitated, and the streets were densely crowded with women of all social classes. Our Landsturm and the Police had to arrest six women who were being downright rebellious. The cause: shortly before a troop of fresh French prisoners (600–800 strong) was marched to the Citadel. It was as if the women had gone quite mad, they threw everything conceivable to the 'Piou-Pious' and wanted to free them. I heard that it was all down to the fact that there were many young men from Lille among the prisoners. In many cases mother and child had recognised the father of the house as he passed by. Today news was received that from now on we are to form the staff of the 116. Inf.-Brig. within the 58. ID, and have to be in Cambrai on Sunday 6 March.

Friday 5 March 1915
I reported to corps and divisional HQ. It is typical that neither Laffert nor Krug said a word of thanks. Well old chap, don't get yourself worked up and don't expect so much out of life!

Sunday 21 March 1915

My path took me along the canal, where there was a good deal of merriment. Everywhere there were boats full of soldiers, enjoying a trip on the water and playing the mouth organ – songs from the Elbe, the Donau and the Neckar. I let myself be photographed with a group of Württemberg soldiers, to their great delight. In a few of the boats pretty girls were sitting beside our *feldgrauen*. The relationship between Württembergers and Saxons is pretty good. Recently though one drunken Württemberger came into the barracks of the 9. Komp. / IR 107, and asserted that they were his own quarters. When they threw him out he got carried away, and committed assaults against superiors. Technically he should have been sentenced to death, but received only three years in prison. ...

Following the loss of his two sons General d'Elsa[23] has sought death himself, and was wounded together with his chief of staff Eulitz.

Saturday 17 April 1915

I drove with Tümmler by motor car to Ostend. Took a stroll along the world-renowned seafront, packed with magnificent palaces and millionaires' hotels, and now redeveloped along its entire length with trenches and barbed wire obstacles. Visited Kapitänleutnant Neudeck's '*Batterie Caecilie*', four long-barreled 15cm *ringkanonen*. Breakfasted merrily in

the officers' mess in the dunes. Continued our journey along the beach as far as Middelkerke, where we came within range of the English artillery at Nieuport. Trip to see the '*Dicke Bertha*', which took its last shot on 7 April and is set up under cover of an artificial wood. I was most impressed by the 42cm projectile, which was bigger than my *ordonnanz-offizier* Tümmler. We ate in the *marinekasino* at the market in Ostend. Here everything has a naval character. I was received by Prince Heinrich of Prussia[24], who had just arrived and amicably shook my hand. Continued our journey as far as Zeebrügge, on a lovely road with countless heavy coastal batteries alongside. Inspected the U-boat pens and the mole. Here we witnessed the 3. Matrosen-Regiment parading before Prince Heinrich. The machine-guns were drawn by dogs. Return journey via Courtrai, where at the railway station, which has been furnished with German economy, we drank a good glass of *Märzenbier*.

Sunday 25 April 1915

I visited the grave of Achim Peter in Ledeghem, and found it handsomely cared for and located in a tranquil spot in the churchyard. I contemplated the young life which had met its end here, then drove to Roulers where I spent a most diverting hour, since a huge crowd of captured Canadians had just arrived in the marketplace via the narrow-gauge railway. They all looked very much the worse for wear. The eight officers

The *Küstenbatterie Hindenburg* at Ostende, part of the coastal defences controlled by Marinekorps Flandern.

who marched at the head of the group made a reasonable impression. At the marketplace I met the staff officer of the division, my old friend from the *Kriegsakademie* General von Runckel[25]. I briefly visited him and heard some details of the fighting which is still raging north-east of Ypres, in which von Watzdorf's Saxon division was also involved. When the trenches were stormed many of the enemy were captured in an insensible condition, poisoned by the gas, together with many others who gave themselves up without any resistance. ...

On the return journey I broke down a short distance from Courtrai. In the village in question[26] there is a Saxon *etappen-fuhrpark-kolonne* under the command of Graf Schimmelmann, where I spent an hour or so. Just eight days ago the famed aviator Ltn. Garros was captured here[27]. Flying his machine-gun armed craft alone without an observer, he had shortly before brought down a German *Taube* and then proceeded to drop a bomb on the railway station. To this end he had descended to a height of 600 metres, and was at that very moment spotted by men of the Landsturm, shot at and forced into a steep glide. Immediately after landing he had burned his machine and concealed himself in a ditch, where he was discovered. The French papers are greatly mourning the loss of this man, the best of their aviators, who had also made a most favourable and gentlemanly impression on Schimmelmann.

Tuesday 4 May 1915

Our own shrapnel balls and machine-gun bullets, fired at enemy aircraft, are now causing us considerable discomfort. They fly past one's nose in quarters and on the street alike, and have already been the cause of numerous unfortunate losses.

On 9 May the French launched a major offensive (the Second Battle of Artois or *Lorettoschlacht*), with the aim of retaking the vital high ground of Vimy Ridge. Simultaneously, the BEF attacked further north (Battles of Aubers Ridge and Festubert). In accordance with its role as a strategic reserve, 58. ID was rushed southwards by railway and committed piecemeal to the defence against the French onslaught between Givenchy-en-Gohelle and Neuville-Saint-Vaast, reinforcing the critically threatened I. bRK. After over a month of heavy fighting north and south of Lens, its units were gradually withdrawn between 19 and 27 June, and transferred to 4. Armee in Flanders. According to '*Sachsen in großer Zeit*', this battle cost the Saxon elements of the division alone 688 killed (including twenty-nine officers), 2,211 wounded (including sixty officers), 477 missing (including ten officers) and three men confirmed captured.

Based from 28 June at Ingelmunster and then from 13 July in Roubaix, the battered division spent a further week regrouping and rebuilding before departing for the Eastern Front on 20 July.

Wednesday 7 July 1915

Attended an early morning meeting at divisional HQ. Gersdorff[28] presented a very interesting report on the riots in Lille and Roubaix. They were inspired by inflammatory and mendacious French reports which had been smuggled in by prohibited means. Aircraft had also scattered leaflets, according to which the French Army would be entering Lille on 12 July. Everywhere strict measures have been taken. A few ringleaders have been shot. Our old mayor in Lambresart, Herr Bonte[29], has also been imprisoned.

Friday 9 July 1915

I took an early morning ride through the Flemish countryside, which could be described as nice but dull. The people here are also exceedingly unlovely. The women are all of the broad-nosed and paunchy Dutch Gobelin-type. In comparison the French or Walloon women are prettier. I don't find the Flemish menfolk congenial either: they are scruffy, slovenly and dull-witted. The population is of course also very poor – everything reeks of poverty.

Sunday 11 July 1915

I drove once again to Gent, and am staying here near the square on which the band plays, where I see many pretty faces and elegant women and eat at Crangale's wine bar. On this day in other years during peacetime, there was a great town festival in Gent over the course of three days, where all classes mingled and danced publicly in the town squares. I have already found that relations between the population and us Germans in Gent are really harmonious. We are politely avoided, and they observe us with curiosity but no hostility – on the contrary, many of the pretty girls smile at one.

Saturday 17 July 1915

Exercise with IR 106 at Hem. In the afternoon I took a stroll to Lambresart and met Herr Bonte, the mayor. He told me sadly how he had been interned for 14 days as a hostage. The people of his community had refused to sew sandbags for the Germans. A fine had then been imposed and he was detained until payment was received.

Tuesday 20 July 1915

Last day in Lille. At 12 o'clock in the evening our train leaves the Gare de la Madeleine, heading in a direction which remains secret. Hurrah!

The Tragedy of Hans Brückner

Survived the war as a POW, only to die of illness within days of his return home

Hans Georg Brückner was born on 6 March 1889 in Zwickau. After completing his studies he worked in Freiberg, Oschatz and Bautzen as a teacher. The *Gedenkbuch den früheren Schülern des Bautzner Gymnasiums* (a memorial book for the former pupils of that school) describes his military career as follows: '*following the outbreak of war he was called up in October 1914. … after three months' training in Freiberg he joined the 8. Kompanie/Reserve-Infanterie-Regiment 242 at the front before Ypres. He remained in the trenches there for nearly a year and a half save for a few short breaks, and took part in offensive operations on numerous occasions. He served from the bottom up as an ersatz-reservist, and only donned the braids*[1] *at the urging of his family. He was wounded twice… At Hooge he was awarded the Iron Cross 2nd Class. After serving with his regiment in France for half a year as an unteroffizier and vizefeldwebel and completing the officer's course at Lockstedter Lager, he went to Galicia as a minenwerfer specialist*[2] *and served as an officer in the subsequent advance to the Zbrucz; at the end of 1917 however, he was back on the Western Front. In the terrible fighting at Nouvron fate overtook him; he went into French captivity and remained there, at Albertville and Courtine, for over a year and a half. Finally, late in the evening of 16 February 1920, he returned to his parental home. There on 23 February he succumbed to pneumonia, which he had already contracted before his return, having been taken ill in the transit camp. On 26 February 1920, amid a large crowd of well-wishers, he was laid to rest at the Taucherfriedhof* [in Bautzen].'

Hans was one of thousands to die when the third wave of 'Spanish flu' hit Germany in January–March 1919. As in the similarly lethal second wave of autumn 1918, the young were worst hit. Only those who had caught the far milder '*Kemmelfieber*' earlier in 1918 were immune.

Oberstudienrat (senior secondary school teacher) Max Brückner from Bautzen, who preserved his son's war letters for posterity by transcribing them in his diaries.

Hans Brückner (standing, right) training with the Ersatz-Bataillon of Infanterie-Regiment 182 at the *König-Friedrich-August-Kaserne* in Freiberg, winter 1914/1915.

Extracts from the diary of Dr Max Brückner, regarding his son's experiences with RIR 242 in 1915

This letter dated **29 January** reached us on **4 February** and states that it was posted in Keiberg. I will copy the contents here almost in their entirety:

Today I send you my first greetings from the front. I'm on field sentry duty in the gap between the front lines of the 242ers and the 244ers. To start with then, our accomodation – we're being housed, all 28 of us (three full sections, a feldwebel, two unteroffiziers and a gefrei-ter), in a shot-up building with only two small rooms still intact. For my own part, I'm stuck with ten other men in the cellar of the building, which is 2 metres wide by 2.5 long and 1.5 in height. So we can't do more than sit down, even at night. Naturally the little room is beauti-fully warm and cosy. When we are cooking or heating something up during the day, we stand in the other more airy rooms as well. Right now we have a bit less room than we used to, since a shell recently hit the house and de-stroyed the so-called bedroom. In fact, the shell splinters nearly destroyed the roof of our little room in the cellar – in one place the ceiling had to be propped up. So as you can see from this account, we are living quite well under the circumstances. We are not allowed out of the house during the day unless we are on watch, since we are not to needlessly expose ourselves to danger – namely, the rifle bullets which are continually hammering away all around us. This evening while I was standing on watch from 6 to 8 o'clock, they were forever whizzing past us; the old sweat who was with me said, that from this you could tell that the English were in the front line again; the French don't shoot so wildly. Shells too are constantly landing in the vicinity, which is clearly why the copse behind which our house stands is known to the soldiers as *Granatwäldchen* ['Shell Copse'] Hardly any tree is still unscathed, every-where the treetops have been beaten down by the shells – it is a sad sight. Numerous corpses are still lying out there too, since no-one has found the time to retrieve them yet; meanwhile they have been laid out in hollows in the ground, and covered with foliage, brushwood and bark fragments. At my post by night I had a really good view of the French flares going up, and could clearly see that they are equipped with parachutes, so that they hang in the air for a particularly long time. So far as I know, our own flares are unfortunately not fitted with this device. Our chaps cook potatoes to their heart's content, together with the chickens which wander freely on a neighbouring

(abandoned) estate and are snatched during the night. So far I have not yet taken part in this myself, preferring instead to catch up on some sleep in our little cellar room; however in recent nights I've almost invariably had to stand watch or carry entrenching supplies to the front, last night for instance 265 sandbags brought up by lorry, which took up all my time from 7:30 to 12 midnight! As a result today I have only stood watch from 6 to 8 am, and will scarcely get another moment's peace 'til the evening.

That same day, to our amazement, a second letter from our boy arrived, which was dated **30 January** on field watch near Keiberg, and read as follows:

You will probably already have received my first letter from field watch. Since then much has happened, but first to set your minds at rest I should say that I remain unhurt. Yesterday afternoon about 2:30 our house took a direct hit from a shell. The effect was dreadful, as it penetrated the guardroom. One comrade is dead, the other seven who were with him in the room are severely wounded; in the adjacent room another man was severely and two men lightly wounded. Those of us in the cellar however escaped wholly unhurt on this occasion. One of our sentries on field watch was also severely wounded at the same time. I must decline to describe the scene in greater detail. We used our 58 field dressings[3] at once as emergency bandages, while one of us (already decorated with the Iron Cross) set out on the difficult journey to notify the *sanitäts-kompanie*. An hour later they came, at the greatest risk to their own lives (as soon as they were visible, the French shelled them!), bandaged the wound-ed properly and wanted to evacuate them immediately. However this proved to be impossible, owing to the immediate resumption of the shelling. So they had to wait until 6:30 and the approach of nightfall. In any case, their self-sacrifice deserves the highest praise. Access to our position by daylight is reckoned impossible, at most a patrol can approach unnoticed by crawling on the ground. Nevertheless they came jogging forward through the shelling across open ground, over a dozen strong, with the unterarzt (who did not strictly need to accompany them!), the feldwebel and numerous unteroffiziers, just to help their comrades! That takes the highest courage! Apart from this there is nothing to report from our field watch or my own duties; I stood watch from 8 to 10 o'clock yesterday evening and from 10 to 12 this morning, with-out noticing anything beside a few aircraft. Naturally the bullets still constantly whizz about us, and this afternoon the shells too are once again crashing horribly all around the house. Replacements for the twelve men came immediately from our company last night, so that we are back to our old strength again.

29 April. Today the following detailed letter arrived from Moorslede, dated **24 April**:

Tonight at 1:15 am our battalion is to be marched out into the battle once more, and unfortunately I am to stay behind in our quarters to guard the backpacks, on the orders of the *korpora*l and the feldwebel! Whenever anything is going on I am not there! I must be considered very valuable indeed, that they should take such pains to keep me away from serious operations – as if they thought me so indispensible later in civilian life? The ring around the Englishmen closes ever tighter, only a few kilometres are left for them to escape encirclement. North and south of us the Germans have stormed forward, and indeed with great success. Naturally I must not reveal more at present. As a result of the pressure from the north and south, a breakthrough attempt was feared in our sector. Hence we had to be on our feet day and night at duties just as arduous as if we were in the trenches. A test had to be undertaken, to see whether the fighting strength of the English opposite us had also been shaken. So our regiment made a mock attack. We set up dummies here, by hanging greatcoats on scaling ladders with helmets tied on the top. At 9 pm precisely we held them up a little above the parapet – as if we intended to launch an assault – and when the whistle sounded the entire battalion occupying the regimental positions began to bellow '*Hurra!*'[4] The effect was fearful; almost at the same instant flares went up from the English lines, and when they saw the figures 'leaping over' the parapet an appalling rifle and artillery fire ensued. The machine-guns hammered on the steel shields of our loopholes, making a fearful din. A few minutes later the English artillery also joined in; one shrapnel round after another, one shell after another, one sulphur bomb[5] after another, one hand grenade after another, one rifle grenade after another came flying over. Fortunately all of these projectiles overshot us, since the English were not shooting into our fighting trenches but rather into our communication trenches, as they wanted to hit the reserves (non-existent, as it was a mock attack). Admittedly a few fell damned short, so that we were covered with a dense shower of earth and splinters. It was pandemonium. Even the old sweats who had survived the heavy assault of 25 October 1914 (where after one night only 500 were left from 2,800 men of the regiment) said that the fire back then had been nowhere near as bad. We all crouched as low to the ground as possible and nestled in the trench, unable to move. If we had attacked in earnest, scarcely a man of us would have got as far as 10 metres forward from our line. We lived through this witches' cauldron for over half an hour, then the English judged that the attack had been beaten off and ceased fire. That was our mock attack, which I will be unable to forget for the rest of my life. God grant that I never have to go through one like it for real! Soon enough the English must have pulled some lovely faces and worked themselves up into a lovely rage, when they saw that they had been fooled and that not a single corpse lay in front of our trench, instead of the hundreds that they could have expected there from a real attack! Their fury was clearly apparent from their fire over the course of the following day. Under such circumstances our leadership declined to make a further 'assault test' of this sort, which should have taken place at 2 o'clock, as well as a real attack in the morning, and so our position only has to be held against a breakthrough.

Meanwhile our attacks north and south of Ypres have already led to great successes. Many thousands of Englishmen have already been captured; earlier, 296 prisoners came through here with 2 officers. They all looked horribly dirty, but the majority were the sort I wouldn't care to have to face in close combat, over half of them big broad-shouldered types, real sportsmen. The rest were younger, and among them a lot of really villainous faces. Both kinds were pretty unappealing. There were a few Highlanders and Scotsmen, the greater part however were Canadians. Their uniforms were consistently excellent and practical, thick clay-yellow fleece coats which are obviously very practical. Some of them had been stuck in the trenches for over 2½ weeks without relief, und were thus almost happy to have been captured. It is also said that in one part of the line the English must have been so demoralised by our artillery fire, that they ran to meet our skirmish lines with raised arms and without weapons, their belt equipment (with the cartridge pouches) already removed, to let themselves be taken prisoner. Their artillery too is believed to have run out of ammunition in places, so that we only incurred losses from infantry fire. Now hopefully it will carry on like this, so that we succeed as soon as possible in closing the sack around Ypres. Hopefully I'll soon rejoin the company at the front; however there is little chance of this for the moment! Best wishes to all.

Open-air church parade in Moorslede, home to the rest quarters of Reserve-Infanterie-Regiment 242 in 1914/1915. The chaplain's pulpit can be seen on the left of the photo, and the bandstand in the background on the right.

On **18 May** Hans gave a detailed account of his experiences in a letter from Verlorenhoek, which I will quote in full.

In the trenches, 3km east of Ypres, 15 May 1915. The rain has just more or less stopped drumming on my ground-sheet-roof in our reserve trench, where I crouch on a little sack of straw, wrapped up in two greatcoats against the abominable cold, while English shrapnel rounds fly overhead at short intervals and strike home all around us. So I'd like to use this brief rest period to finally give you the long-intended detailed account. It was 7 o'clock on the morning of 4 May and I was on watch, when suddenly the report came from the left that the English trenches opposite us were empty. Immediately we went forward, once it had been confirmed by the *pioniere* that the English had not laid mines about, to blow us sky-high when we ventured onto the site. Everything over there had been abandoned in the greatest haste and disorder. Masses of ammunition and provision crates lay scattered about, and we quickly replenished our supplies with army biscuits,

corned beef and jam, insofar as the tins were still intact— the English had punctured many of them with bayonets, to render them inedible by letting the water in – and then proceeded by forced march to Zonnebeke, where we arrived about 9:45. West of the town our advance guard were already engaged in a fierce battle with the withdrawing enemy. For us too the order was the same: spread out and advance. The first enemy shots passed over us on the way. We dug in behind a copse and lay there until evening. Then we went back to Zonnebeke where, as I wrote to you before, we stayed for two days in the convent school. Here too of course the English did not leave us in peace; they repeatedly bombarded the town with sulphur shells[5], once so heavily that everyone had to flee into the surrounding fields and we also had a few losses. Meanwhile the advance continued west of Zonnebeke, despite the desperate resistance of the English. All the same they finally managed to get dug in again on a ridge, while our chaps laid out new trenches opposite. As I wrote previously, we then occupied a reserve trench in the rear for two days.

Early on the 8 May, as I was getting up, reinforcements suddenly appeared everywhere: today we were to attack. About 8 am a fearful artillery barrage opened up. The English line was discernible only as a single continuous cloud of smoke. This lasted for two hours, then there was dead silence – the calm before the storm, which soon gave way to a heavy fire from English rifles and machine-guns: our first line had begun the assault on the English positions! My company was to advance as the second wave, so first we had to reach the front line via the communication trench. In doing so we already had dreadful losses from shrapnel fire. Then the call came: over the top! We were greeted with terrific fire. But it was all the same to us; it had to be done, no matter the cost! Only a moment's thought for our loved ones at home, and then forwards. Unfortunately I lost my glasses while clambering out of the trench, so for the moment I had to storm forward like that, despite my shortsightedness. Soon I realised that this wouldn't do. So I threw off my backpack to retrieve my spare pair. Under the awful fire, in which com-

rades were going down to the left and right of me, I could not take the time to don the backpack again – so I stormed forward again without it. Soon the English trench was reached; admittedly it could hardly be called a trench any more but rather a series of shell holes, our artillery having done their preparatory work brilliantly! The Englishmen shot like maniacs until we were within about 10 metres, then they turned to flee, and at the sprint it's no easy matter for any us us to outrun these sportsmen! On and on we advanced, until finally we came under such heavy fire that for the moment it was impossible to continue. So the order was given: 'stellung!'[6] At once we began to dig ourselves in, to obtain some cover from the shrapnel fire. One can dig very quickly, when one's head is on the line! In a good hour our new trench was ready; very wet and muddy, but what of it? We stayed in it for a day and a half, until we were relieved. Already on the first night the English tried to wrest the trench from us with strong forces; our rapid rifle fire and our machine-gun soon broke up the attack. Over the day and half when we were still

Hans and his friend Willy Ulbrich (right) in a photographer's studio in Roulers. Willy was killed at Hooge in early August 1915 by a direct hit on his dug-out.

Hans convalescing at hospital in Gent from a light calf wound, inflicted by a shrapnel ball near Zonnebeke on 24 May 1915. He was also suffering from scabies.

in the front line we had much to endure under the enemy artillery fire, for hours we crouched on our knees (despite the mud) in the trench, our heads (as the most precious body part) pressed against the ground, while the shells hammered down all around and showered us with lumps of dirt. We went no further forward here, as it was first necessary for the troops on our flanks to catch up. After our relief we first lay for a further day and a half in reserve in the old English dug-outs at Zonnebeke, then as I wrote previously we went on to Moorslede.

On the night of the 12th–13th we occupied the dug-outs at Zonnebeke again. On the 13th the English launched a ferocious assault, we had to rush forward as quickly as possible as reinforcements to the second line (our former first line, as our positions had been pushed forward another 400 metres closer to Ypres in the mean time) and now we crouch here for a third day in the fiercest shrapnel and small-arms fire as reserves, until we are needed! So much for today!

On **11 July** our boy's detailed letter from St. Eloi of **8 July** arrived, which I reproduce below in full, save for the short introduction and closing words:

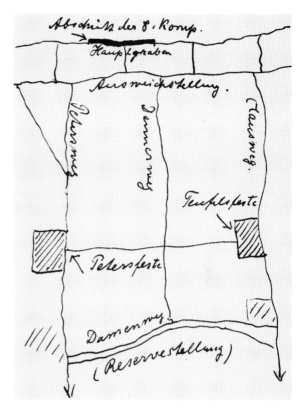

Last night we were sent for a day's rest in the reserve positions. We arrived there about 12 midnight. Then we were immediately ordered to fall in again, to carry a self-assembly dug-out forward to the front line! We returned from this task about 3 o'clock at night, after which I indeed slept soundly right through to 1 o'clock in the afternoon today, in spite of the hundreds of flies. Today we remain here still, getting a thorough rest (the time which isn't devoted to eating and sleeping is occupied with writing letters, cleaning our rifles etc.). This evening however we are to go forward into the trenches again for a day, then we are to go once more into reserve for a further two days. The Bavarian[7] trench which now forms our position is wonderfully constructed, with hundreds of thousands of sandbags. About 50 to 100 metres behind this trench is the alternate position, likewise impeccably constructed throughout with sandbags, loopholes and dug-outs. If the enemy should ever break into the first trench, the garrison are to fall back in the first instance to the alternate position and put up further resistance here. About 1½ km further back along the three communication trenches are two proper little fortresses, the *Petersfeste* and the *Teufelsfeste*, which are to be occupied when necessary by the troops waiting in reserve in the dug-outs on the *Damenweg*. Beyond this reserve position

the communication trenches continue for another 2km further back before reaching open ground. So, for once you get some idea how such a well-developed position is laid out. The Bavarians have also built up the reserve position perfectly; proper little wooden blockhouses, in places even little wooden villas for the officers! Anyhow the position itself is flawless. Now maybe you have still been worrying yourselves over the account of the mine detonation. However that is a commonplace occurrence here. For our own part we are also diligently undermining the enemy; in our company sector alone there are two galleries, which are being driven forward about 5 to 8 metres underground. In the solid clay of this area such mole-work is quite feasible. The passageways are lined with planks, the ground water which leaks through is sucked up and carried away by great pressure-pumps. I once climbed down into the gallery myself in my free time and had a look at everything. To our left there remains a gigantic mine crater, 20 metres in diameter and almost 10 metres deep. Previously on a small hill here the English had set up machine-guns, with which they inflicted heavy losses on the Bavarians by enfilading their trenches. Without hesitation the Bavarians blew this place up into the air together with everything on it, and incorporated the place into our positions. Naturally the English too are no slouches at undermining. However I reckon that the recent detonation was no ordinary one. Anyhow, they had somehow heard us digging and driven forward a lateral gallery, so that by exploding it they could break into our mine passage and 'pinch it out' – as the technical term puts it. Thus in any case it only produced a very small mine crater on the surface, 15 metres in front of our trench.

13 August. Finally the tension has been relieved again, this morning a card and a letter arrived together from Hooge, which informed us that we had been worrying with good reason. The card written on **10 August**, which should have reassured us in the first instance, reached us alas at the same time as the detailed letter, but one could also argue this was fortunate. It reads:

Today just a note to say that I am entirely unharmed. The previous day was the hardest to date in the field. For fifteen hours we lay under the heaviest English artillery fire, to which our company lost about thirty men! On top of that, nothing to eat or drink!

The contents of the letter were as follows:

As you may have gathered from [postcard] Nr. 186, I got through the previous day unhurt. Our company has now lost about forty men in eight days, including ten dead! Yesterday it was most especially bad. The English made a desperate breakthrough attempt at Hooge Chateau, also aiming to recapture their recently lost positions. At 3:30 am the artillery battle began, all available batteries right up to the heaviest fired away incessantly. About 5:30 we were alerted: the English had succeeded in breaking into our positions in the neighbouring sector (IR 126 and IR 132) which could no longer be held under the artillery fire. We were called upon as reinforcements, and went forward post-haste along the communication trenches. However these had been partially collapsed by the heavy shells, so that in places we had to go across open ground. In doing so we were observed, and immediately received the heaviest artillery fire, from which we had considerable losses; for example the man right behind me was severely wounded by a shrapnel ball, which struck a metre to my rear. Having got into a forward trench, it was necessary to tackle the mine crater which the English had reoccupied, using hand grenades. Together with many others I drove forward a sap toward the crater. Here too we had losses. I had scarcely been relieved from shovelling

when my replacement, my friend Miethe, was hit in the shoulder blade by a bullet. Besides myself he was the only one in my section who got through the attack of 8 May unscathed! Then until about 2 o'clock I was with the forwardmost machine-gun. The heavy shells came crashing down incessantly all around us; one 2 metres in front of the gun, one 3 metres behind, and still uninjured! A metre closer and all ten of us would have gone to the devil. About 2 o'clock we were moved further to the right. However it was no better there either with the shells. They struck repeatedly right in front or behind the trench, and showered us with clumps of dirt and iron splinters. About 6 pm the artillery fire slackened off somewhat; about 10 pm we were relieved and returned to our reserve dug-outs. I had nothing to eat from morning to evening (I hadn't had a chance to grab anything before the alarm was sounded that morning) and nothing to drink but my canteen full of coffee, most of which however was drunk by the wounded and the 132ers, who had already had nothing to drink for a day. It was lucky that I had at least pocketed thirteen cigars, and puffed through most of them! Thus passed this heaviest day to date in the field! On account of this we are lying today in complete rest in reserve. Indeed according to plan we should get relieved this evening, but it isn't likely to happen, we will probably still remain here as reserves. The English breakthrough has failed, although they have succeeded in recapturing some of their lost positions; nevertheless a heavy fight is still raging for this part, and I don't believe they'll be able to hang onto it…

In a later letter Hans adds the following concerning the fighting on **9 August**:

That our conduct in the fighting on 9 May was most especially commendable is also shown by the fact that our I. Batl. and 8. Komp., the only one from our battalion which was called to the front line, have been granted twenty-five Iron Crosses 2nd Class and one 1st Class for this day alone! Senior officers are also said to have remarked that the position to our left was only held thanks to the 8. Komp., which was swiftly on the scene in spite of the tremendous volume of fire and considerable losses, and by their calm demeanour did much to bolster the morale of the other companies. Once again RIR 242 in general gave the appearance of being an elite regiment, which even surpassed other active regiments in daring and bravery! Well, we can certainly be satisfied with this testimony!

Trenches at Hooge after the fighting of August 1915, from the regimental history of Württemberg Infanterie-Regiment 126 (39. ID / XV. AK).

After the fighting at Hooge. Hans (top right) was promoted to unteroffizier. In October 1915 he was sent to Lockstedt in Schleswig-Holstein (the *truppenübungsplatz* of Prussian IX. AK) to take the *offiziers-aspiranten-kursus*. Going by helmet numbers alone, most of the 'aspirants' pictured here are fellow Saxons

Three fallen brothers

The cruel fate of the Krebs family

The Krebs family of Mittweida in Saxony had three young sons, all of whom went to war and none of whom returned. The first to fall was Fritz, who was serving with **Grenadier-Regiment 101** from Dresden when reported missing on 4 September 1916, at Chaulnes on the French part of the Somme battlefront. His brothers Kurt and Karl were both killed in action in Flanders within a few weeks of each other in October 1917. Karl fell on 9 October in Prussian service, leading a machine-gun team of Silesian **Jäger-Bataillon 5** near Passchendaele, and Kurt on 27 October with the 7. Kompanie of **Infanterie-Regiment 179** near Gheluvelt. At about this time poor Herr and Frau Krebs also received an official death notice for Fritz, although to date he still has no known grave. Karl was buried at De Ruyter and later re-interred at the *Deutscher Soldatenfriedhof Menen* (Block B Grave 1041). Kurt remains in his original resting place at the *Soldatenfriedhof Halluin*, among hundreds of other victims of the *Dritte Flandernschlacht.*

Grenadier Fritz Krebs (right) and friend in July 1915 on the fortress walls at Laon. This was the HQ city of 7. Armee, to which XII. AK was subordinated during its lengthy stay on the Aisne northwest of Reims.

Karl Krebs (left) and a comrade in 1914, during training with the 1. or 2. Ersatz-MGK of V. AK in Silesia. These units recruited and trained gunners (*MG-schützen*) for all arms of service; as his *pickelhaube* indicates, Karl is not yet a *jäger.*

On the death of Karl Krebs

....

In 1917 Jäger-Bataillon 5 (with the likewise Silesian Jäger-Bataillon 6, and Pommeranian Reserve-Jäger-Bataillon 2) was serving as part of Jäger-Regiment 6. Together with its sister Jäger-Regiment 8 (Reserve-Jäger-Bataillone 4, 16 and 24) and Reserve-Infanterie-Regiment 233 it belonged to the 195. Infanterie-Division, which had begun formation in Flanders in July 1916 before a hasty transfer to the Eastern Front to counter the Brusilov Offensive. It returned in late April 1917, taking over a sector on the Menin Road about the 26th and remaining in Flanders until transferred southwards in August. On 2 October the

Oberjäger Karl Krebs in the field with Jäger-Bataillon 5, posing in fatigue dress with an MG 08 on an improvised anti-aircraft turntable. For this role the gun was more usually removed from its 'sledge' and fitted to a simple rotary mount bolted on top of a sturdy pole.

units of 195. Infanterie-Division, then resting near Caudry, received the grim news of its assignment to *Gruppe Ypres* of 4. Armee.

On the night of the 5–6 October Jäger-Bataillon 5 took over the front line in the new regimental sector on the divisional right flank, with Reserve-Jäger-Bataillon 2 in *bereitschaft* (immediate support) and Jäger-Bataillon 6 further back in reserve. The front extended for about a kilometre along the Passchendaele Ridge, from 100 metres south of Wallemolen cemetery to the Gravenstafel road. These landmarks were largely notional in a hellish landscape of flooded craters, some of which served as the *vorpostenlinie* (outpost line), the first of three lines forming a defensive zone 600–800 metres deep. The 1. and 2. MGK, with six heavy MG 08 each (organised in two-gun platoons), were largely deployed at the back of this zone to secure the *hauptwiderstandslinie* (or 'HWL', the main line of defence) along the Bellevue Spur, which boasted a system of battered but serviceable ferro-concrete pillboxes. Further forward the defence depended on the 'light' machine-guns (MG 08/15) of the rifle companies.

The bombardment began in earnest on the evening of the 7th, followed on the 8th by apparent attempts to probe forward on the left of the battalion, as the Tommies struggled toward their start line under torrential rain. On 9 October the British launched their next major attack, later known as the Battle of Poelcappelle. 195. Infanterie-Division was attacked by two brigades each from two British divisions under the command of II. ANZAC Corps, 49th (West Riding) Infantry Division to the north and 66th (2nd East Lancashire) Division to the south. Hampered by the inundated ground and uncut wire 25–40 metres deep, the 49th Division became bogged down in the pre-planned killing zone in front of the HWL; by the end of the day they had made little progress at a cost of 2,500 casualties. Further south however and on more solid ground, the 66th Division broke through towards Passchendaele in the Reserve-Infanterie-Regiment 233 sector. On Jäger-Bataillon 5's left flank, where the 3. Kompanie was holding the high ground of Höhe 704 ('Bellevue' on British maps) above the Gravenstafel road, Karl Krebs and his MG 08 team also became pivotally involved in countering this threat. British accounts of the day's fighting would emphasise the role of the machine-guns at Bellevue, both in repelling the 49th Division and later in forcing the 66th to withdraw (following a counter-attack by elements of Reserve Infanterie-Regiment 233 and Jäger-Regiment 8). However Karl himself would not live to see it.

From the account of Leutnant Kaczynski, a *zugführer* (platoon commander) with the **1. MG-Kompanie / Jäger-Bataillon von Neumann (1. Schlesisches) Nr. 5**, as it appears in the published battalion history, pp. 163–164. Oberjäger Karl Krebs was a *gewehrführer* (gun commander), one of two under Kaczynski's command.

The action of my heavy MG platoon was closely connected with the fighting on the fronts of our 3. Kompanie and the neighbouring [Reserve-] Jäger-Bataillon 16. The Englishman had barely redirected his drum-fire to our rear and already the MGs were being readied for action, in order to support the *jägers* to our front in the defense with overhead fire. However the first attack by the English assault troops was completely repulsed[1]. Then at 9 o'clock a very heavy drumming started up again, and while the shell splinters were still whizzing past our ears, the MGs began hammering further forward and the crackle of rifle fire rang out along the whole front. A second massed attack launched from the channel of the Stroombeek broke against our lines. As the smoke and fumes cleared, we saw that dense waves of attackers were pushing forward against the left flank. *Gewehr Schreinert*

immediately took them under fire and shot at 600 to 800 metres into the slowly advancing English. With binoculars it was possible to observe the effects of the burst on the opposition; the leading waves disintegrated.

Meanwhile *Gewehr Krebs* was still lying inactive further to the right, since the HWL at Höhe 704 was still secure in the hands of the 3. Kompanie, and all attempts to advance there had been repelled. On the other hand dense English columns were advancing on the front of the 16. [Reserve-] Jägers to our left. There on the flank of Jäger-Regiment 8 and above all by Reserve-Infanterie-Regiment 233 they had succeeded in breaking in, and by clever use of the streambed (which lay in a dead angle), in pushing strong forces forward there through the mire. The breach had widened, the infantry were under pressure from flanks and rear, and the heights on the western outskirts of Passchendaele were occupied by the enemy. From there well-aimed English MG fire struck the 16. [Reserve-] Jägers and our left wing in the flank, and inflicted heavy losses. The danger that the battalion in contact on our left would be trapped by a flanking movement grew ever greater.

The six *gewehrführer* of 1. MGK / Jäger-Bataillon 5 plus a friend, in front of their quarters in Galicia on 14 April 1917 – two days later the battalion was informed of the transfer to the Western Front. Unless otherwise noted, all held the rank of *oberjäger* at the time – from left Scholz I., Krebs (gefreiter), Geil, Lorenz, Seidel, Eckert (gefreiter, not a *gewehrführer*) and Scholz II.

Karl in 'Scottish' fancy dress during a hospital stay in 1916, at the Vereinslazarett Moltkefels in Niederschreiberhau (Silesia).

Meanwhile English waves were also advancing by bounds on the ruins of Passchendaele village, and here the bullets were already glancing off the street halfway from the rear. One messenger after another ran back by [Reserve-] Jäger [Batl.] 16 across the crater field. The situation was becoming increasingly dangerous, so I decided to send Oberjäger Krebs across the [Gravenstafel] road to deploy over there behind [Reserve-] Jäger [Batl.] 16, to counter any move to roll the position up from the flank. Under vicious English MG fire, and a rain of bullets from the shrapnel shells bursting at house-height above the street, the machine-gun crew sprang forward. The muddy crater field impeded their progress; but if they got just a bit further they would gain a better field of fire. Then suddenly the situation took a turn for the worse and before he could give the order 'stellung'[2], the brave *oberjäger* toppled forward. With a few strides Sanitäts-Feldwebel Peucker was beside him, but even so help had sadly come all too late. A shot to the heart had snuffed out the life of the young Saxon, a swift and painless death.

On the death of Kurt Krebs

Less than 5 miles to the south on 9 October, 24. ID beat off a local diversionary attack for the assault on the Passchendaele ridge. For three weeks from the night of 7–8 to 28 October, the division held '*Abschnitt Zandvoorde*' on the right of *Gruppe Wytschaete* (see pp. 135–136). There it was steadily ground down by nightmarish conditions, incessant bombardment and localised infantry attacks (notably on 22 October). By the evening of the 25th it was exhausted and significantly understrength. Unfortunately the next day would bring the opening of the Second Battle of Passchendaele, and a large-scale diversionary attack by British X Corps; on the British right, 7th Division would advance on both sides of the Menin Road.

The following extracts are taken from the published history of **14. Kgl. Sächs. Infanterie-Regiment Nr. 179**, pp. 201–202. The regiment was on the Saxon right, immediately to the south of the Menin Road (now no more than a line of craters) with its right flank just ahead of the ruins of Gheluvelt, the British 7th Division's objective.

During the night of the 25–26 October, forward patrols from the 'a' and 'b' company[3] observed a lively traffic and feverish activity behind the enemy lines. Immediately MG fire was brought to bear on the locations that had been identified. ... The enemy artillery fire seemed to increase in intensity.

... The companies in the front line had gone on the alert on their own initiative, due to strong enemy movements. A little before 5 am a wounded Englishman from the 7th Division (Regiment Queen [sic])[4] was brought in by the 1. Kompanie, having been shot by one of our sentries manning a light MG. He belonged to an English storm detachment.

This was conclusive evidence of an English attack, which promptly materialised. 10 minutes after the onset of the murderous drum fire at 6.30 am, which had rampaged across the whole of our sector as well as those of IR 133 and 139 and severely thinned our ranks, the deeply-echeloned stormtroops of the English 7th Division advanced on both sides of the Menin Road. On the left by the 4. and 1. Kompanie the attack broke down a short distance from our lines, thanks to the cool-headedness of our fellows and the muddy ground. ... on the right by the 2. Kompanie the situation was taking a far more serious shape. By our right-hand neighbour IR 69 the enemy had got as far as Gheluvelt Chateau. Our right flank was in the air. Heavy losses had also been incurred

Kurt and Karl at home in Saxony in early 1917. Fritz has already been reported missing, while Kurt has probably not yet enlisted.

among the men, and of the five MGs only two were still serviceable. Thus we were powerless to prevent the enemy penetrating as far as the western edge of Gheluvelt, where he pushed column after column into the gap.

The 7. Kompanie to which Kurt Krebs belonged, together with its parent II. Bataillon, was in rest quarters at Halluin, but was immediately alerted on account of the situation. Partly by narrow-gauge railway and partly by truck the battalion moved forward again, and took up position in reserve. In the course of the 26 Oct. the I. and III. Batl./IR 179, together with the III. Batl./RIR 31, succeeded in stabilising the line with high losses. Fortunately for the Saxons, the battle was now effectively over in their sector – Kurt Krebs would be killed in action on the 27th in the 'normal' course of trench warfare.

In order to have fresh troops in the front line the next morning in case of a new English attack, and since the III./RIR 31 had to go back to Halluin, a relief of the 'A' battalion (which had been assembled from the severely depleted remnants of the 1., 2., 3., 4., 9., 10., 11. and 12./179 together with a few men from III./RIR 31) by the less worn out II./179 was conducted. ... the fighting strength of the III. Bataillon amounted to only two officers, twelve NCOs and fifty-eight men, that of the I. Bataillon to two officers, four NCOs and twenty-eight men. Throughout the night the enemy's disruptive artillery fire continued across the whole sector, and in the morning rose again in strength to an enormous intensity. ... there was little infantry activity. ... after daybreak the level of aggressive action on both sides slackened somewhat. ... In the afternoon the firing resumed on both sides. Enemy snipers made their presence uncomfortably felt in our lines. During the following night the relief of the regiment began.

On 29 October the regiment entrained at Wevelgem for transport to the Arras front.

Kurt Krebs before the war at a photographic studio in Mittweida, and ca. 1917 in training with the II. Ersatz-Bataillon/Reserve-Infanterie-Regiment 104, probably in Burgstädt. The black mourning band on his sleeve signifies the death of a close family member, quite possibly Fritz.

Plötzlich und unerwartet erhielten wir zum 2. Male die schmerzliche Nachricht, daß unser hoffnungsvoller, lebensfroher Sohn, lieber Bruder, Schwager und Neffe,

der Oberjäger

Karl Krebs,

I. Masch.-Gewehr-Komp. in einem Jäger-Btl.,

Inhaber des Eisernen Kreuzes II. Kl.,

am 9. 10. in Flandern den Heldentod gefunden hat.

Im tiefsten Weh:

Ferdinand Krebs u. Frau
Dora Thalheim geb. Krebs
Kurt Krebs, z. Z. im Felde
Erwin Thalheim, z. Z. im Felde
Frieda verw. **Krebs** geb. Kräuter
nebst übrigen Verwandten.

Mittweida, am 16. Oktober 1917.

Gestern erhielten wir die fast unglaubliche Nachricht, daß auch unser dritter und letzter Sohn, lieber Bruder, Schwager und Neffe,

Kurt Krebs,

Soldat in einem Infanterie-Regiment,

am 27. 10. den Heldentod in Flandern gefunden hat. Drei Söhne, all unser Stolz und unsere Hoffnung, haben wir dem Vaterlande opfern müssen.

In unsagbarem Schmerz

Ferdinand Krebs u. Frau
Dora Thalheim geb. Krebs
Erwin Thalheim, z. Zt. im Felde
Frida Krebs geb. Kräuter
und übrige Verwandte.

Mittweida und Frankenberg,
November 1917.

In 1936 friends of the family were able to visit the grave of Karl Krebs at De Ruyter. This cemetery held 2,806 war dead, and was closed with the establishment of the three great 'collecting' cemeteries in 1954; Karl was then reburied at Menen. The pre-printed postcard (provided by the VDK, the German war graves charity) assures his parents that Karl's numbered grave has been inspected by patrons of the cemetery and that '*our dead have found a worthy resting place here*'.

Werner Mühle, Gefreiter

A teenage volunteer's diary of the war in Flanders, 1917

By the end of 1916 the class of 1918 was being called up, and the class of 1919 would follow in May and June. Born in Löbau on 4 April 1899, Werner Mühle was already working for the war effort at the family firm (which produced horse-drawn vehicles, and later shells) when he decided to join up early. Like the volunteers of 1914 he was anxious to see action before the war ended, but also to ensure that his family was represented at the front again after two cousins had been killed in action and a third invalided out. After being turned down by 'several artillery regiments and the *jägers*', Mühle signed up as an *einjährig-freiwilliger* with the infantry, reporting for training with II. Ersatz-Bataillon / **Infanterie Regiment 102** in Löbau on 22 January 1917. This depot unit was dissolved (together with the second ersatz battalions of both 'active' grenadier regiments) on 25 April due to increasing manpower shortages, and Mühle completed his training with the I. Ersatz-Bataillon in Zittau.

On 19 July he entrained for the Western Front, reaching his regiment a few days before 32. Infanterie-Division was transferred to Flanders. Bored with the grim routine of trench warfare, he volunteered for his company's *stoßtrupp* that Autumn. This made him a member of the regimental *sturmkompanie* and of **Sturmabteilung der 32. Infanterie-Division** when these units were required. In February 1918 he was training for the upcoming offensive with the battalion-strength *sturmabteilung* when he suffered an accidental injury to his hand requiring treatment in Germany. After service as an instructor in Zittau and promotion to unteroffizier, he completed an officers' training course in Libau (now Liepaja, Latvia) in June, returning to Zittau a vizefeldwebel and *offizier-aspirant*. However his hopes of a reserve commission and of seeing out the war in Saxony were dashed that October when he was assigned to 241. ID, recently all but obliterated north of St. Quentin. With the severely understrength **Infanterie Regiment 474** he took part in desperate defensive fighting against the Americans north of Verdun in the last week of the war. On 25 November he was pleased to receive the Iron Cross 2nd Class, a visible token that he had 'done his bit'. After a long journey home and a brief stay in hospital, he was demobilised in Chemnitz on 17 March 1919.

We entrained right behind Le Chatelet. Before our departure however Ltn. Groß informed us of the latest army report from 31 July, which spoke of the offensive the English had just launched in Flanders, to which he added a comment on the tough times the company would face etc. etc. So what, we already knew that well enough. We didn't exactly board the train in higher spirits. I have nothing to report from the journey. I sat in our cattle wagon right at the back, and caught an impression of woods and quite nice little villages flashing past. On the morning of 2 August we detrained in Moeskroen. I don't have cheerful memories of this town, as I got to know it on a really wet and gloomy day. At any rate, it looked more pleasant and fit for human habitation than the French villages of the Champagne. Here I also saw the first civilians, with even a couple of passably attractive girls amongst them. I could no longer quite imagine such beings, as for weeks I had only seen *landsers*. So it meant more to me under the circumstances.

Flanders made an excellent impression on me in spite of the miserable rainy day. However this was to a great extent due to the contrast with the bleak Champagne. Long sprawling villages with nice houses, numerous civilians, open shops and lots of estaminets. Everywhere brisk activity. One could believe we were on manouvres somewhere in lower Germany.

We'd already passed through Lauwe, Wevelghem and Menin. Now we followed the road across open country. Night had fallen, it was pretty much pitch-dark and still raining. So it was anything but cosy. The village was called Gheluwe. One of the larger villages, it had already been subjected to the English long-range bombardment and taken several hits. One consequence of this was that the inhabitants had fled, and had been obliged to leave almost everything behind. The rich harvest of fruit, beans, greens and potatoes was of particular benefit to the German *landser*, who soon plundered it thoroughly. I too savoured the peas, pears and apples, although almost all of them were still unripe. At the front all hell had lately broken loose, but when I arrived it was already quiet again. The company lay in barracks on raised ground in a wood. It was near Koelenberg. We incurred no losses, save a couple of men lightly wounded. There was almost nothing to do. We just wired the wood and our camp. Then we were relocated further back at a farm. We lay in a hayloft, but we could live with that. We only had a lot to put up with from the flies. It was impossible to sleep without covering ourselves completely, and that in turn was uncomfortable on account of the heat. The first lice were also pestering me in earnest. We usually went forward about 3 or 4 o'clock at night as far as field railway station *Nachtigall* for wiring duty, and returned at the crack of dawn. Then we mooched around for the whole day and sunned ourselves in the nearby meadows. Besides a few roll calls that was all we did, when the fighting at the front was at its usual intensity. When it was spitting up front though, as it was more often than we'd have liked, we didn't get a moment's peace either. By day or in the middle of the night – Tommy was really inconsiderate like that – we were drummed out and had to occupy our immediate reserve position [*bereitschaftsstellung*]. This was near our earlier camp, to the left of a heroes' cemetery where two 21cm *mörsers* now sat. A house had once stood there, but only its foundation walls could still be seen. We now sought cover along the hedge which surrounded the garden, where we stared into space, cursed whenever one of the 21ers near us let rip, and waited to find out whether we'd be going back soon. For the most part this waiting in the open air was not at all pleasant, since the weather was very unsettled – and more often than not long showers of rain were pelting down, so that we were beastly cold. The nights in particular were exceedingly unpleasant.

About the end of August the situation grew steadily more frantic, so that no day went by without being alerted and we were almost constantly squatting outside. For a few days I'd been feeling really unwell, with a high fever and pain in the limbs. So one evening I reported sick, just as we were going on alert again. I was presented to the medical officer with a 39.5° fever, and taken post-haste to the *sanitäts-kompanie*. While I was squatting in the medical dugout, the companies moved up to the front line and immediately took some losses too, from which only our company in immediate reserve was spared[1]. The English had the strange and much-loved habit of only shooting at our positions just after we had left, but then he knocked some tidy great dents in them. Small houses would have fitted inside the craters. Nevertheless it was quite uncomfortable enough for us when their target was 100 or 200 metres away, as then the splinters still pattered and howled about our ears. Well, for the moment I was saved and could pity my comrades from my place of safety.

After I had spent half the night huddled with the *sanitäts-kompanie*, a car arrived to carry me and the others away. We were unloaded at a casualty clearing station [*kranken-sammelstelle*] beyond Menin, which was housed in a magnificently furnished chateau, and after being really well fed with sandwiches and *glühwein* we were examined. I was transferred to *Krankensammelstelle Courtrai*. In the morning the car journey continued. Courtrai was bustling with activity. There were a lot of wounded men about. In the afternoon a trainload of light sick cases would be leaving for Germany. Since I too was seated among them, I was already revelling in the wildest hopes of soon being back at home. Sadly though it

turned out otherwise. Our train stopped in Gent, and once again a thorough medical examination was conducted. Then they picked me out and stuck me in *Kriegslazarett Kerkhove* near Gent. Farewell, homeland. Although we arrived in the middle of the night and were dog-tired, we were still bathed before we were allowed to go to our beds. We had to hand in our uniforms and were given linen smocks in return. I had already left the rest of my equipment at the *sanitäts-kompanie* and in Courtrai. I only had left what was on my person, plus a sandbag with my personal things. I slept marvellously on the first night in hospital. Bathed, in clean clothes and a freshly made white bed – in short, what more could you wish for? Well, to remain here. The sisters – they were Catholic nuns – were very friendly. As far as the doctor was concerned there was nothing to complain about either, I just found his frequent enquiries whether I would like to return to my unit rather disagreeable.

My condition rapidly improved, the fever had subsided after the first few days and the diarrhoea had stopped. With time my stay grew really dull, reading no longer interested me and we weren't allowed to go out. So I had ample opportunity to polish up my memories. One of them is still as clear to me today as if it had happened yesterday. We were still at the farm outside Gheluwe, once again lolling idly in the sun, when Tommy began shooting. The shells were landing steadily closer to us. Well, that had never happened before. Luckily he now shot further to the right, so our farm remained undamaged. 'So, now he's got something.' He had hit the neighbouring farm, about 400 metres away. Appeased, he now ceased fire. Over there however there was hell to pay. The whole farm was full of munitions. And now small arms ammo was crackling and popping, and hand grenades banging away, while the farm blazed fiercely and black fumes rose into the sky. Now it was the turn of the flare cartridges. It was the most beautiful fireworks display. Yellow, green, red and white flares shot out into the air in all directions. Then suddenly an ear-splitting crash, and an enormous pillar of fire rose upward. Instinctively we threw ourselves down as the first stones and wooden beams came flying. When we glanced up again, a monstrous cloud of smoke over a hundred metres high stood out against the sky, with an aircraft circling around – and there wasn't a trace of the farm to be seen. A stockpile of heavy *minenwerfer* bombs had exploded.

My comrades in hospital were for the most part agreeable. I associated especially with another *einjähriger*, a Rheinländer from Viersen named Heinz Heynen. His father was a partner in Kaiser's Kaffee-Geschäft[2]. My liking for him was not however entirely selfless, because as you would expect Heynen got all sorts of tasty treats sent to him, which he shared freely with me. As I already said there was no going out. I only managed to get into the town twice, as a result of reporting that I had toothache and being sent to the dental ward. Lord how I (the feral *frontmensch*) boggled at everything there.

Hospital life suited me well enough, so I was anything but indifferent when the doctor finally discharged me with a recommendation for fourteen days' convalescent leave. That was my hope, and my consolation was that Heynen had to pack up his things at the same time as me. I also had the good luck of grabbing a quite new, so-called universal greatcoat instead of my old front-line coat. Then the two of us reported to the *Kaiser-Wilhelm-Kaserne*, where we were issued marching rations and fresh kit. In order to look suitably needy, we completely wrecked our trousers by tearing great rents through them with a knife. Unfortunately however, our new things were no better than the old ones had been to start with. We wanted to spend one more carefree day in Gent, but had no money. Finally an idea came to us. Heynen gave me his ankle boots and my new, freshly issued pair were 'flogged'. The proceeds were fairly divided.

On the following morning we had to bid farewell [to Gent]. I had become *transportführer*[3] for two other men belonging to the 32. [Infanterie-] Division. One parted company from me again at Courtrai. I reached Menin that evening with the other, and from there we continued on foot via Halluin to Roncq, where the divisional staff was based. Sadly the rumour that the division was to be relieved from Flanders had not been confirmed, it had only been moved to the left. We stayed overnight in Roncq, and on the following morning resumed our march to Bousbeque, where the first shells came to greet us. That was rather unpleasant, but the reunion with the *kompaniefeldwebel* after three weeks' absence was still more so. Once again he kept me from getting bored over the next few days. However I didn't stay there long, but rather went on to Werwicq, where the rest billets for the companies were located. I now had ample opportunity to get to know this area thoroughly, as we stayed here until early January.

The company returned from the line that same evening, and I was able to renew almost all of my old acquaintances. The *einjährigen* were all still there except for Schöfer, who was in hospital with alleged gas-poisoning, and Hoffmann, whom I had met again in the sick bay where he was still suffering from the effects of that shrapnel shot.

The five rest days were soon up, and now we were told to move forward again. I certainly had little enthusiasm for it. Our route took us through shot-up Comines, which was still under heavy fire, so that – puffing and panting, sweating and cursing – we rushed through at the gallop. We then occupied the reserve positions in front of Comines, and after three days moved further to the left into the company's old forward positions. It was the first time that I had taken part in a relief

under such circumstances, so I was full of nervous excitement. In single file we went silently forward through the trenches, until they came to an end. Bent over double, we scurried across the open field, taking pains not to make any noise. At each post the men were relieved in a whisper. Then we went onward, until an English flare forced us to throw ourselves flat again.

Finally I too had reached my shell-hole. Swiftly my comrade and I prepared our position. We checked the hand grenades, quickly oriented ourselves and then strained our ears into the night. In front of us was the ghostly outline of our wire, beyond which nothing more could be seen. We guessed that the English lines were somewhere over there, where the flares were going up. To the right a trench had been started toward the nearest post, behind us a narrow trench ran to our neighbours on the left. The line here almost presented a right angle, with our shell hole at the point. While I was staring into the night, my comrade was at work. Then suddenly from the neighbouring post on our left came shouting, and the flash and bang of a hand grenade. Then silence fell, in the moonlight I saw the silhouettes of the two sentries. Again fire sprayed out and a hand grenade boomed. I sent a few pot-shots across, in what I guessed was the direction of the English patrol.

Dead silence broken only by the heavy artillery shells sighing past overhead, then the flaming tail of a mortar bomb tracked across the sky and detonated over there in the English trenches with a monstrous crash. Then that was it for the first night, we listening posts pulled back into the trenches. How I gaped when we arrived in front of our dugout. The wall of the trench had been cut out to create a four-cornered hole, over which a corrugated iron ceiling, some tar paper and a foot of earth had been thrown. We hung a *zeltbahn*[4] in front of our bedchamber, lay the other one on the mud floor and, with the backpack for a pillow and covered with the greatcoat, slept the sleep of the just. But not for long. The hole was just too narrow, we lay rolled up in a ball like hedgehogs, all our limbs ached. We attempted to enlarge the 'pit' a little, but before we had finished we were ordered to go creeping out and scouting again.

The next two nights went by at work and on watch. Then I came to another post, in an especially isolated location. Here one had to be doubly on one's guard. Occasionally noises would tempt us into taking shots in the dark. Soon however one grew accustomed to the danger, and at dawn we would amuse ourselves by sticking beer bottles and spent shrapnel shells on the stakes of the wire obstacle and shooting them down. Unfortunately the English field artillery became uncomfortably active here.

The weather was persistently pleasant but already noticeably cool, especially in the mornings. Then the hour of our relief came round, we were supposed to be going into rest billets. Supposed to be. But the next day we were already on the march again, to act as reserve for a breakthrough attempt to the right of our sector.

So weeks and weeks went by. I also came to know and fear the so-called *bereitschaftsstellung*, as it was from here that transport parties set out to take essential supplies to the troops in the front line. We crouched there in a cellar with a concrete cupola all the live-long day, outside the rain spattered – no, poured – down, turning the roads into a quagmire, and the shell-holes into ponds. At dusk the ration carriers arrived and brought the provisions. These were rapidly shared out and eaten, and a cigarette smoked. And that would be the moment to try and grab a quick nap. One would just be dozing off pleasantly, then: 'Fall out! *Transport!*'[5] A long and elaborate oath. Outside the rain lashed at our faces as we trudged sullenly through the swamp. Now and then a half-suppressed curse when someone slipped and fell into a shell-hole. Darkness all around, too dark to see your own hand in front of your eyes. The darkness was illuminated only for seconds at a time by the glare of the muzzle flashes and the light of the flares. We collected our loads further back at a shot up farmstead outfitted as a *pionierpark*. Portable wire entanglements, rolls of barbed wire, duckboards and bags of charcoal. Then we went forward again.

The target area for English defensive barrages began at our immediate reserve zone. One shell-hole after another, filled with water by the rain that pelted down for days on end. The ground in between was a bottomless swamp. Thus we wheezed our way forward weighed down with our burden, stumbled, fell and cursed. The things were dumped at the front, and in lighter spirits we returned to our dugout. 'What, another one?' There were one or two transports per night.

To escape from monotonous watch duty, and for the opportunity to get to know something different, I had reported to the company's *stoßtrupp*. This had the task of reconnaissance in front of our lines, setting up the barbed wire, occasionally doing some digging on the trenches and in thick fog, which is not uncommon in Flanders, forming an advanced skirmish line in front of our own outposts. So a highly varied routine. Admittedly I didn't find my comrades to my liking, most of them were rough young lads with no inclination for close comradeship, but nevertheless I got myself settled. One has to howl in the company of wolves. In the *bereitschaftsstellung* we had our own dugout to ourselves. It wasn't up to much, but at least one could lie down properly. However one day it was flooded out by the ever-annoying rain, and we had to move. That was a nice surprise, when we woke one morning to find ourselves lying in water, which rose slowly and steadily higher. We found a new refuge in a cellar. When we were in

forward positions we were on patrol every night, or else wiring and digging. At least we got more rest than the other men. I never came into contact with the English, nor did I ever get into the enemy trenches. It almost happened on only one occasion, and then by accident. We were lying in front of the English wire, and simply wanted to make our way back along a collapsed trench, which had previously led to the now lost German positions and which we had already used occasionally for the purpose. Disorientated by numerous light signals, we followed it in the wrong direction. After some time we came to a wire entanglement and clambered cheerfully through, expecting we would soon be back in our dugout. When – '*stop!*'[6] A flare went up, a couple of shots cracked out, the machine-gun chattered away. We got back in our trench like the devil and kept as quiet as mice, then back we went on all fours. '*Stupid Tommy!*' If you had only waited, you could have boasted of having captured six Germans[6]. On this occasion the whole business concluded happily, sadly this would not always be the case.

The best time to work was in the morning, when it was light, but the usual morning mist still impeded visibility. We – and naturally Tommy too – made full use of this period. On a couple of occasions we managed to surprise our opponents and send a couple of 'blue beans'[7] in their direction. Unfortunately we could not determine whether we had scored any hits.

One day we were working on the wire obstacle line again. It was admittedly already getting perilously light, but we were keen to finish the job. Then there came a crack from over there. Within a second we were in the closest shell-holes and trenches. As I leapt into cover someone cried out behind me, and turning I saw a man fall backwards into the wire entanglement. After seconds of anxious waiting we slid ourselves slowly, virtually flat to the ground, over to the casualty. His tunic and undervest were quickly torn open. Poor comrade, the shot had ricocheted through your gasmask and gone right through your chest. We tried to haul him back into the trench. Then something whistled past my hand, and the man next to me cried out faintly and began crawling toward the trench. The rest of us now had to drag the wounded through the tangle of barbed wire. Our clothes were torn, our hands bloody, the moisture and filth soaked right through to our skin. After an hour-long effort we slid the wailing man down the wall of the trench. Poor, poor comrade. Our efforts were all in vain, he died on the transport. On the following morning my friend Wildau fell victim to a shell from our own artillery. That's the war for you.

But there were also some amusing episodes. My friend Krohe discovered an English two-man post. 'We had to capture them, because we would get 14 days' leave.' No sooner said than done. Softly and soundlessly they crept forward, the hand grenades were ready. Then all at once the English two-man post was revealed to be nothing but a few huge cabbage leaves.

Thus October and November went by. The autumn and approaching winter made themselves felt. The weather had now become exceedingly bad. The rain poured incessantly, and the eagerly awaited sun rarely appeared through the clouds. The trenches became streams, and the cratered landscape an almost impassable swamp. No matter how much we bailed and dug drainage trenches, the water always gushed in again, brought the mud walls slipping down and blocked the trenches with a tough, pulpy mass in which one sank up to the eyes and could only pull onself free with difficulty. In our pits we froze like young dogs. To be sure, we made a fire of wood chips in tins – but the heat did not last long, for the cold rain-damp air streamed in through all of the many cracks and holes in the *zeltbahn*, no matter how well we plugged them. The smoke brought tears to our eyes and made us cough incessantly. The provisions became really meagre; that was when I learned what hunger really is, as I lay shivering, frozen through with frost on the damp mud floor, and waited for the ration carriers. All in all a truly miserable existence.

Slowly Christmas drew nearer. Wistful thoughts turned to the warm, bright room at home. It was our misfortune that we were to be in the line even at Christmas. Even though it could in no sense be called a rest, for we were abused from dawn to dusk with labouring, exercises and roll calls, at least we had a roof over our heads in the evening, a warm oven and electric lighting. I still had it quite good, as while we were in immediate reserve I was with a signal flare post. I was housed with three comrades and the crew of a heavy machine-gun in a dugout built from concrete blocks. I did not have to take part in the harrowing 'transports', but only to stand post for two hours every six hours.

Christmas Eve came round. The day before the English were still firing heavily and shot two of our munitions depots ablaze, but today it was appreciably quieter. In our dugout we burned every stub of candle we could find, and sang one Christmas carol after another. In all of us there reigned a wistful, heightened, almost solemn mood – especially me, as I had received the buttons[8] the day before. The eagerly awaited parcels too arrived on the first day of the holiday, and now once more we were able to celebrate Christmas with cakes and good strong grog. But five wretched days in the front line still beckoned.

Snow had fallen, and an intense cold prevailed. Admittedly little stoves had been installed in our pits in recent weeks, but there was a lack of fuel. They were not to be lit during the day so as not to betray our positions, and at night one spent the least amount of time in the dugout. So one just froze. Our limbs were stiff and painful, our feet seemed to want to burst out of our wet boots. At New Year the hour of salvation struck, and we slipped and tumbled over indescribably treacherous ice back to Werwicq – for the last time. Farewell, *Flandernstellung*. I gladly turn my back on you. Farewell, Comines, you that have fallen victim to the British shells. For the last time I hurried through the silent streets, the shattered walls gaping at me. In Werwicq the New Year was cheerfully celebrated amid the crack of hand grenades, the rattle of rifles and the glow of signal flares. The company held its belated Christmas party, then on 10 January 1918 we withdrew from Werwicq, which had become thoroughly familiar to us over many long weeks. For the most part the houses were admittedly still standing – but they were no longer human dwellings, merely lifeless piles of stones. An extinct city of the dead, into which only the German *landser* brought any life. How might you look now, after the war has thundered across you again? Have you suffered the fate of Comines, which I saw ablaze in the distance when at night (if I could not sleep) I gazed from your high church tower across the Flemish countryside?

The view from the church tower in Werwicq / Wervik in autumn 1917, much as it must have appeared to Mühle. Although little damage is visible, some houses had already fallen to shelling in 1916.

Due to his hand injury and subsequent assignments, Mühle never rejoined 32. Infanterie-Division in the field. For the division's part in the spring offensives of 1918 we must turn to the field correspondence of Robert Reichel, a company commander with Infanterie-Regiment 103.

Robert Reichel, Leutnant der Reserve

Letters to his mother during the *Georgette* Offensive

Robert Reichel was a lawyer from Dresden, and had completed his service with Schützen-Regiment 108 long before the war. In August 1914 he was recalled to the colours as an *offiziersstellvertreter* with **Landwehr-Infanterie-Regiment 102** (45. Ldw. Brig.), and soon commissioned. After over two years east of Verdun and on the Eastern Front, he completed a machine-gun course at Königsbrück early in 1917 and took over the MGK of Infanterie-Regiment 621. Together with its sister 'regiment' 622 (which only reached battalion strength) this was formed in January 1917, as Saxony's contribution to defence against potential invasion via Denmark or Holland. IR 621 was dissolved on 10 June without leaving Germany, and Reichel returned to the field. He commanded **2. MGK / Infanterie Regiment 103** (32. ID) throughout the Third Battle of Ypres, the subsequent winter in the trenches, and the *Georgette* Offensive of April 1918 (see pp. 157–158).

Four of his many letters to his mother (nicknamed 'Schecke', meaning a dappled mare!) vividly illustrate his volatile moods during this critical period, and certainly reflect the feelings of many at the time. His casual indifference to censorship is also typical. As he writes elsewhere: '*You haven't quite got the picture yet concerning "censorship". This is the business of the so-called military postal monitoring authorities [postüberwachungsstellen]. They are constantly at work, but in general only via random spot checks. Therefore you will only occasionally find that letters have been inspected. This inspection only extends to military matters, troop movements, offensive preparations and the like. You wouldn't believe how even officers – despite constant admonition and instruction – write everything in letters home; even the smallest details. Well, this is all by the by.*'
On 17 July 1918 Reichel's beloved brother-in-law Ltn. d. R. Adolf ('Alf') Rohde was killed in action at La Chapelle with Leibgrenadier-Regiment 100. Reichel himself survived to return home to Saxony that December.

13 April 1918
Dear Schecke, on the 9th we attacked at Armentières and by today we'd already got a good distance further forward. But Tommy is making a tough fighting withdrawal (please: he doesn't 'flee'). Today the Kaiser is visiting. There is so much to eat, that everyone is twice as fat as they were. And champagne: Cliquot!
My Ltn. Krause (the teacher) has fallen; the officer casualties overall are very heavy; all of the regimental staff wounded. My company lost two dead and seven wounded. We hope to get some rest today or tomorrow. I have shot at the English myself with the MG and they just tumbled. Their losses are heavier than ours, not to mention the prisoners. The whole thing is quite splendid! Our lads simply capital! Good morale all round!
Regards R.

18 April 1918
Dear Schecke, today a few more lines. You've probably already read of our deeds in the *Anzeiger*[1]. The lads have exceeded all possible praise. Sadly very great losses; Hptm. Loeser dead, [Ltn.] Bourquin lost both legs and is probably beyond hope too[2]. Besides me there are only four officers of my battalion left at the front. I don't care to write more about this here. The brigade took Bailleul the day before yesterday. Very bitter fighting, but very honourable. Soon we are to go into rest quarters. I haven't taken my things off in four weeks. Tremendous stockpiles have been captured; the English have a

real surplus of food, there isn't a trace of the U-boat emergency to be seen. Coffee, meat, butter, wine, champagne, chocolate, biscuits etc., unfortunately one doesn't get to send much of it on. There's a really huge amount of corned beef.
Your letter came yesterday; many thanks. My fountain pen and everything else I had in my pocket were completely smashed on the first day, when a shrapnel ball hit me right there. Apart from that I only have a bruise to show for it. My Ltn. Hoffmann took a ball to the head, but it only dented his helmet. Weather cold and wet, morale good.
Regards R.

19 April 1918
Dear Schecke, my poor Bourquin has died! I feel so isolated, as if among complete strangers. It is too dreadful! This lively fellow, ever cheerful and healthy! I have just written to his poor parents and brother; an agonising task. And what overall losses! Six officers dead, including the regimental adjutant and my battalion commander, Hptm. Loeser; 33 wounded! But the newspapers will say that the losses are low.
Don't worry any more on my account; if you have this letter, we are most likely already in rest quarters. These days are full of honour but hard, and a heavy trial for one's mental powers of endurance. This hateful Bailleul! And everything has ground to a halt, at least for now. I am yearning again for quarters fit for human habitation; for four weeks now nothing but old heaps of straw and musty cellars! The war, this

British POWs help to carry the wounded to the regimental dressing station (*regimentsverbandsplatz*) at Croix Maréchal south of Armentières on 9 or 10 April 1918. In a cellar near Bailleul on 20 April, a single aerial bomb all but wiped out the medical personnel of Infanterie-Regiment 103 and Sanitäts-Kompanie 28 – including Regimentsarzt Dr Barth, Bataillonsarzt Dr Müller and numerous stretcher-bearers. Only Bataillonsarzt Dr Monse and one other man could be rescued (albeit badly injured) from a total of almost thirty trapped in the rubble.

systematic obliteration of human beings (what wounds one has to see here) must nauseate anyone who isn't just sitting in the *etappe*.

Regards R.

30 April 1918

Dear Schecke!

Two smaller parcels of soap are on their way to you at the same time as this letter. Rice, macaroni and white flour will follow, all war booty. So they cost nothing. Hopefully it will all reach you alright. I enclose here the letters from Bourquin's parents and brother, and ask that you save them for me.

I am not in particularly good spirits. Yet again I haven't received the Iron Cross 1ˢᵗ class, although the regiment had put me forward for it. Although the troops are always promised mountains of gold before big shows, afterwards those promises look flimsy. Now I'm to receive the *Verdienstorden*, which is naturally a poor substitute.

Life here is devoid of joy or anything to lift the spirits. After the splendid advance we are bleeding to death by degrees; there won't be much left at this rate. Yesterday the attacks on the Kemmel failed, because a sudden wind dispersed our gas.

And we have only had our successes with the aid of the gas, which stops the enemy batteries from shooting.

Unfortunately we still can't reckon on any rest. Understandable, because fresh troops are always needed for other purposes at the moment. But the morale of the troops has suffered so much that it will take more than a few days to restore it. The food consists of pearl barley, groats and dehydrated vegetables, with a bit of gristle swimming in the soup by way of meat. The stuff is no good to eat in the long run. All is no longer well here. But still the newspapermen write that the troops do not wish to be relieved.

Shortly a gentleman from Dresden will be visiting us, you'll already have guessed who[3].

The only thing that ever puts me in a better mood is your correspondence. Otherwise it is cheerless. Now Sturm[4] too has fallen. There are ever fewer of us. The thought is constantly with us: when we marched out we were so many, today there are only five left. The day before yesterday this one fell, yesterday that one was wounded, now it'll be your turn soon. And despite it all one must bolster the morale of one's men. It is not easy.

Regards R.

Fritz Wittig, Gefreiter

Sudden death on the Kemmelberg in May 1918

Fritz Wittig from Leipzig was a professional *monteur* (electrical fitter). As such, he trained in early 1915 as a field telephonist at Dresden and Zeithain with Ersatz-Abteilung / Telegraphen-Bataillon 7 (the depot unit for all Saxon telephone and radio troops until 1917). In April he was sent to France with **Fernsprech-Doppelzug 58** of the newly formed 58. Infanterie-Division. This 'double platoon' comprised a *bauzug* and a *betriebszug*, responsible respectively for construction and operation of the telephone system linking divisional and brigade headquarters with each other and their subordinate units. Each of the latter maintained its own connections with sub-units up to the front line. Although further back, the divisional *bauzug* often had to work under fire, since breakages were usually the result of shelling. In January 1917 the unit gained a third platoon and became **(Divisions-)Fernsprech-Abteilung 58**. Later that year it was joined by a *funker-abteilung* (wireless detachment) and subordinated to a *nachrichten-kommandeur* (signals command staff).

Amongst other places his service took Fritz to Lille, Wilna (now Vilnius, Lithuania), Saarburg, the *Caillettewald* near Verdun, Molenhoek, Valenciennes, Balaschi (on the shore of Lake Narocz in Belarus) and Hooglede. For his conduct in the Battle of Verdun he was awarded the Iron Cross 2nd Class in April 1916, and was promoted to gefreiter in summer 1917. By 1918 he had acting command of a *trupp* (section). This was an unteroffizier's post, and Fritz had been scheduled for further promotion when he died. On 27 May 1918 the dug-out near Kemmelberg where he worked and slept took a direct hit; it was several days before his body could be recovered from the rubble. He was buried at the *Ehrenfriedhof* in Linselles, but later disinterred; his final resting place is at the *Kriegsgräberstätte* in St.-Laurent-Blangy (Block 6 Grave 45).

Fritz Wittig (second right) in civilian life as a *monteur*, during work at Schloss Otterwisch near Grimma in 1913.

Fritz ca. February 1916, wearing his unit's insignia on a Prussian *waffen-rock* (most likely issued as a replacement at a non-Saxon hospital).

Korps-Fernsprech-Abteilung
des X. Res.-Korps.
(Res. Fernsprech-Abteilung Nr. 4)
Kommando.

K.H.Qu.,7.4.1916.

Vorläufiger Ausweis.

Im Namen Sr.Majestät hat Sr.Exzellenz der kommandierende
General des X.Res.Korps heute auf Vorschlag des Abteilungs –
Kommandeurs und des Doppelzugführers

dem Telegraphisten Fritz Wittig

des Fernsprech-Doppelzuges der 58.Inf.Div.

das Eiserne Kreuz II.Klasse verliehen.

Hauptmann u.Abt.Kommandeur.

Provisional award document for Fritz Wittig's Iron Cross 2nd Class, authorised by X. Reserve-Korps and signed by the commander of its corps telephone detachment. Fernsprech-Doppelzug 58 was temporarily subordinated to this unit while 58.ID was serving under X. Reserve-Korps at Verdun in March–April 1916 (q.v. Kaden, p. 204).

Fritz Wittig (third left) on home leave with his parents and other relatives.

The last photo of Fritz Wittig (right) with note dated 12 May 1918 on the back (see below). Given the small size of the unit, it is likely that the senior NCO in the centre is Sergeant Schuberts (see letter of the 19 June).

12 May 1918

My dears!
Hearty greetings to you, I'm in the best of health here. How are things with you? I'm having a pretty good time of it at the moment. Now farewell 'til we meet again safe and sound. Your Fritze

Whit Monday[1] 1918 (20 May)

My dears!
Many thanks for your dear letter of 12 May. At the moment we are staying in the place where Walter Freitag lies buried, but at rest. I had charge of the *vorkommando*[2], so have been here for six days already and arranged quarters. The rest of the detachment only got here yesterday, and with it I also received my accumulated mail. I got post sixteen times over – perhaps you can imagine what a lot of writing I have stored up to do today, on the second day of the holiday? Writing is the only diversion one has in the field. I probably don't need to tell you that I have taken very good quarters for my own use. A fine furnished room and above all a really choice cask – so I'm almost excessively well provided for. So you know now, that I am feeling quite well off – for the few days of the holiday.

Now to your letter. Uncle Max is ill – well he comes down with something every five minutes, so what's new – hope he gets well soon. It irked me that I have not received any card from the Elster valley – at least Else could take that much time – that's women for you – long on hair but short on understanding, and as soon as the weather turns warm the little bit of brain melts – and then it's all gone. I have probably already confirmed receipt of your 20 marks. You want soap in a hurry? Yes that is fine – I can get enough soap at our end, but leave is still barred, so how should I arrange for this to get to you?[3] You will have to be patient for a while yet. Just now the daughter of my hosts is starting to play the piano – in the evenings I have some quite pleasant entertainment. So now do let yourselves have a good time, for all is well with me here too.
Until we meet again safe and sound I remain
Your Fritze

P. S. Why are you complaining to Süptitz – I have to hear via other fellows, that I have not written for a long time – I've never met Süptitz. I don't like it. Lisa doesn't need to tell Süptitz everything.

Letters from Fritz Wittig's comrades and immediate superiors

In the field, 28 May 1918

Most honoured Herr Wittig,

and most honoured gracious lady!

In writing to you, I discharge the sad duty of reporting the death of your son Fritz Wittig. I know that no words can be sufficient to comfort your anguish as parents; still I must tell you, that in your son I have lost one of my most keen and dutiful *truppführer*[4], who was respected and loved by his subordinates. Due to his competence I had recently put his name forward as an unteroffizier, but fate had not granted that he would live to see his promotion.

It will surely be of some comfort to you, if I might inform you of the fact that he died without any suffering. The direct hit which struck the dug-out resulted in instant death, as confirmed by a medical officer at the scene. Two of his men were wounded. Sadly in spite of all our efforts we have not been able to recover his body, since he is completely buried and the area in question is under heavy fire.

Please be assured that your son was respected by us all as a capable, brave and honourable man and soldier, and as such he will live on in our memory.

Your devoted servant

Alfred Weller, leutnant and *zugführer*

In the field, 1 June 1918

Esteemed Wittig family!

By now you will surely have already had news from our detachment of the calamity that has befallen us, and to which your son Fritz has fallen victim. He was our *truppführer* and we were very sorry to lose him, on account of his good character alone. Hence his passing has affected us all the more painfully, and so we have taken this liberty of expressing our deepest sympathy to you.

He had just laid down on his bunk when our cellar, which served as our [telephone] station, took a direct hit. Naturally there was great confusion, then it was only a matter of a moment and as soon as we saw that Fritz was missing, we set to work right away to dig him out. Sadly this was not to succeed, since the masonry of the house was collapsing and putting us in mortal danger. A medical officer who was present and treated our two wounded, stated that the death of the buried man had occurred instantly and also that further efforts would be useless since the house was still under enemy fire. Then the house took another direct hit – God be thanked it was only a dud, else we would probably all have been buried. So there was nothing for it but for us to evacuate the house. When we returned to the site of the disaster the following morning, aiming at least to recover the body, there was a hauptmann of *pio-*

niere present, who explained to us that we were unlikely to succeed without losing even more of our comrades in the process – and so unfortunately we had to abandon our plans. All of the things that he had about him – watch, money etc. – were buried with him. The calamity happened on 27 May 1918 between 6 and 7 o'clock in the afternoon. The bombardment, which only affected our station (at least we assume so), started up at about 5 o'clock and lasted until about 8.

If there is anything more you wish to know, we hereby declare that we are most ready and willing to help.

With German greeting[5]

Gefreiter Edwin Brause,

on behalf of all of the comrades of our troop

Written 17 June 1918

Esteemed Wittig family!

first of all we beg your pardon, that we have only today got round to replying to your dear letter of the 6 June, but prevailing conditions did not give us a chance to deal with it earlier, as we have only just now been pulled back from the front.

Our comrades Gefreiter Röner and Telegraphist Körner were lightly wounded in the head by flying stones. They were not admitted to hospital but rather treated within the detachment, and both received home leave afterwards. As regards our buried station, well you probably don't have a clear idea of what the war landscape looks like, and it is pretty nondescript. There are no longer any whole houses. So it was a typical shot-up house, where the cellar had been built up as a dug-out. We felt pretty safe, because there was a layer of earth on top about a metre thick. It was splinter-proof in all respects and nothing could happen to us there, unless we received a direct hit. The house lay at the foot of the Kemmel.

Among us from Leipzig there are Telegr. Hans Quelins of Leipzig N., Wissmannstraße, with whom your son was on the occasion of his last leave, and Gefreiter Edwin Brause of Leipzig, Moltkestraße 59 II. The former is expected to be coming home on leave in the near future, and will look you up while he is there to give you further information. Naturally we were also most anxious to dig your dear Fritz out, and recently when the intensity of the fire on the site of the disaster had slackened somewhat, we set to at once on this task. We succeeded, although under difficult circumstances, in digging him out. He lay there still just as he had before the disaster, and there is every indication that he had been totally oblivious, so death occurred straight away and he did not experience any suffering.

Our comrade Telegraphist Kurt Braun had made a coffin and a pretty cross, and so we were in the fortunate situation – if also under difficult circumstances – of being able to carry back our Fritz, who had always been so dear to us. We dug him out early on 12 June and buried him on the 13th with military ho-

A view across the 58. ID sector from the right flank in May 1918, looking over the ruins of Kemmel village toward the Kemmelberg (see sector map on p. 161).

On the lower slope near the left edge of the photo is the site of the *regimentsgefechtsstand* for the Kemmelberg subsector. Seven signals personnel of IR 107 were buried when it was demolished by superheavy shelling on 30 June, three of whom were eventually rescued.

nours. All of the off-duty comrades and officers of the detachment were in attendance, and the funeral rites were performed by our divisional chaplain Pfarrer Weck[6]. He rests at the *Ehrenfriedhof* in Linselles, Grave Nr. 637. A picture was also taken by the *truppführer* Gefreiter Heller with his camera. As soon as we are in possession of the photos we will send you copies, as we are also interested in having such a picture by which to remember our dear Fritz.

We believe that with this letter, we have now written to you everything that is worth your knowing, but we declare that we are most ready and willing to provide any further details you may desire, and remain.

With German greeting and deepest respect
Gefreiter Edwin Brause,
together with all the comrades of the troop

P.S. Fritz had put all of his valuables – such as his watch, wallet and also various writing things – to one side on a shelf attached to the wall, and these were probably buried under the stones together with it, so that none of them could be found when we dug him out. We are therefore most sorry that we could not fulfil his wishes in this respect. All other items which he had not taken forward with him, and so remained in the rear, will be sent on to you within the next few days via our detachment.

In the field, 19 June 1918
To the Wittig family –
Following the communications you have already received from the detachment and from my *zugführer* Herr Ltn. Weller with the sad news of the passing of your dear son Fritz, I would also like to belatedly convey to you my deepest sympathy.

In the last few days it was possible for us, under difficult circumstances, to furnish your dear son Fritz with an honourable resting place. He was interred with military honours at the *Ehrenfriedhof* in Linselles near Roncq. This disaster was a heavy blow for me, just as it was for his comrades. Your dear son served for a long time in my troop, and latterly with my platoon, as a dutiful and conscientious comrade. His memory will always live on in our remembrance. With him I have also lost a good influence in my platoon.

In the course of today I am also sending on his things. Unfortunately the watch and the wallet are still missing, and according to witnesses are not recoverable. Also enclosed are a picture of his grave and a list of the packed items.
Signed, respectfully yours
Schuberts, Sergeant and *Wachtmeister-Diensttuer*[7]
II. Zug / Fernsprech-Abt. 58

In the field, 28 June 1918
Most honoured Herr Wittig, gracious lady –
I am in possession of your letter and can give you a reply, which will hopefully give you a good impression. We recovered your son; his comrades had constructed a very handsome coffin, wound a great wreath of leaves and flowers, and also prepared the cross and the inscription itself. Then we laid him to rest at the *Soldatenfriedhof* Linselles. I entrusted a man with the task of photographing the grave; the pictures will be sent on to you by this man today. I hope that knowing where your dear son lies buried will be some consolation in your great pain!
I remain as always, your most devoted
Ltn. Weller

Most honoured Wittig family!

I am sending you enclosed the three pictures you desired, from the grave of your dear son. The price for all five cards is 1.50 M. Our division is still here at K., and once again fourteen young men full of promise have had to lose their lives buried in the rubble, nine *funkers* and five infantrymen. The Kemmel

19 July 1918

will be completely churned up by the heaviest calibres, nothing will be left there.

When will this miserable war just come to an end? The hardship in dear *Sachsenland* is great again too. God grant that there will still be a peace this year, the hope is however not great.

With the greatest respect, most devoted greetings from

Your Paul Heller

The *Ehrenfriedhof* in Linselles, which held 681 German graves prior to the concentration of the war dead in the giant 'collecting' cemeteries. Fritz Wittig's grave is marked with an arrow (immediately to the left of the monument).

Fritz Wittig's death notice from the supplement to the *Leipziger Neuesten Nachrichten* of 8 June 1918, printed on behalf of his parents, fiancée and extended family.

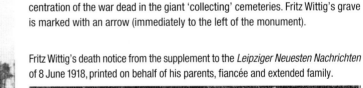

CHAPTER 10
THE HOME FRONT

A one-armed veteran of Infanterie-Regiment 'Kronprinz' 104 proudly wearing his best walking out uniform and Iron Cross 2nd Class on his wedding day in Chemnitz.

Although Saxony was not directly attacked, civilian life in the once-prosperous kingdom grew increasingly bleak as the war dragged on. Under the state of siege established by the British blockade **Stellvertretende Generalkommando XII** (Gen. der Kav. von Broizem) in Dresden and **XIX** (Gen. der Inf. von Schweinitz) in Leipzig exercised virtually dictatorial powers, reporting directly to the Kaiser. As state control of the economy tightened, war production intensified and the *ersatztruppenteile* and home-service Landsturm units under their command proliferated, both staffs steadily expanded. By October 1918 Stv. Genkdo XII had grown from a few dozen to 850 soldiers and civil servants.

In peacetime a quarter of Germany's food was imported. The inevitable shortages under blockade were compounded by the loss of agricultural labour to the army. Although all the physically fit enlisted men were put to work in industry and agriculture, the almost 100,000 P.O.W.s and civil internees held in Saxony by 1918 were yet more mouths to feed. Rationing, food queues and even riots began early in 1915, unappetising 'ersatz' foodstuffs became universal and price controls created a thriving black market. The loss of the potato crop in the freezing autumn of 1916 was followed by the infamous 'Turnip Winter' of 1916–1917, when the basic daily ration fell to 700–900 calories and coal became desperately scarce.

Although often struggling to look after families, women joined the workforce in vast numbers. However the number of skilled industrial workers exempted from conscription increased in 1915–1916, to counter faulty production and accidents caused by excessive use of unskilled labour. Wages rose but were outpaced by inflation, and strikes became a serious problem in 1917. Shortages of strategic materials were a growing and still greater threat to the war effort.

After von Broizem died of a heart attack on 11 March 1918, his successor Gen. der Inf. Götz von Olenhusen (former commander of 40. ID) faced a desperate situation. As hope faded at the front and the influenza pandemic cut a swathe through the starving people it became impossible. In November Dresden, Leipzig and Chemnitz were convulsed by civil unrest. The king refused to respond with force, and the ruined kingdom peacefully became the *Freistaat Sachsen*.

Leatherworkers (*sattler*) employed by Actien Gesellschaft H. Thiele of Dresden-Neustadt in 1914, with some of their wartime products – backpacks and leather headgear. At this early stage most of the workers are still men of military age.

Commemorative photo from a foundry in Potschappel in March 1915, marking the achievement of a production total of 35,000 shells since the outbreak of war. A note on the reverse indicates that the occasion was celebrated with a party for the workforce.

Employees of Wagenfabrik Gnauck & Co. in Dresden celebrate the completion of their thousandth horse-drawn vehicle for the war effort. The factory appears to be producing two different models of baggage wagon (compare with the photo on p. 79).

Sombre group picture of staff at an unidentified factory at Reichenbach in Vogtland; typically for 1918 only two men (both too old even for the Landsturm) remain. As in Britain, the war economy ultimately depended on mass mobilisation of women in traditional male occupations.

The village of Deuben (since 1921 part of the town of Freital, southwest of Dresden) prepares to welcome the homecoming troops in November 1918. Although a fine triumphal arch has been constructed, few civilians are in evidence – at least by the standards of 1914.

APPENDICES

Gefreiter Martin Hagen (left) and comrades of 1. Kompanie / Reserve-Infanterie-Regiment 244 in full marching order, ca. spring 1916. In addition to his *vereinfachte* (simplified) *waffenrock* with plain barrel cuffs, Gefr. Hagen displays another wartime substitution – a Prussian buckle with the motto *'GOTT MIT UNS'* in place of the Saxon *'PROVIDENTIAE MEMOR'*.

NOTES

CHAPTER 2 – THE ROYAL SAXON ARMY AT WAR

1   Prinz Ernst Heinrich von Sachsen, *Mein Lebensweg vom Königsschloss zum Bauernhof* p. 73

CHAPTER 3 – The Year 1914

1   Knoppe, *Die Geschichte des Königlich Sächsischen Reserve-Infanterie-Regiments Nr. 241* pp. 41–42. This may have been Serjeant J.H. Measures of the 1st (Royal) Dragoons, one of three men of this unit killed in action that day and buried at Ledeghem Military Cemetery (Block B Grave 20).
2   Anonymous officer of the Rifle Brigade, letter to the *Times* of 2 January 1915; quoted in Brown and Seaton, *Christmas Truce* p. 84.
3   Karl Artur Baumgarten-Crusius (29 November 1858 – 15 April 1932) was invalided out of the Royal Saxon Army with the honorary (*charakterisiert*) rank of generalmajor. With Oberst z.D. Edmund Hottenroth of the Saxon Kriegsarchiv he produced the quasi-official history *Sachsen in großer Zeit*. His other works include the regimental history of IR 139.
4   *Sachsen in großer Zeit* vol. I p. 62

CHAPTER 4 – The Year 1915

1   Fromm, *Das Württemb. Reserve-Infanterie-Regiment Nr. 120* p. 75
2   Kramer, *Geschichte des Reserve-Infanterie-Regiments 245 im Weltkriege 1914–1918* pp. 22–23
3   According to the French 68e Regiment d'Infanterie the attack was preceded by a short, sharp barrage from 10.5cm howitzers and *minenwerfers* and developed both north and south of Broodseinde. The advance was led by what were believed to be volunteer 'storm troops' in light skirmish order, but fell apart under rifle and machine-gun fire. See Général Alfred Dubois, *Deux ans de commandement sur le front de France 1914–1916* vol. 2 pp. 140–142
4   Knoppe, op. cit. p. 109
5   *Was wir erlebten – 245er Erinnerungen*, vol. II nr. 17–18
6   Kramer, op. cit. p. 64
7   Hay, *The First Hundred Thousand*; quoted in Ashworth, *Trench Warfare 1914–1918* p. 110
8   Fromm, op. cit. p. 55
9   Hitchcock, *"Stand To" A Diary of the Trenches 1915–1918* p. 116
10 Hitchcock op. cit. p. 118
11 Hitchcock op. cit. p. 124

CHAPTER 5 – The Year 1916

1   Blunden, *Undertones of War* Penguin edition 2000 pp. 57–58
2   Mangels, *Königlich Preußisches Reserve-Infanterie-Regiment Nr. 215* vol. II p. 19
3   Stoffleth, *Geschichte des Reserve-Jäger-Bataillons Nr. 18* p. 178
4   Five men were trapped by the *Chemnitz* detonation in a collapsed gallery being worked by 254th Tunnelling Company R.E. Three were rescued late on 23 June, but Sapper William Hackett elected to remain with the badly wounded Private Thomas Collins. Both died, and Sapper Hackett posthumously received the only Victoria Cross of the tunnelling war.
5   All quotes in this paragraph from the war diary of 11th Btn. Royal Scots [WO 95/1773/1]
6   Richter, *Der Königlich Sächsische Militar-St. Heinrichs-Orden 1736–1918* p. 705
7   All quotes in this paragraph from Lt.-Col. Croft's report of 14 May to 27 Infantry Brigade [WO 95/1769/4]
8   Lt.-Col. Croft's report of 14 May to 27 Bde. [WO 95/1769/4]
9   This and the following quote are from a 9th Division report of 15 May [WO 95/1769/4]
10 This probably refers to a metal bar or rail hung up and struck as a crude form of gas alarm.
11 Steel-cored armour-piercing ammunition ('K' for *kern*, meaning 'core'). Originally developed for use against armoured loophole plates in the trenches, they also proved effective against early tanks at close range. From late 1916 a reserve was commonly held in the front line in case of tank attack.
12 Conventional small-arms (rifle) ammunition.

CHAPTER 6 – The Year 1917

1   Abteilung IB of Generalkommando XIX. AK was the department for 'rearward connections and facilities', with primary responsibility for billeting. Note that administration of military justice and courts martial was handled by a different department (Abteilung III).
2   Oberstltn. Otto Ritter und Edler Herr von Berger, commander of IR 181 from 7 September 1916 to 27 March 1917. Born in Hanover on 23 November 1868, von Berger was chief of the *Abteilung für Landesaufnahme* (mapping department) of the Saxon General Staff before the war. He was awarded the MStHO(R) on 15 March 1915 as a staff officer with 19. Ersatz-Division, and appointed *Chef des Generalstabes* with Etappen-Inspektion 3 after his service with IR 181. He ended

the war in command of 246. Inf. Brig. (241. Inf. Div.), in which capacity he was awarded the MStHO(K2) on 9 November 1918.
3   Hptm. Alfred Thomas, commander of III. Batl. / IR 104 from 25 October 1916 to 14 March 1917. Originally with IR 134, he was awarded the MStHO(R) on 31 August 1916 for his leadership of 11. / IR 134 at Martinpuich and High Wood, and briefly commanded I. Batl. / IR 134 in September. From 8 June to 15 August 1917 he returned to command III. Batl. / IR 134, and survived to serve with the *Reichswehr* after the war.
4   Major Alfred Hanson, probably commander of II. Batl. / IR 181 (a position he definitely held in September 1916). This highly distinguished officer was awarded the MStHO(R) as a hauptmann on 23 October 1914 for his leadership of 2. / IR 181 in the Battle of the Marne, and died in 1923.
5   Hauptmann Johann Pflugbeil, probably the machine-gun officer on the staff of IR 181 mentioned under point 13 of the operational order. Already serving with MGK / IR 181 in peacetime, he was awarded the MStHO(R) as its commander on 31 August 1916. By October 1917 he commanded III. Batl. / IR 181, and was awarded the MStHO(K2) on 3 November 1918 for personally leading the battalion's successful counter-attack near Zandvoorde on 28 September, although severely wounded (see p. 170). He survived the war and subsequently served with the *Reichswehr*.
6   The protruding 'nose' in the German line west of the *Fransecky-Hof*, visible on the map on p. 121.
7   Codename for the battalion battle HQ in IR 181's right-hand sub-sector. This may be the location marked with a flag northwest of the *Steinbauer-Hof* on the map on p. 121.
8   This unit was still present in June 1917 and took part in the Battle of Messines.
9   Generalleutnant Traugott Freiherr Leuckart von Weissdorf, former Saxon military attaché in Berlin and commander of 23. Reserve-Division from February 1917 until some point in 1918.
10 Three members of this ancient noble house, all born in the old Kingdom of Hanover, served as Saxon generals during the war and received both the MStHO(R) and MStHO(K2). Otto commanded 23. Kavallerie-Brigade, then 8. KD and 45. LD. Friedrich commanded IR 134 and Detachement von der Decken (see p. 40) in 1914, and 96. ID throughout its existence.
11 German sources contain conflicting references to both Sturm-Bataillon 4 (the organic assault battalion of 4. Armee) and the famous Sturm-Bataillon 5 'Rohr'. Since the published death list for the latter shows no losses in Flanders around this time, the unit involved was almost certainly Sturm-Bataillon 4.

CHAPTER 7 – The Year 1918

1   Prinz Ernst Heinrich von Sachsen, *Mein Lebensweg vom Königsschloß zum Bauernhof* pp. 102–105
2   A.E.F. General Staff, *Histories of Two Hundred and Fifty-One Divisions of the German Army Which Participated in the War* p. 445. This source was compiled in 1919, incorporating intelligence from the other Entente armies.
3   Ltn. d. R. Hermann Weber (born 22 February 1889) was an Austrian from Tetschen in Bohemia, and taught at a vocational school (*Gewerbeschule*). When awarded his MStHO(R) on 13 September 1918 he was acting commander of 8. / IR 392. The citation states that in the counterattack which he had initiated Weber took his second prisoner in two days.
4   The official 'order of the day' for the entire German armed forces.
5   A.E.F. General Staff, op. cit. p. 340; 23. RD is nevertheless ranked in the third of four classes. Its resistance on 31 October 1918 is especially remarkable given that it had never faced tanks before.

CHAPTER 8 – Independent Units

1   Palmer, *My Year of the War* (Project Gutenberg online edition) p. 55

CHAPTER 9 – Saxon Lives and Deaths in Flanders

Curt Penther, Vizefeldwebel

1   From (at the latest) Summer 1915 until the corps moved further south in 1916, all new recruits for the infantry or *jägers* of 53. or 54. RD were first assigned to the *Feldrekrutendepot des XXVII. RK* in Oudenaarde, where their training would be completed under field conditions. By 1916 the depot had at least nine companies, several of them purely Württemberg (for RIR 246–248).
2   106. RIB was attached to 40. ID / XIX. AK as of 1 October (see p. 49).
3   Genmaj. Gustav von der Decken, commander of 106. Reserve-Infanterie-Brigade and not in fact an 'excellency' (at his rank he would be addressed as '*herr general*' rather than '*euer excellenz*'). In 1914 he commanded Leibgrenadier-Regiment 100, and was promoted and transferred when 53. Reserve-Division formed a second brigade staff in November. He was awarded the MStHO(R) on 25 May 1915, and later commanded 32. Infanterie-Division (see p. 152).
4   Limeflower tea was (and is) popularly drunk for its health benefits as well as its flavour. Penther is implying that the King looked like he really enjoyed his beer! And indeed, His Majesty's face still adorns bottles of *Radeberger Pils*, who proudly advertise their status as a *Kgl. Sächs. Hoflieferant* (the equivalent of 'by royal appointment').

5   We have found no other instance of this slang term ('treacle jar') in the contemporary literature.
6   Here, *'die Herren'*. Tommies were often referred to humorously as *'die herren'* or even *'die Gentlemen'*.
7   This refers to Penther's period of training on the *Offiziers-Aspiranten-Kursus* at Lockstedter Lager in Schleswig-Holstein, the main training area of the (Prussian) X. Armee-Korps. c.f. Brückner (p. 219).
8   A popular herbal liqueur (32 % abv) from Stonsdorf in Lower Silesia, made primarily from blueberries.
9   A traditional Saxon pound cake.
10 The table reserved for regulars in a local pub, or figuratively the group which meets there.
11 The naval equivalent of a *soldatenheim*.
12 The war diary of 2nd Btn. Royal Inniskilling Fusiliers records two killed, fourteen wounded (including an officer) and three missing between 25 and 28 August. Pte. 25597 R. Birnie and Pte. 27729 D. McPhail were both killed on 27 August and are buried at Cambrin Churchyard Extension (graves Q 51 and Q 52).

Max Conrad, Gefreiter

1   By 'Frenchmen' here Conrad means Francophone Belgians, i.e. Walloons. The Germans anticipated that they would as a whole be more likely than the Flemings to remain loyal to the Walloon-dominated Belgian state, and certainly more likely voluntarily to take up arms on its behalf.
2   The Garde Civique was a militia formed in 1830 to defend the Belgian state and maintain civil order, and was organised in local companies. It called (with exemptions for medical and family reasons) upon all male citizens aged 21–50 without other military obligations. In peacetime the Garde functioned as a gendarmerie (controlled by the Ministry of the Interior rather than the Ministry of War), and was mobilised on several occasions against riots and political violence by the far left. In August 1914 all units were mobilised under military control. The entire organisation was dissolved by King Albert I on 31 October due to German complaints that some guardsmen were fighting in civilian clothing (and therefore liable to be summarily shot as *Francs-tireurs*), and the threat that the legal combatant status of all guardsmen would be disregarded. In fact the two younger classes of the Garde were uniformed; the third class (volunteers aged over 50) served in a support role and were issued with neither uniforms nor weapons. Belgian sources acknowledge that, due to the massive disruption of their supply system during the invasion, some war volunteers did fight in civilian clothing – however, these were not necessarily members of the Garde. (see p. 190).
3   In all four German national armies a *Landwehr-Bezirkskommando* (Landwehr district command) was responsible for the administration and wartime mobilisation of the Landwehr and Landsturm in its designated area. In peacetime its role was limited to registering and monitoring those liable for service, hence the comparison with the role of the *Meldeamt*. The men liable for German service mentioned in the text would presumably have been German subjects resident in Belgium at the outbreak of war.
4   German law until 1974 (and both Belgian and French law to this day) recognised three categories of offense based on the severity of the punishment incurred. In descending order of severity these were *verbrechen* ('crime' – punishable by death, imprisonment with hard labour or confinement to a fortress for more than five years), *vergehen* ('misdemeanour' – punishable by ordinary imprisonment, confinement to a fortress for up to five years or a fine in excess of 150 marks) und *übertretung* ('contravention' – punishable by arrest for a maximum of six weeks or a fine of up to 150 marks). *Ordnungsvergehen* ('public order misdemeanours') and *polizeivergehen* ('police misdemeanours') were apparently lesser and greater degrees of *vergehen*.

Richard Kaden, Generalmajor

1   At this time Richard's younger brother Oberstltn. Alfred Kaden commanded FAR 77. Alfred was appointed divisional artillery commander of 40. ID in 1916, and awarded his own MStHO(R) on 27 November for his performance in this role during the Battle of the Somme.
2   Genmaj. Kaden was awarded the MStHO(R) on 15 October 1914 for his leadership in the battles of August and September. As noted earlier he received the *Komturkreuz 2. Klasse* (which could only be awarded to existing holders of the *Ritterkreuz*) in 1916.
3   IR 139 was facing the left flank of British 17th Brigade (6th Division). IR 179 had forced 2nd Btn. the Leinster Regt. out of Prémesques on 20 October, then taken Wez-Macquart the next day whilst JB 13 attacked L'Epinette. IR 139 was in the centre, and advanced via La Hongrie to help clear Prémesques and Wez-Macquart from the north.
4   La Houssoie was defended by British 16th Brigade (6th Division), primarily 1st Btn. the Leicestershire Regt. As genuine 'Old Contemptibles' of the regular British Army, they could certainly be described as an élite. IR 107 gradually fought their way into the village on 25 October, supported by Hessians of RIR 118 (25. RD) on the flank, together with Saxon *pioniere* and artillery from both divisions. The Leicesters abandoned their remaining positions in La Houssoie as untenable during the night.

5   Genltn. Adolf von Carlowitz was officially on convalescent leave for a heart condition as of 27 October 1914, and did not return to active service until August 1916. Nevertheless in 1917 he was again given command of a corps (XIX. AK), and in 1918 of two successive armies (9. and then 2. Armee). His command of XXVII. RK during the battle has come in for heavy criticism ever since, but the anecdote related by Kaden on 1 November can be neither proved nor disproved.
6   General der Kavallerie Hans Krug von Nidda was in fact promoted to that rank as of September 1914 (though this may have been backdated). He commanded 24. ID from July 1911 to May 1916, when he went on convalescent leave and was on the semi-retired list (*zur disposition*) for a year. Returning to active service in June 1917, he spent the remainder of the war as a corps commander (XXVII. RK and later XII. AK).
7   General der Kavallerie Maximilian von Laffert commanded XIX. AK continuously from November 1912 until his death from heart failure in July 1917.
8   Major Johannes Kretzschmar was a divisional staff officer and Major Adolf von Zeschau divisional adjutant, positions they already held under Genltn. Krug von Nidda in peacetime. Both subsequently commanded infantry regiments, respectively IR 178 and IR 183.
9   Almost certainly Hptm. Armin Mirus, who served in peacetime with PB 12, PB 22 and at the fortress of Strassburg. During the war he eventually reached the position of senior *pionier* officer on the staff of 3. Armee. The full-size round for the 25cm *minenwerfer* actually contained about 47 Kilos of TNT, equivalent to a couple of hundred field gun shells. According to the published history of IR 107, two of these (at the time still scarce) weapons were deployed in their sector on the night of 9–10 November.
10 According to the published history of IR 107, Major Gustav Freiherr von Bodenhausen had to return to Germany to recuperate after the heavy fighting on 11 November, and was replaced by the same Hptm. Hans Schreiber mentioned in Kaden's entries for 13 November and 25 December. The major clearly made a full recovery since he served as regimental commander from 16 July 1915, until given command of 47. Ersatz-Infanterie-Brigade (with 219. ID on the Eastern Front) on 28 August 1918.
11 Most likely Hptm. Ernst von Schweinitz, adjutant to Prince Friedrich Christian (his brother Wolfgang was adjutant to Prince Ernst Heinrich). The older prince was the art expert of his generation, following the example of his uncle Prince Johann Georg and a long tradition in the House of Wettin. After the war Prince Friedrich Christian completed a doctorate in law and worked as a private teacher of art history. He became the heir apparent when Crown Prince Georg joined the Jesuit priesthood in 1923, and head of the Saxon royal house upon his father's death in 1932.
12 Genmaj. Hans von Watzdorf, commander of 53. RD until July 1915. He is not to be confused with Genmaj. Bernhard von Watzdorf of 46. IB / 23. ID (later commander of 23. RD, 46. LD and from September 1917 last commander of XXVII. RK) or with Maj. Georg von Watzdorf of LGR 100.
13 Undoubtedly the *Seminar für Orientalische Sprachen* at the Friedrich-Wilhelms-Universität in Berlin (known since 1949 as Humboldt University). It is possible that this interview was partly or wholly for academic purposes; in the period 1915–1918 the distinguished linguist Wilhelm Doegen would record a vast (and now invaluable) sound archive of the numerous languages and dialects found in German POW camps.
14 'Fat Minna', an affectionate nickname for the 25cm *minenwerfer*, analogous to the much more familiar '*Dicke Bertha*' (the 42cm super-heavy siege howitzer).
15 It is interesting to note that both British and German accounts of the Christmas Truce usually claim that the other side made the first move, presumably due to concerns about potential disciplinary action. Ltn. Horst von Gehe of IR 107 later transferred to the *Luftstreitkräfte*, and was killed in action as a fighter pilot with Kampfstaffel 26 at Mercy le Bas (Woëvre-Ebene) on 17 March 1916.
16 The war diary of the Queen's Westminster Rifles (16th Btn. the London Regt.) opposite IR 107 records with considerable embarrassment that three men (Riflemen Byng, Goude and Pearce) went missing on Christmas Eve. During the fraternisation on Christmas Day, the Saxons informed the QWRs that they had wandered into the German trenches in a drunken state and been detained, having seen too much of the German defences to be released. The regimental history of IR 107 (which likewise claims that a British officer initiated the truce) refers to the 'capture' on Christmas Eve of two successive groups, of four and two Tommies respectively. The other three have been identified as Corporal Thomas Latimer and two men of 3rd Btn. The Rifle Brigade.
17 The Krampus is a comic demon who traditionally accompanies St. Nicholas (Father Christmas) in many parts of Germany and the former Austro-Hungarian Empire. While St. Nicholas rewards good children with presents, Krampus punishes bad children with 'gifts' of coal, or even carries them off in his sack.
18 Possibly Hptm. Gottfried Schröter (with a 't') of IR 106, killed in action near Neuville St. Vaast on 13 May 1915.
19 Genmaj. Georg Bärensprung, at this time commanding 88. IB / 40. ID, and from July 1915 commander of 23. ID for the remainder of the war.
20 OHL was based at Charleville-Mézières from 25 September 1914 to 19 September 1916. The Kaiser's birthday was 27 January.
21 Königin Elisabeth Garde-Grenadier-Regiment Nr. 3, often known colloquially as '*Regiment Elisabeth*'.

22 Oberst William Kohl commanded IR 106, and later 47. Infanterie-Brigade. His regimental adjutant Oltn. Friedrich Olbricht was promoted to hauptmann and adjutant of Kaden's old brigade after Verdun, later serving on the staffs of XIX. AK and 3. Armee. He is far better known for his heroic (and often under-appreciated) role in the Second World War, as unofficial leader and tireless organiser of the military resistance to Hitler. Following the failure of the bomb plot of 20 July 1944, he was summarily shot alongside Graf von Stauffenberg and others in the courtyard of his headquarters on the Bendlerstraße (now Stauffenbergstraße) in Berlin.

23 General der Infanterie Karl Ludwig d'Elsa commanded XII. AK from March 1910 to April 1916, when he was given command of Armeeabteilung 'A' in the Vosges. We have been unable to substantiate Kaden's story, but both of d'Elsa's sons had indeed been killed in action in 1914, Hptm. Walter d'Elsa with GR 101 at Rosée on 24 August and Ltn. Karl d'Elsa with LGR 100 at Bertoncourt on 30 August. Both regiments belonged to 23. ID / XII. AK, and were thus under their father's command at the time. After the war the general was pursued by the Entente as an alleged war criminal for the destruction of Dinant in this phase of the campaign, but died peacefully in July 1922.

24 Prince Heinrich had pursued a naval career, and at this time held the rank of *großadmiral* and command of German naval forces in the Baltic.

25 Prussian Genmaj. von Runckel, who had commanded 43. RD in Flanders since October 1914 (contrary to some published lists). Like all Saxon staff officers, Kaden had attended the Prussian *Kriegsakademie* in Berlin.

26 Lendelede, about four miles north of Courtrai / Kortrijk.

27 Sous-lieutenant Roland Garros had been a passionate aviation pioneer before the war, and was serving at this time with Escadrille MS 26. He is sometimes erroneously described as the first 'ace', although he only scored four confirmed aerial victories. He did however achieve the first ever aerial 'kill' by a fighter firing through a tractor propeller on 1 April 1915, with a system of deflector plates of his own design fitted to the blades. Interned in a series of POW camps, he managed to escape in February 1918 and return to service, only to be shot down and killed aged 29 on 5 October. The unit which downed his aircraft in 1915 was 1. Kompanie / Landsturm-Infanterie-Bataillon 'Wurzen' XIX.9, tasked with the defence of Lendelede railway station (though a Württemberg cavalry division claimed credit for his capture). Although this is one of only two Saxon Landsturm battalions with a full published history, it has remarkably little to say beyond noting that Fwltn. Schlenstedt, Ldstm. Arnold (I.) and Ldstm. Brömme all received the Iron Cross 1st Class for their achievement.

28 Genltn. Georg von Gersdorff commanded 58. ID from its formation until relieved due to illness in April 1917, as a result of which he died on 11 May of that year.

29 Auguste Bonte was mayor of Lambresart from 1897 to March 1916. During the war he was imprisoned as a hostage on three occasions – for his community's alleged involvement in the deaths of German officers (in October 1914, for fourteen days), refusal to sew sandbags for the Germans (as described in Kaden's entry of 17 July 1915) and finally the alleged concealment of carrier pigeons in the town. He died on 25 July 1916 at the age of 63, almost certainly in part due to the stress and privations he had endured.

The Tragedy of Hans Brückner

1 To 'don the braids' (*die Schnüre anlegen*), meaning 'to become an NCO' is still common parlance in the Bundeswehr.

2 i.e. with the regimental *minenwerfer-abteilung* (later expanded to a full company).

3 Every German soldier was issued with one field dressing (*verbandspäckchen*), carried in a special pocket inside the front left skirt flap of the tunic.

4 Pre-war training prescribed the battle-cry *'Hurra'* for bayonet charges (*sturm-angriff mit hurrarufen*).

5 'Sulphur bombs' (*schwefelbomben*) and 'sulphur shells' (*schwefelgranaten*) were common German terms for British high explosive shells filled with Lyddite. This mixture of picric acid and guncotton produced noxious fumes and a powdery yellow residue as by-products of detonation.

6 Roughly 'into [static] positions!', an order to occupy a trench or (if necessary) create one.

7 This sector had been held since the onset of trench warfare by Bavarians of 3. bID / II. bAK.

Three fallen brothers

1 The guns had been set up to provide, in British terms, a 'machine-gun barrage' ahead of the *hauptwiderstandslinie*. In the event the advance was apparently checked before 49th Division could enter the barrage zone.

2 See Brückner, note 5. For an MG team this would mean 'deploy', i.e. 'set up the gun here'.

3 This system of designating companies by lower-case ('a', 'b' etc.) and battalions by upper-case ('A', 'B' etc.) letters refers to the company and battalion sectors, and only by extension to the specific sub-units occupying them at any given time. i.e. any battalion holding sector 'B' would be *designated 'B Bataillon'* for as long as it remained there.

4 As Jack Sheldon has noted, this prisoner must have belonged to 2nd Btn. the Queen's (Royal West Surrey Regt) of 91st Brigade / 7th Division.

Werner Mühle, Gefreiter

1 In summer 1917 Mühle's company (1. / IR 102) seems to have been the luckiest in its battalion (I. / IR 102), which itself spent a considerable period in reserve behind the line.

2 Kaiser's Kaffee Geschäft AG was a highly successful chain of coffee shops founded by Josef Kaiser in Viersen in 1880, with over a thousand branches by 1914. It also sold tea, biscuits and confectionary – hence Heynen's bounty and Mühle's toothache. Since 1971 the company has been part of the supermarket chain Kaiser's Tengelmann GmbH; the premises in Viersen closed in 2010.

3 An NCO or gefreiter temporarily responsible for a group of men travelling by rail.

4 The contemporary *zeltbahn* or *zeltplane* was a waterproof brown or grey canvas sheet (1.7 metres square) intended as half a tent or a rain cape, and often used as a stretcher or burial shroud (see the order on p. 148). Second World War and later versions are smaller and triangular in shape.

5 '[Form a] carrying party!'

6 The words 'stop' and 'Germans' here appear in English in the original text.

7 'Blue beans' (*blaue bohnen*) is still common German soldiers' slang for bullets.

8 To 'receive the buttons' (*die Knöpfe bekommen*) meant to be promoted to the rank of gefreiter.

Robert Reichel, Leutnant der Reserve

1 The *Dresdener Anzeiger* was the kingdom's paper of record, founded in 1730 and forcibly merged under Nazi rule. Its modern successor is the *Dresdner Amtsblatt*.

2 At La Bourse north of Bailleul on 16 April the battalion staff of II. / IR 103 fell victim to a direct hit. While their commander Hptm. Georg Loeser died quickly, Reichel's friend Ltn. d. R. Leonhard Bourquin suffered horrific injuries to both legs from a shell splinter and died the next day at the divisional dressing station (*hauptverbandplatz*) aged only 19. Reichel's letters show that he had developed a deep paternal affection for Bourquin since becoming his company commander in August 1917, and his loss was especially hard to bear. The many dead of 16 April also included Vfw. Barth, the *bataillons-tambour* (drummer) and one of the last of the old regulars from 1914.

3 Reichel is probably alluding to the announcement of H.M. the King of Saxony's visit, which proved to be the monarch's last to the 32. ID. The parade was held on 15 May south of Fleurbaix near Rue Petillon, site of the division's break-through on 9 April and now of a British cemetery with a total of 881 known graves.

4 The 'Sturm' mentioned by Reichel is probably Oltn. Hans Sturm, a fellow Dres-dener and the only known Saxon officer of this name to die in the war. A former artilleryman (FAR 78), Oltn. Sturm was serving as a pilot with Riesenflugzeug-Abteilung 501, a 'giant' bomber unit which had conducted raids on London since September 1917. His air-craft, Staaken R VI R 34/16 (with a wingspan of 42.2 metres) was a unique variant with a fifth engine driving a revolutionary supercharger. On 21 April 1918 it set out to bomb the British airfield at Saint-Omer, only to be shot down by AA fire near Westrozebeke with the loss of all seven crewmen. The wreck was unearthed in 1981, but not identified until 2007.

Fritz Wittig, Gefreiter

1 Whit Monday (*Pfingstmontag* – the second day of Pentecost) is still a public holiday in Germany, as it was in Britain until 1967. For the troops in the field this was an occasion for religious observance, various traditional festivities (which could be quite raucous) and commemorative photos.

2 In all arms of service a *vorkommando* (roughly, 'advance party') would routinely be sent ahead when moving to a new sector, to make accommodation and other arrangements for the rest of the unit.

3 By 1918, *liebesgaben* from home had become a thing of the past. Due to the acute shortages resulting from the British naval blockade, practically everything was strictly rationed and many goods were reserved for the men at the front. It was now the turn of the soldiers to provide their families with even basic necessities, such as soles for shoes (cut from old boots and covertly posted home).

4 The organisation of a *fernsprech-abteilung* below platoon level is unclear from the available sources, but it is evident that the *trupp* was the smallest sub-unit, and would therefore theoretically be commanded by an unteroffizier. A gefreiter was not an NCO, and could only exercise temporary authority delegated to him by a superior for a specific task. By 1918 many such 'temporary' arrangements had become the norm.

5 'Mit deutschem Gruß', a phrase more familiar from the Hitler period, when it would act as the written form of the Nazi salute (the so-called 'German greeting'). In 1918 it evidently expressed a more nebulous patriotic sentiment.

6 The smallest field formation with an official 'padre' was the division, which was authorised one *divisionspfarrer* (divisional pastor) of the majority denomination – invariably Protestant in Saxon divisions. This *etatsmäßige divisionspfarrer* was supplemented in wartime by volunteer *hilfspfarrer*, so that a typical division would have one Roman Catholic and one Protestant chaplain. A total of about thirty Jewish *feldrabbiner* (field rabbis) were attached at higher headquarters throughout the German armies.

7 This unusual title translates to 'acting wachtmeister'; like Gefr. Wittig (and Heller), Sergt. Schuberts is serving 'temporarily' in a position officially above his substantive rank. Unlike *stellvertreter* ('deputy'), the status of *diensttuer* was not formally recognised.

INDEX

---

* page(s) contain one or more relevant images
° index of places only; page(s) contain one or more relevant maps

BIBLIOGRAPHY

UNPUBLISHED SOURCES

The National Archives, London – British Army war diaries 1914–1922 (series WO95)
Sächsisches Hauptstaatsarchiv Dresden – records filed under the following shelfmarks (signaturen): 11300 (Sanitätskompanien); 11351 (Generalkommando des XIX. Armeekorps); 11356 (Generalkommando des XII. Reservekorps); 11358 (Generalkommando des XXVII. Reservekorps); 11359 (Infanteriedivisionen, Infanterieregimenter, Infanteriebataillone); 11362 (Feldartilleriebrigaden / Artilleriekommandeure); 13180-13245 (artillery, individually shelfmarked by unit)
Original diaries, correspondence and photographs from the authors' collections

PUBLISHED WORKS

AEF General Staff, Histories of Two Hundred and Fifty-One Divisions of the German Army Which Participated in the War, Washington, 1920
Albrecht, O., Das Königlich Sächsische Reserve-Jäger-Bataillon Nr. 25 im Weltkriege, Dresden, 1927
Anon., Evangelisches Militair-Gesang- und Gebetbuch – Ausgabe für die Königlich Sächsischen Truppen, Leipzig, Ca. 1900
Anon. (collaborative work), Kgl. Sächs. Infanterie-Regiment Nr. 178, Dresden / Kamenz, 1935
Ashworth, T., Trench Warfare 1914–1918: The Live and Let Live System, London, 1980
Baker, The Battle for Flanders: German defeat on the Lys 1918, Barnsley, 2011
Bamberg, G., Das Reserve-Infanterie-Regiment Nr. 106 (kgl. sächs.) im Weltkrieg, Dresden, 1925
Barton, P., Doyle, P & Vandewalle J., Beneath Flanders Fields – The Tunnellers' War 1914–18, Stroud, 2007
Baumgaertel, M., Das Kgl. Sächs. 14. Infanterie-Regt. 179, Leipzig, 1931
Baumgarten-Crusius, A., Das 2. Kgl. Sächsische Husaren-Regiment Nr. 19 "Kronprinz Wilhelm des Deutschen Reiches und von Preußen", Leipzig, 1930
Baumgarten-Crusius, A., Das Königlich-Sächsische 11. Infanterie-Regiment Nr. 139 (1914–1918), Dresden, 1927
Baumgarten-Crusius, A. & Hottenroth, J.E., Sachsen in großer Zeit, Leipzig, 1918–1920
Bayerisches Kriegsarchiv, Die Bayern im Großen Kriege 1914–1918, Munich, 1923
Bean, C.E.W., Official History of Australia in the War of 1914–1918 (vol. III), Sydney, 1929
Berger, E., Die 204. (S.W.) Infanterie-Division im Weltkrieg 1914–18, Stuttgart, 1922
Beumelburg, W., Die Schlacht um Flandern 1917, Oldenburg, 1928
Beumelburg, W., Ypern 1914, Oldenburg, 1925
Bierey, R., Das Kgl. Sächs. Reserve-Feldartillerie-Regiment Nr. 40, Dresden, 1927
Blades, G.D., The Battles of the Lys – The British Army on the Defensive in April 1918 (M.Phil thesis), London, 1999
Blohm, E. et al., Das Kgl. Sächs. Schützen-Regiment "Prinz Georg" Nr. 108, Dresden, 1926
Blunden, Undertones of War, London, 1928
Bolze, W., Das Kgl. Sächs. 1. Feldartillerie-Regiment Nr. 12, Dresden, 1927
Bolze, W., Das Kgl. Sächs. 7. Feldartillerie-Regiment Nr. 77, Dresden, 1924
Bossert, H., Das 4. Unter-Elsässische Infanterie-Regiment Nr. 143 im Frieden und im Weltkrieg (vol. I), Berlin, 1935
Böttger, K., Das Kgl. Sächs. 7. Infanterie-Regiment König Georg Nr. 106, Dresden, 1927
Bramsch, D. et al., Das Kgl. Sächs. 2. Ulanen-Regiment Nr. 18, Dresden, 1928
Braun, Das Reserve-Infanterie-Regiment 104 im Weltkriege 1914–1918, Leipzig, 1921
Brown, M. & Seaton, S., Christmas Truce, London, 1994
Brueckner, J., Das Kgl. Sächs. Ersatz-Feldartillerie-Regiment Nr. 45 und seine Stammabteilungen, Dresden, 1937
Bucher, Dienstunterricht des Königlich Sächsischen Infanteristen, Dresden, 1910
Busche, H., Formationsgeschichte der Deutschen Infanterie im Ersten Weltkrieg 1914–1918, Owschlag, 1998
Butterworth, H.M. & Cooksey, J. (ed.), Blood and Iron: Letters from the Western Front, Barnsley, 2011
Byrne, A.E., Official History of the Otago Regiment, N.Z.E.F. in the Great War 1914–1918, Dunedin, 1921
Cleaver, A., Park, L. et al., Not a Shot was Fired: Letters from the Christmas Truce 1914, Raleigh, 2008
Cron, H., Die Organisation des Deutschen Heeres im Weltkrieg, Berlin, 1923
Cron, H., Imperial German Army 1914–18: Organisation, Structure, Orders-of-Battle, Solihull, 2006
Deutschen Offizier-Bund, Ehrenrangliste des ehemaligen Deutschen Heeres auf Grund der Ranglisten von 1914 mit den inzwischen eingetretenen Veränderungen, Berlin, 1926
Dubois, A., Deux ans de commandement sur le front de France 1914–1916, Paris, 1921
Duguid, A.F., Official History of the Canadian Forces in the Great War 1914–1919 (vol. I), Ottawa, 1938
Edmonds, Sir J.E., [British Official History] Military Operations France and Belgium, 1914 (vol. II), London, 1925
Edmonds, Sir J.E. & Maxwell-Hyslop, R., [British Official History] Military Operations France and Belgium, 1918 (vol. V), London, 1947
Ewing, J., The Royal Scots 1914–1919, Edinburgh / London, 1925
Ferro, M., Brown, M. et al., Meetings in No Man's Land: Christmas 1914 and Fraternization in the Great War, London, 2007
Friedag, B., Führer durch Heer und Flotte, Berlin, 1914

Friedel. P., *Geschichte des Königlich Sächsischen Infanterie-Regiments Nr. 416*, Leipzig, 1926

Fromm, F., *Das Württembergische Reserve-Infanterie-Regiment Nr. 120 im Weltkrieg 1914–1918*, Stuttgart, 1920

von Funke, A., *Unser tapferes Regiment. Das Kgl. Sächs. 8. Feldartillerie-Regiment Nr. 78 im Großen Kriege*, Dresden, 1931

Glogowski, E., *Das Königlich Sächsische 6. Infanterie-Regiment Nr. 105 König Wilhelm II von Württemberg*, Dresden, 1929

Glück, E. & Wald, A., *Das 8. Württembergische Infanterie-Regiment Nr. 126 Großherzog Friedrich von Baden im Weltkrieg 1914–1918*, Stuttgart, 1929

Gray, J.H., *The New Zealand Division in France and Flanders, May 1916 to November 1918*, Christchurch, 2005

Grill, Dr. A., *Das Sächsische Reserve-Infanterie-Regiment 241 im Weltkriege 1914 / 1918: Kriegserinnerungen eines Truppenarztes*, Dresden, 1922

Guéno, J. (ed.), *Paroles de poilus: lettres et carnets du front 1914–1918*, Paris, 2001

Herkenrath, A., *Das Württembergische Reserve-Inf.-Regiment Nr. 247 im Weltkriege 1914–1918*, Stuttgart, 1923

Herrmann, H., *Geschichte des Königlich Sächsischen Leibgrenadier-Regiments Nr. 100*, Zittau, 1927

Heydenreich, F., *Das Kgl. Sächs. Feldartillerie-Regiment Nr. 245*, Dresden, 1921

Hitchcock, F.C., *"Stand To" A Diary of the Trenches 1915–1918*, London, 1937

Hoffmann, *Die sächsische Armee im Deutschen Reich 1871 bis 1918* (D. Phil dissertation), Dresden, 2007

Joermann-Düsseldorf, *Geschichte des 4. Lothringischen Infanterie-Regiments Nr. 136*, Duisburg, 1933

Jones, S., *World War I Gas Warfare Tactics and Equipment*, Oxford, 2007

K.S. Kriegsministerium, *Rangliste der Königlich Sächsischen Armee für das Jahr 1914*, Dresden, 1914

Kaden, R., *In der Alte Armee*, Leipzig, 1933

Kastner, H., *Geschichte des Königlichen Sächsischen Reserve Infanterie-Regiments 242*, Zittau, 1924

Kees, H., *Das Kgl. Sächs. Feldartillerie-Regiment Nr. 115*, Dresden, 1928–1934

Kleeberg, A., *Das Infanterie-Regiment Nr. 354 im Weltkriege 1914–1918*, Oldenburg, 1923

Klitzsch, J., *Kriegstagebuch 1914–1918 des Kgl. Sächs. Reserve-Infanterie-Regiments Nr. 101*, Dresden, 1934

Klotz, D., *Das Württembergische Reserve-Feldartillerie-Regiment Nr. 54 im Weltkrieg 1914–1918*, Stuttgart, 1929

Knoppe, P., *Die Geschichte des Königlich Sächsischen Reserve-Infanterie-Regiments Nr. 241*, Dresden, 1936

Krämer, K., *Geschichte des Reserve-Infanterie-Regiments Nr. 245 im Weltkrieg 1914–1918*, Leipzig, 1923

Kruspe, H., *Das Kgl. Sächs. 12. Infanterie-Regiment Nr. 177*, Dresden, 1924

Kuehn, W., *Das Kgl. Sächs. Landsturm-Infanterie-Bataillon Wurzen XIX / 9*, Dresden, 1938

Lehmann, H., *Das Königlich Sächsische Reserve-Jäger-Bataillon Nr. 26*, Dresden, 1923

Lucas, A.R. & Lucas, M.J., *Loos to St. Eloi – the Experience of the Saxon 123. Infanterie-Division on the Western Front, 1915–16, Stand To!* (issues 96–98), January–September 2013

Lucas, M.J., *The Journey's End Battalion*, Barnsley, 2012

Luxford, J.H., *With the Machine Gunners in France and Palestine*, Auckland, 1923

Machate, F., D*as Kgl. Sächs. Reserve-Feldartillerie-Regiment Nr. 32*, Dresden, 1932

Marix-Evans, M., *1918 – The Year of Victories*, London, 2002

Martin, A., *Das Kgl. Sächs. Grenadier-Regiment Nr. 100*, Dresden, 1924

Maude, A.H., *The History of the 47th (London) Division 1914–1919*, London, 1922

Mertens, P., *Die militärische "Nebenregierung" in Dresden 1914–1918*, Militärhistorisches Museum der Bundeswehr in Dresden (vol. 10), January 2006

Meyer, A., *Das Kgl. Sächs. 2. Grenadier-Regiment Nr. 101 "Kaiser Wilhelm, König von Preußen"*, Dresden, 1924

Monse, R., *Das 4. Königl. Sächsische Infanterie-Regiment Nr. 103 im Kriege 1914–18*, Dresden, 1930

Niemann, J., *Das 9. Königlich Sächsische Infanterie-Regiment Nr. 133 im Weltkrieg, 1914–18*, Hamburg, 1969

Orgeldinger, L., *Das Württembergische Reserve-Infanterie-Regiment Nr. 246*, Stuttgart, 1931

Otto, K., *Das Kgl. Sächs. Feldartillerie-Regiment Nr. 246*, Dresden, 1928

Pache, A., *Das Kgl. Sächs. 16. Infanterie-Regiment Nr. 182*, Dresden, 1924

Palmer, F., *My Year of the War*, New York, 1915

Partzsch, M., *Das Kgl. Sächs. 3. Feldartillerie-Regiment Nr. 32*, Dresden, 1939

Pflugbeil, H., *Das Kgl. Sächs. 15. Infanterie-Regiment Nr. 181*, Dresden, 1923

Pohland, F.T., *Das Kgl. Sächs. Reserve-Infanterie-Regiment Nr. 103*, Dresden, 1922

Reddemann, Dr. B., *Geschichte der Deutschen Flammenwerfer-Truppe*, Berlin, 1933

Reichsarchiv, *Ruhmeshalle unserer alten Armee*, Berlin, 1927

Reimer, K., *Geschichte der Abteilung Reimer: sächs. Ers. Abt. FAR 68, I. sächs. Res. FAR 54 u. III. sächs. Res. FAR 32*, Dresden, 1927

Reinecke, A. & Steiglehner, W., *Das Königlich Preußische Straßburger Feld-Artillerie-Regiment Nr. 84*, Oldenburg, 1934

Reinhardt, E., *Das Württembergische Reserve-Inf.-Regiment Nr. 248 im Weltkriege 1914–1918*, Stuttgart, 1924

Richter, G., *Der Königliche Sächsische Militär-St. Heinrichs-Orden 1736–1918*, Frankfurt, 1964

Robinson, J. & Robinson, J., *Handbook of Imperial Germany*, Bloomington, 2009

Sachse, J., *Die Sächsische Pioniere*, Dresden, 1923

s.K.H. Prinz Ernst Heinrich von Sachsen, *Mein Lebensweg vom Königsschloss zum Bauernhof*, Dresden / Basel, 1995

Schatz, *Das 10. Kgl. Sächs. Infanterie Regiment Nr. 134*, Dresden, 1922

Scheer, C., *Flandern-Regiment 413, 30 Monate Westfront – Das Württembergische Infanterie-Regiment Nr. 413 im Weltkrieg 1916–1918*, Stuttgart, 1936

Schmacht, F., *Geschichte des Kgl. Sächs. Reserve-Feldartillerie-Regiments Nr. 24*, Dresden, 1926

Schmaler, M., *Das Königlich Sächsische Infanterie-Regiment Nr. 415 im Weltkriege*, Dresden, 1928

Schmidt, E., *Die Geschichte des Infanterie-Regiments Graf Werder (4. Rhein.) Nr. 30 im Weltkrieg 1914–18* (vol. 4), Zeulenroda, 1932

Schoene, M., *Das I. Bataillon des 2. Kgl. Sächs. Fußartillerie-Regiments Nr. 19*, Dresden, 1925

Schuck, F., *Die Kgl. Sächs. Divisions-Funker-Abteilung Nr. 15 im Weltkrieg*, Mylau, 1934

Schwarte, M., *Der Weltkampf um Ehre und Recht*, Leipzig, 1921–33

Freiherr von Seckendorff-Gudent, E., *Das Königlich Sächsische 8. Infanterie-Regiment "Prinz Johann Georg" Nr. 107 während des Weltkrieges 1914–1918*, Dresden, 1928

Sheldon, J., *The Gas Attacks – Ypres 1915*, Barnsley, 2009

Sheldon, J., *The German Army at Passchendaele*, Barnsley, 2007

Sheldon, J., *The German Army on the Western Front 1915*, Barnsley, 2012

Sheldon, J., *The Germany Army at Ypres 1914*, Barnsley, 2010

Spagnoly, T. & Smith, T., *A Walk Around Plugstreet*, Barnsley, 2003

Strasheim, R., *Beute-Tanks* (vol. 2), Erlangen, 2011

Stuhlmann, F., *Das Kgl. Sächs. 6. Feldartillerie-Regiment Nr. 68*, Dresden, 1927

Trümper-Bödemann, M., *Das Königl. Sächs. Reserve-Infanterie-Regiment Nr. 102*, Dresden, 1929

Turner, A., *Messines 1917: The Zenith of Siege Warfare*, Oxford, 2010

U.S. Army War College, *Vocabulary of German Military Terms and Abbreviations*, Washington, 1917

Ulbricht, W., *Die Geschichte des Königlich Sächsischen Reserve-Infanterie-Regiments 244 im Weltkriege 1914–1918*, Chemnitz, 1920

Unruh, K., *Langemarck – Legende und Wirklichkeit*, Koblenz, 1986

Freiherr von Uslar-Gleichen, K., *Das Kgl. Sächs. 2. Jäger-Bataillon Nr. 13 im Weltkriege*, Dresden, 1924

Various authors, *Was wir erlebten – 245er Erinnerungen*, Leipzig, 1921–1942

Wagner, E., *Das 5. Kgl. Sächs. Feldartillerie-Regiment Nr. 64*, Dresden, 1922

Walde, H., *Im Weltkrieg unter dem Sachsenbanner*, Dresden, 1917

War Office (Great Britain), *Handbook of the German Army 1914*, London / Nashville, 2002

War Office (Great Britain), *The German Army Handbook of 1918*, Barnsley, 2008

Whitton, F.C., *A History of the Prince of Wales's Leinster Regiment (Royal Canadians)*, Aldershot, 1924

Winzer, R., *Das Königliche Sächsische Reserve Infanterie-Regiment Nr. 243 im Weltkrieg 1914–1918*, Dresden, 1927

Wolff, L., *Das Kgl. Sächs. 5. Inf.-Regiment "Kronprinz" Nr. 104*, Dresden, 1925

Wolff, L., *In Flanders Fields: The 1917 Campaign*, New York, 1958

Zipfel, G., *Das 3. Kgl. Sächs. Infanterie-Regiment Nr. 102 "König Ludwig III. von Bayern" im Weltkriege 1914–1918*, Dresden, 1925

SELECTED ONLINE SOURCES

Commonwealth War Graves Commission – http://www.cwgc.org/
GenWiki – http://wiki-de.genealogy.net
Great War Forum – http://1914-1918.invisionzone.com
Indre 14-18 – http://indre1418.canalblog.com
Landships (Google) – https://sites.google.com/site/landships/home
Landships II – http://www.landships.info/landships/index.html
The Long, Long Trail – http://www.1914-1918.net/
Menenwald – www.menenwald.be
Onlineprojekt Gefallenendenkmaler – http://denkmalprojekt.org
The Royal Sussex Living History Group – http://www.royalsussex.org.uk/
The Tunneller's Memorial, Givenchy – http://www.tunnellersmemorial.com/

PICTURE CREDITS

Andrew Lucas Collection 8, 9 (creation), 10, 17, 18, 20, 21, 29 top left, 31 bottom, 35, 36, 41 (creation), 56 top, 59, 68 top, 69 bottom, 70 top right & bottom right, 72, 73, 98, 107 top, 111 bottom right, 112, 115, 118 top, 122 top, 125, 135, 143 bottom, 145, 147 bottom, 149 bottom, 150 top, 154 top, 157, 164, 169, 175 bottom, 179 top, 180 top right & left, 245

Jürgen Schmieschek Collection 5–7, 11–15, 19, 22, 23, 25–28, 29 top right, 30, 31 top, 32–34, 37–40, 42, 43, 45, 47–55, 56 bottom, 57, 58, 60–67, 68 bottom, 69 top, 70 top left & bottom left, 71, 74–87, 88 top, 89, 91–97, 99–104, 106, 107 bottom, 108–110, 111 top & bottom left, 113, 114, 117, 118 bottom, 119–121, 122 bottom, 123, 124, 126–131, 133, 136 bottom, 137, 140–142, 143 top, 144, 146, 147 top, 148, 149 top, 150 bottom, 151–153, 154 bottom, 155, 158–163, 166 left, 167, 168, 170, 171, 173, 174, 175 top, 176, 177, 178 left, 179 bottom, 180 bottom right, 181–189, 193, 194, 196, 198–203, 205, 206, 208, 210, 212, 215–217, 219–227, 232, 234, 235–237, 239–244

Jan Vancoillie Collection 44, 88 bottom left & right, 136 top

Margot Hemmings 16

Volksbund deutscher Kriegsgräberfürsorge 166 right, 178 right,

GLOSSARY

TIME

German time is used as standard throughout this book. Due to the adoption of different daylight saving schemes during the war, the British-German time difference varied significantly from 1916 onwards. To convert British to German time apply the following modifiers:

+1 hour: Until 1 May 1916, 14 June to 30 September 1916, 1 October 1916 to 24 March 1917, 16 April to 17 September 1917, 7 October 1917 to 9 March 1918, 15 April to 16 September 1918, 6 October 1918 onwards

+2 hour: 1 May to 14 June 1916

nil: 30 September to 1 October 1916, 24 March to 16 April 1917, 17 September to 7 October 1917, 9 March to 15 April 1918, 16 September to 6 October 1918

RANK

Rank	Abbreviation	British Equivalent
GENERALE (generals)		
Generalfeldmarschall	GFM	Field Marshal
Generaloberst		'Colonel-General'
General der Infanterie (... Artillerie / ... Kavallerie)	Gen. der Inf. (... Art., ... Kav.)	General
Generalleutnant	Genltn.	Lieutenant-General
Generalmajor	Genmaj.	Major-General
STABSOFFIZIERE (staff officers)		
Oberst	Oberst	Colonel
Oberstleutnant	Oberstltn.	Lieutenant-Colonel
Major	Maj.	Major
HAUPTLEUTE UND SUBALTERNOFFIZIERE (captains and subalterns)		
Hauptmann/Rittmeister[1]	Hptm.	Captain
Oberleutnant	Oltn.	1st Lieutenant
Leutnant	Ltn.	2nd Lieutenant
Feldwebelleutnant[2]	Fwltn.	'Sergeant-Lieutenant'
PORTEPEE-UNTEROFFIZIERE (snr. NCOs, entitled to an officer's sword knot)		
Feldwebel / Wachtmeister[3]	Fw.	Sergeant-Major
Vizefeldwebel / Vizewachtmeister[4]	Vfw.	'Vice Sergeant-Major'
UNTEROFFIZIERE OHNE PORTEPEE (jnr. NCOs)		
Sergeant	Sergt.	Sergeant
Unteroffizier / Oberjäger[5]	Uffz.	Corporal
MANNSCHAFTEN ('other ranks'; no command authority)		
Gefreiter	Gefr.	Lance-Corporal
Soldat[6]	Sold.	Private

1 'Rittmeister' in the cavalry and train only.
2 A senior career NCO promoted to officer rank.
3 'Wachtmeister' in the cavalry, *feldartillerie* and *train* only.
4 'Vizewachtmeister' in the cavalry, *feldartillerie* and *train* only.
5 'Oberjäger' in the *jäger* only.
6 'Soldat' was the title for a private in the Saxon infantry only. Alternative titles in different units and arms of service included: fahrer ('driver' – artillery and *train*), funker (radio units), gardist (Garde-Reiter and Prussian Garde), grenadier, husar, infanterist (Bavarian infantry), jäger, kanonier ('gunner' – artillery), karabinier, musketier (Prussian infantry), pionier, schütze ('rifleman' – SR 108 and machine-gunners with all units), telegraphist and ulan.

SPECIAL RANKS AND SERVICE CATEGORIES

... außer Dienst (a. D.) Rank suffix for retired officers ('out of service'); often re-called in wartime; **... der Landwehr (d. L.)** Suffix for ranks in the (trained) second-line reserve; divided by age into two 'bans' (Landwehr I and II). In peacetime ORs would pass into the Landsturm at the age of 39; **... der Reserve (d. R.)** Suffix for ranks in the (trained) first-line reserve. In peacetime ORs would pass into the Land-wehr at about the age of 27; **... zur Disposition (z. D.)** Rank suffix for semi-retired officers (half pay); usually recalled in wartime; **Arzt** Medical officer; ranks included assistenzarzt, oberarzt and stabsarzt; **Beamte** Uniformed (military) civil servant; **Einjährig-Freiwilliger (Einj. Frw.)** One-year volunteer; a man who reported to a unit before his active call-up and paid for his own kit and expenses, with the aim of becoming a reserve officer. Served actively for only one year (rather than up to three) in peacetime; **Ersatz-Reservist (Ers. Res.)** An untrained man of military age, passed over for active service in peacetime (included about half of those eligible to serve before the war); **Fahnenjunker** Prospective officer (with variable rank up to uffz.); formerly *avantageur*; **Fähnrich** Prospective officer (with variable rank up to vfw.); **Hornist** Trumpeter; **Kapitulant** Re-engaged (career) soldier; the main source of NCOs in peacetime; **Krankenträger** Stretcher-bearer (private); **Kriegsfreiwilliger (Kr. Frw.)** War volunteer; a man who reported to a unit before his ersatz-reserve, Landsturm or active call-up. If not immediately killed, such men often enjoyed rapid promotion; **Landsturmmann (Ldstm.)** Landsturm infantry private (either a reservist aged 39–45 or an untrained man aged 17–45 without other military obligations); given ranks 'der Landwehr' if promoted; **Obergefreiter** Rank between gefreiter and unteroffizier, used only in the *fussartillerie* for a qualified gun-layer (*richtkanonier*); **Reservist** Infantry private in the (trained) first-line reserve; **Sanitäts- (San.)** Prefix for medical NCOs and ORs; **Tambour** Drummer; **Wehrmann** Infantry private in the (trained) second-line reserve; **Sanitäter** Medical orderly (private); often yelled as a call for medical assistance (like "stretcher bearers!" on the British side)

APPOINTMENTS

Bataillonsarzt (Batl. Arzt) Battalion medical officer; commanded a deputy (unter-arzt) and numerous *sanitäter* and *krankenträger*; **Chef** Honorary colonel-in-chief (often royalty); **Etatsmässiger Feldwebel** Company sergeant-major; **Führer (Fhr.)** Leader; acting commander (if an officer); **Kommandeur (Kdr.)** Commanding officer (formally appointed); **Offiziers-Stellvertreter (Offz. Stv.)** NCO formally 'deputising' in a subaltern's post (typically a vizefeldwebel); **Ordonnanz (-Offizier)** Orderly officer; **Regimentsarzt (Regts. Arzt)** Regimental medical officer

DECORATIONS

Eiserne Kreuz 1. Klasse (EK1) Iron Cross 1st Class (Prussian); **Eiserne Kreuz 2. Klasse (EK2)** Iron Cross 2nd Class (Prussian); **Pour le Mérite (PLM)** Pour le Mérite ("Blue Max"; the highest Prussian gallantry award); **Militär-St. Heinrichs-Orden (MStHO)** Military St. Henry Order (highest Saxon and oldest German gallantry award); **Komturkreuz des MStHO (MStHO[K])** Commander's Cross of the above (for senior officers, two classes); **Ritterkreuz des MStHO (MStHO[R])** Knight's Cross of the above (for officers); **Militär-St. Heinrichs-Medaille (MStHM)** Medal of the above (for enlisted men, in silver and gold); **Friedrich-August-Medaille (FAM)** Friedrich August Medal (for enlisted men, in silver and bronze)

REGIMENT AND BATTALION

The basic unit of infantry, cavalry and artillery was the regiment. An infantry regiment normally comprised three battalions, designated with Roman numerals (I–III). Each battalion had four rifle companies, designated with Arabic numerals in a single regimental sequence (1–4, 5–8 and 9–12 in battalions I–III respectively); in 1914 the single machine-gun company was unnumbered; later each battalion had an MG company with a matching Arabic number (1–3 MGK). Companies in *jäger* and *pionier* battalions were likewise designated with Arabic numerals, as were the (typically four) squadrons of a cavalry regiment. Most artillery regiments in 1914 had two battalions, designated with Roman numerals and each with three (*feldartillerie*) or up to four (*fussartillerie*) batteries; like companies, these were designated with Arabic numerals in a single regimental sequence. The system for referring to sub-units is quite intuitive and best explained via examples; the prefix of the parent unit (e.g. 'IR') is only ever dropped where the context excludes any possibility of confusion.

Long form	Shortest form	Translation
II. Bataillon / Infanterie-Regiment 102	II./102	2nd Battalion, IR 102
2. Kompanie / Infanterie-Regiment 102	2./102	2nd Company, IR 102
I. Abteilung / Feldartillerie-Regiment 48	I./48	1st Battalion, FAR 48
II. Bataillon / Fußartillerie-Regiment 12	II./12	2nd Battalion, FußAR 12
4. Batterie / Feldartillerie-Regiment 48	4./48	4th Battery, FAR 48
3. Eskadron / Husaren-Regiment 19	3./19	3rd Squadron, HR 19

MAIN GLOSSARY

Abschnitt Sector; **Abteilung (Abt.)** 1. Battalion (field artillery); 2. detachment (other arms); **Armee** Field army; **Armee-Korps (AK)** Corps (active); **Armee-oberkommando (AOK)** Staff of an armee; **Armierungs-Bataillon (Arm. Batl.)** Unarmed labour battalion; **Artillerie (Art.)** Artillery; **Artillerie-Kommandeur (Arko)** Divisional artillery command staff;

Ballon-Abwehr-Kanone (BAK) Anti-balloon gun (ca. 1914–15); **Bataillon (Batl.)** Battalion; **Batterie (Battr.)** Battery; **Bereitschaft** Immediate reserve ('readiness') **Bereitschaftstruppen-Kommandeur (BTK)** 1. CO of the immediate reserve battalion in a sector (see p. 132); 2. his HQ dugout; **Brigade (Brig.)** Brigade; **Brückentrain (Br. Tr.)** Bridging train (carried pontoons for the pioniere)

Division (Div.) Division; **Divisions- (Div.-)** Divisional; **Divisions-Nachrichten-Kommandeur (Divkonach)** Divisional signals command staff

Eingreif- Intervention (by counterattack or reinforcement); **Ersatz-Bataillon (-Abteilung, -Eskadron) (Ers. Batl. [-Abt., -Esk.])** Replacement and training depot, normally immobile in Germany but sometimes converted into a provisional mobile unit.; **Ersatz-Division (Ers. Div., ED)** Ersatz division (formed of mobile ersatz units); **Ersatz-Infanterie-Regiment (Ers. Inf. Regt., EIR)** Ersatz infantry regiment (formed of mobile ersatz battalions); **Eskadron (Esk.)** Squadron (cavalry and train); **Etappe (Et.)** Lines of communication (rear area behind the fighting troops); also a prefix for rear-area units, often dismissed as *etappenschwein* (REMFs) by combat troops; **Etappen-Inspektion (Et. Insp.)** Command staff of the etappe behind a specific Armee

Feldartillerie (Feldart., Felda.) Field (light) artillery; armed with 7.7cm FK and 10.5cm lFH; **Feldartillerie-Regiment (Felda. Regt., FAR)** Field artillery regiment; **Feldgendarmerie** Military police; **Feldgrauen** (slang) 'our boys in field grey', the main contemporary nickname for German soldiers; **Feldhaubitze (Feldhaub.)** Howitzer, typically 'light' (10.5cm) or 'heavy' (15cm); **Feldkanone (Feldkan., FK)** Field gun; **Feldkompanie (Feldkomp., FK)** Field company of a pionier battalion; **Feldpost** 1. the field postal service; 2. item(s) of post sent via same; **Feldrekruten-Depot (Feldrekr. Depot)** Field recruit depot (used in 1915–18 to complete training of recruits in the field); **Fernsprech-Abteilung (Ferna)** Telephone detachment; **Fernsprech-Doppelzug (Fern. Dopp. Zug)** Telephone 'double platoon' (see p. 235); **Flieger-** Aviation; **Flieger-Abwehr-Kanone (FLAK)** Anti-aircraft gun (term replaced BAK); **Freiwillige Krankenpflege** Uniformed civilian medical volunteers (from the Red Cross and other organisations); **Friedhof** Cemetery; **Frontschwein** (slang) 'Front Pig', an infantryman; similar in spirit to 'poor bloody infantry'; **Funker-Abteilung (Funka)** Radio detachment; **Fußartillerie (Fuße., Fußart.)** Foot (heavy/siege) artillery; **Fußartillerie-Regiment (Fuße. Regt., FußaR)** Foot artillery regiment

Garde-Reiter-Regiment Horse guards regiment; before 1867 all Saxon cavalry regiments were 'reiter' (horsemen); **Gefechtsstand** Battle HQ of a battalion, regimental or higher staff; **Geheime Feldpolizei** Secret (plainclothes) field police; **gemischt (gem.)** Mixed (can mean 'all arms'); **General-Gouvernement (Gen. Gouv.)** Military government (of occupied territory behind the *etappe*); **Generalkommando (Genkdo)** Staff of a corps; **Generalstab** General staff; **Gewehr (Gew.)** Rifle; also short for 'maschinengewehr'; **Graben** Trench; **Grenadier-Regiment (Gren. Regt., GR)** Grenadier regiment; **Gruppe (Gr.)** 1. Section; 2. geographical 'group' controlled by a corps staff (see p. 132)

Handscheinwerfer-Trupp (HSwT) Hand-held searchlight troop; **Hauptwiderstandslinie (HWL)** Main line of resistance (1917–18); **Höherer Kavallerie-Kommandeur (HKK)** Cavalry corps (used in the West only in 1914); **Husaren-Regiment (Hus. Regt., HR)** Hussar regiment

Infanterie-Division (Inf. Div.; ID) Infantry division; **Infanterie-Regiment (Inf. Regt., IR)** Infantry regiment (usually of three battalions); **Intendantur** Commissariat (military administration)

Jäger-Bataillon (Jäg. Batl., JB) Light infantry ('hunters') battalion; **Jäger-Regiment (Jäg. Regt., JR)** Wartime regimental grouping of *jäger* battalions; not historically abbreviated as 'JR' due to confusion between 'I' and 'J'

Kampftruppen-Kommandeur (KTK) 1. CO of the battalion holding the front line in a sector and primarily responsible for organising its defence (see p. 132); 2. his HQ dugout; **Kaserne** Barracks; **Kasino** Officers' mess; **Kavallerie (Kav.)** Cavalry; all regiments were identically trained and equipped despite their many different titles, uniforms and traditions; **Kavallerie-Division (Kav. Div., KD)** Cavalry division; **Kavallerie-Schützen-Division (KSD)** Dismounted cavalry division; **Kolonne (Kol.)** Column (artillery and train); **Kommando (Kdo.)** 1. (Corps or army) command staff; 2. party detailed for a task; **Kompanie / Kompagnie (Komp.)** Company (both spellings were in common use); **königlich bayerisch (kgl. bayer., b.)** Royal Bavarian; **königlich preussisch (kgl. preuss., p.)** Royal Prussian; **königlich sächsisch (kgl. sächs., s.)** Royal Saxon; **königlich württembergisch (kgl. württ., w.)** Royal Württemberg; **Korporalschaft** Section, commanded by an unteroffizier (known before 1867 and colloquially as a '*korporal*'); **Kraftfahr-** Motor transport; **Kriegsministerium** War ministry

Landser / Lanzer (slang) German soldier, a term of probable Saxon origin which grew more widespread during and after the Great War. Possibly from Landsmann (fellow countryman) or Landsknecht.; **Landsturm (Ldst.)** Home guard / militia; **Landwehr (Ldw.)** (Trained) second-line reserve; **Landwehr-Division (Ldw. Div., LD)** Landwehr (infantry) division; **Landwehr-Infanterie-Regiment (Ldw. Inf. Regt., LIR)** Landwehr infantry regiment; **Lausoleum** (slang) punning term for a steam delousing oven; **Lazarett** Military hospital; **Leib-Grenadier-Regiment (Leib Gren. Regt., LGR)** "Body" (life guard) grenadier regiment; **leichter (l-)** Light (of weapons); **Liebesgaben** Charitable gifts from the home front (for collective distribution)

Maschinengewehr (Masch. Gew.) Machine-gun; **Maschinengewehr-Kompanie (MGK)** Machine-gun company; **Maschinengewehr-Scharfschützen-Trupp (MGSST)** Machine-gun marksman troop; **Matrosen-Regiment** Naval infantry regiment; **Minenwerfer** Trench mortar, firing *wurfminen*; **Minenwerfer-Kompanie (Mw. Komp., MwK)** Trench mortar company; **mittlerer (m-)** Medium (of weapons); **Mörser** Howitzer (21cm or larger); **Munitions-Kolonne (Mun. Kol., MK)** Ammunition column

Nachrichten (Nach.) Signals (1917–18)

Oberste Heeresleitung (OHL) Supreme (imperial) command staff; **Orts-kommandantur** Office of the town major

Pionier- (Mineur-) Kompanie (Pi. (Min.) Komp.) Tunneling company; **Pionier-Bataillon (Pi. Batl., PB)** Engineer / pioneer battalion; **Pionier-Kompanie (Pi. Komp., PK)** Engineer / pioneer company

Radfahrer-Kompanie (Radfahr-Komp.) Cyclist company; **Regiment (Regt.)** Regiment; **Regiments-Musik** Regimental band; **Reitende Abteilung (Reit. Abt.)** Horse artillery battalion (of a FAR); **Reserve (Res.)** (Trained) first-line reserve; **Reserve-Division (Res. Div., RD)** Reserve (infantry) division; **Reserve-Infanterie-Regiment (Res. Inf. Regt., RIR)** Reserve infantry regiment; **Reserve-Jäger-Bataillon (Res. Jäg. Batl., RJB)** Reserve jäger battalion; **Reserve-Kompanie (RK)** Reserve company of a *pionier* battalion; **Reserve-Korps (RK)** Reserve corps; **Ringkanone** Obsolete (non quick-firing) siege gun

Sanitäts-Kompanie (San. Komp., SK) Divisional medical (bearer) company; **Scheinwerfer-Zug (SwZ)** Searchlight platoon; **Schützen-Regiment (Schützen Regt., SR)** Rifle regiment; **schwerer (schw., s-)** Heavy (of weapons); **Soldatenheim** Soldiers' mess; **Stab** Staff / HQ element; **Stellung** (Defensive) position; trench system; **Stoßtrupp / Sturmtrupp** Assault troop (at regimental or lower level, often ad-hoc); **Sturmabteilung / Sturmkompanie (Sturmabt. / Sturmkomp.)** Divisional assault detachment / company (references before 1916 are synonymous with 'sturmtrupp'); **Sturmbataillon (Sturmbatl.)** Independent assault battalion ('stormtroops')

Tank-Gewehr Mauser 13mm anti-tank rifle; **Telegraphen-Bataillon** Telegraph battalion (peacetime); **Train (Tr.)** 1. The supply service; 2. a unit of same; **Trichter** Crater / shell hole

Ulanen-Regiment (Ul. Regt.) Uhlan (lancer) regiment; **Unternehmen** Undertaking (military operation)

verstärkt (verst.) Reinforced (with extra units attached); **Vorpostenlinie** Outpost line (1917–1918)

Wache Sentry (post)

Zug (Zg.) Platoon (infantry etc.) or two-gun section (artillery and MGs); the lowest command for an officer and only official one for an *offiziers-stellvertreter*